W9-BOA-273

Jewett and Her Contemporaries

Jewett and Her Contemporaries

Reshaping the Canon

Edited by Karen L. Kilcup and Thomas S. Edwards

University Press of Florida

GAINESVILLE · TALLAHASSEE · TAMPA · BOCA RATON

PENSACOLA · ORLANDO · MIAMI · JACKSONVILLE

04 03 02 01 00 99 6 5 4 3 2 1

LIBRARY OF CONGRESS CATALOGING-IN-PUBLICATION DATA

Jewett and her contemporaries: reshaping the Canon / edited by Karen L. Kilcup and Thomas S. Edwards.
p. cm.
Includes bibliographical references and index.
ISBN 0-8130-1703-3 (cloth: alk. paper)
1. Jewett, Sarah Orne, 1849–1909—Criticism and interpretation. 2. Women and literature—United States—History—19th century. 3. Women and literature—United States—History—20th century. 4. American literature—Women authors—History and criticism. 5. Jewett, Sarah Orne, 1849–1909—Contemporaries. 6. Maine—In literature. 7. Canon (Literature). I. Kilcup, Karen L. II. Edwards, Thomas S.
PS2133.J49 1999
813'.4—dc21 99-40599

The University Press of Florida is the scholarly publishing agency for the State University System of Florida, comprising Florida A&M University, Florida Atlantic University, Florida International University, Florida State University, University of Central Florida, University of Florida, University of North Florida, University of South Florida, and University of West Florida.

University Press of Florida
15 Northwest 15th Street
Gainesville, FL 32611-2079
http://www.upf.com

This volume is dedicated to Karen's mother, Mary Gove Kilcup, New Englander to the core, wishing her always "the clear sunshine and blue sky" of the country of the pointed firs; and to Tom's family, Barbara, Emily, and Liam: "Trailing clouds of glory do you come."

Contents

Acknowledgments

The resources of many people and institutions have been important in the completion of this volume. We wish to thank Westbrook College, now part of the University of New England, for honoring Karen with the 1996 Dorothy M. Healy visiting professorship for research, enabling her work in the Maine Women Writers Collection. We appreciate the sponsorship by the college and by the Society for the Preservation of New England Antiquities (SPNEA) of the Jewett centennial conference that Karen directed, and we are grateful to the more than 125 participants from North America, Europe, and Japan who gathered to share their ideas, providing the context from which the essays in the collection emerged. In addition to Tom, associate director of the conference, many other people were important in making the conference—and thus this collection—come to pass: Ron Morrison, dean of the college; Roberta Gray, librarian of the college; Nancy Noble, the Maine Women Writers Collection librarian; and the staff of the library and the college grounds. Offering crucial initial support for the conference, Richard Roberts of Westbrook College has been the source of special wisdom, insight, and friendship for Tom.

Warm thanks are also due to many people at the University of North Carolina at Greensboro: Jim Evans, head of the English Department; Walter Beale, dean of the College of Arts and Sciences; the staff at the Office of Research Services, especially Beverley Maddox-Britt, Charna Howson, and Nelda French; the members of the Research Grants Committee, who provided Karen with a Regular Faculty Grant that enabled the completion of the introduction; the excellent staff at the Walter Clinton Jackson Library; graduate research assistants Anna Elkins, Greg Tredore, and Drew Perry; and UNCG office manager Lydia Howard, for contributions both tangible and intangible.

We would also like to thank the following individuals at Castleton State College: Martha K. Farmer and Joseph T. Mark, for their support of the project; Nancy Stearns, for keeping us on track; and Anne Tabor, for her excellent editorial support and her keen eye. Meredith Trude deserves special thanks for her work on the index. Also, our editor at the University Press of Florida, Susan Fernandez, has been enthusiastic and generous throughout the process, and the other staff members at the press have been prompt and helpful.

Confronting Time and Change

Jewett, Her Contemporaries, and Her Critics

Karen L. Kilcup and Thomas S. Edwards

> No such beautiful and perfect work has been done for many years; perhaps no such beautiful work has ever been done in America.
>
> —*Alice Brown*

> If I were asked to name three American books which have the possibility of a long, long life, I would say at once, "The Scarlet Letter," "Huckleberry Finn," and "The Country of the Pointed Firs." I can think of no others that confront time and change so serenely.
>
> —*Willa Cather*

Like Alice Brown's early praise for Jewett's masterpiece, Willa Cather's famous comparison of *The Country of the Pointed Firs* to *The Adventures of Huckleberry Finn* and *The Scarlet Letter* represents both a judgment on the aesthetics of Jewett's finest work and a prediction of its place in American literary history. Yet Jewett's "importance" has been the subject of much discussion, from the first appearance of her sketches to the present. If, using Cather's phrase, to "confront time and change . . . serenely" is to be continually appreciated, then *The Country of the Pointed Firs*, like the writer herself, has enjoyed anything but an unambiguous reputation.[1] One of Jewett's supporters, Richard Cary, has remarked upon the mixed reviews that the writer's earliest productions received. A Deephaven sketch published in the *Atlantic* in 1873 drew the observation from a *Nation* reviewer that it was "very agreeable reading" that was "more like talk than reading, and talk of a very fresh, unaffected kind." Only four years later, a reviewer for the *New York Times* judged *Deephaven* itself to be thin and unsophisticated, concluding, "it is by some mistake, doubtless, that it got into print at all."[2] These reviews demonstrate that from the beginning Jewett criticism was characterized by a split, what June Howard terms a "curiously mingled tone of respect and depreciation." This mingling emerged perhaps most famously in Henry James's assessment of Jewett's "beautiful little quantum of achievement."[3]

A number of recent critics have attributed the ambivalence of much previous Jewett criticism to her participation in the supposedly limited genre of regionalism; June Howard observes, "suggestions that Jewett's work is fine but slight are usually linked to her regional subject matter and often (at least by implication) to her status as a woman writing mostly about women."[4] Howard's remarks suggest that such relegation of Jewett to "minor" status is grounded in the politics of literary criticism rather than in any consensual and enduring standards for literary merit. As Judith Fetterley underscores in a recent essay on nineteenth-century American women's writing more generally, criticism performs a series of political gestures that themselves confront time and change.[5] The political inflection of current Jewett criticism is evident in the conflict between two warring perspectives;[6] this debate is noteworthy for its intensity, especially the rhetoric that surrounds and motivates it. To better understand the writer herself, as well as the situation of nineteenth-century American women's writing more broadly, we need to investigate this intensity. What are the sources of its power and anxiety? Why is Jewett at the center of this turbulence? What, finally, is at stake?

Some answers to these questions emerge when we look at the history of Jewett criticism; what becomes clear is that an important subtextual element in the conflict is the role of sentimentalism, both in Jewett's own writing and in scholarly accounts of her work. After the writer's death, Jewett criticism developed in four overlapping stages. In a preliminary stage, critics confined themselves predominantly to a review of Jewett's life, tending (in their positive incarnation) to eulogize the writer and reading her principally as a New England regionalist (and hence somewhat limited in scope). In the second, feminist stage, critics frequently affirmed Jewett's value as a woman writing about women. These early feminist critics contrasted their positive, even utopian, views of Jewett with the preliminary readings that depicted her as limited, pointing out their predecessors' critical shortcomings and characterizing Jewett as a responsive and evocative artist. In the third, corrective stage, later critics, some feminist and some traditional, reacted to what they perceived as the idealization of Jewett by the second-stage critics; they have tended to emphasize the limitations of her work, especially her representation of the ethnic, racial, and class "other." Although the motives of the two groups participating in this corrective stage vary, the sources of their anxiety about the earlier feminist stage are allied. Finally, in the present stage, the criticism appears to be returning to equilibrium, with Jewett acknowledged as a writer of continuing cultural power whose postmodern elements, among others, offer new opportunities for criticism and appreciation.

Jewett, the Rhetoric of Sentiment, and the Sentiment of Rhetoric

Two of Jewett's most influential early critics, F. O. Matthiessen and Van Wyck Brooks, published narratives of her life that embody the nostalgic perspective of the preliminary stage. A distant relative, Matthiessen emphasized the romantic qualities of Jewett's early life and career. Describing one of her journeys with her father, he creates a scene that would appeal to a certain kind of reader: "They stopped at one or two other places farther along. Sarah observed how almost every house had plots of gay flowers out front, carefully hedged with barrel staves to keep out miscreant hens. Calves were tethered in shady spots, and puppies and kittens were adventuring from doorways."[7] Although the context for this description is the death of a farmer struck by lightning, the overall effect is one of profound nostalgia, underscored by the young animals who figure in it so conspicuously.[8]

In a similar vein, Van Wyck Brooks tells of Jewett's childhood, where "she had grown up in a world of square, white houses, picket fences—some of them ornamental, with high posts and urns,—and yards overflowing with larkspurs, petunias and asters, with hollyhocks and borders of box. When the fences were torn down, and the old reserve went with them, she felt that she belonged to an age that was passing." He speaks of the writer's appreciation of houses in the woods that were "deserted and empty": "She liked these silent, long-lost places, with a few bits of bright colour relieving the green of the woods or the white of the snow. She seemed to die out of the world in this forest quiet, where everything was merged in the life of nature." Finally, he describes Jewett's visits to Tenant's Harbor, where she "hired the schoolhouse for fifty cents a week and strolled to her morning's work through a bayberry pasture. In this 'country of the pointed firs', with its long frost-whitened ledges and its barren slopes where flocks of sheep moved slowly, she found the Dunnet shepherdess and Mrs. Todd, the herbalist, and many of the scenes and persons of her finest stories,—or sketches, rather, light as smoke or wisps of sea-fog, charged with the odours of mint, wild roses and balsam."[9]

For many of today's readers, Matthiessen's and Brooks's descriptions sentimentalize Jewett and intimate the backward-looking element of her work. Rooted in the past, she is, they suggest, a delightful representative of an earlier generation more attuned to nature and to a disappearing New England legacy than to the requirements of an urgent present.[10] In constructing Jewett and her work in this way, Matthiessen and Brooks unwittingly consign her to the status of a "minor" writer describing a narrow domain. Ironically, however, Matthiessen contrasts the implicitly declining New England to Jewett's continuing power: "She has withstood the onslaught of time, and is secure within her limits, because she achieved a style."[11] Perhaps there was some pleasure in considering Jewett to be "secure within her limits," for even her later advocate Richard Cary would affirm that "Miss Jewett's finished art is deficient in some of the significant phases of a mature culture"; he concluded his 1962 critical biography with the faint praise that "it is not too much to claim that Sarah Orne Jewett is without peer among her contemporaries in the reliable depiction of her chosen time, place, and personalities."[12] Significantly for our discussion, the suggestion of immaturity was leveled against many women writers in this period, in part as a way of dismissing their apparently disproportionate investment in emotion rather than (mature and masculine) reason.[13]

Although the theme of New England in decline was well established in literature by Jewett's time, appearing in such culturally normative periodicals as *Harper's Magazine*,[14] Matthiessen and Brooks were not merely reiterating a myth, they were creating one. Like depictions of Emily Dickinson as a half-cracked virgin poetess, this myth had considerable appeal and durability. While it echoed Cather's depiction of *The Country of the Pointed Firs* as confronting time and change serenely, it also suggested that Jewett was irretrievably bound to a limited past rather than looking outward to a lively and masculine future. One of the last preliminary-stage critics, Warner Berthoff, focused more on Jewett's work and less on her life than Matthiessen and Brooks, but his observations articulated a common attitude. Berthoff's narrative made explicit what Matthiessen and Brooks only suggested. In a section of *The Fer-*

ment of Realism entitled "Regionalism, Local-Color Realism," Berthoff situated Jewett as "the best" of the New England "story-tellers" but asserted that she "had very nearly the narrowest range." Claiming that Jewett's early sketches for the *Atlantic* revealed her "miniature competence," he resurrected a crucial issue framing the rose-tinged portraits of Matthiessen and Brooks: "There were . . . many temptations to sentimentality and archness in her materials. . . . In the best of the stories she was writing in the 80's and early 90's . . . these temptations are more and more firmly mastered." Berthoff continued to discuss "the beautiful book," *The Country of the Pointed Firs*, in terms that were ambiguous at best: "Once imaginatively secured, this legendary world became, for Sarah Jewett, more actual than that of her own time. It thus renewed the risks of sentimentality."[15]

We will return later to a discussion of Jewett's vulnerability to the charge of sentimentalism, but underline here that, for some readers at least, the idealized elements of *Pointed Firs* recalled Jewett's alliance with novels like Stowe's *The Pearl of Orr's Island*, which she claimed explicitly as a precursor. Berthoff's remarks remind us that the literary past was imbricated in sentimentalism; as Shirley Samuels has observed, "sentimentality is literally at the heart of nineteenth-century American culture. . . . As a set of cultural practices designed to evoke a certain form of emotional response, usually empathy, in the reader or viewer, sentimentality produces or reproduces spectacles that cross race, class, and gender boundaries."[16] Apparently for preliminary-stage critics, this emotional response was not secure across gender boundaries. For, in spite of Richard Cary's approving remark about Jewett's "beguiling sentimentality," to affiliate a writer with sentimentalism, however indirectly, especially in this era of New Criticism, would destine her work to minor status at best and obscurity at worst.[17] Even though realist-regionalist writers such as Rose Terry Cooke and Mary E. Wilkins Freeman wrote in part to counteract earlier depictions of New England and domestic life as idyllic, a later generation of writers would reject their work (along with that of Jewett herself, Alice Brown, and a feminized Howells) as sentimental. As Suzanne Clark has so aptly observed, "In the United States, this reversal against the sentimental helped to establish beleaguered avant-garde intellectuals as a discourse community, defined by its adversarial relationship to domestic culture."[18]

With the rise of feminist literary criticism it became possible once again to tell affirmative stories about the feminine, the domestic, and, ultimately, the sentimental. It is no coincidence that a certain strain in Jewett criticism intensified at the moment in which sentimentalism was rediscovered—or reinvented—as a respectable area for literary studies.[19] This second, or feminist, stage was anticipated in 1973 by Richard Cary's important collection, *Appreciation of Sarah Orne Jewett*, which brings together appreciative essays from the beginnings of Jewett criticism. Susan Allen Toth's contribution forecasts the flowering of the feminist stage of Jewett criticism. Toth points toward Jewett's older characters as an indication of the writer's realism, yet her emphasis resides on the strength and power of her old women: "Old women, rather than men, seem to have acquired this feeling for the rituals of everyday life, perhaps because they have lived closest to the center of family and household life. Among women, Miss Jewett chose to write about spinsters or widows, for they are the ones who concentrate with single-mindedness on maintaining and celebrating the bonds of community, whether attending a reunion or preparing a tea-table."[20]

Here we see the affirmation of a woman-centered aesthetic that emerged in the work of the early feminist critics of the 1980s as they responded to the limited and disempowering view of Jewett constructed by their precursors. Inaugurated in force by Josephine Donovan's *New England Local Color Literature: A Women's Tradition* (1983), this critical stage celebrates Jewett's accomplishments as it places her principally in a domestic or "feminine" world. Acknowledging that Jewett's portrait of Maine is elegiac and not idealized, Donovan nevertheless tells a relatively utopian story about that world as the writer depicts it: "The world of rural Maine, the land of the pointed firs, however, emerges as a place on the edge of historical time; it is an almost timeless female realm that stands as a counterreality to the encroaching male world of modern technology." The nostalgia for this realm emerges even more explicitly in Donovan's conclusion: "Sarah Orne Jewett created a symbolic universe which expressed the longing of late-nineteenth-century women that the matriarchal world of the mothers be sustained. . . . Hers is perhaps the last fully female-identified vision in women's literature." Painting a nostalgic portrait of women's literature, Donovan nevertheless feels it necessary to open her chapter on Jewett with an assertion that would attempt to remove the writer from the very tradition that she has constructed: "Jewett incorporated the perceptions of women's literary realism developed by her predecessors in the local color school to produce an authentically female-identified vision of her own that moved beyond their limits."[21] This characteristic of transcendence represents an effort to elevate Jewett into another ("major") category, in effect ensuring that her reputation would "confront time and change . . . serenely."

This utopian moment is not limited to Donovan but includes important work such as Marcia McClintock Folsom's "'Tact Is a Kind of Mind-Reading': Empathic Style in Sarah Orne Jewett's *The Country of the Pointed Firs*" (1982); Elizabeth Ammons's "Going in Circles: The Female Geography of *The Country of the Pointed Firs*" (1983); Sandra Zagarell's "Narrative of Community: The Identification of a Genre" (1988); and Sarah Way Sherman's *Sarah Orne Jewett: An American Persephone* (1989).[22] In each of these readings, even when Jewett is regarded as ambivalent or elegiac, she is presented affirmatively, as a representative of an important feminine tradition. Exploring such matters as Jewett's innovative formal structures and her invention of a textured language of "silence beyond language," as Sherman puts it, "rich with emotion and full of meaning," the critics work out of the assumption that in Jewett's writing, "women find voice, the marginal becomes central, and immanence is a means to transcendence." For many critics, an important part of the recovery of women's voices and community in Jewett's work was its investment in what some called a lesbian vision.[23]

The early feminist critics were likely to regard her work affirmatively for obvious and significant reasons. From the distance of a decade, we can more readily acknowledge that recovery work has its dangers, one of which is a representation of earlier writers geared to contemporary tastes, whether in the selections that scholars make for anthologies or in the novels we select for republication and emphasize in our criticism. This dilemma might translate, on the one hand, into a taste for grim, psychologically realistic stories of women and hardship amenable to modernist-inflected criticism, or, on the other hand, into a desire for representations of utopian female communities that invite empowering feminist readings. In some sense, feminist critics must depict their writers in valorized contemporary terms or risk what we might call their "redisappearance"; certainly, it is in critics' interest to advance the best face of their writers, whether male or female.

From one perspective, the perspective that would appear in later corrective views, even feminist ones, this early feminist portrait of the writer has itself come to be seen as nostalgic or even sentimental. As Joanne

Dobson has pointed out in another context: "connection, commitment, community: out of these priorities sprang both domestic sentimentalism and a realist/regionalist aesthetic."[24] In their emphasis on women's power and women's communities, Jewett's early feminist critics were responding in affirmative fashion to the resonant emotional content of her work that Berthoff had called "sentimental" but that they themselves would call evocative or intimate. In spite of the recovery of sentimentalism as a useful term for critical discourse, it nevertheless threatened to contaminate the writer's reputation. Although feminist critics might appreciate her sentimentalism—though it rarely appears explicitly or in a sustained fashion in most accounts of the writer—it was crucial to de-emphasize it in the selection of Jewett's stories for recovery, and in the interpretation of some, like "Martha's Lady," that clearly work out of a sentimental tradition.[25] Some of the more familiar texts by Jewett—like "Too Late" and "Mrs. Flint's Married Experience" by Cooke and "The Revolt of 'Mother'" and "Old Woman Magoun" by Freeman, all of which have been regularly anthologized in the last fifteen years—could be recuperated into a (tough-minded) modernist aesthetic, even though they clearly retained strong elements of the sentimental tradition. Such Jewett stories include "The Queen's Twin," "The Foreigner," and "A White Heron."

More recent Jewett criticism has been, to reconfigure Cather's praise of her friend, less than serene and more confrontational. Whether in conscious response to the idealizing evident in much early feminist work or not, Margaret Roman's study of Jewett offers a transition to the next stage of Jewett scholarship. From one perspective, Roman appreciates the work of her predecessors, as is apparent in her early assertion that "Jewett creates a woman's imaginative universe. She turns the tables and subverts the male-dominated form." This acknowledgment expands into a discussion of how Jewett allows both men and women to escape from socially constructed norms—in the words of the subtitle, "reconstructing gender"—as Roman attempts to make Jewett more "universal," to expand the scope of her vision, and, at the same time, to counterbalance (while she paradoxically reinforces) the putatively sentimental vision of the writer articulated by her feminist predecessors.[26]

Other recent criticism, especially of Jewett's racial and ethnic politics, reflects greater detachment, and at some level it may indicate academic readers' desire to remove themselves from the emotional response to

Jewett in which some readers can so easily become submerged. That is, we can see these later responses as a form of self-criticism—a correction of the impulse to sentimentalize, to see the writer "subjectively" and hence to miss the racial-ethnic politics embedded in her work. Working in this vein, writers like [Kilcup] Oakes (1992), Ammons (1994), Zagarell (1994), and Gillman (1994) would take Jewett to task for her limited, even exclusionary nationalist vision.[27]

Zagarell's comparison of two passages in *The Country of the Pointed Firs*, the first in which Jewett invokes Mrs. Blackett and "the golden chain of love and dependence" that unites the country farms, and the second in which one guest at the Bowden family reunion compares Mari' Harris to "a Chinee," is representative: "Reading the first passage, one may savor the empathic understanding of community that has made Jewett's *Country* so moving for so many readers, myself included. Reading the second, with its use of the racist slur 'Chinee' to dismiss a woman unpopular among Dunnet Landing folk and excluded from the community celebrated in her famous narrative, probably makes other readers as uncomfortable as it makes me. Most commentators seem to have responded simply by ignoring it."[28] Historicizing the use of the racial slur within the context of the recent passage of the Chinese Exclusion Acts, Zagarell observes that "invoked as it is at the Bowden reunion, this appellation asserts absolute difference not only between Mari' and the community but also between her and the nation for which the community is a model."[29] In this narrative of Jewett's fall from the ideal, perhaps the only counternarrative that can rescue her is a representation of the writer as national rather than (merely) regional. Ammons's and Gillman's analyses of Jewett as the creator of a narrative of empire and nationalism, respectively, parallel this strategy.[30]

If the paradox for early feminist critics was that in attempting to defend Jewett from an explicit or implicit affiliation with (reductive) sentimentality, they themselves engaged in a form of sentimentalization, then for later feminist critics the paradox was that in critiquing Jewett's cultural politics, they would inevitably be opening the way for Jewett's redisappearance from the canon. It is worth noting that even Judith Fetterley, one of the writer's strongest advocates, expresses disappointment with *The Country of the Pointed Firs*'s elision of the lesbian narrative more overtly present in *Deephaven*.[31]

Nonfeminist critics such as Richard Brodhead responded to the incipient sentimentality in Jewett's writing—and the putative sentimentalization of feminist criticism about it—by disparaging both, citing the jacket copy from Sherman's book as an example of how "feminist criticism has supplied Jewett with her most successful rescue plan to date." He goes on to claim that "the feminist reconception of regionalism has tended to repeat the autonomy fantasies of the nineteenth-century ideology of separate spheres. . . . Similarly, in disclosing concerns specific to nineteenth-century women's life, this criticism has tended to forget that no culture is ever specified by its gender dimension alone."[32] Brodhead seeks not only to complicate the feminist account but also to counteract its emotional investment in the affirmative elements of Jewett's writing. Like Fetterley, but with a very different perspective and set of goals, Brodhead situates literary criticism and canon revision in particular within a political framework—here the Civil Rights movements—and affirms the necessity to conduct "an inquiry into the history of literary access: a systematic asking by what means and by virtue of what circumstances different potential authors have been able to lay claim to different powers in the literary realm." In this context, regionalism proves particularly illuminating, for a growing audience for such writing ensured that "in the later nineteenth century, regionalism was so structured as to extend opportunity above all to groups traditionally distanced from literary lives." This opportunity allowed a wide range of writers to penetrate elite outlets like *Scribner's*, *Century*, and the *Atlantic*, as elite *readers* engaged in a kind of literary tourism. In extending this overarching narrative to Jewett herself, Brodhead focuses on her self-conscious participation in the creation of a ("minor") high art that ensured her place among a group of "master" artists.[33]

Brodhead's account has considerable power and allure, especially, if paradoxically, for some feminist readers conscious of their "sin" of idealizing the writer. But the rhetoric of this account is, to say the least, somewhat off-putting for such readers. In his opening discussion of Sherman and others, after noting feminists' "rescue plan" for Jewett, Brodhead observes:

> Jewett's critics have been able to lift her out of the "minor" project of regional genre painting and into the "major" one of articulating women's culture. A book like *The Country of the Pointed Firs* is now said to detail the particulars of simple life in rural Maine to the end

> of realizing a world where women are capable and men are dysfunctional; where children stay bound to their mothers and inherit their mothers' powers; where female community supplants self-assertive masculine individuality; and where the feminine is seen as the outlet to the divine.

The distaste, anger, or revulsion (depending on the observer's perspective) shading this passage is palpable; the forces that appear to energize it include Brodhead's anxiety about the (emasculating) gender politics of such fictional worlds and his implicit sense of earlier feminist critics' sentimental attitude toward the writer.[34]

These tensions resurface later in the narrative, where Brodhead affirms that he sees "Jewett's regionalism as produced not in some weakly specified women's culture but in the culture of a quite specific late-nineteenth-century upper class, a class that organized a certain world for women (the chief performers of its leisure) but that was defined by a host of other social relations at the same time."[35] Again the reference to "some weakly specified women's culture" represents a stab at earlier feminists' idealizing view (presumably because it was not historically grounded) of the writer's work and life. He acknowledges this indirectly later, when he observes that "the problem Jewett has always presented for her admirers is how to value her achievement without inflating the dimensions of her achievement."[36] Because Brodhead rejects the rhetoric of sentiment surrounding the writer, he is more able to reject claims of the magnitude of her achievement and consign her to the status of great "minor" writer.

We see this gesture enacted elsewhere in his discussion of Jewett's work itself. In contrast to criticism (presumably feminist) attempting to link Jewett with sentimental precursors like Susan Warner and Harriet Beecher Stowe, Brodhead detaches her from the domestic-sentimental tradition by highlighting the writer's rejection of both the child-centered world of these precursors and their moral grounding in liberal Protestant religious belief. Unlike her predecessors, he argues, Jewett's understanding of "the literary" is detached from, not continuous with, projects of cultural amelioration. Paradoxically, this rejection precipitates Jewett's ascent into the world of high art at the same time that it ensured her status as "a minor literary figure."[37] What is contested is not her presence in the canon but in effect her "importance."

We can unpack this discussion of "major" and "minor" further if we consider some of the resonances of these terms. When we speak of individuals being "minors," for example, we are indicating their less than "grown-up" status; the contrasting term signifies adulthood, the age of "majority." As we pointed out earlier, one method of consigning women writers (and critics) to a diminished position or even obscurity is to claim that they have not grown up, that sentiment rather than reason informs their actions and articulations. Readers before Brodhead have discussed Jewett's self-diminishment, and the early feminist critics attempted to controvert this minimization, not so much by Jewett herself but by their critical predecessors who subscribed to her self-assessment. Brodhead acknowledges that "Jewett's compulsive self-miniaturization may be thought to display a general syndrome afflicting women writers, the self-undermining bred by enculturation systems that mark assertion and achievement as proper provinces only for men."[38] What both groups fail to explore, however, is the degree to which Jewett may have been transvaluing the terms of the discussion, where "small" becomes a term of approbation rather than criticism. This possibility becomes clearer when we juxtapose Jewett to Emily Dickinson (a volume of whose poems had been published only a few years before the appearance of *The Country of the Pointed Firs*); no one would any longer take the "small" poet at her word, especially after Paula Bennett's persuasive discussions of clitoral power in Dickinson's oeuvre. While their situations clearly differ in a variety of ways, both writers created compelling fictions in which "small" often represented a term of affirmation.[39]

Fetterley's response to Brodhead, as rhetorically intense as his, indicates the passion within the corrective moment of Jewett criticism. For example, while she approves of his including Jewett in his broader discussion, she criticizes his self-presentation as "the first scout to enter an unknown territory" and his "use of class and race as categories of analysis that cancel rather than complicate attention to gender." She is understandably concerned that "if white women are understood simply as sites of race and class privilege, then one cannot argue that recovering their texts is an act of enfranchising the disenfranchised. Indeed, if one accepts this model, then one can only recover these texts to critique them. And in such a climate, why bother to read them at all?" That is, "inclusion serves as the occasion for orchestrating their redismissal and for effecting their continued exclusion from further literary or historical consideration." As the relative paucity of scholarship on nineteenth-century American women's writing suggests, these are clearly legitimate concerns. Ironically, however, some of the recent feminist scholarship on Jewett discussed above is vulnerable to the same critique: if Jewett excludes the racial or ethnic "other," then why should we (if "we" is conceived in multicultural terms) continue to value her? Why should "women" in particular value her?[40]

There are two perspectives from which we can more fully comprehend this clash. For one thing, we could take Brodhead's account to task on its own terms, namely, the investigation of the role played by class in the cultures of letters. In spite of the late nineteenth century's well-documented segregation of "high" and "low" culture—and the acceptance by many current literary critics of this split—writers like Jewett continued to participate in a wide range of cultural activities, even when they valued the former more than the latter.[41] The question that needs to be asked of Jewett and her contemporaries is: Why do critics talk principally of these writers' "high art" and relation to "high culture"? Even Brodhead's historically informed account omits discussion of Jewett's investment in popular culture outlets such as newspapers (in which she published many "sentimental" stories) and children's literature journals, to which she was a regular contributor. In this light, we have to question his claim that Jewett rejected the child-centered world of her sentimental precursors, for even beyond her children's literature, a significant number of her stories, such as "The Girl with the Cannon Dresses," "The Honey Tree," and "A Garden Story," focus on children and on the relationship between child and adult worlds.[42]

In terms of Jewett criticism—and indeed, in the context of recovery work on a number of other women writers—another consequence of the necessity to protect the writer's reputation, beyond highlighting more "modern" work, has been this elevation of what we might call "elite" over "popular" work: the concentration on her *Atlantic* stories and her masterpiece, *The Country of the Pointed Firs.* Contemporary Jewett criticism (that is, the work of the last twenty-five years) has to a certain degree internalized the popular-elite split and its affiliated valorizations. Yet, as one of us has argued elsewhere, to separate "popular" from "academic" readers is problematic, for the latter can be as readily construed as a subset of or adjacent to the former. In this context, what we might call her "aesthetic merit" is divorced from her "cultural work," although aesthetics *themselves* perform cultural work.[43] We tend to forget that Jewett, like her "contemporary" Dickinson, was popular with a wide readership and to ignore her popular productions.

In addition to this problem with what we have called the corrective stage of Jewett criticism, both feminist and nonfeminist rejections of the second stage represent attempts to disavow "emotional" responses to the writer. Such counternarratives are unconsciously invested in anti-feminine strategies. In spite of the recuperation of sentimental literature by feminist critics, the interrogation of the role of emotion (easily converted to "sentimentality") in literary criticism itself has a relatively short history. Olivia Frey writes of the conventions of mainstream literary criticism: "these conventions include the use of argument as the preferred mode for discussion, the importance of the objective and the impersonal, the importance of a finished product without direct reference to the process by which it was accomplished, and the necessity of being thorough in order to establish proof and reach a definitive (read 'objective') conclusion." She concludes that criticism is propelled by the need to "get it right" rather than the desire to connect with readers.[44] This adversarial method excludes the use of emotional response as part of its process of understanding. Citing Alison Jaggar, Jane Tompkins speaks of these problems in a larger context: "Western epistemology . . . is shaped by the belief that emotion should be excluded from the process of attaining knowledge. Because women in our culture are not simply encouraged but *required* to be the bearers of emotion, which men are culturally conditioned to repress, an epistemology which excludes emotions from the process of attaining knowledge radically undercuts women's epistemic authority."[45]

What this bifurcation means for literary criticism is that writers (men as well as women) who speak out of emotional responses to texts risk losing interpretive authority: they risk being seen as (what Tompkins implies but does not say directly) sentimental. That is, the regulatory force of the term extends well beyond the domain of literary texts themselves and into the critical region. In this light, the criticism of Jewett by Matthiessen and Brooks, as well as that by early feminist readers, resides outside of the mainstream interpretive domain. Although the former are buffered somewhat from the charge of sentimentality by their gender, the latter can be readily dismissed using dominant critical standards.

Interestingly, *both* camps in the corrective moment of Jewett criticism seem to retreat to a less vulnerable position, which suggests another explanation for Jewett criticism's avoidance of her more "popular" writing: the fact that it more often and more explicitly seeks from its readers the kind of emotional response upon which her predecessors relied for social transformation.[46]

If a text enables a form of virtual reality, we need to ask what kinds of realities these putatively different kinds of texts enable or foster and how our vision interacts with these perspectives.[47] Unlike in scientific disciplines, in literary criticism the replication of data is regarded as "derivative" rather than confirming. It is not surprising, then, that the most recent stage of Jewett criticism performs a reaction to the reaction. Responding explicitly to the critical war surrounding the writer, Louis Renza and Jack Morgan's recent collection of Jewett's Irish stories represents her in a more balanced and, some might say, optimistic light than its immediate predecessors.[48] Although they acknowledge the possibility of Jewett's participation in the elevation of middle-class values, they argue that the stories "serve to undo the 'Paddy' stereotype of the Irish favored in nineteenth-century discourse" and they compare Jewett's views to the ethnocentrism of writers like Hawthorne, Emerson, and Thoreau.[49]

This comparison suggests an important and neglected point in relation to the critiques of Jewett for racism, classism, and ethnocentrism: women writers as a whole seem to be held to a higher standard than their male contemporaries. In fact, few nonethnic white writers' views in the nineteenth century would withstand careful scrutiny, and to interrogate only women writers' contributions on this basis is, as Morgan and Renza argue, extremely problematic. Perhaps this situation has arisen because we still consider (or desire) women to be the moral exemplars for American culture, but such a claim is unfair at best and represents idealization and sentimentalization of another sort. Morgan and Renza's account of the interaction between men and women in Jewett's work and her sympathy for men suggests another kind of balance needed in studies of Jewett (and hence of nineteenth-century American women writers more broadly). Finally, they conclude by affirming "Jewett's respect for Irish cultural otherness. Her considerable optimism about Irish success in America is balanced by her recognition of their rootedness in the world of their native island and her respect for their own traditional view of themselves—as exiles."[50] In Morgan and Renza's account, difference in Jewett does not necessarily translate to disparagement.

Several answers finally emerge to the questions posed at the beginning about the virulence of the debate surrounding the ostensibly calm—even "serene"—work of Jewett. The terms and tones of this discussion provide a useful touchstone for understanding critical conversations on nineteenth-century American women writers more generally, for they indicate that even a writer like Jewett who, relative to many of her peers, has enjoyed a remarkably stable readership and positive reputation, can be vulnerable to a disabling (if covert) affiliation with sentimentality. That is, the renovation of sentimentalism's reputation—as well as the delineation of its contours and resonances—is far from complete. Moreover, the voice of the critic herself, and her epistemological stance, remain fair game in the critical competition; another way for conservative critics to stifle dialogue is to extend the charge of sentimentalism, metonymically and sometimes covertly, to critics who regard Jewett's work affirmatively. A third damaging strategy, in which feminist critics have themselves participated, is to critique the racial, ethic, class, or sexual politics of a writer like Jewett, setting forms of cultural disadvantage against each other in a hierarchical calculus rather than exploring the fact that, as Fetterley underscores, "nineteenth-century black and white women writers emerge from and represent in their work complex combinations of privilege and disadvantage, of acceptance and critique."[51] What is at stake is the power to name and configure the "literary" itself, to determine whose stories ("literary" as well as "critical") will continue to possess cultural authority. In this context, work on writers like Jewett becomes even more crucial, for it represents the possibilities for continuing intervention into questions of interpretive perspective as well as aesthetic value.

Jewett, Time, and Change

As the preceding discussion suggests, just as Jewett's writing has endured heated debates about form and content, Jewett scholarship has itself been suffering from "category crisis," a term that Marjorie Pryse uses in a different context in the opening essay of this volume. *Jewett and Her Contemporaries: Reshaping the Canon* attempts to return consideration of the writer to equilibrium. Although the impetus for this volume came from the 1996 conference "Sarah Orne Jewett and Her Contemporaries: The Centennial Conference," which brought together scholars from all over the world to celebrate the centennial of the publication of *The Country of the Pointed Firs*, the revised and expanded essays represented here reach far beyond that occasion. This collection investigates Jewett's hospitality to current and contemporary theoretical concerns, to "difference," to historicity, and to context—literary, biographical, and geographical. Offering a wide continuum of views, from critical to celebratory, from "popular" to "academic," "visitor" and "native," the contributors create a conversation that assumes a wide range of epistemic authority. This conversation does not oppose historical to celebratory perspectives, and it reaffirms without apology the value of positive views of—and personal, even emotional responses to—the writer's work. Morgan and Renza's account suggests that many of today's critics value Jewett's masterpiece both for its ability to "confront time and change . . . serenely" and for the opposite: its uncertainties, gaps, and unspoken messages, where Jewett "confronts time and change" more assertively. The appeal of Jewett's work as a whole resides for many readers in its ability to mediate between independence and community, isolation and relationship, tradition and change. These tensions were as endemic to Jewett's time as to our own, and it is perhaps this parallel that helps to endow her work with continuing resonance.[52]

Beyond the significance of Jewett to individual readers, her importance to contemporary literary studies emerges in a recent essay by Judith Fetterley. Fetterley highlights Jewett's implied challenge to the canon, arguing that the writer's "regionalism . . . deconstructs the 'national', revealing its presumed universality to be in fact the position of a certain, albeit privileged, group of locals."[53] Indeed, as we have seen, Jewett's work has helped fuel lively debates in contemporary literary studies about the meaning and shape of "American" literature, and the affiliation (or disjunction) between "regional" and "national" literature.[54] Placed in this context, her writing—not merely *The Country of the Pointed Firs*, but her other novels and short fiction—illuminates and interrogates that of her peers.[55] In *Jewett and Her Contemporaries* the writer's work serves as a touchstone for the other writers discussed here, who include Celia Thaxter, Willa Cather, Edith Wharton, William Dean Howells, Fanny Fern, Henry James, and nineteenth-century American women doctors. The continuing challenge, which this volume takes up, is to prevent what Fetterley calls the "revanishing" of Jewett and her "unAmerican" contemporaries, acknowledging their shortcomings but affirming their continuing power and importance, where "importance" extends beyond the literary domain of "major" and "minor" writers.

The first part of this collection, "Contexts: Readers and Reading," not only establishes Jewett as a writer deeply conscious of contemporary literary trends and underscores her manipulation of market influences, but also interrogates the concept of "regionalism" itself. Marjorie Pryse's essay points to Jewett's "continuing to imagine regionalism as an alternative cultural vision" via a radical reinvention of the interwoven categories of gender, class, and sexuality. Depicting Jewett as a border-crosser, one who destabilizes boundaries of both nationalism and regionalism, Pryse recuperates the writer as a powerful model for cultural and theoretical transformation. Working in a historical frame, Donna M. Campbell resituates Jewett in the company of peers like Mary Noialles Murfree, Bret Harte, and Hamlin Garland, providing a contextualization for the late nineteenth-century discussions swirling around regional and national literature and asking, "What did Jewett's audiences understand by 'local color'?" Audience and the marketplace also figure centrally in Melissa Homestead's essay, which explores the development at the end of the nineteenth century of a new concept of authorship. Homestead argues that whereas "earlier literary practices represent the author as present in personal service to the reader," later realist practices invoke the author as "powerful, distant, and independent." Representing another kind of border-crosser for Paul R. Petrie, Jewett emerges as a writer of conscience who translates and undercuts the nascent and briefly dominating Howellsian ethic into a "reader-participatory, metaphysically evocative narrative experience." Like all of the essays in this section, Petrie's provides a perspective informed by the tensions between history and myth, readers and writers, regionalism and nationalism.

Extending the connections established in the first part, part II, "Contemporaries: Jewett and the Writing World," links the writer to both famous and unknown contemporaries, advancing discussion of women writing within (an increasingly) masculine tradition. Complicating the idea of the author and the reader, Judith Bryant Wittenberg explores the intertextual relations between Jewett's *A Country Doctor* and contemporary medical autobiographies by women, arguing that such an exploration "reveals the textual strategies all of them employ to function in partial compliance with [and partial challenge to] some of the prevailing notions about gender, education, and professionalism." Marcia B. Littenberg's essay identifies some connections between regionalist writers like Jewett and Celia Thaxter and their Transcendentalist precursors, exploring these women's gendered transformations of masculine concepts and ideologies and their mediation between Transcendentalism and contemporary ecofeminism. Focusing on the important relationship between Jewett and Willa Cather, Ann Romines casts light—and shade—on the resistance of the younger writer to her mentor. Often depicted as a utopianized connection between women, the Cather-Jewett relationship contains far more ambivalence for Cather, an ambivalence embodied in her works after Jewett's death. Similarly, Priscilla Leder maps out Edith Wharton's admiring yet uneasy reinventions of her predecessor's work, reinventions embedded in Wharton's discovery of her own authority as a writer and in her uneasy relationship to the social class in which she was raised. Domesticity and art figure as antagonists in this process, which is very much a process of self-engendering.

Part III, "Conflicts: Identity and Ideology," explores further tensions in Jewett's work that open out into the culture as a whole. "Whiteness," and the representation of a racialized self, form the center of Mitzi Schrag's discussion of "The Foreigner." Moving beyond the boundaries of Jewett's story into both contemporary theory and literary history, Schrag investigates the consequences of "reading for whiteness," one of which is the potential for "loss": of community, of self, of other, of authority. Extending Schrag's concern with race, Alison Easton's essay takes on another aspect of identity, social class. Easton offers a carefully historicized view of Jewett's sometimes ambivalent and ambiguous representations of class divisions, highlighting the writer's sensitivity both to the dehumanizing "processes of capitalism" and the consequences of class divisions for individuals. Class and gender come together in Sarah Way Sherman's contribution on a relatively unexplored area, Jewett's children's literature, as Sherman explores the unsettled and unsettling divisions between an alluring and culturally subversive "bad girl" and her rich, beautiful counterpart. Sherman reads in this conflict "the difficulty of overcoming class differences and the penalty paid on both sides for failure." In all of these essays, the cultural conflicts explored have national, not merely regional, significance.

Part IV, "Connections: Jewett's Time and Place," situates Jewett in the context of concrete location, family and cultural history, and social location, also offering two more personal responses that effectively circle back to the beginning and Marjorie Pryse's discussion of "category crisis." Graham Frater's essay picks up where Sherman's leaves off, with discussion of the writer's children's literature. Here, however, this writing becomes more a resource for continuity than a source of fragmentation. Frater's account of community, commemoration, and celebration is not utopian, however, for it concludes that "Jewett's dream of order was largely self-subverting"; and it returns us to the writer's investment in the difficult development of an American national identity. Writing from a personal place, Patti Capel Swartz provides a more affirmative view of the writer, highlighting the empowerment that Jewett offers her as a lesbian reader. The empowerment occurs not merely because Jewett celebrates connections between women, but also because she acknowledges the need for difference. Finally, fiction writer Carol Schachinger explores the writer's connection to place and time; acknowledging Jewett's own "difference," her inner nonconformity to social norms, Schachinger highlights the writer's courage to be simply and fully herself, a resident both of Berwick and the world.

As these brief descriptions suggest, the dialectics between identity and difference, tradition and transformation, and, finally, regionalism and nationalism form the central matrices for the collection. A writer for whom place is central, Jewett ultimately remains both alluringly accessible and notoriously difficult to "place"; this elusive quality renders her particularly effective as a representative of nineteenth-century American women's writing in these discussions, which explore the permeability and tenacity of such boundaries as race, class, sexuality, region, period, and gender. Itself confronting time and change, *Jewett and Her Contemporaries* engages energetically in the ongoing discussions about nineteenth-century American literature, women's literature, and canon criticism, in the process complicating and celebrating the "beautiful and perfect," "American" and "unAmerican" work of Sarah Orne Jewett.

Notes

1. In 1994, Judith Fetterley articulated a wide-ranging vision of the field of nineteenth-century American women's writing. Beyond appreciation of the ongoing recovery work taking place, Fetterley expressed disappointment about the relative absence of secondary materials such as critical biographies, literary histories, and criticism. The situation has changed little since this essay was published; still, Jewett's current position in American literary studies is an enviable one if we consider the fate of many nineteenth-century American women writers. For example, among the writers included in the Rutgers American Women Writers Series, which Fetterley highlights, Alice Cary, Harriet Prescott Spofford, Maria Cummins, and Caroline Kirkland are virtually absent from the *MLA Online Bibliography* (encompassing the period from 1963 to 1998), with three, eight, ten, and sixteen entries respectively. Although admittedly this resource is incomplete, it provides a useful baseline. We should compare these figures to those for Hawthorne (2,871 entries) and Twain (1,137). See Fetterley, "Commentary: Nineteenth-Century American Women Writers and the Politics of Recovery," *American Literary History* 6.3 (1994): 600–11.

2. Cited in *Appreciation of Sarah Orne Jewett: Twenty-nine Interpretive Essays*, ed. Richard Cary (Waterville, Maine: Colby College Press, 1973), ix.

3. June Howard, "Introduction: Sarah Orne Jewett and the Traffic in Words," in *New Essays on* The Country of the Pointed Firs, ed. Howard (Cambridge: Cambridge University Press, 1994), 3; Henry James, "Mr. and Mrs. James T. Fields," *Atlantic Monthly* 116 (July 1915): 30.

4. Howard, "Introduction"; see also, for example, Stephanie Foote, "'I feared to find myself a foreigner': Revisiting Regionalism in Sarah Orne Jewett's *The Country of the Pointed Firs*," *Arizona Quarterly* 52.2 (1996): 37–61; Josephine Donovan, *New England Local Color Literature: A Women's Tradition* (New York: Frederick Ungar, 1983); Judith Fetterley and Marjorie Pryse, Introduction to *American Women Regionalists, 1850–1910* (New York: Norton, 1992); Joanna Russ, *How to Suppress Women's Writing* (Austin: University of Texas Press, 1983).

5. Fetterley, "Commentary," 608.

6. In an effort to defuse the situation and open lines of discussion between the two camps, June Howard in a recent essay calls the two perspectives the "celebratory" and the "historical." We believe that a return to Jewett's earlier critical situation provides an important context within which to understand the resonances of the current conflict. See Howard, "Unraveling Regions, Unsettling Periods: Sarah Orne Jewett and American Literary History," *American Literature* 68.2 (1996): 365–84. We are expanding significantly the period encompassed by Howard's account as well as exploring the sources for the rhetorical vehemence of the debate.

7. F. O. Matthiessen, *Sarah Orne Jewett* (Boston: Houghton Mifflin, 1929), 17.

8. In this connection, Richard Reed remarks that the poems in Robert Frost's *A Boy's Will* "are marred by several shortcomings," one of which is "excessive sentimentality"; he claims that "the sentimentality evident in so many of these early poems is often evoked through the presence or absence of animals." Reed, "The Animal World in Frost's Poetry," in *Frost: Centennial Essays II*, ed. Jac Tharpe (Jackson: University Press of Mississippi, 1976), 159, 160.

9. Van Wyck Brooks, *New England: Indian Summer, 1865–1915* (New York: Dutton, 1940), 348, 350, 353.

10. As Richard Brodhead has pointed out, regional fiction was invested in the creation of rural history, especially in the myth of the decline of country life. See Brodhead, *Cultures of Letters: Scenes of Reading and Writing in Nineteenth-Century America* (Chicago: University of Chicago Press, 1993), 121. See also Steven Hahn and Jonathan Prude, eds., *The Countryside in the Age of Capitalist Transformation: Essays in the Social History of Rural America* (Chapel Hill: University of North Carolina Press, 1985), especially the essay by Hal S. Barron; and Barron, *Those Who Stayed Behind: Rural Society in Nineteenth-Century New England* (New York: Cambridge University Press, 1984).

11. Matthiessen, *Sarah Orne Jewett*, 145.

12. Richard Cary, *Sarah Orne Jewett* (New York: Twayne, 1962), 157–58, 159; on fencing Jewett in, see Howard, "Unraveling Regions."

13. Perhaps the most famous attack came from John Crowe Ransom, who had written of Edna St. Vincent Millay that "Miss Millay is rarely and barely very intellectual, and I think everybody knows it," remarking that the poems of *Second April* reveal an "author [who] at twenty-nine is not consistently grown up." Ransom, "The Poet as Woman," in *The World's Body* (1938; rpt., Baton Rouge: Louisiana State University Press, 1968), 76, 78, 104.

14. See Brodhead, *Cultures of Letters*, 150–52.

15. Warner Berthoff, *The Ferment of Realism: American Literature 1884–1919* (New York: Free Press, 1965), 94, 97, 98.

16. Shirley Samuels, Introduction to *The Culture of Sentiment: Race, Gender, and Sentimentality in Nineteenth-Century America* (New York: Oxford University Press, 1992), 4–5.

17. Richard Cary, Introduction to *The Uncollected Stories of Sarah Orne Jewett* (Waterville, Maine: Colby College Press, 1971), xi. In an 1890 essay for *Century Magazine* poet and critic Helen Gray Cone had blasted sentimentalism. See Cone, "Woman in American Literature," *Century Magazine* 40.6 (1890): 922.

18. Suzanne Clark, *Sentimental Modernism: Women Writers and the Revolution of the Word* (Bloomington: Indiana University Press, 1991), 1. Clark's observation points us toward another element of sentimentalism that doomed its participants to oblivion in the twentieth century: its popularity and its affiliation with mass culture. Andreas Huyssen has argued that "Modernism constituted itself through a conscious strategy of exclusion, an anxiety of contamination by its other: an increasingly consuming and engulfing mass culture." He further

asserts that "[i]t is indeed striking . . . how the political, psychological, and aesthetic discourse around the turn of the century consistently and obsessively genders mass culture and the masses as feminine, while high culture, whether traditional or modern, clearly remains the privileged realm of male activities." Of course, the emphasis of modernism on inventiveness (we might say novelty) itself indicates the commodification of "high art" and hence its own participation in mass culture, but, as Huyssen affirms, in spite of attempts to destabilize "the opposition between modernism and mass culture [this opposition] has remained amazingly resilient over the decades." Andreas Huyssen, *After the Great Divide: Modernism, Mass Culture, Postmodernism* (Bloomington: Indiana University Press, 1986), vii, 47.

Several recent writers have explored how the modern university was central for creating and reinforcing the distinction between "high" and "low" culture. See, for example, Thomas Strychacz, *Modernism, Mass Culture, and Professionalism* (Cambridge: Cambridge University Press, 1993), 1–44; see also Gail McDonald, *Learning To Be Modern: Pound, Eliot, and the American University* (Oxford: Clarendon Press, 1993); Leslie Fiedler, *What Was Literature? Class Culture and Mass Society* (New York: Simon and Schuster, 1982); and John Guillory, *Cultural Capital: The Problem of Literary Canon Formation* (Chicago: University of Chicago Press, 1993), 139–41.

19. Most will agree that although Ann Douglas was the first contemporary critic to take sentimentalism seriously, Nina Baym and Jane Tompkins were the first to attempt to renovate the term. Douglas, *The Feminization of American Culture* (New York: Avon, 1977); Baym, *Woman's Fiction: A Guide to Novels by and about Women in America, 1820–1870* (Ithaca: Cornell University Press, 1978); Tompkins, *Sensational Designs: The Cultural Work of American Fiction, 1790–1860* (New York: Oxford University Press, 1985).

20. Susan Allen Toth, "The Value of Age in the Fiction of Sarah Orne Jewett," in *Appreciation*, ed. Cary, 259.

21. Donovan, *New England Local Color Literature*, 113, 118, 99. Donovan is very careful to say that Jewett herself is not utopian; see 99.

22. Marcia McClintock Folsom, "'Tact Is a Kind of Mind-Reading': Empathic Style in Sarah Orne Jewett's *The Country of the Pointed Firs*," *Colby Library Quarterly* 18.1 (1982): 66–78; Elizabeth Ammons, "Going in Circles: The Female Geography of Jewett's *The Country of the Pointed Firs*," *Studies in the Literary Imagination* 16.2 (1983): 83–92; Sandra Zagarell, "Narrative of Community: The Identification of a Genre," *Signs: Journal of Women in Culture and Society* 13 (1988): 498–527; Sarah Way Sherman, *Sarah Orne Jewett: An American Persephone* (Hanover, N.H.: University Press of New England, 1989). As we observed earlier, the chronology of the interpretive moments is not strict; we see the utopian moment expressed after Sherman's book appeared. See, for example, Elizabeth Ammons, *Conflicting Stories: American Women Writers at the Turn into the Twentieth Century* (New York: Oxford University Press, 1991), 44–58; Karen

[Kilcup] Oakes, "'All that lay deepest in her heart': Reflections on Jewett, Gender, and Genre," *Colby Quarterly* 26.3 (1990): 152–60; Ann Romines, *The Home Plot: Women, Writing, and Domestic Ritual* (Amherst: University of Massachusetts Press, 1992), 3–90; Marjorie Pryse, "Archives of Female Friendship and the 'Way' Jewett Wrote," *New England Quarterly* 66.1 (1993): 47–66; and Joseph Church, *Transcendent Daughters in Jewett's "Country of the Pointed Firs"* (Rutherford, N.J.: Fairleigh Dickinson University Press, 1994).

23. Sherman, *An American Persephone*, 2. On Jewett, same-sex friendships, and lesbianism, see Sherman, 69–84; Judith Fetterley, "Reading *Deephaven* as a Lesbian Text," in *Sexual Practice/Textual Theory: Lesbian Cultural Criticism*, ed. Susan J. Wolfe and Julia Penelope (Cambridge: Blackwell, 1993), 164–83; Josephine Donovan, *Sarah Orne Jewett* (New York: Frederick Ungar, 1980), 14; Donovan, "The Unpublished Love Poems of Sarah Orne Jewett," *Frontiers: A Journal of Women's Studies* 4.3 (1979): 26–31; and Lillian Faderman, *Surpassing the Love of Men: Friendship between Women from the Renaissance to the Present* (New York: William Morrow, 1981), 197–203.

24. Joanne Dobson, "The American Renaissance Reenvisioned," in *The (Other) American Traditions: Nineteenth-Century Women Writers*, ed. Joyce W. Warren (New Brunswick, N.J.: Rutgers University Press, 1993), 167.

25. On Jewett and sentimental tradition, see Sherman, *An American Persephone*, 7–15; for an opposing view (which we discuss below) see Brodhead, *Cultures of Letters*, 159–63.

26. Margaret Roman, *Sarah Orne Jewett: Reconstructing Gender* (Tuscaloosa: University of Alabama Press, 1992), xi.

27. Karen [Kilcup] Oakes, "'Colossal in Sheet-Lead': The Native American and Piscataqua-Region Writers," in *"A Noble and Dignified Stream": The Piscataqua Region in the Colonial Revival, 1860–1930*, ed. Sarah L. Giffen and Kevin D. Murphy (York, Maine: Old York Historical Society, 1992), 165–76; Elizabeth Ammons, "Material Culture, Empire, and Jewett's *Country of the Pointed Firs*," in *New Essays*, ed. Howard, 81–99; Zagarell, "*Country*'s Portrayal of Community and the Exclusion of Difference," in *New Essays*, ed. Howard, 39–60; Susan Gillman, "Regionalism and Nationalism in Jewett's *Country of the Pointed Firs*," in *New Essays*, ed. Howard, 101–17. Howard also observes feminist critics' omission of class differences in depictions of Jewett ("Unraveling Regions," 377).

28. Zagarell, "Community and Difference," 39. Zagarell cites only one source for sustained discussion of Jewett's views on race: Ferman Bishop, "Sarah Orne Jewett's Ideas of Race," *New England Quarterly* 30.2 (1957): 243–49. She also points to several writers who discuss Jewett's racial politics in "an aside": Warner Berthoff, "The Art of Jewett's *Pointed Firs*," *New England Quarterly* 32.1 (1959): 53; Josephine Donovan, *Sarah Orne Jewett*, 94–97; and Sherman, *An American Persephone*, 48–49. Jack Morgan and Louis A. Renza cite Van Wyck

Brooks's mention of Jewett's Irish stories; see Morgan and Renza, Introduction to *The Irish Stories of Sarah Orne Jewett* (Carbondale: Southern Illinois University Press, 1996), xvix. See also Cynthia J. Davis, "Making the Strange(r) Familiar: Sarah Orne Jewett's 'The Foreigner'," in *Breaking Boundaries: New Perspectives on Women's Regional Writing*, ed. Sherrie A. Inness and Diane Royer (Iowa City: University of Iowa Press, 1997), 88–108.

29. Zagarell, "Community and Difference," 47.

30. In relation to Jewett's nationalism, see also Amy Kaplan, "Nation, Region, and Empire," in *Columbia Literary History of the United States*, ed. Emory Elliott (New York: Columbia University Press, 1988), 240–66.

31. Fetterley writes that in comparison to *Deephaven*, "*The Country of the Pointed Firs* appears regressive, for it backs off from exploring how the relationship between mother and daughter might be solved by the daughter's adult relationship with a female peer." Fetterley, "Reading *Deephaven*," 182.

32. Brodhead, *Cultures of Letters*, 143, 144. Fetterley sees Michael Bell and Eric Sundquist as participants in this move to discredit feminist criticism of Jewett; Fetterley, "'Not in the Least American': Nineteenth-Century Literary Regionalism as UnAmerican Literature," in *Nineteenth-Century American Women Writers: A Critical Reader*, ed. Karen L. Kilcup (Malden, Mass., and Oxford: Blackwell, 1998), 18–19. See Bell, *The Problem of American Realism Studies in the Cultural History of an American Idea* (Chicago: University of Chicago Press, 1993); Sundquist, "Realism and Regionalism," in *Columbia Literary History of the United States*, 501–24; and Bell, "Gender and American Realism in *The Country of the Pointed Firs*," in *New Essays*, ed. Howard, 61–80.

33. Brodhead, *Cultures of Letters*, 107, 109–10, 116, 152–58. For another account of Jewett's place in "local color" literature, see Donna M. Campbell, *Resisting Regionalism: Gender and Naturalism in American Fiction, 1885–1915* (Athens: Ohio University Press, 1997), esp. chapter 2, "Necessary Limits: Women's Local Color Fiction."

34. Brodhead, *Cultures of Letters*, 143. Brodhead may also be responding to feminists' "emasculated" portraits of men in Jewett's work; see Oakes, "'All that lay deepest'."

35. Brodhead, *Cultures of Letters*, 149. Sherman appears to respond to this charge; see Introduction to *The Country of the Pointed Firs and Other Stories* (Hanover, N.H.: University Press of New England, 1997), xviii–xix.

36. Brodhead, *Cultures of Letters*, 167.

37. Brodhead, *Cultures of Letters*, 159, 160–61, 163 (Brodhead's emphasis). Brodhead accomplishes this narrative of Jewett's detachment by ignoring the work of critics such as Richard Cary and Margaret Roman, who discuss both her popular and children's literature. See Cary, Introduction to *The Uncollected Stories of Sarah Orne Jewett;* Roman, *Reconstructing Gender*, esp. 25–32. It is also worth noting that for several decades after her death, Jewett was taught on a

regular basis in "elite" universities; see Stanley T. Williams and Nelson F. Adkins, *Courses of Reading in American Literature with Bibliographies* (New York: Harcourt, Brace, 1930).

38. Brodhead, *Cultures of Letters*, 164.

39. Paula Bennett, "'The Pea That Duty Locks': Lesbian and Feminist-Heterosexual Readings of Emily Dickinson's Poetry," in *Lesbian Texts and Contexts: Radical Revisions*, ed. Karla Jay and Joanne Glasgow (New York: New York University Press, 1990), 104–25; Bennett, "Critical Clitoridectomy: Female Sexual Imagery and Feminist Psychoanalytic Theory," *Signs: Journal of Woman in Culture and Society* 18.2 (1993): 235–59. On critics' obsession with Jewett's "size," see also Bell, "Gender and American Realism," 66. Jewett's most recent biographer, Paula Blanchard, seems to continue in the vein of Jewett's self-minimization when she affirms, "When [Jewett] reached beyond herself and produced *The Country of the Pointed Firs* or a story on the level of 'The Foreigner' or 'The Queen's Twin', she was not able to analyze the work and see where its strengths lay—or indeed to recognize that it had unusual strengths at all." Blanchard, *Sarah Orne Jewett: Her World and Her Work* (Reading, Mass.: Addison-Wesley, 1994), 337.

40. Fetterley, "Commentary," 609, 610, 608. Fetterley observes that "Brodhead explicitly positions himself in opposition to feminist efforts to recuperate as resistant writers like Sarah Orne Jewett" (608).

41. On the separation of American culture into "high" and "low," see Lawrence Levine, *Highbrow/Lowbrow: The Emergence of Cultural Hierarchy* (Cambridge, Mass.: Harvard University Press, 1988).

42. On Jewett's newspaper publications, see Charles Johanningsmeier, "Sarah Orne Jewett and Mary E. Wilkins (Freeman): Two Shrewd Businesswomen in Search of New Markets," *New England Quarterly* 70 (1997): 57–82. On her writing for children, see, in addition to the work by Cary and Roman noted above, [Kilcup] Oakes's discussion of "York Garrison, 1640," in "'Colossal in Sheet-Lead'." "Woodchucks" is reprinted in Karen L. Kilcup, ed., *Nineteenth-Century American Women Writers: An Anthology* (Cambridge, Mass., and Oxford: Blackwell, 1997), 379–84.

43. For a discussion of the continuity between "popular" and "elite" readers, see Karen L. Kilcup, *Robert Frost and Feminine Literary Tradition* (Ann Arbor: University of Michigan Press, 1998), especially chapter 1; see also Brodhead, *Cultures of Letters*, 152.

44. Olivia Frey, "Beyond Literary Darwinism: Women's Voices and Critical Discourse," in *The Intimate Critique: Autobiographical Literary Criticism*, ed. Diane P. Freedman, Olivia Frey, and Frances Murphy Zauhar (Durham: Duke University Press, 1993), 44–45, 45.

45. Jane Tompkins, "Me and My Shadow," in *The Intimate Critique*, 25–26.

46. Even Richard Cary talks about recovering the "best" of Jewett, which (as his discussion makes clear) customarily means the least sentimental, and the

elite rather than the popular. See Cary, Introduction to *The Uncollected Stories of Sarah Orne Jewett.*

47. See Howard, "Unraveling Regions," 380.

48. Morgan and Renza, Introduction to *The Irish Stories of Sarah Orne Jewett*, xli–xliii. Cary discusses Jewett's Irish stories briefly; see Introduction to *The Uncollected Stories of Sarah Orne Jewett*, xii–xiii.

49. Morgan and Renza, xxxvii–xxxix; xxi, xxiv, xliii.

50. Ibid., xxxiv, xliii–xliv.

51. Fetterley, "Commentary," 608.

52. On the continuity between the *fin-de-siècle* and gender anxiety, see Rita Felski, "Fin de Siècle, Fin de Sexe: Transsexuality, Postmodernism, and the Death of History," in *Centuries' Ends, Narrative Means*, ed. Robert Newman (Stanford: Stanford University Press, 1996), 226; see also Elaine Showalter, *Sexual Anarchy: Gender and Culture at the Fin de Siècle* (New York: Viking, 1990).

53. Fetterley, "'Not in the Least American'," 27.

54. For a discussion of regionalism and nationalism, see the discussions by Gillman, Kaplan, and Sundquist cited earlier; see also David Jordan, ed., *Regionalism Reconsidered: New Approaches to the Field* (New York: Garland, 1994).

55. The exchanges about genre, for example, which have been central to Jewett studies for many years, form a matrix for discussion in collections such as *The (Other) American Traditions* and *Nineteenth-Century American Women Writers* and monographs like Elizabeth Ammons's *Conflicting Stories.* Moreover, *Jewett and Her Contemporaries* contributes to another movement in contemporary literary studies influenced strongly by women-of-color scholars like Gloria Anzaldúa: "border crossings" across such boundaries as race, class, sexuality, region, age, gender, and period. In this connection, Henry B. Wonham's collection, *Criticism on the Color Line: Desegregating American Literary Studies* (New Brunswick, N.J.: Rutgers University Press, 1996) reintegrates African American and "mainstream" American literature; and collections such as John Idol and Melinda Ponder's *Hawthorne and Women: Engendering and Expanding the Hawthorne Tradition* (Amherst: University of Massachusetts Press, 1999) and Karen L. Kilcup's *Soft Canons: American Women Writers and Masculine Tradition* (Iowa City: University of Iowa Press, 1999) help to resituate female-authored literature alongside canonical male writing.

Part I

Contexts

Readers and Reading

Sex, Class, and "Category Crisis"

Reading Jewett's Transitivity

Marjorie Pryse

A century after the publication of *The Country of the Pointed Firs* (1896), Sarah Orne Jewett continues to attract critics while eluding their classificatory schemes, since her fiction does not fit traditional literary categories: she was unable to sustain plot in the traditional sense, as she herself acknowledged, and her attempts at novels[1] have been considered less significant and less successful than her other works; she wrote sketches instead of short stories. Both *Deephaven* and *The Country of the Pointed Firs* are often treated as collections of sketches rather than sustained narratives with their own form;[2] and her rural, female, unmarried or widowed, poor, and often elderly fictional characters live well outside the centers of power and urban social hierarchies common in fiction by her realist contemporaries. Since the early 1980s feminist critics have contributed to a revaluation of Jewett and her work; indeed, feminist perspectives have allowed readers to understand Jewett's fiction and its regionalism as a deliberately minor literary mode that avoids reliance on sexist, racist, or classist stereotypes in the depiction of character and, in the process, creates an alternative narrative space that shifts the reader's perceptions to the margins of cultural influence.[3]

However, a critique of Jewett's work has emerged in the 1990s, building in part on Amy Kaplan's reading, which associates the ability of Jewett's urban narrator to move in and out of rural life in *The Country of the Pointed Firs* with "literary tourism."[4] This analysis appears to reflect new critical and theoretical directions in American literary studies, but has often constructed its case much less on careful rereadings of Jewett's texts than on the politics of critical reception itself. As the introduction to this volume explores from a different perspective, some of the new readings have faulted feminist criticism for failing to historicize racism, classism, and imperialism in Jewett, and in the ostensible project of informing readers that Jewett's fiction is not as transformative as feminist critics have claimed, have reduced Jewett's complexity and destabilized the power of her work for an analysis of gender relations. I am interested in reading Jewett again in light of these charges because I see her work as continuing to imagine regionalism as an alternative cultural vision—a vision Philip Fisher describes, before proceeding to discredit it, as "the counterelement to central myths within American studies."[5] I am also interested in examining the question of Jewett's critical reception in the 1990s as symptomatic of the way "new" directions in theory do not necessarily offer socially progressive alternatives. Rather, decentering gender as a framework for analysis can serve conservative interests by once again relegating a writer like Jewett to the margins of literary history. On the grounds that instead of critiquing emerging nationalism and imperialism at the turn of the twentieth century her work is rather complicit in consolidating these efforts, the radicalism of her representation of gender relations and the implications of this representation for understanding cultural and political power can itself be overwritten.

Jewett's resistance to traditional categories produces a salutary crisis for critics. To critique simplistic categorical and reductionist readings of Jewett is to argue for blurring and creating new categories of analysis, or at least understanding the way new categories transform old ones. Thus, when we are trying to understand a body of work as resistant to classification as Jewett's, we learn fluidity in our own critical frameworks. In the essay that follows, I will begin by examining the curious and recent reaction to Jewett and to feminist criticism of her work as a way of reading what I will characterize, in analyses of "An Autumn Holiday," "Martha's Lady," and other works in the second and third parts of this essay, as Jewett's transitivity, particularly in terms of her fiction's response to the consolidation of sex and class as modern categories at the end of the nineteenth century. Critics who fault Jewett for racism and classism have attempted to "overwrite" feminist criticism of her work, but find their own arguments subsequently outmoded by frameworks of analysis that straddle intersections of class and sexuality. Feminist criticism itself, and indeed the very articulation of the politics of criticism, also become transformed by such frameworks. Since emerging readers in a critical universe of theory are likely to argue that their own new categories have been "always already" on the horizon, and since the power of their critical lenses may add categories and compelling new readings as well, complicating our own reductive approaches to Jewett may help us move toward the very transitivity her work demonstrates—and without which we cannot follow her.

I

When Henry James damned *The Country of the Pointed Firs* by terming it Jewett's "beautiful little quantum of achievement,"[6] he also relegated Jewett to the category of "minor literature," which continued to characterize the critical reception of Jewett's work prior to the 1980s. Such a category, according to Louis Renza, can have the effect of interrupting the production of major literature, and thereby of resisting becoming culturally representative. Thus, "minor literature" would appear to have the potential for occupying a newly privileged critical status. Renza writes, "To this end, it enacts a passive-aggressive strategy that promotes parts over the whole and in this way exists in the process of becoming 'the third linguistic world', a literature that de facto sabotages whatever social or systematic code happens to control the means of major literary production at the moment."[7] Invoking Deleuze and Guattari's understanding of minor literature,[8] Renza proposes to evaluate the extent to which Jewett may be read as a "minority writer" writing a resistant "minor" literature, a project that might seem to be a strategy for elevating Jewett's critical status.

However, while he suggests that this "nineteenth-century American, regionalist, and woman writer" (32) might have produced such a resistant literature, he concludes that we should not view Jewett as a "minority" writer at all because her works "manifest the desire to reterritorialize their incipient politically minor or 'collective' minority context" (35). In other words, while Jewett did write "minor literature," she ought not be viewed as a writer whose work "sabotages" the social codes because she creates regional characters only in order to "reterritorialize" or recolonize them once again. Renza both raises the possibility of Jewett as literary saboteur and rejects it, arguing finally that while "minor literature originates in the comparative binary context of major and minor literature," Jewett "outlines a nondialectical category of minor literature," one "accidentally located in the 'district' of regionalist, feminist, pastoral, and sketchy modes of literary production" (167). It is only "accidentally" as well that Jewett occupies a category of literary production with potentially ideological content and therefore, for Renza, her work cannot be said to occupy the "third linguistic world." While Renza is arguably the first critic other than the feminists to consider Jewett as resistant to the hegemonic visions of "major" American literature, he nevertheless continues the pattern established by Henry James, that of raising the question of Jewett's cultural significance only to ascribe "little" value to her achievement. Indeed, Renza goes beyond James by suggesting that Jewett deliberately contains her own potential power. In Renza's reading Jewett was determined to remain a "minor," like the young protagonist of her sketch "A White Heron," despite what he describes as efforts to understand her work "as a scene of minor or major feminist *righting*" (97).

Renza's attempt to deconstruct both Jewett and feminist criticism of Jewett anticipated by a decade more recent critiques that have ironically done more than feminist criticism itself to bring Jewett decidedly into critical and theoretical focus. Although these critiques have produced some intriguing new directions for understanding Jewett's work, they have also once again curiously emphasized the limitations of her ideological vision, an argument that works very hard to contain Jewett's value. Here I wish to revisit the debate outlined in the introduction to this collection, focusing on the critical self-reversals in recent Jewett scholarship and on some historical and political contexts for these reversals. Such an investigation is central in order to articulate my own view that Jewett's work itself provides us with a theoretical model that is more sophisticated and nuanced than those applied to her work, and that this model offers an important direction that Jewett scholarship—and, indeed, feminist theory more broadly—should pursue.

Some recent critics have argued, echoing Renza's reading, that Jewett "reterritorializes" her rural Maine communities by the racist, classist, and imperialist attitudes she purportedly brings to her fictional representations.[9] In the most intense of the recent critical attacks on Jewett to date, in which in the process she repudiates her own earlier writing about *The Country of the Pointed Firs*, Elizabeth Ammons argues that when Jewett's readers "eat the word(s) and swallow the house" in the Bowden reunion scene, "what we commemorate . . . is white imperialism."[10] In what she admits is a "disconcerting" interpretation of the reunion, Ammons describes "the subtle but clear protofascist implications of all those white people marching around in military formation ritualistically affirming their racial purity, global dominance, and white ethnic superiority and solidarity." Thus, for Ammons, "there is no escaping that the communion at the end of *The Country of the Pointed Firs* is about colonialism."[11] Sandra Zagarell, whose interest in exploring what she calls Jewett's "hierarchical racialized thinking" is an attempt to complicate her own earlier view of *Pointed Firs* as a "narrative of community,"[12] concurs that while "Jewett would never have employed . . . crude, derogatory racial categories," nevertheless *Pointed Firs* "does echo the more genteel advocacy of racial exclusion articulated by members of Jewett's Boston circle."[13]

Discussion of Jewett's ideas about race preceded the new interest in "racialized thinking" in her work in the 1990s. Ferman Bishop as early as 1957 finds references in her work to the view that the population around Berwick possessed "inherent worth" through their supposedly Norman lineage and that "those more especially singled out for approbation were certain members of the local aristocracy, who presumably enjoyed a less adulterated Norman inheritance than their lesser brethren."[14] Writing from the 1950s, Ferman Bishop appears an uncanny predictor of 1990s assertions, like those by Ammons and Zagarell, of Jewett's imperialism and implicit racism.[15] However, differences between Bishop's claim for Jewett's Nordicism and Ammons's assertions of Jewett's racism rest in the political stakes that have accompanied revaluation of Jewett's work in the 1980s and 1990s that were not present during the 1950s, when Jewett and her fiction remained safely marginalized.[16]

In 1957, Bishop could raise the question of Jewett's "aristocratic emphasis upon the racial inequalities of mankind" while also acknowledging "her admiration for Whittier and Harriet Beecher Stowe," early-nineteenth-century abolitionists; and although he mentions Jewett's reference to Negroes in "A War Debt" (1895), he does not find it necessary to analyze Jewett's representation of Caesar in *The Tory Lover* (1901) and the few other African Americans mentioned in her fiction, or the French-speaking Mrs. Captain Tolland in "The Foreigner" (1900), or the characters in Jewett's Irish stories, that might allow a closer examination of race in Jewett's texts. When Bishop explains Jewett's interest in a "theory of 'race'" after the 1880s by suggesting that "the time-spirit must have done its work,"[17] he may be alluding to attitudes that would culminate in *Plessy* v. *Ferguson* (1896). We might be able to infer Jewett's critique of such attitudes from her representations of the Irish, which Jack Morgan and Louis Renza, in a recent collection of Jewett's Irish stories, characterize as performing "a kind of specific cultural-historical work. Not least, they serve to undo the 'Paddy' stereotype."[18] Although Morgan and Renza consider Jewett's treatment of the Irish "ethnographically problematical," at the same time they comment that Jewett's stories represent "the first serious treatment of the Irish in America by an important literary figure and a prescient engagement with what today we would term the issue of multiculturalism" and end by invoking Jewett's "respect for Irish cultural otherness."[19] Writing within a context informed by emerging attitudes toward Civil Rights in the years following *Brown* v. *Board of Education* (1954), Bishop could assert his own awakening interest in issues and representations of race. Nevertheless, despite his contention that "after all allowance has been made, [Jewett] must still be counted a consistent adherent to the ideas of nordicism,"[20] Bishop does not equate Jewett's pride in what she believed was her Anglo-Norman and French heritage with a form of white supremacy.[21]

In contrast with Bishop, Susan Gillman in 1994 does associate Jewett with white supremacy of the most egregious kind when she writes, referring again to the Bowden reunion scene from *The Country of the Pointed Firs*, "the Bowden family might as well be one of the many fraternal organizations—among them the Knights of Columbus and the Ku Klux Klan—that flourished during this period of growing U.S. interest in expansion overseas."[22] If the Bowden family "might as well be" the Ku Klux Klan, then Jewett's fiction does promote white supremacy. It may appear that discrediting feminist interpretations of Jewett would serve as a corrective response to inadequacies in feminism itself, one that characterizes second-wave U.S. feminism as primarily white and middle class and, following on the critiques of African American and other theorists, would fault both feminism and the critical projects of early feminist criticism as racist and classist.[23] If Jewett were truly complicit in promoting white supremacy, most readers in the 1990s would not be interested in reading, much less writing about, her work. Ironically, demonstrating Jewett's racism and imperialism can become a move to exonerate the critic from similar charges while allowing him or her to continue to write about Jewett and thereby to suggest the importance of reconsidering her work.

Gillman makes a symptomatic gesture toward feminism that suggests her uneasiness in collocating the Bowden family and the Ku Klux Klan and that helps explicate the politics of 1990s critiques of Jewett. She argues that because the Bowden clan is "predominantly female," they can "supplant" a Klan vision with "a road of their own, or what amounts to a feminist nationalism" that allows the "Bowden militarism to partially undercut itself" (113–14). She finds evidence, in the feast's abrupt end, that "the whole reunion episode contains its own critique," and that "Jewett's feminism locates a place where she can be critical of the culture within which she speaks" (114). But what kind of nationalism is a "feminist nationalism," and is it a better or a worse kind? And since Gillman argues that recent feminist criticism, what she describes as work by "revisionist feminists" (115), "has tended to construct an essentialized rather than historicized conception of woman" (103), how does she herself escape essentialism in her description of the "predominantly female" (and therefore implicitly "feminist") Bowden "clan"? Gillman's argument itself appears to "supplant" feminist criticism of Jewett by focusing on her fiction's nationalism and racism, yet ends by invoking a concept of feminism that will disavow "a specifically female world of love and ritual" in order to admit both literary readings of regionalism and "celebratory" feminist critics "back into the fold of their dialogue with the dominant culture" (115). A gendered critique of that culture, her essay implies, becomes "celebratory" or what Zagarell terms "informed appreciation" of Jewett:[24] for Gillman, only a critique that subsumes feminism into a critique of nationalism will allow for a "fully historicized" reading of Jewett.

The difficulty lies in the fact that subsuming a feminist critique, or terming it merely "celebratory," may lead readers to wonder why the feminists have tried to make such a "major" issue of Jewett's marginalization, and why we should bother to read Jewett at all if she only "partially undercuts" the racism and nationalism of her fiction. Judith Fetterley cites Richard Brodhead as a critic who "explicitly positions himself in opposition to feminist efforts to recuperate as resistant writers like Sarah Orne Jewett and chooses instead to present nineteenth-century American women writers from Warner to Stowe to Alcott to Jewett as simply complicit in a variety of cultural projects designed to consolidate their own race and class privilege."[25] The operative word here is "simply," for Brodhead's claims about class in Jewett as well as Ammons's,

Zagarell's, and Gillman's assertions of Jewett's imperialism and racism seem to emerge from the premise that a writer's analysis of race, class, and empire can be readily determined without a thorough historicizing that ought to include close readings of texts in their contextual complexity. Brodhead, however, as Fetterley observes, uses "class and race as categories of analysis that cancel rather than complicate attention to gender," thereby understanding white women writers "as sites of race and class privilege" and making it impossible, therefore, to argue "that recovering their texts is an act of enfranchising the disenfranchised."[26] For Brodhead and Ammons in particular, Jewett's race and class enroll her in social and cultural categories that render any analysis of her resistance to those categories suspect.

In compiling the collection titled *New Essays on "The Country of the Pointed Firs,"* June Howard occupies the position of attempting to resolve the apparent contradiction between feminist criticism and critiques that would supplant that work. Howard underscores the existence of "two separate bodies of literary criticism" concerning Jewett, urges her readers not to be misled "into thinking that the literary culture they describe was so thoroughly segregated,"[27] and describes her collection of essays as a "dialogue rather than a consensus," one that will "combine the insights of feminist readings of Jewett with the new analysis of regionalism that has emerged in the past few years."[28] And in an even more recent acknowledgment of critical controversy, Howard addresses what she describes as a binary opposition between two critical approaches to Jewett's work, the "historicizing" and the "feminist."[29] Kaplan, Brodhead, and the essays by Ammons, Zagarell, and Gillman included in Howard's own recent collection all fall into the "historicizing" category.[30] Howard characterizes the conflict as "the opposition between celebration and critique" (370), as "the strongly opposed current views of Jewett as an empathetic artist of local life or as a literary tourist" (377), and as a "hermeneutic of restoration" set against "a complementary hermeneutic of suspicion" (378). As a result of specifying her "disagreements with [Brodhead's] account of Jewett" (370) and presenting her reading of Jewett's 1878 story "A Late Supper," Howard concludes that neither the historicizing view nor what she terms "the celebratory view" is adequate to understanding Jewett, just as she began by admonishing critics to avoid what she calls "interpretation by classification" (365).

As a closer analysis of classification in Jewett's fiction reveals, rather than consolidating social categories her work asks us instead to "leap the fence" of classificatory systems (as her narrator does in one of the sketches I will discuss in the second part of this essay, "An Autumn Holiday"). What has created the apparent oppositionality within recent Jewett criticism may indeed be, as Howard notes, the critics' tendency toward "interpretation by classification." Jewett's own work creates what Marjorie Garber has termed "category crisis"—or rather, the critical controversy her work has elicited in the 1990s reflects the extent to which many critics themselves continue to endorse restrictive boundaries contained in modern understandings of social structures and literary hierarchies.[31] The real crisis lies elsewhere—not in Jewett's fiction but in the critics' inability to fully incorporate Jewett's strategies into their own reading practices. Destabilizing gender as a framework for analysis masquerades as a critical strategy; in fact it reinforces gender as a cultural binary and, as Brodhead does, locates women themselves and especially nineteenth-century American women writers as complicit in establishing and maintaining the terms of their own oppression.

Although the sex-gender classifications of the critics Howard sets in opposition to one other may appear to deflect the relationship between current critical controversy and gender because several in the "historicizing" group are women, Howard's categories in fact reinforce a gender binary. The category of "feminist" criticism is clearly figured as "feminine" in Howard's account and the "historicizing" as "masculine." For example, in Howard's narrative of regionalism's complicity in the "drive towards national unification" ("Unraveling Regions," 368), the (masculine) "historicizing" interpretations correct the (feminine) "limited horizons" (367) of "celebratory" interpretations of women's friendships.[32] In this implicitly gendered critical binary, "the historicizing view *distances* Jewett, looking back and finding difference; the celebratory view *embraces* her, finding similarity" (380; emphasis added). Surely it is time to recognize that feminist criticism of the 1990s has become historicized, that gender remains a necessary component of any historical analysis of literary and cultural texts, and that to be sufficiently explanatory, critical arguments must center gender as well as other categories of analysis—race, class, imperialism, and, as I will suggest, sexuality. Because her work does not fit readily into any category, whether those of traditional literary history or that of a newly "historicized" model, Jewett creates a crisis in American literary criticism.

In the second and third sections of this essay, I will demonstrate that a much more complex reading of Jewett emerges when we locate her within an historical moment in which the very categories of analysis fascinating to late-twentieth-century critics began to be consolidated in modernism. What would perhaps have troubled Jewett most about the reductionism of critics who insist on viewing her "simply" as a site of race and class privilege is that Jewett herself, writing during the transition to modernism, reflects a concern with categories—especially, as I will suggest, with the categories of sex and class—even though much of her work appears to resist the very concept of category. We can thus make a case for Jewett as a resisting minor(ity) writer: although her fiction may not fully anticipate critical concerns of the 1990s, it does shift the reader's focus away from social and cultural categories to the fluid, permeable movement *across* and *between* borders. This movement may be understood most clearly in Jewett's analysis of sexuality and the way sex and class interact to limit women's freedom. Despite efforts of Jewett's critics and biographers to "locate" her, she will not be confined within any category that 1990s critics attempt to impose on her work in the name of historicism.[33]

2

Eve Sedgwick uses the term "transitivity" to describe what she terms "inversion models" of homosexuality that "locate gay people—whether biologically or culturally—at the threshold between genders."[34] "Transitivity" also describes Jewett's own liminality and her resistance to being confined, whether as narrator in "An Autumn Holiday" explaining her unexpected visit to someone she knows far from the village ("It was too pleasant to stay in the house, and I haven't had a long walk for some time before");[35] as a storyteller whose lack of plot defies genre if not form; or as an artist whose writing was inextricable from her love for women[36] and who resisted being confined by her culture's construction of gender. "Transitivity" also offers a term for the kind of reading practice Jewett's work invites, one that encourages us to avoid substituting one category for another and also to be less reductive, more attuned to the borders across and between the categories we construct as critics, whether we understand these categories to be literary modes ("realism," "local color," "regionalism"), subject positions (race, class, gender), or narrative forms (story, sketch, novel).

In a letter to Willa Cather in 1908, Jewett comments on Cather's story "On the Gull's Road." While she praises the story's "feeling," she suggests to Cather that the dying woman's lover in the story, whom Cather made a man, might have been more convincing as a woman. Sexuality, for Jewett, was not a fixed category. The letter suggests Jewett's own awareness, as a reader, of the way Cather's insistence on a heterosexual frame for her story confines its potential power. "The lover is as well done as he could be when a woman writes in the man's character,—it must always, I believe, be something of a masquerade. I think it is safer to write about him as you did about the others, and not try to be he! And you could almost have done it as yourself—a woman could love her in that same protecting way—a woman could even care enough to wish to take her away from such a life, by some means or other."[37] Whether we understand Jewett to be describing a "long-lived, intimate, loving friendship between two women"[38] or the kind of same-sex relationship that the sexologists at the turn of the century were calling "sexual inversion," her advice to Cather resists pathologizing same-sex love and holds out the possibility of sexual indeterminacy as a source for creativity.

Jewett's resistance to rigid sexual categories in this letter emerged from the context within which both Jewett and Cather were writing, as women who formed primary emotional and relational bonds with other women at the turn of the century. According to Lillian Faderman, as women gained freedom in the United States people began to fear that "the distinction between the sexes would be obliterated." This cultural anxiety fostered a belief that women who sought equality with men were "inverts" and thus "love between women was metamorphosed into a freakishness."[39] For Faderman, the medical interest in homosexuality had political motivation; "love between women had been encouraged or tolerated for centuries—but now that women had the possibility of economic independence, such love became potentially threatening to the social order" (240). "The sexologists thus created a third sex, which, they said, was characterized by a neurotic desire to reject what had hitherto been women's accepted role" (248).

The central force in the emergence of the turn-of-the-century pathologizing of same-sex love was not Freud, although Freud did contribute to the new visibility of homosexuality in his 1905 essays,[40] but Havelock Ellis, whose *Sexual Inversion* appeared in 1897.[41] Paul Robinson claims that Ellis's larger work, *Studies in the Psychology of Sex*, the first six volumes of which were published between 1897 and 1910, "established the basic moral categories for nearly all subsequent sexual theorizing."[42] For Robinson, "sexual modernism represented a reaction against Victorianism" (2), a reaction that moved beyond morality to the construction of new categories. In a curious way, then, modernism both expanded our understanding of sexuality by exploring the existence of homosexuality and women's sexuality in general and confined our understanding by categorizing it. Modernism, Faderman argues, gave us sexual categories women had not been aware of before—and then pathologized them. Love between women "became a condition for which women were advised to visit a doctor and have both a physical and mental examination" (252). Robinson offers evidence that supports Faderman's concern, noting that Ellis "argued that the prime objective of the Women's Movement ought to be not equality with men but official recognition of the distinctive needs that resulted from woman's physical and psychological constitution" (35).

The dates of Ellis's and Freud's contributions to turn-of-the-century sexology might be said to indicate that Jewett had already accomplished her major work before modernist categories of sexuality were constructed. However, as Josephine Donovan has convincingly argued, Jewett's *A Country Doctor* (1884) suggests that she was aware of the work of the German physicians (especially Richard von Krafft-Ebing), "who had been publishing their theories about female inverts since 1869."[43] Donovan's article cites several passages in *A Country Doctor* that provide evidence that Jewett had read Krafft-Ebing's *Psychopathia Sexualis*, published in Europe in 1882, the same year Jewett and Annie Fields made their first European trip. Donovan cites the manuscript obituary that Jewett wrote for her father, Theodore Herman Jewett, in which Jewett identifies him as a specialist in "obstetrics and diseases of women and children" (26); and notes that Dr. Leslie in *A Country Doctor*, Dr. Jewett's analog, "has an extensive medical library, subscribes to the latest medical journals, and rejects European medical opinion. . . . Nan herself occasionally reads these works but generally with similar disregard" (26). Donovan concludes, "[I]t seems likely that Dr. Jewett would have been aware of the sexologists' theories and that he and Sarah may have discussed them. Her own proclivities could have readily identified her with this 'new type' of woman that European theorists were condemning as a pathological freak" (26). Jewett and her father, Donovan argues, along with Dr. Leslie and Nan in *A Country Doctor*, rejected those theories. Jewett's fiction supports Donovan's conclusion.[44]

In her depiction of the transvestite Captain Dan'el Gunn in her 1880 story "An Autumn Holiday," Jewett seems to anticipate the work of both Josephine Donovan and Marjorie Garber. "Category crisis" is Garber's term for "a failure of definitional distinction, a borderline that becomes permeable, that permits of border-crossings from one (apparently distinct) category to another: black/white, Jew/Christian, noble/bourgeois, master/servant, master/slave" (16). Garber notes that "category crises can and do mark displacements from the axis of *class* as well as from *race* onto the axis of gender," and she reads transvestism in particular as "the disruptive element that intervenes, not just a category crisis of male and female, but the crisis of category itself" (17). She argues that the transvestite challenges binary thinking about gender, "putting into question the categories of 'female' and 'male', whether they are considered essential or constructed, biological or cultural" (10), and often takes shape "as the creation of what looks like a third term. . . . But what is crucial here . . . is that the "third term" is *not* a *term*. Much less is it a *sex*. . . . The "third" is a mode of articulation, a way of describing a space of possibility" (11). For Garber, the "third" is something "that challenges the possibility of harmonious and stable binary symmetry" (12), that "puts in question identities previously conceived as stable, unchallengeable, grounded, and 'known'" (13): "[T]he transvestite figure in a text . . . that does not seem, thematically, to be primarily concerned with gender difference or blurred gender indicates a *category crisis elsewhere*, an irresolvable conflict . . . that displaces the resulting discomfort onto a figure that already inhabits, indeed incarnates, the margin" (17).

One of Jewett's fascinations includes her own challenge to binary thinking, one in which the "third" not only articulates a "space of possibility" but appears to realize its potential. Jewett's "An Autumn Holiday" begins with the narrator springing over stone walls and "shaky pasture fences" and expressing her delight in the new, the unexplored, even the transgressive. She writes: "I am very fond of walking between the roads. One grows so familiar with the highways themselves. But once leap the fence and there are a hundred roads that you can take, each with its own scenery and entertainment. Every walk of this kind proves itself a tour of exploration and discovery, and the fields of my own town, which I think I know so well, are always new fields" (141). As the sketch opens, Jewett's sense of discovery appears to invoke Thoreau more readily than to merit an application of Marjorie Garber—until she arrives at the home of Miss Polly Marsh. Polly Marsh tells the story of Captain Dan'el Gunn who "got sun-struck" during his time in the militia "and at last he seemed to get it into his head that he was his own sister Patience that died some five or six years before: she was single too, and she always lived with him" (153). When he starts wearing his sister's clothes, people begin to call him "Miss Dan'el Gunn," and Polly reports that "The neighbors got used to his ways, and, land! I never thought nothing of it after the first week or two" (155).

Polly describes his unexpected entrance into church meeting one afternoon:

> "But to see him come up the aisle! He'd fixed himself nice as he could, poor creatur; he'd raked out Miss Patience's old Navarino bonnet with green ribbons and a willow feather, and set it on right over his cap, and he had her bead bag on his arm, and her turkey-tail fan that he'd got out of the best room; and he come with little short steps up to the pew: and I s'posed he'd set by the door; but no, he made to go by us, up into the corner where she used to set, and took her place, and spread his dress out nice, and got his handkerchief out o' his bag, just's he'd seen her do. He took off his bonnet all of a sudden, as if he'd forgot it, and put it under the seat, like he did his hat—that was the only thing he did that any woman wouldn't have done—and the crown of his cap was bent some. I thought die I should." (158)

The narrator asks, "What did they say in church when the captain came in," and Polly tells how "a good many of them laughed," but "[a]fter the first fun of it was over, most of the folks felt bad. . . . I see some tears in some o' the old folks' eyes: they hated to see him so broke in his mind, you know" (159–60). For the townspeople, Gunn is "broke in his mind," not someone deliberately challenging categories of sex and gender; yet Polly ends with "the greatest" story—the afternoon he was "setting at home" when the Deacon stopped in to see the captain's nephew Jacob about a fence but stayed to tea at the captain's urging. "And when he went away, says he to [cousin] Statiry, in a dreadful knowing way, 'Which of us do you consider the deacon come to see?' You see the deacon was a widower" (162). "The greatest" moment, for Polly, is the one in which "Miss Dan'el Gunn" thinks (s)he might elicit a proposal; indeed, marriage, while perhaps a laughing matter for Polly in this situation, would become the mark of success for the transvestite, what a woman "ought" to want.

Telling the story about the captain reveals Polly's own displaced discomfort about gender. When she describes his appearance at meeting, Polly says, "He hadn't offered to go anywhere of an afternoon for a long time," then adds, "I s'pose he thought women ought to be stayers at home according to Scripture" (157). And when (s)he decides next week to attend the Female Missionary Society meeting dressed in sister Patience's clothes, Polly reports that the ladies "treated him so handsome, and tried to make him enjoy himself," although she wonders "if some of 'em would have put themselves out much if it had been some poor flighty old woman" (161). Jewett suggests that Polly can accommodate a potential disruption of gender norms—although the transvestite provokes her to contrast the power of the cross-dressing man with the powerlessness of actual women. Captain Gunn's transvestism does not trouble the community—but it does "trouble" the category-ridden reader by adding sexuality to Jewett's interest in gender.

It also problematizes an analysis of the class difference between the narrator of "An Autumn Holiday" and Polly herself. The narrator's father is a country doctor; Polly is a country nurse, who without medical training has become "one of the most useful women in the world" and had spent the winter taking care of the narrator during a "very painful illness." Like the narrator, she is also a storyteller: "There was no end either to her stories or her kindness" (148). Thus when the narrator arrives at Polly Marsh's house and describes it as "low and long and unpainted" and its hollyhocks as "bowed down despairingly" (145) in a day that otherwise "brought no thought of winter" (139), she is establishing contrasts between nurse and doctor, oral storyteller and writer-narrator, that we read as class markers. The figure of the transvestite in the sketch destabilizes these markers by bringing into focus other forms of gender transgression that end by linking Polly and the narrator.

"An Autumn Holiday" appears, like much of Jewett's work, to lack form, as if the sketch's arrival at the figure of the transvestite is a roundabout effect of the narrator's "tour of exploration and discovery" and her unexpected visit with Polly Marsh. When the narrator arrives, Polly has just had a very pleasant encounter with the narrator's doctor-father, and, demonstrating "an evident consciousness of the underlying compliment and the doctor's good opinion" (147), she and her sister Mrs. Snow are happy to stop their spinning and gossip with the narrator. After a fashion reminiscent of the narrator's own roundabout walk, Polly eventually recalls the man for whom "a cousin o' my father's" kept house and whom she visited for a season when she was growing up (152). Mrs. Snow then encourages her sister to tell the narrator the story of Captain Dan'el Gunn: "Do tell her about him, Polly; she'll like to hear" (152). The question the story raises at this point is how Mrs. Snow knows that our narrator would "like to hear" the story about the transvestite. If the narrator had a reputation for enjoying the quaint, the queer, the "local color," and if the women believed that her "autumn holiday" provided her merely with an opportunity to collect material for her sketch-book, it seems unlikely that they would welcome her so warmly, or that they would trust her to withhold judgment when Polly tells her story; for despite the fact that Polly reports laughing at the transvestite, the narrator does not laugh upon hearing the story and seems to realize that Polly is not really telling it for her entertainment. The figure of the transvestite in the sketch calls our attention to another dynamic that leads the narrator to refer to the women as "my friends" (146).

Once Polly begins to tell her story, the narrator rarely speaks and then only to ask questions that encourage her to continue. When the story ends, so does the narrator's visit. However, when the women see the doctor returning along the road and Polly hurries out to stop him, Mrs. Snow confides to the narrator that the Captain's nephew had "offered to Polly that summer she was over there, and she never could see why she didn't have him" (162). The story about the transvestite's deviance displaces Polly Marsh's own, for she has remained an unmarried woman, even, Mrs. Snow hints, a marriage resister: "Polly wasn't one to marry for what she could get if she didn't like the man" even though "there was plenty that would have said yes, and thank you too, sir, to Jacob Gunn" (162). Although it is Mrs. Snow who finally tells the narrator this story about Polly, the intimacy and trust the story conveys suggests that, in Garber's terms, Polly's sharing the story about the transvestite "displaces the resulting discomfort onto a figure that already inhabits, indeed incarnates, the margin" (17)—the marginal-because-unmarried woman. Read symptomatically, Polly's story about the captain displaces the queerness of resistance to marriage—which she recognizes, in telling the story, gives her common ground with the narrator. The recognition conferred by the doctor's "good opinion" and the narrator's unexpected visit; the implied connections between Jewett's unmarried narrator and Polly Marsh; and the women's shared approach to storytelling in which one observation can "link it in my thoughts with something I saw once" (143) somewhere else allows the sketch itself to "leap the fence."

"An Autumn Holiday" becomes a hybrid even in Jewett's canon, neither quasi-autobiographical diary entry nor short story, but a "third" form in which transgressive status and narrative strategies link country nurse and former patient to disrupt class boundaries. As the narrator rides home with her doctor-father, the sketch's final sentence suggests that the narrator gives Polly's story, and Polly's situation, a great deal of thought: "It was a much longer way home around by the road than by the way I had come across the fields" (162). In Garber's understanding of "category crisis," the transvestite in "An Autumn Holiday" shows Polly something about the way men and women are accorded differential power that she might not otherwise have seen, thereby allowing the story to critique both gender (despite the community's way of explaining the captain's transvestism by claiming he was "broke in his mind") and class, as the unmarried "queer" status of Polly Marsh finds common ground with the fence-crossing doctor's daughter from town, who can afford to spin sketches rather than yarn.

Although transvestism does not recur in Jewett's work (except as a joke in "Hollowell's Pretty Sister"),[45] Jewett does not portray gender as a binary construction. Rather, Jewett's characters inhabit the "third" space of possibility in which gender is a category many of them resist. Indeed, as feminist critics have observed since the 1970s, Jewett's major fiction deliberately blurs gender distinctions.[46] In *The Country of the Pointed Firs* Jewett creates a world in which men and women behave in ways that do not necessarily conform to categories of masculine and feminine and where gender does not determine the valences of power in the community. Jewett imagines a society constructed not on an imbalance of power between men and women but on a recognition of the values of a prepatriarchal and preindustrial world symbolized most clearly in Mrs. Todd, whose stature in the community of Dunnet Landing derives from her skills as a healer and herbalist who, like Polly Marsh, maintains cordial professional relations with the medical doctor.

Among the 1990s critics hostile to feminist interpretations of Jewett, Richard Brodhead is perhaps the most scathing in his rejection of what he calls the feminist critics' "rescue plan" for Jewett.[47] Brodhead wants us to move beyond, in his terms, "the feminist rehabilitation of regionalism" to read Jewett in the context of "a nineteenth-century leisure-class culture" whose primary relation to rural life becomes that of the vacationer. When the narrator of *The Country of the Pointed Firs* travels to Dunnet Landing, Brodhead writes, "she is an urbanite, a native of the world of 'anxious living'—the world of stressful modernity and its social arrangements" (145). She has financial resources that the Dunnet Landing residents do not share: "she can command someone else's home as a second home for her leisure, and does so with a confident exercise of her rights" (146).

Brodhead's argument is provocative in reminding us to examine class distinctions in Jewett, yet it may benefit from the same kind of historicizing he recommends for her. Brodhead accurately depicts Jewett's narrator as belonging to a different world—a different socioeconomic class—than Mrs. Todd; what he fails to give Jewett credit for, however, is her resistance to such categories as "urban world" and "social class" and her fiction's struggle to remain always on the borders that create barriers within such categories. Amy Kaplan reminds us that tourism began as an industry at the end of the nineteenth century; and Jewett herself, in her preface to the 1893 edition of *Deephaven*, describes Kate Lancaster and Helen Denis as "pioneers" of an urban life that "had made necessary a reflex current that set countryward in summer."[48] Yet Kate and Helen's summer in Deephaven, like the narrator's extended visits to Dunnet Landing in *The Country of the Pointed Firs*, complicates a construction of the tourist as urbanite vacationer; Kaplan's and Brodhead's readings do not distinguish between those outsiders to rural life who come to gawk and those whose perspective alters to take in the lives of rural people, a distinction Judith Fetterley and I have elsewhere characterized as the difference between "local color" and regionalist fiction: "Because regional narrators identify with rather than distance themselves from the material of their stories, regionalist texts allow the reader to view the regional speaker as subject and not as object and to include empathic feeling as an aspect of critical response . . . [by] shifting the center of perception."[49] In "An Autumn Holiday," when the narrator withholds laughter and listens empathically, she is modeling for her own readers an enlarging critical response. The dramatic moment in the fiction, which allows us to reread the sketch and its transvestite, occurs at the end, when Mrs. Snow tells the narrator the story of Polly Marsh's refusal to marry and we can then understand the basis for the cross-class relationship.

In *The Country of the Pointed Firs*, Mrs. Todd's economic situation blurs rather than reifies class distinctions. Mrs. Todd diversifies her occupations in order to earn her living: she gathers and sells herbs and herb products, provides a form of psychotherapy to many patients who come to her for herbal healing, and takes in lodgers such as Jewett's narrator. Mrs. Todd's employment thus follows the pattern for rural New England women throughout the nineteenth century. Providing lodging, in particular, was one source of income for women, one that remained located within the household even after industrialization had removed most production from the home.[50] Taking in summer lodgers makes it possible for Mrs. Todd to continue her more important work, and when Jewett's narrator describes the "two dollars and twenty-seven cents" she has collected one day during Mrs. Todd's absence, she calls herself Mrs. Todd's "business partner" (6). Mrs. Todd regrets the narrator's decision to move her own "literary employments" (7) to the schoolhouse. "'Well, dear', [Mrs. Todd] said sorrowfully, 'I've took great advantage o' your bein' here. I ain't had such a season for years, but I have never had nobody I could so trust. All you lack is a few qualities, but with time you'd gain judgment an' experience, an' be very able in the business. I'd stand right here an' say it to anybody'" (7).

Yet the "business" Mrs. Todd alludes to here involves more than the narrator's ability to mind the store; it also includes her potential as a good listener, which forms the heart of Mrs. Todd's "psychotherapy" practice. The text makes it clear that Mrs. Todd does more than dispense herbal remedies. As the narrator observes, Mrs. Todd's remedies often require "whispered directions" and "an air of secrecy and importance" because "[i]t may not have been only the common ails of humanity with which she tried to cope; it seemed sometimes as if love and hate and jealousy and adverse winds at sea might also find their proper remedies among the curious wild-looking plants in Mrs. Todd's garden" (4). The "plot" of *The Country of the Pointed Firs* goes beyond its portrait of the narrator's development from an isolated urbanite to a person capable of human connection; it also demonstrates the narrator's implicit apprenticeship to Mrs. Todd. Mrs. Todd helps the narrator acquire the "few qualities" that allow her to "gain judgment an' experience"—but within the context of the narrator's "literary employments," she becomes not an herb-dispensing healer but rather a narrator who views border-crossing between urban and rural worlds as psychically healing—both for her own readers and for the residents of Dunnet Landing about whom Captain Littlepage says, "In the old days, a good part o' the best men here knew a hundred ports and something of the way folks lived in them. They saw the world for themselves, and like's not their wives and children saw it with them. They may not have had the best of knowledge to carry with 'em sight-seein', but they were some acquainted with foreign lands an' their laws, an' could see outside the battle for town clerk here in Dunnet; they got some sense o' proportion" (20). In the relationship between Jewett's narrator and Mrs. Todd, which Jewett continues to explore in her late stories "The Queen's Twin" and "The Foreigner," she suggests the empathic exchange characterized by careful listening as a method of border-crossing.

Brodhead attempts to locate Jewett as an elite member of the world of early modernism, arguing that as "a virtual native of the social world that sponsored nineteenth-century high culture," she was complicit in that culture's acceptance of social and artistic stratification (174). Yet although Jewett certainly did publish in the "high culture" journals of the period, Charles Johanningsmeier has identified what he refers to as her "lost" newspaper writings and has discovered that Jewett reached millions of readers, including readers at every rural post stop, with the stories she sold to syndicated newspapers—hardly the act of someone interested only in "high culture."[51] The complexity of Jewett's resistance to social stratification and to the categories of sexual modernism reveals itself most clearly in those fictions in which she represents cross-class relationships between women directly, neither as a transvestite effect as in "An Autumn Holiday," nor as the result of an economic exchange, as in *The Country of the Pointed Firs*.

In one of Jewett's most subtle fictions, "Miss Tempy's Watchers," for example, Jewett dramatizes the process of careful listening and comfort one character offers another—and situates this action in the liminal region of the richer woman's anxieties about death and the poorer woman's sensitivity to her companion's distress. Jewett's drama "takes place" on the class border that separates the characters and allows the dead woman, Miss Tempy, to intervene, using her own death as the crisis that precipitates the moment of connection between the living women, fulfilling Miss Tempy's hope that "the richer woman might better understand the burdens of the poorer."[52] "Miss Tempy's Watchers" combines Jewett's belief in empathic listening as the highest form of human action with her dramatization of a cross-class relationship in formation.

In Jewett's fiction, a crisis precipitates connections between people, usually women; it is not disruptive, in the postmodern use of that word, but rather facilitative. Nevertheless, as "An Autumn Holiday" suggests, sharing queerness disrupts class boundaries. We see this most clearly in those fictions—like "Miss Tempy's Watchers," *Deephaven*, *The Country of the Pointed Firs*, and especially the late story "Martha's Lady"—in which Jewett's portraits of close, even romantic (some have argued lesbian) relationships between women cross class borders. *Deephaven*, for example, presents Helen Denis and Kate Lancaster as young women of, respectively, the middle and upper classes, who discover that Kate's deceased Aunt Katharine had inspired devotion in her poor but proud neighbor, the Widow Jim. Yet only in "Martha's Lady" does Jewett foreground rather than mute class differences. The question "Martha's Lady" raises is whether the hinted sexual disruption displaces class and thereby flags an unexamined classism, or whether Jewett uses the class difference between the women in order to contain anxieties about same-sex relationships that, despite her letter to Cather, could not be openly represented in fiction. In my analysis of "Martha's Lady" (1899), I will suggest that even by asking the question this way we confine our readings of Jewett to precisely those modernist categories that her fiction not only resists but also critiques.

3

The most extensive critical discussions of "Martha's Lady" have treated it as a portrait of a romantic, even a lesbian, friendship.[53] Yet from the perspective of class analysis, the story is one of Jewett's most disturbing because of its portrait of the maid, Martha. While Helena is described as a "beauty" and a "light-hearted girl" of "good breeding,"[54] Martha has a "tall, ungainly shape," and possesses a "simple brain" that is "slow enough in its processes and recognitions" that her employer Harriet Pyne calls her as "clumsy as a calf" (261). Yet after Martha meets Harriet's niece Helena, who establishes "friendly relations" with her, Martha's eyes become "as affectionate as a dog's, and there was a new look of hopefulness on her face; this dreaded guest was a friend after all, and not a foe come from proud Boston to confound her ignorance and patient efforts" (260). Read as a story about class relations, "Martha's Lady" appears to reinforce the separation of the beautiful, rich, generous, kind, and imaginative upper-class Helena and the unattractive, poor, dull, insecure, and slow-to-learn maid Martha; to make matters worse, the story's action shows Martha learning her job as maid and looking "almost pretty and quite as young as she was" under the influence of her increasing love and devotion to serving Helena (263). As Jewett writes, "All for love's sake she had been learning to do many things" (265). Helena becomes Martha's fairy godmother—until she leaves to get married. Forty years separate the two friends. At the end of the story, Helena returns dressed in black, apparently widowed, and the two women discover that except for their own aging, their feelings for each other remain the same. For Martha, Helena has simply returned; for Helena, the moment marks a recognition of Martha's feelings: "Oh, Martha, have you remembered like this, all these long years!" (277).

Glenda Hobbs notes that "Martha's Lady" "is one of the few Jewett stories to focus on women before they reach old age."[55] Thus, as she does in *Deephaven*, Jewett chooses to begin her story just prior to the time in young women's lives when they are expected to marry. Yet as Judith Fetterley notes in "Reading *Deephaven* as a Lesbian Text," this moment creates "lesbian anxieties."

> Though Kate obviously loves Helen enough to select her as the special friend with whom she wishes to spend her summer, Helen is telling the story, and the story she tells is the story of her love for Kate. Indeed, the very qualities that Helen identifies as making Kate so lovable—her class and family status, her tact, her sociability—equally identify Kate as preeminently marriageable. Moreover, while Helen, by writing *Deephaven*, can be imagined as beginning a career that will displace marriage, no such alternative interest seems present for Kate. Thus Kate figures in the text as heterosexual, and thus *Deephaven* presents a classic lesbian experi-

> ence: a lesbian woman in love with a heterosexual woman who is willing to take time off before getting married to play, but only to play, with an alternative. The shadow of eventual separation hangs over Helen's summer, providing sufficient cause in itself for her pervasive depression.[56]

If we apply Fetterley's lesbian argument to "Martha's Lady," Helena's class position becomes a liability. Precisely because she possesses, like Kate Lancaster, class and family status (for which her tact, beauty, and sociability become metonymic), she is "eminently marriageable," and in Victorian society, thus "heterosexual." Helena's class position, like Kate's in *Deephaven*, prevents her from imagining, much less choosing, a rural retreat and a life with Martha; Helena's construction as an upper-class heterosexual woman means that she cannot conceive Martha. Martha, on the other hand, is presented as having a choice. She can either work for Harriet and love Helena at a distance or follow the footsteps of her aunt, who formerly worked for Harriet Pyne "but lately married a thriving farm and its prosperous owner" (260). Jewett's phrasing here is quite deliberate: Martha can marry a house or she can marry a farm, and at least marrying the house offers her an opportunity to love. Helena has no choice but to marry a diplomat. In a world in which fathers and husbands define women's class positions, class barriers between women eliminate for most of them the possibility of same-sex love and commitment. Not having her aunt's reason to remain unmarried—Miss Pyne, the youngest in her family, "had been the dutiful companion of her father and mother in their last years, all her elder brothers and sisters having married and gone" (256)—Helena really has no socioeconomically viable choice *but* to marry, just as Martha has no choice but to keep her position if she does not wish to marry a farm. As Martha tells Helena, she is the sole support of her own mother and younger brothers: "[W]e're dreadful hard pushed" (266). In "Martha's Lady," it is class that separates the two women and prevents the fictional realization of their relationship; however, Jewett seems to be suggesting that it is *only* women's lack of economic independence and therefore lack of economic choice that does so.

Thus, rather than using female friendship to obscure class issues, Jewett is calling attention to the pathology of class—not of sexual object choice—as the reason for the forty-year deferral of Martha and Helena's final kiss. This story provides us with an excellent example of how the categories with which we read can obscure other categories in (or other readings of) texts. Reading the story through the lens of sexuality—as a lesbian text—mutes the category of class and the class differences between Martha and Helena. However, reading the story as a conservative and even sentimental treatment of class displaces Jewett's lesbian critique. Jewett's unwieldy and uncomfortable interweaving of sex and class creates "category crisis" for the critic. Forced to choose between reading the story as about sex *or* about class, we become the category-ridden readers Jewett will not accommodate and wishes to challenge. Jewett presents class not as a quasi-essentialist barrier to lesbian love but as a socioeconomic identity that constructs a woman as either marriageable (and therefore heterosexual) or not (and therefore boylike, as Martha becomes when she climbs the tree to pick cherries for Helena).

Jewett made it clear at the turn of the twentieth century, even before the cultural consolidation of modernism, that categories themselves undermine women's agency. What allowed both Jewett and Annie Fields, her companion for more than twenty years, to realize their own commitment to each other was not an option Jewett imagined as possible for most women in her historical moment. Jewett had to care for her aging and ill mother with her sister Mary but inherited enough money to support herself; Fields was safely widowed and therefore controlled her own money. "Martha's Lady" suggests that it is precisely class-based economic differences that *prevent* most women from enjoying the kind of "Boston marriage" that she and Fields were able to afford. Without question, Jewett's class position gave her different choices than were available to her contemporaries such as Mary E. Wilkins Freeman, to cite just one writer whose need to support herself with her work restricted her choice of subject matter in much of her fiction. However, to move from a recognition of Jewett's class privilege to associating her, as Brodhead does, with the values of "high culture" creates a symptomatic gap in interpretation: it elides the passage Jewett takes through gender as the site where sexual identity and class position converge to limit women's choices.

Jewett suggests in "Martha's Lady" that Helena's forty years of marriage (her world traveling as the wife of a diplomat, the births and deaths, and the marriage of her children) were worth writing home about, but that she has been, as Harriet tells Martha, "a good deal changed . . . she has had a great deal of trouble, poor girl" (274). As Jewett writes Helena's life, these years become a parenthesis to the moment she wants to get to, when Martha and Helena both have lived beyond the years in which women are constructed as heterosexual or marriageable. That they do so—and that, as Helena says, "Oh, Martha, have you remembered like this, all these long years!"—articulates much more than the possibility of lesbian love. At the end of the story, Jewett, with Helena, portrays the high cost of the social construction of woman-as-marriageable-heterosexual. Helena's cousin Harriet clarifies the price when she attends Helena's wedding, "but not without some protest in her heart against the uncertainties of married life." In Harriet's view, "Helena was so equal to a happy independence and even to the assistance of other lives grown strangely dependent upon her quick sympathies and instinctive decisions, that it was hard to let her sink her personality in the affairs of another" (268).

In "Martha's Lady," Jewett suggests that lesbianism is not a medical condition but an economic one. The pathologizing of same-sex love at the end of the nineteenth century supported the privilege of the emerging professional class of white male doctors with medical specialties who practiced in urban centers—the kind of privilege and professional practice Dr. Leslie, in *A Country Doctor*, explicitly rejects as a career path for himself. His rural practice and his concomitant encouragement of Nan Prince's desire to become a doctor like him, a "country doctor," reinforces Jewett's view that it is the modern economy that is pathological for women, not sexual object choice or the choice either to heal or write as a vocation. Jewett's own class position made her "equal to a happy independence," and she used that position to move across the border between rural and urban life, between premodern and the modern, between a moment in which women yet retained a certain agency and autonomy (represented best in Almira Todd) and their modern struggle "against the wind" of the new society represented in *A Country Doctor*. Only in Nan Prince—whose mixed class origins also allow her to move between upper-class relatives and patrons and rural patients—does Jewett make her own position explicit; Nan hopes Dr. Leslie will not consider her decision to become a doctor (and a "country doctor" at that, a metonym for the way Jewett conflates social movement across class borders and geographical movement across regions) "a freak of which she would soon tire." Jewett knows that she is violating increasingly rigid gender conventions when she writes about Nan, "She had the feeling of a reformer, a radical, and even of a political agitator, as she tried to face her stormy future."[57] By choosing regionalism as her mode, Jewett also used her own position of class privilege, and her experience moving in and out of Boston's literary world, to keep open a discursive space for writing that resists modern categories of "high" and "low"—for what Garber calls a "third" term. Establishing regionalism as such a "third" term calls into question the literary categories of local color and realism, both of which have long been used to devalue regionalist texts and their place in the classroom.[58]

New readings of Jewett's work that attempt to bypass her analysis of gender demonstrate the same myopia that afflicts the upper-class citizens of Dunport in *A Country Doctor*, who are disappointed in their conservative hopes that George Gerry's arrival on the scene will serve as "the most powerful argument for their side of the debate" over Nan Prince's future, despite her refusal to marry.[59] Like Brodhead, these citizens refuse to take into account Nan Prince's (and Jewett's) compelling critique of gender as a binary social structure. The citizens of Dunport, and some of the "new (Jewett) critics" of the 1990s, have not yet learned to read gender as the site where sexual identity and class position come together to limit women's choices. Jewett's description of Nan Prince reveals her own resistance to the modernist categories of sex, class, and gender in particular: "It must be confessed that every one who had known her well had discovered sooner or later the untamed wildnesses which seemed like the tangles which one often sees in field-corners, though a most orderly crop is taking up the best part of the room between the fences."[60] Choosing to remain in the field-corners of American regionalist fiction, Jewett was willing to present the tangles of class and the "untamed wildnesses" of lesbian sexuality for an audience that might have preferred a more "orderly crop," and even for critics who read Jewett as complicit in the very process of categorizing sex and class that her work moves through gender to critique. That she managed to insert such "tangles" despite the fact that "a most orderly crop [was] taking up the best part of the room between the fences" makes it possible to read her work for its resistance to the urban, upper-class, and "high culture" world to which she became a regular visitor from her home in Maine. More than a tourist in Boston, Jewett occupied her "Fields-corner" (at 148 Charles Street) but always returned to South Berwick. Transitivity much more than tourism serves as our figure for understanding Jewett's border-crossing about a century before such practices might be theorized by literary critics, although they have long been fully understood by readers who have loved Jewett beyond the boundaries of academic discourse.

Notes

I delivered a shorter version of this paper (without section 1) as the keynote address at "Sarah Orne Jewett and Her Contemporaries: The Centennial Conference," held at Westbrook College in Portland, Maine, June 21–23, 1996. I am indebted to conference participants for comments, as well as to Sarah Way Sherman, whose incisive reading of the conference draft has helped me think further about Jewett's relation to gender and class in particular. Sherman's own new introduction to *The Country of the Pointed Firs* has just appeared (Hanover, N.H., and London: University Press of New England, 1997). I also thank Judith Fetterley for her (always) careful and critical reading.

1. *A Country Doctor* (New York: Grosset and Dunlap, 1884) and *The Tory Lover* (Boston: Houghton Mifflin, 1901).

2. For example, when Willa Cather edited Jewett's *The Country of the Pointed Firs* and wrote a preface that, as Paula Blanchard describes it, "has become a classic of Jewett criticism" (*Sarah Orne Jewett: Her World and Her Work* [Reading, Mass.: Addison-Wesley, 1994], 360), she incorporated three of the later Dunnet Landing sketches into Jewett's 1896 text, apparently not perceiving the original as complete in itself. For fuller discussion of Cather's role in editing Jewett, see Marjorie Pryse, Introduction to Sarah Orne Jewett, *The Country of the Pointed Firs and Other Stories* (New York: Norton, 1981), vi–vii; Blanchard, 360–61; and June Howard, "Introduction: Sarah Orne Jewett and the Traffic in Words," in *New Essays on "The Country of the Pointed Firs,"* ed. Howard (New York: Cambridge University Press, 1994), 20–21.

3. See Elizabeth Ammons, "Going in Circles: The Female Geography of Jewett's *Country of the Pointed Firs*," *Studies in the Literary Imagination* 16 (Fall 1983): 83–92; Pryse, Introduction to *The Country of the Pointed Firs and Other Stories*; Josephine Donovan, *Sarah Orne Jewett* (New York: Ungar, 1980); Judith Fetterley, "'Not in the Least American': Nineteenth-Century Literary Regionalism," *College English* 56 (December 1994): 877–95; Judith Fetterley and Marjorie Pryse, Introduction to *American Women Regionalists, 1850–1910*, ed. Fetterley and Pryse (New York: Norton, 1992), xi–xx; Marcia McClintock Folsom, "'Tact Is a Kind of Mind-Reading': Empathic Style in Sarah Orne Jewett's *The Country of the Pointed Firs*," *Colby Library Quarterly* 18 (1982): 66–78; Marilyn Sanders Mobley, *Folk Roots and Mythic Wings in Sarah Orne Jewett and Toni Morrison* (Baton Rouge: Louisiana State University Press, 1991); Sarah

Way Sherman, *Sarah Orne Jewett: An American Persephone* (Hanover, N.H.: University Press of New England, 1989); and Cecilia Tichi, "Women Writers and the New Woman," in *Columbia Literary History of the United States*, ed. Emory Elliott (New York: Columbia University Press, 1988), 589–606.

4. Amy Kaplan, "Nation, Region, and Empire," in *The Columbia History of the American Novel*, ed. Emory Elliott (New York: Columbia University Press, 1991), 252.

5. Philip Fisher, "American Literary and Cultural Studies since the Civil War," in *Redrawing the Boundaries: The Transformation of English and American Literary Studies*, ed. Stephen Greenblatt and Giles Gunn (New York: MLA, 1992), 232.

6. Henry James, "Mr. and Mrs. James T. Fields," *Atlantic Monthly* 116 (July 1915): 30.

7. Louis Renza, *"A White Heron" and the Question of Minor Literature* (Madison: University of Wisconsin Press, 1984), 33. Subsequent quotations are cited in the text.

8. Gilles Deleuze and Félix Guattari, *Kafka: Pour une littérature mineure* (Paris: Editions de Minuit, 1975).

9. See Susan Gillman, "Regionalism and Nationalism in Jewett's *The Country of the Pointed Firs*," in *New Essays*, ed. Howard, 101–17; Sandra Zagarell, "*Country*'s Portrayal of Community and the Exclusion of Difference," in *New Essays*, ed. Howard, 39–60; Richard H. Brodhead, *Cultures of Letters: Scenes of Reading and Writing in Nineteenth-Century America* (Chicago: University of Chicago Press, 1993); and Kaplan, "Nation, Region, and Empire."

10. Elizabeth Ammons, "Material Culture, Empire, and Jewett's *Country of the Pointed Firs*," in *New Essays*, ed. Howard, 91–92.

11. Ammons, "Material Culture," 97.

12. Sandra Zagarell, "Narrative of Community: The Identification of a Genre," *Signs* 13 (1988): 498–527.

13. Zagarell, "*Country*'s Portrayal," 47.

14. Ferman Bishop, "Sarah Orne Jewett's Ideas of Race," *New England Quarterly* 30 (1957): 249.

15. Zagarell writes that she is "much indebted" to Bishop's article ("*Country*'s Portrayal," 57).

16. It is important to acknowledge several scholars and biographers who did take an interest in Jewett during the 1950s and 1960s and without whose work Jewett scholarship would be much impoverished. See in particular Perry D. Westbrook, *Acres of Flint: Writers of Rural New England, 1870–1900* (Washington, D.C.: Scarecrow Press, 1951); John Eldridge Frost, *Sarah Orne Jewett* (Kittery Point: Gundalow Club, 1960); and Richard Cary, *Sarah Orne Jewett* (New York: Twayne, 1962). Before publishing their books, Westbrook and Frost had written dissertations on Jewett—Westbrook for Columbia University (1951) and Frost for New York University (1953). During this period as well,

F. O. Matthiessen's 1929 biography of Jewett was also reprinted (*Sarah Orne Jewett* [Gloucester, Mass.: Peter Smith, 1965]). See also Gwen L. Nagel and James Nagel, whose bibliographical work in *Sarah Orne Jewett: A Reference Guide* (Boston: G. K. Hall, 1978) makes it possible to trace Jewett's slow emergence from the margins of literary history.

17. Bishop, "Sarah Orne Jewett's Ideas of Race," 244.

18. Jack Morgan and Louis A. Renza, *The Irish Stories of Sarah Orne Jewett* (Carbondale: Southern Illinois University Press, 1996), xxi.

19. Ibid., xix, xliii.

20. Bishop, "Sarah Orne Jewett's Ideas of Race," 249.

21. In an essay Bishop published two years later, he complicates his earlier argument by noting that at the end of Jewett's *The Story of the Normans* (1887), a volume of history Jewett was commissioned to write for young people, she "tempered her observations with criticism" of the Normans ("The Sense of the Past in Sarah Orne Jewett," in *Appreciation of Sarah Orne Jewett*, ed. Richard Cary [Waterville, Maine: Colby College Press, 1973], 139; rpt. from *University of Wichita Bulletin* 41 [1959]).

22. Gillman, "Regionalism and Nationalism," 113. Subsequent quotations are cited in the text.

23. By invoking this view of "inadequacies" in feminism, I do not mean either to subscribe to it or to refute it. By now, this view of "second-wave" feminism has become a cliché, often unexamined. Although across the body of their work, African-American feminist critics and theorists (Audre Lorde, Barbara Smith, bell hooks, and others) have critiqued racism in the (white) women's movement, some white women from the 1970s and early 1980s have done significant work to expand feminist analysis well beyond the cliché. One of the earliest was Adrienne Rich, in "Disloyal to Civilization: Feminism, Racism, Gynophobia," in *On Lies, Secrets and Silence* (New York: Norton, 1979). Other white feminists who have invoked racism (and its extensions into classism and imperialism) as a focus for feminism include Charlotte Bunch, Minnie Bruce Pratt, and Robin Morgan.

24. Zagarell, "*Country*'s Portrayal," 56.

25. Judith Fetterley, "Commentary: Nineteenth-Century American Women Writers and the Politics of Recovery," *American Literary History* 6 (Fall 1994): 608.

26. Fetterley, "Commentary," 609–10.

27. Howard, "Introduction," 15.

28. Ibid., 23.

29. June Howard, "Unraveling Regions, Unsettling Periods: Sarah Orne Jewett and American Literary History," *American Literature* 68 (June 1996): 369. Subsequent quotations are cited in the text.

30. Michael Davitt Bell's essay in the collection is the only one that terms the feminist readings "new," examines *The Country of the Pointed Firs* as a book that

moves beyond the "rigid bifurcation" of American realism, and argues for moving beyond gendered readings of Jewett to the extent that these "reimpose these bifurcations on *The Country of the Pointed Firs,* even in the interest of finding in it an *inversion* of realist values" ("Gender and American Realism in *The Country of the Pointed Firs,*" in *New Essays,* ed. Howard, 77).

31. Marjorie Garber, *Vested Interests: Cross Dressing and Cultural Anxiety* (New York: HarperCollins, 1992), 16. Subsequent quotations are cited in the text.

32. See also Howard's discussion of visiting and friendship between women in her Introduction to *New Readings,* 6–8.

33. Jewett's biographers themselves have either ignored Jewett's sexuality, have attempted to deflect attention from her possible lesbianism, or have argued that she was not a lesbian. Margaret Roman describes the "lifelong relationship of support and comfort" that Jewett and Annie Fields enjoyed and writes that "neither Fields nor Jewett took on a specific male or female role in their association" (*Sarah Orne Jewett: Reconstructing Gender* [Tuscaloosa: University of Alabama Press, 1992], 145); Elizabeth Silverthorne argues that "attempts have been made to interpret [the relationship between Jewett and Fields] in terms of late-twentieth-century ideology," which has "led to confusion and controversy, since it modifies and extends the dictionary definition of lesbianism" even though "it is doubtful that Sarah or her friends knew the term 'lesbian' at all" (*Sarah Orne Jewett: A Writer's Life* [Woodstock, N.Y.: Overlook Press, 1993], 105–6); and Paula Blanchard concludes that Jewett "was not, in the strictest sense of the term" a lesbian because Jewett's love for other women "belongs in a category hardly imaginable to the modern sensibility, that of romantic friendship" (54). For critics more willing to consider Jewett's (sexual) love for women and its influence on her work, see Josephine Donovan, "The Unpublished Love Poetry of Sarah Orne Jewett," *Frontiers: A Journal of Women Studies* 4 (January 1980): 26–31; Lillian Faderman, "Boston Marriage," 190–203, and "The Contributions of the Sexologists," 239–53, in *Surpassing the Love of Men: Friendship between Women from the Renaissance to the Present* (New York: William Morrow, 1981); Judith Fetterley, "Reading *Deephaven* as a Lesbian Text," in *Sexual Practice/Textual Theory: Lesbian Cultural Criticism,* ed. Susan J. Wolfe and Julia Penelope (Cambridge: Blackwell, 1993), 164–83; and Marjorie Pryse, "Archives of Female Friendship and the 'Way' Jewett Wrote," *New England Quarterly* 66 (March 1993): 47–66. See also Sherman, *Sarah Orne Jewett,* esp. 78–84.

34. Eve Kosofsky Sedgwick, *Epistemology of the Closet* (Berkeley: University of California Press, 1990), 88.

35. Sarah Orne Jewett, "An Autumn Holiday," in *Country By-Ways* (Boston: Houghton Mifflin, 1881), 147. Subsequent quotations are cited in the text.

36. See Marjorie Pryse, "Archives of Female Friendship and the 'Way' Jewett Wrote," *New England Quarterly* 66 (March 1993): 47–66.

37. *Letters of Sarah Orne Jewett,* ed. Annie Fields (Boston: Houghton Mifflin, 1911), 246–47.

38. Carroll Smith-Rosenberg, "The Female World of Love and Ritual: Relations between Women in Nineteenth-Century America," in her *Disorderly Conduct: Visions of Gender in Victorian America* (New York: Oxford University Press, 1985), 53.

39. Faderman, *Surpassing the Love of Men*, 239–40. Subsequent quotations are cited in the text.

40. Sigmund Freud, *Three Essays on the Theory of Sexuality* (1905), trans. James Strachey (New York: Basic Books, 1962).

41. Havelock Ellis, *Sexual Inversion* (London: Wilson and Macmillan, 1897).

42. Paul Robinson, *The Modernization of Sex* (New York: Harper and Row, 1976), 3. Subsequent references are cited in the text.

43. Josephine Donovan, "Nan Prince and the Golden Apples," *Colby Library Quarterly* 22 (1986): 26. Subsequent references are cited in the text.

44. When Faderman wrote that Jewett's 1908 letter to Cather "must have made Cather blush—but Jewett probably would not have known what she was blushing about" (*Surpassing the Love of Men*, 202), she was not taking into account Donovan's research, which suggests that Jewett knew very well what she was talking about, whether or not it made Cather "blush."

45. Mrs. Fosdick in *The Country of the Pointed Firs* also tells a story about going to sea with her family at the age of eight and having to wear her brother's clothes because her mother has forgotten to bring the basket in which hers were packed. Until they reach their first port she wears trousers, which represented for her "quite a spell o' freedom"; when her mother makes her a new skirt and she feels the hem at her heels, she feels "as if youth was past and gone" (*Pointed Firs*, 61). Subsequent references to *The Country of the Pointed Firs and Other Stories* will be to the 1981 edition (New York: Norton) and are cited in the text.

46. See Ammons, "Going in Circles"; Donovan, "Nan Prince" and "The Unpublished Love Poetry"; Josephine Donovan, "Jewett and Swedenborg," *American Literature* 65 (December 1993): 731–50; Folsom, "'Tact Is a Kind of Mind-Reading'"; Mobley, *Folk Roots;* Marjorie Pryse, Introduction to Sarah Orne Jewett, *The Country of the Pointed Firs and Other Stories;* and Sherman, *Sarah Orne Jewett.*

47. Brodhead, *Cultures of Letters*, 143. Subsequent quotations are cited in the text.

48. Sarah Orne Jewett, *Deephaven and Other Stories* (New Haven: College and University Press, 1966), 31.

49. Fetterley and Pryse, Introduction to *American Women Regionalists*, xvii–xviii; see also our discussion of "The Circus at Denby" in *American Women Regionalists*, 186–87. See also Fetterley, "'Not in the Least American'," esp. 887; and Pryse, "'Distilling Essences': Regionalism and 'Women's Culture'," *American Literary Realism* 25.2 (Winter 1993): 1–15, and "Reading Regionalism and the 'Difference' It Makes," in *Regionalism Reconsidered: New Approaches to the Field*, ed. David Jordan (New York: Garland, 1994), 47–63.

50. Cf. Christine Stansell's description of this economic shift, which took place earlier in New York City, in *City of Women: Sex and Class in New York, 1789–1860* (Urbana: University of Illinois Press, 1987), esp. 11–18.

51. Charles Johanningsmeier, "Sarah Orne Jewett and Mary E. Wilkins (Freeman): Two Shrewd Businesswomen in Search of New Markets," *New England Quarterly* 70 (March 1997): 57–82. See also *Fiction and the American Literary Marketplace: The Role of the Newspaper Syndicates in America, 1860–1900* (Cambridge: Cambridge University Press, 1996).

52. Sarah Orne Jewett, "Miss Tempy's Watchers," in *The Country of the Pointed Firs and Other Stories*, 243.

53. In 1980, Glenda Hobbs interpreted the friendship as "passionate, but not necessarily erotic" ("Pure and Passionate: Female Friendship in Sarah Orne Jewett's 'Martha's Lady'," *Studies in Short Fiction* 17 [1980]: 21–29; reprinted in *Critical Essays on Sarah Orne Jewett*, ed. Gwen L. Nagel, [Boston: G. K. Hall, 1984], 103). In 1981, Lillian Faderman described the relationship between upper-class Helena Vernon and her cousin Harriet's maid, Martha, as "what would be called lesbian love in our times" (*Surpassing the Love of Men*, 203); and Susan Koppelman includes the story in her anthology of lesbian fiction, *Two Friends* (New York: Meridian-Penguin, 1994), 124–40.

54. Sarah Orne Jewett, "Martha's Lady," in *The Country of the Pointed Firs and Other Stories*, 257. Subsequent quotations are cited in the text.

55. Hobbs, "Pure and Passionate," 99.

56. Fetterley, "Reading *Deephaven*," 167.

57. Sarah Orne Jewett, *A Country Doctor*, 130, 173, 174.

58. In addition, as Chris Gallagher has commented, regionalism foregrounds "category crisis" both as an oppositional term in the triad "realism, regionalism, and naturalism" as well as in Amy Kaplan's "Nation, Region, and Empire." Gallagher has noted that while "empire" in Kaplan's triad seems to foreground "nation" and "region" as domestic concepts, this move obscures the way "reading regionalism" (see Pryse, "Reading Regionalism") works against a domestic U.S. agenda. In unpublished working notes (here quoted with permission), Gallagher writes: "regionalist texts, of course, are not often—if ever—*about* U.S. external imperialism, but . . . they do often invoke the colonizing gesture in an attempt to resist and ultimately to reject it. They also seek to represent the marginalized stories—of women, of people of color, of lower-class people—in ways that not only avoid appropriating, but resist appropriative gestures themselves, thus countering U.S. exceptionalism by foregrounding U.S. *internal* imperialism. In these ways, the category and practice of "regionalism" can contribute to the study of empire, as a project which itself puts into question the binary between 'region' and 'empire'."

59. Jewett, *A Country Doctor*, 286.

60. Ibid., 269–70.

"In Search of Local Color"

Context, Controversy, and *The Country of the Pointed Firs*

Donna M. Campbell

When *The Country of the Pointed Firs* appeared in 1896, it received "Jewett's usual favorable reviews" as a piece of local color fiction, the "minor" genre that nonetheless had become popular in the pages of the *Century*, the *Atlantic*, and *Harper's Monthly*.[1] To judge from these literary journals of the day, however, the genre into which Sarah Orne Jewett's masterpiece fit so recognizably was, paradoxically enough, becoming dismantled even at the cultural moment that produced its finest single work. *The Country of the Pointed Firs* was published at the historical juncture when local color had reached its peak and American naturalism was about to become a force on the literary horizon. Its serial run in the *Atlantic Monthly* from January through September 1896 thus placed the work not only within the women's tradition described by Marjorie Pryse, Sarah Sherman, and Josephine Donovan, the "reversal of realism" discussed by Michael Davitt Bell, Richard Brodhead's "upper-class-based universe of high-cultural understandings," and the discourses of nationalism proposed by Susan Gillman and Sandra Zagarell, but within a critical debate on local color that challenged cultural interpretations of the term itself.[2] What did Jewett's audiences understand by "local color"? An examination of the term as it is used by Jewett's contemporaries Hamlin Garland, Charles Dudley Warner, Brander Matthews, and James Lane Allen indicates that during the few short years from 1894 to 1897, local color became fragmented while it was almost simultaneously promoted as the key to a "national" literature, rejected as a literary fad, reworked as a variety of proto-naturalism, and, most damaging of all, redefined and marginalized as what James Lane Allen termed the "Feminine Principle" in American fiction before it disappeared into a host of other movements, including historical romance.[3]

The first of these responses, the promotion of local color as a "national" literature, appeared initially to be a logical culmination of its particular brand of cultural dominance, for the "minor" genre was one of the day's most recognizable literary forms. From the date of its inception at the close of the Civil War, local color literature had been popular, promoted in its infancy by William Dean Howells and nourished by the steady exposure given it in such prestigious journals of the day as the *Atlantic Monthly*, *Harper's Monthly*, and the *Century*. For example, in his February 1887 "Editor's Study" for *Harper's Monthly*, Howells had praised the "sketches and studies by the women" short story writers as being "faithfuler and more realistic than those of the men, in proportion to their number. Their tendency is more distinctly in that direction, and there is a solidity, an honest report of observation, in the work of such women as Mrs. Cooke, Miss Murfree, Miss Jewett, and Miss Woolson which often leaves little to be desired."[4] Whereas naturalistic authors Frank Norris and Jack London each published just one short piece in the *Atlantic* between 1889 and 1901, Jewett alone published thirteen stories and two book-length works in the *Atlantic* during the same period. Later critical writings by local colorists, such as Jewett's 1893 preface to *Deephaven* (1877), Bret Harte's "The Rise of the American 'Short Story'" (1899), and James Lane Allen's "Two Principles in Recent American Fiction" (1897), all suggest that local color had indeed become, in Edward Eggleston's words, "the most significant movement in American literature in our generation."[5] Defined as a literature of margins, local color instead occupied a central place in the cultural climate of late-nineteenth-century America.

In 1894, the movement gained a theorist and apologist in regional writer Hamlin Garland, whose *Main-Travelled Roads* (1891) had staked out the hardscrabble farms of the Midwest as his own literary territory. Anticipating the criticism that would be leveled at local color, Garland's *Crumbling Idols* (1894) distinguishes legitimate local color fiction, which he termed "veritism," from the rest: "I am using local color to mean something more than a forced study of the picturesque scenery of a State. *Local color in a novel means that it has such quality of texture and background that it could not have been written in any other place or by any one else than a native.*"[6] Garland tried to shock the literary establishment by announcing that the local novel "is sure to become all-powerful" and "will redeem American literature"; but about regional fiction, at least, Garland assumes a radical stance not justified by the essays. As Paul Shorey noted in his 1896 *Atlantic* essay "Present Conditions of Literary Production," "the novel of local color . . . [is] the most prosperous [form] of literature to-day and contain[s] the most promise for the immediate future."[7] And Charles Miner Thompson, the reviewer who eight years later would write "The Art of Miss Jewett" for the same journal, gives a tongue-in-cheek portrait of Garland as a "literary anarchist" whose aim as a "literary Jingo" is to promote "[o]ur literature—right or wrong";[8] he treats Garland's piece as bombastic grandstanding, a defense of local color rendered unnecessary by virtue of the genre's popularity. Reviewers generally refused to rise to the bait of his pugnacious tone, for, as they saw it, Garland was preaching to the converted.

In furthering this "literary jingoism," however, Garland and his contemporaries Edward Eggleston and Frank Norris chipped away at the integrity of local color's preservationist ethos. They sought to legitimize and also to colonize the hitherto self-enclosed islands of local color fiction by uniting them under the all-encompassing banner of John W. DeForest's "Great American Novel." "The 'great American novel', for which prophetic critics yearned so fondly twenty years ago, is appearing in sections," Edward Eggleston declared in his preface (1892) to *The Hoosier Schoolmaster*.[9] Norris at first vacillated between disappointment that American novelists had not written an epic treatment of their great land and defensiveness about the lack of a "primitive" stage that would make such an epic possible. Finally, however, he announced that "the possibility of *A*—note the indefinite article—*A* Great American Novel is not too remote for discussion. But such a novel will be sectional."[10] Garland took a similar stand, believing that, just as impressionism uses bits of color to form an overall picture or impression, so bits of regional writing, united by veritist theories of composition and presentation, would create an overall picture of the nation. Charles Dudley Warner's "Editor's Study" column in the December 1892 *Harper's Monthly* likewise promotes this idea: "So, while we have been expecting the American Literature to come out from some locality, neat and clean, like a nugget . . . there are coming forth a hundred expressions of the hundred aspects of American life. . . . And all these writers . . . are animated by the free spirit of inquiry and expression that belongs to an independent nation, and so our literature is coming to have a stamp of its own that is unlike any other national stamp."[11] Rather than existing as finished products, the sketches and stories of the local colorists now become redefined as ore or raw material, gaining value only through being refined and stamped into a national literary coinage. The nationalist and normalizing enterprise implicit in these perspectives fits perfectly into the era's political agenda, yet this assimilationist ethos inflated, and nearly obliterated, the movement's original impetus, its lack of pretension and focus on preservation of the individual. Nearly twenty years later, Howells, fighting a rearguard action, again invoked Jewett, Freeman, Garland, and even Norris as "localists who have done and are doing far better work than any conceivable of a nationalist" before concluding "We for our part do not believe that the novel of the United States ever will be, or ever can be, written, or that it would be worth reading if it were written."[12] Although the refiguring of local color in this fashion may have served the aims of nationalism, the literary version of manifest destiny wherein the local became the national could not succeed aesthetically, causing as it did the "local" in local color to be both transformed and subdued, rendered subordinate to a purpose that it had not sought and could not support.

By the time Garland wrote *Crumbling Idols*, in fact, the converted were rapidly becoming the disenchanted. According to Charles Dudley Warner in the May 1896 *Harper's Monthly*, local color had suffered the fate of other popular literary movements, a downhill road leading from stylistic excess to literary faddishness to dangerous self-parody:

> We do not hear much now of "local color"; that has rather gone out. . . . "Local color" had a fine run while it lasted. . . . [S]o much color was produced that the market broke down. It was an external affair, and its use was supposed to serve the gospel of Realism. . . . The author had only to go to the "locality" that he intended to attack and immortalize . . . in order to pick up the style of profanity there current, the dialect, if any existed; if not, to work up one from slovenly and ungrammatical speech, procure some "views" of landscape and of costume, strike the kind of landscape necessary to the atmosphere of the story . . . and the thing was done. As soon as the reader saw the "local color" thus laid on he knew that the story was a real story of real life.[13]

Warner's metaphors are telling: the relationship of writer to subject is that of conquest as the author sets out to "attack and immortalize" his subject, not to "under[stand] . . . without speaking" as Jewett's narrator does with Mrs. Blackett (a method, incidentally, that Edith Wharton's narrator adopts later with Mrs. Hale in *Ethan Frome*).[14] Gone, too, is the sense of stories shared for their own sake: the text itself enters the realm of naturalistic economic exchange as the writer "works up," procures, and exploits the raw materials of this colonial "locality"; and mass-produces the commodity until "the market [breaks] down." In such a system of standardized production, a smattering of authenticating "local color" dialect guarantees the middle-class reader a commodity at once safely standardized and suitably exotic.

Significantly, in *The Country of the Pointed Firs* Jewett focuses not on the written product but upon her narrator's writing process—or, rather, the deferral of the writing process: "One afternoon when I had listened . . . with an idle pen in my hand . . . I reached for my hat, and, taking blotting-book and all under my arm, I resolutely fled further temptation. . . . The way went straight uphill, and presently I stopped and turned to look back" (9). The reader sees the creative process but not the published work itself, an authorial decision that downplays the commodified nature of the narrator's exchanges, although Jewett links her narrator's labor with Mrs. Todd's by a kind of doubling: "it was not until I felt myself confronted with too great pride and pleasure in the display, one night, of two dollars and twenty-seven cents which I had taken in during the day, that I remembered a long piece of writing, sadly belated now, which I was bound to do" (6). Deferring the production of her work and resisting its consumption, Jewett's narrator clearly exemplifies a different sort of writer than the author who created her; and, despite Jewett's more overt presence in the marketplace, Warner does not target Jewett, a friend, in his attack. Yet to have the features of the genre held up to dismissive scrutiny in a contemporary journal halfway through the publication of *The Country of the Pointed Firs* not only demarcates the quality of Jewett's piece but surely also complicates audience assumptions about the viability of local color itself.

A third perspective on the genre provides further insight into contemporary nuances through which to view Jewett's work. As early as the mid-1890s, the term "local color" had regained its more general sense of "qualities of a region" as it encompassed more urban settings and grew into a kind of naturalism. "In Search of Local Color," one of the "Vignettes of Manhattan" series that Brander Matthews wrote for *Harper's*

Monthly (June 1894), depicts just such a cynical process of gathering copy. In its surface features, at least, the story parallels "Along Shore," chapter 20 of *The Country of the Pointed Firs.* In Jewett's work, the narrator waits to speak with Elijah Tilley, an "elderly, gaunt-shaped great fisherman," and silently walks beside him until, by a subtle shifting of a fishing basket, she understands that her "company was accepted" (114, 118). Visiting him later that afternoon, she observes his "careful housekeeping" (122) and sympathizes with his bereavement as he knits and tells the tale of his "poor dear," his wife who died eight years previously. By the end of the afternoon, after she has silently "read the history of Mrs. Tilley's best room from its very beginning" (124) and thereby come to understand its owner, the narrator and Elijah Tilley cement their relationship as they discuss Almira Todd and laugh together "like the best of friends" (127).

Like *The Country of the Pointed Firs,* "In Search of Local Color" features an upper-class, educated writer who asks a friend, a native of the region, for an introduction to some of its inhabitants; after meeting a laconic widower employed in keeping up domestic pursuits after his wife's death, the writer learns the story of the man's marriage. Only in these essentials, however, does Matthews's local color story resemble Jewett's. In Matthews's proto-naturalistic sketch, the literary enterprise is overt, the quest after "copy" and color foregrounded, as Harvard-educated man-about-town Rupert de Ruyter asks settlement worker John Suydam to help him find "a little local color" for "a series of New York stories for the *Metropolis.*" With some hesitation, Suydam takes him to the Italian immigrant neighborhood in Mulberry Bend, a neighborhood made famous four years earlier as the "foul core of New York's slums" in Jacob Riis's pioneering study *How the Other Half Lives.*[15] Like Jewett's narrator, who finds classical analogues in Mrs. Todd's "look of a huge sibyl" (8) and her standing like "Antigone alone on the Theban plain" (49), De Ruyter draws on his classical education to see "faces . . . of a purer Greek type" in the tenement-dwellers. Suydam cuts him short, however, with an observation based in the spurious racial science pervasive at the turn of the century: Sicilians are the "hottest tempered Italians" (36), a comment that at once denies the reason and culture implicit in "purer Greek type" and imputes a dangerous rage and lack of control to the immigrant underclass. Compressing De Ruyter's aesthetic distance and burgeoning sympathy into a clinically dispassionate objectivity, Suydam's comment separates subject from observer in a way more common to naturalistic than to local color works. Its function is to differentiate between classes rather than to blur the distinctions, as Jewett's text attempts to do. If, as Amy Kaplan, Richard Brodhead, and others have suggested, the local color movement "compose[ed] a certain version of modern history" and "[rendered] social difference in terms of region" so that "social conflicts of class, race, and gender made contiguous by urban life could be effaced," then the redefinition of local color in Matthews's sketch and other such Bowery tales aggressively codifies ethnicities and overtly reinscribes the conflicts of class and race.[16]

Gone is the tact with which Jewett's narrator approaches characters such as Elijah Tilley, for here local color conversation becomes naturalistic observation, and then invasion: the two men throw open the doors of apartments without knocking because, according to Suydam, most of the Italian immigrants "have no sense of home" and "don't know what privacy means" (38). Finding one such resident, Pietro Barretti, a "tall, dark Italian with fiery eyes," the two question him as he cooks "macaroni with ropy cheese over an oil lamp" and laconically tells them that his wife is dead (39). Learning later that the man has killed his wife, De Ruyter feels neither sympathy, as does Jewett's narrator, nor horror; he is instead satisfied that he now has "lots of color" (39) and a suitably sensational ending to his tale. Depicted as more interested in her subject than in her writing, Jewett's narrator "turn[s] to the half-written page" (15) with a sigh and, despite differences in class, counts Elijah Tilley among her friends. By contrast, in his quest for "copy" (39), De Ruyter, whose Dutch family name links him with New York's "old stock," reverses the process. His vision, like Suydam's now mired in ethnic stereotypes (Barretti eats exotic food and has an "eye like a glass stiletto" [40]), De Ruyter preserves a journalistic detachment from his subject that distinguishes naturalistic observation from local color sympathy. In the character of De Ruyter, Matthews, like Charles Dudley Warner, censures only the local color hack and the commodification of experience into fodder for the presses. The basic enterprise, however, remains the same in both tales: the exploration, appropriation, and inscription of a foreign, oral culture by an educated observer. Matthews's tale critiques in uncomfortable ways the construction of class bias, "old stock" ethnicity, and the privileged position of the educated author/observer in *The Country of the Pointed Firs*, however sympathetic Jewett's own treatment may be.

Perhaps the most damaging development to the status of local color in this period was the shift in attitude described by James Lane Allen in "Two Principles in Recent American Fiction," which appeared in the *Atlantic* one year after *The Country of the Pointed Firs.* Allen reports that literature has become divided into two distinct and opposing "principles":[17] the first, characterized by "Refinement, Delicacy, Grace, Smallness, Rarity, [and] Tact" (433), has, he believes, for too long dominated American short-story writing as its practitioners "sought the coverts where some of the more delicate elements of our national life escaped the lidless eye of publicity, and paid their delicate tributes to these" (433). Allen's language here suggests the local colorists, but his term for this genre is telling: he calls it the "Feminine Principle" and hails its departure in favor of the "approaching supremacy" of its opposite, the "Masculine Principle." Allen's description of the Masculine Principle reads like a naturalist's manifesto: its "Virility, Strength, Massiveness, Largeness, Obviousness, and Primary or Instinctive Action" will bring "more masculinity and also more passion" to the overcivilized, fragile literature "of effeminacy, of decadence" nurtured by the Feminine Principle (483). Anticipating the nativist racial theories of Jack London and Frank Norris, Allen claims that the Masculine Principle will promote a more accurate vision of the "Anglo-Saxon race" as it moves "from the thin-aired regions of consciousness which are ruled over by Tact to the underworld of unconsciousness . . . [and] . . . instinct" (435). When "tact," the hallmark of Jewett's narrator in *The Country of the Pointed Firs,* becomes redefined from "a kind of mindreading" (46) to the emblem of an effete, exhausted literary tradition, the marginalization of local color, clearly well underway even before the century's end, appears inevitable.

This response to the "Feminine Principle," and the gendered quality of the antagonism that naturalists like Norris, Crane, and Dreiser expressed for what Norris called the "drama of the broken teacup," rendered the virtual disappearance of local color in its original meaning all but inescapable. Neither Allen's intention nor his method demanded exact proof; he affirms throughout that he writes an exposition or description of the temper of the times, not a polemic. His reflections on the masculine principle lack documentation because he assumed that the sentiments expressed were universally held.[18] His carefully phrased but damning report on the Feminine Principle and the local colorists rested on the same assumption. Nor was Allen misguided in his beliefs. As late as 1904, the persistent connection between "littleness" and femininity that Allen had emphasized recurs in Gertrude Atherton's "Why Is American Literature Bourgeois?" Atherton attacks the magazines that promote "anaemic" literature and stifle originality, pausing along the way to ridicule those of "slender equipment" who, like Matthews's De Ruyter, are "always running about looking for copy, for local color," but whose "eyes are closed to the great things."[19] The equation of "local color" with "copy," suggesting that each is mere fodder for the presses, shows the extent to which the reputation of local color had declined. Indeed, a more satiric approach to the same issue, Jack London's "Local Color" (*Ainslee's*, October 1903), addresses similar themes, as a "copy-gathering" excursion into hobo life yields "local color, wads of it," including an unflattering portrait of a police judge. When the writer, Leith Clay-Randolph, is mistakenly arrested for vagrancy and appears before the judge, he is told, "Young man, local color is a bad thing. I find you guilty of it and sentence you to thirty days' imprisonment."[20]

As the style and method of local color became the subject of parody, one obvious transformation resulted as its themes of retreat into the recent past merged with, or became transmogrified into, the full-blown escape possible in historical romances. Works such as Charles Major's *When Knighthood Was in Flower* (1898) and George Barr McCutcheon's *Graustark* (1901) fed on the public's taste for exciting events set in remote eras, much as Richard Harding Davis's adventure novels, including *Soldiers of Fortune* (1897), satisfied its craving for exotic places. Denouncing the undeserved neglect of Filipino author Jose Rizal's *An Eagle Flight*, Howells underscored the imperialist myth at the heart of these novels by referring to the day's bestsellers by satiric titles such as *The Flaming Sword* and *Buckets of Blood.*[21] Noting that "historical romances, in fact, were the major best-sellers on the earliest published lists from 1895–1902," Amy Kaplan demonstrates convincingly that the performance of such fantasies of empire effects the revitalization of masculinity through a nostalgic "escape to a distant frontier . . . that . . . allows the American man to return home by becoming more fully himself."[22] In such a shift in literary taste, nostalgia for a redemptive atavism and conquest thus replaces local color's rhetoric of civilization and inclusion.

Confronted by this trend, even the best of the local colorists did not escape contamination by the rage for romance.[23] In what seems a belated effort to meet this challenge, local colorists such as Jewett, Freeman,

Garland, Mary Hartwell Catherwood, and others turned to writing historical romances. In 1900, Mary Wilkins Freeman (then Mary E. Wilkins) published *The Heart's Highway: A Romance of Virginia in the Seventeenth Century;* a year later, Sarah Orne Jewett came out with *The Tory Lover.* These two departures from their early work drew this response from an exasperated Henry James, who wrote to Howells on January 25, 1902: "Mary Wilkins's I have found no better than any other Mary, in the fat volume; and dear Sarah Jewett sent me not long since a Revolutionary Romance, with officers over their wine etc., that was a thing to make the angels weep."[24] Addressing Jewett herself on October 5, 1901, James had tried a more tactful vein, though one that binds Jewett inescapably with her former works: "Go back to the dear country of the *Pointed Firs, come* back to the palpable present-*intimate* that throbs responsive, and that wants, misses, needs you, God knows, and that suffers woefully in your absence."[25] But neither Jewett nor Freeman was to repeat her previous success. The 1902 carriage accident that incapacitated Jewett rendered moot the question of her burgeoning career as a romance writer, and the decidedly pedestrian quality of Mary Wilkins's romances failed to regain for her the acclaim she had received as a local colorist.

To write a masterpiece such as *The Country of the Pointed Firs,* then, at the very moment when the genre of local color threatened, like Dunnet Landing itself, to stand "high above the flat sea for a few minutes" before sinking "back into the uniformity of the coast" (132), suggests a multiply ironic perspective. Local color did not sink without a trace, of course. As its retreat into the past allied local color with historical romance, so too did its insistence on accurate representation, on the interdependence of character and milieu, on "old stock," and on the observer's narrative gaze applied to a humbler class of people become subsumed into the competing genre of naturalism. As a brief review of the evidence indicates, however, the meaning as well as the reputation of local color was far from stable in the years surrounding *The Country of the Pointed Firs.* James had criticized Jewett for moving toward the market-based form of historical romance, but, given the circumstances, it is difficult to blame her for what, in retrospect, seems such a departure from serious, realistic local color fiction. Dislocated by the passage of time, by shifting tastes, and now by ideology from the local color movement she had represented for so long, Jewett may well have felt that she had nowhere else to go in a genre that the 1890s saw altered almost beyond recognition.

Notes

I would like to thank Elaine Sargent Apthorp, Karen Kilcup, Ann Romines, Ann C. Morrissey, Kevin Hearle, and others at the Sarah Orne Jewett Centennial Conference for their comments and encouragement on an earlier version of this paper.

1. Paula Blanchard, *Sarah Orne Jewett: Her World and Her Work* (Reading, Mass.: Addison-Wesley, 1994), 304.

2. Richard H. Brodhead, *Cultures of Letters: Scenes of Reading and Writing in Nineteenth-Century America* (Chicago: University of Chicago Press, 1993), 162. Over the past twenty years, critics have contextualized Jewett's work by reading it within a host of traditions. Among the many feminist critics exploring Jewett's vision of female community and place within a tradition of women's authorship, see especially Marjorie Pryse, "'Distilling Essences': Regionalism and 'Women's Culture'," *American Literary Realism* 25.2 (Winter 1993): 1–15; Sarah Way Sherman, *Sarah Orne Jewett: An American Persephone* (Hanover, N.H.: University Press of New England, 1989); and Josephine Donovan, *Sarah Orne Jewett* (New York: Ungar, 1980), *New England Local Color Literature: A Women's Tradition* (New York: Ungar, 1983), and *After the Fall: The Demeter-Persephone Myth in Wharton, Cather, and Glasgow* (University Park: Pennsylvania State University Press, 1989). Defending the central position of regionalism in "'Not in the Least American': Nineteenth-Century Literary Regionalism," Judith Fetterley further defines the movement through its "efforts to dismantle and deconstruct hierarchies," its "commitment to empathy," and its "different model of storytelling" (*College English* 56 [December 1994]: 888, 889, 891).

Other recent works seek to reclaim Jewett for more mainstream traditions. Michael Davitt Bell's *Problem of American Realism: Studies in the Cultural History of a Literary Idea* (Chicago: University of Chicago Press, 1993) places Jewett within the context of realism, whereas Brodhead situates her writings within the "topoi of travel writing" and cultural tourism. The revisionist readings in June Howard's *New Essays on "The Country of the Pointed Firs"* (New York: Cambridge University Press, 1994), especially Sandra Zagarell's "*Country*'s Portrayal of Community and the Exclusion of Difference," Susan Gillman's "Regionalism and Nationalism in Jewett's *Country of the Pointed Firs*," and Elizabeth Ammons's "Material Culture, Empire, and Jewett's *Country of the Pointed Firs*," place Jewett within the late-nineteenth-century discourses of ethnicity, immigration, and the creation of a national culture.

3. June Howard suggests that "Jewett ought to be read not just with other regionalists but with other authors of the late nineteenth and early twentieth centuries who are striving to tell a 'story of civilization' (often a racialized and racist developmental narrative)—with, for example, Jack London." Howard, "Unraveling Regions, Unsettling Periods: Sarah Orne Jewett and American Literary History," *American Literature* 69 (1996): 379. The present essay focuses

more specifically on the aesthetic implications than on the political valences of the term "local color."

4. Howells, "Editor's Study," *Harper's New Monthly Magazine* 74 (1886): 485. According to Frank Luther Mott's *History of American Magazines* (Cambridge, Mass.: Harvard University Press, 1957, 2:383), *Harper's New Monthly Magazine* changed its name to *Harper's Monthly* in 1900; for the sake of consistency, the latter title has been used throughout.

5. Edward Eggleston, Preface to the Library Edition (1892) of *The Hoosier School-Master* (New York: Grosset and Dunlap, 1913), 6.

6. Hamlin Garland, *Crumbling Idols: Twelve Essays on Art Dealing Chiefly with Literature, Painting and the Drama*, ed. Jane Johnson (Cambridge, Mass: Belknap Press of Harvard University Press, 1960), 59, 53–54. Subsequent references are cited in the text.

7. Paul Shorey, "Present Conditions of Literary Production," *Atlantic Monthly* 78 (1896): 164.

8. Charles Miner Thompson, "New Figures in Literature," *Atlantic Monthly* 76 (December 1895): 840. In the *Atlantic Monthly*, this feature is unsigned. Charles L. P. Silet, Robert E. Welch, and Richard Boudreau, editors of *The Critical Reception of Hamlin Garland 1891–1978* (Troy, N.Y.: Whitson, 1985), identify Thompson as the author. Subsequent references are cited in the text.

9. Eggleston, Preface, 6.

10. Frank Norris, "The Great American Novelist," in *The Responsibilities of the Novelist and Other Literary Essays* (New York: Doubleday, Page, 1903); reprinted in *Literary Criticism of Frank Norris*, ed. Donald Pizer (Austin: University of Texas Press, 1964), 123.

11. Charles Dudley Warner, "Editor's Study," *Harper's Monthly* 86 (December 1892): 150.

12. "The Future of the American Novel," *Harper's Monthly* (March 1912); reprinted in *Criticism and Fiction*, 348, 347. Howells wrote in response to Arnold Bennett's attack in "The Future of the American Novel."

13. Charles Dudley Warner, "Editor's Study," *Harper's Monthly* 92 (May 1896): 961.

14. Jewett, *The Country of the Pointed Firs and Other Stories*, ed. Mary Ellen Chase (New York: Norton, 1981), 54. Subsequent references to this edition are cited in the text.

15. Brander Matthews, "In Search of Local Color," *Harper's Monthly Magazine* 89 (June 1894): 33–40; Jacob Riis, *How the Other Half Lives* (New York: Scribners, 1890), 55. Subsequent references to both works appear in the text. In addition to plays, novels, and criticism, Matthews published three collections of New York local color stories: *Vignettes of Manhattan* (1894), *Outlines in Local Color* (1898), and *Vistas of New York* (1912).

16. Brodhead, *Cultures of Letters*, 120; Amy Kaplan, "Nation, Region, and

Empire," in *The Columbia History of the American Novel*, ed. Emory Elliott (New York: Columbia University Press, 1991), 251.

17. James Lane Allen, "Two Principles in Recent American Fiction," *Atlantic Monthly* 80 (October 1897): 433–43. In his "Editor's Study" column for November 1891, Howells had similarly identified "two tendencies, apparently opposite, but probably parallel: one a tendency toward an elegance refined and polished, both in thought and phrase, almost to tenuity; the other a tendency to grotesqueness, wild and extravagant, to the point of anarchy"; Longfellow exemplified the first and Whitman the second. *W. D. Howells as Critic*, ed. Edwin H. Cady (London: Routledge and Kegan Paul, 1973, 210).

18. The same matter-of-fact tone occurs in Alexander Harvey's book *William Dean Howells: A Study of the Achievement of a Literary Artist* (1917; rpt., New York: Haskell House, 1972): "Unless we perceive clearly the reasons which have raised Howells to sovereignty over the sissy school of literature, the dominant American one, we shall miss the point of his distinction between the romanticist and the realist" (184). The "sissy school" of realism reflects a feminine "attitude of receptivity" that reflects things as they are, whereas "[t]the novelist whose genius happens to be masculine will never submit to the trammels of such a female conception of his function. He will inevitably stamp himself upon the wax of life in patterns of his own temperament" (184–85). Harvey's explanation of the difference between realism and romance sounds much like Norris's.

19. Gertrude Atherton, "Why Is American Literature Bourgeois?" *North American Review* 178 (May 1904): 781.

20. London, "Local Color," in his *Moon-Face and Other Stories* (New York: Grosset and Dunlap, 1906), 41, 55.

21. "The Editor's Easy Chair," *Harper's Monthly* (April 1901); reprinted in *W. D. Howells as Critic*, ed. Cady, 352–60.

22. Kaplan, "Romancing the Empire: The Embodiment of American Masculinity in the Popular Historical Novel of the 1890s," *American Literary History* 2.4 (1990): 660, 671.

23. For example, Mary Hartwell Catherwood, whose 1870s local color stories of the Great Lakes were later collected in *The Queen of the Swamp and Other Plain Americans* (1899), had long since turned to historical fiction set in eighteenth-century Quebec by the time the volume appeared. A frequent contributor to the *Atlantic* during the 1890s, her works published there include a novel, *The Lady of Fort St. John* (July–November 1891), and fifteen other pieces published between 1893 and 1899.

24. Henry James, *Letters of Henry James*, ed. Leon Edel (Cambridge, Mass.: Belknap Press of Harvard University Press, 1984), 4:222–23. The "other Mary" may be Mary N. Murfree, who had written a series of Southern historical romances including one called *The Story of Old Fort Loudon* (1899).

25. James, *Letters of Henry James*, 4:209.

"Links of Similitude"

The Narrator of *The Country of the Pointed Firs* and Author-Reader Relations at the End of the Nineteenth Century

Melissa Homestead

"Practically, there *is* no author; that is for us to deal with. There are all the immortal people—*in* the work; but there is nobody else."

"Yes," said the young man—"that's what it comes to. There should really, to clear the matter up, be no such Person."

"As you say," Gedge returned, "it's what it comes to. There *is* no such Person."

—*Henry James, "The Birthplace" (1903)*[1]

. . . the trouble with most realism is that it isn't seen from any point of view at all, and so its shadows fall in every direction and it fails of being art.

—*Letter of Sarah Orne Jewett to Thomas Bailey Aldrich (1890)*[2]

The narrator of *The Country of the Pointed Firs* is an elusive figure. A narrator who is also a character in the fiction, she nevertheless reveals very little about herself as a character in the course of her narration. She is the unnamed speaking "I," and she is "you" to Mrs. Todd and other characters. Although the narrator apparently travels to Dunnet Landing from a city, we don't know where she lives the rest of the year; and we can only *assume* from her time spent in the schoolhouse engaged in "literary employments" that she writes for pay. But critics (and I happily include myself) find the narrator as a character irresistible, and they expend much effort on constructing her from scant internal evidence and on reading *Pointed Firs* as a story of her personal development. To name just a few examples, critics have highlighted the narrator's apprenticeship to Almira Todd in the healing arts, the primal female love between the narrator and Mrs. Todd, the narrator's relearning female-identified relational living and returning to teach living to an emotionally starved male-identified culture, the story's ritual enactment of the Demeter-Persephone myth (with the narrator taking the role of the daughter Persephone to Mrs. Todd's motherly Demeter), and, least flatteringly, the narrator's role as tourist, traveling to the country to write about the quaint folk to amuse her cosmopolitan audience and to reinforce its hegemonic power.[3]

My own analysis focuses on the narrator's most clearly defined characteristic: her profession. In the context of the literary field in the American 1890s, why did Sarah Orne Jewett choose to tell the stories of *The Country of the Pointed Firs* through a first-person narrator who happens to be a female author?[4] What does Jewett's literary practice tell us about her construction of herself as an author and of her relationship to the marketplace and her readers through that authorial persona? Although the practitioners of high realism in Jewett's own time, and the New Critics following their example, counseled that we should not look for authors and authors' intentions in literary texts, nineteenth-century American readers clearly *did* read for the author in literary texts.[5] Exactly what did they expect to find? That is, for a nineteenth-century American reader, what was an author, and what was an author supposed to do?

These meanings and expectations did not remain constant over the course of the century, and I want to map out here two different cultures of authorship, one on the wane and the other on the rise, in order better to describe the position Jewett takes in relation to both with *The Country of the Pointed Firs.* The 1890s literary field represented, in many ways, a radical break from the past as the literary market grew exponentially and as authors increasingly became national celebrities. Daniel Borus has argued that as authors became powerful, wealthy public figures, realism paradoxically advocated a withdrawal of the author's personal presence in the literary text.[6] Before this withdrawal, however, fiction writers, and particularly popular women writers of the 1850s through the 1870s, used literary strategies that actively encouraged readers to imagine novel reading as an immediate, personal communication with the author. These two cultures of authorship produced markedly different literary texts, which also embody radically different visions of the nature of author-reader relations; while realist practices have the effect of representing the author as powerful, distant, and independent, the earlier literary practices represent the author as present in personal service to the reader.[7]

Before I explicate where Jewett's practices in *Pointed Firs* fall on the continuum between these two poles, I want to outline the very different terrains of these two cultures of authorship. Novels by the "literary domestics," to use Mary Kelley's apt name for the popular women novelists of mid-century, encode both thematically and formally expectations that books are personal communication both produced and consumed within domestic space.[8] On a formal level, the novelists often use what Robyn Warhol has labeled an "engaging narrator," a narrator who uses direct address to the reader ("dear reader" or simply "you") to engage the reader's sympathy.[9] Harriet Beecher Stowe's engaging narrator of *Uncle Tom's Cabin* is a classic example, with her many direct pleas to her readers to sympathize with the plight of the slaves.[10] Arguing from the evidence of book reviews, Nina Baym has made a persuasive case that nineteenth-century readers routinely identified the narrator with the author and approached "the novel as an expression of authorial voice as well as the recital of story."[11] That is, the narrator herself, whom nineteenth-century readers would have closely identified with the author, becomes a kind of character in the novel, even though she does not take part in the action.

Thematically, many of these novels take on the question of author-reader relations directly by creating sympathetic heroines who are authors and who work valiantly to serve their readers despite the often conflicting demands of domestic responsibility. Indeed, the primary subject of these novels featuring author-heroines is this conflict between authorship and domesticity, and the resolution of this conflict determines the resolution of the plot. In Fanny Fern's *Ruth Hall*, Ruth takes up writing after her husband's death leaves her penniless. Combining authorship and domesticity is both an absolute necessity for Ruth and a nearly impossible task, especially in the face of opposition from family members who give her no financial support yet who find her writing for pay indecorous. Out of necessity, she writes in the thick of her very small domestic space, with her child sleeping beside her and "her *mother's heart* . . . goading her on."[12] Her twin motivations are to earn a better home for her children and to improve the home lives of her readers through her writing. When she receives a fan letter from a man who says he is "a better brother, a better husband, and a better father, than I was before I commenced reading your articles" (183), Ruth breaks down in grateful tears. Eventually she manages to balance all of her obligations, writing morally instructive sketches that both please and instruct her readers and thus earning more than enough money to provide a secure home for her two daughters.

In Marion Harland's *The Hidden Path* (1853), one of the two heroines, Isabel Oakley, faces a conflict between authorship and domesticity that is not financially determined like Ruth's, but that nevertheless drives the plot of the novel. Isabel writes from within a financially secure domestic space; as the unmarried daughter of a wealthy Philadelphia man who supports her intellectual pursuits, she claims as her space for writing "a small room in the rear of the family parlor," separated from the main room only by a curtain rather than a door.[13] The narrator lovingly lingers on the "neatness" and good taste of the room, "a pleasant boudoir, its light convenient furniture; pictures and books kept in perfect order" (232). Significantly, Harland chooses to represent a moment when the desk "wheeled directly in front of the [open] door" is "piled with letters," the answers to which "engaged Isabel's nimble fingers" (222), much as if she were sitting in the family parlor doing needlework. As in a similar scene in which Ruth Hall sorts through her fan letters, those that most engage Isabel are not those from the famous or letters of the "inquisitive and mercenary" classes. Instead, the letters that "warm the heart and kindle the eye" are "far more humble tributes from obscure or unknown readers—her 'friends' she loved to style them; blessings and thanks from the sick, the weary, the oppressed to whom the touch of her flowery sceptre had brought ease and strength and rest" (223).

From *within* that domestic authorial sanctuary, however, she witnesses her own undoing, as she unintentionally observes the man she loves proposing to another woman, a woman whom she urged him to entertain because her authorial duties kept her too busy. In an elaborately worked out continuing metaphor, Isabel becomes a figure of the female author as Christ, suffering an emotional crucifixion when her devotion to her readers causes her to lose the man she loves ("She wears the prickly Cavalry crown of Fame; / And praises follow all her steps, but sobbing, / Through the blank night, she breathes one hoarded name" [297]). Eventually, her beloved recognizes his mistake, and Isabel manages to combine marriage with authorship (although actually representing this balancing act seems to be beyond Harland's own authorial talents, despite her ability to represent at *great* length Isabel's experience of the conflict between the two). But before that reconciliation takes place, once again a letter from a humble reader consoles and sustains Isabel. The reader, a female invalid, writes to Isabel describing Isabel's authorship in language vaguely echoing the Twenty-third Psalm's description of the protective, parental benevolence of a loving God:

> I was weary, and you have rested me;—suffering, and you have soothed;—hopeless, and you have taught me hope;—and so, in my loneliness, I come to you in gratitude. Books are my friends now. Once they were a study, and a passion and a pride; but in ceasing to be these, they are more—constant and sympathizing companions. . . . [O]verwrought nerves shrink from spoken words of counsel and hope, and yet find them gratefully upon the printed page. And so, your book came to my couch a stranger, and lies beside me now—a friend, seeming, as every true book must—but a part of its author. (319)

Out from Isabel's parlor study went her book, which this reader takes as a metonym for Isabel's body, entering the reader's home and lying on her couch with her. In Isabel's moment of need, this reader returns the favor, providing Isabel with consolation.

I hope these brief examples make clear the congruence between the imagined scenes of production and of reception in these fictions of female authorship, with literature flowing from the author's home to the reader's home and improving the lives of both.[14] In other fictions of female authorship of the period, the same tropes of author-reader relations appear repeatedly: the author as teacher, mother, or sister to her readers in need of guidance, the work of writing as sewing, cooking, or other forms of nurturing domestic labor which takes place within the home in service to the family.

As literacy rose and the variety of reading materials proliferated, an entire genre of advice literature arose to guide reader consumers in their selection and consumption of books, to help them choose, as it were, which books to take in as friends to lie on their couches with them. As these advice books make clear, however, readers did not see themselves as selecting books or texts—independent, abstract objects separated from their creators—but as selecting the personal companionship of the people who wrote the books. In his *Books and Reading; or What Books Shall I Read and How Shall I Read Them?* the published version of his popular lectures on the topic, Noah Porter, president of Yale University, tells readers that they should ask authors who "solicit our attention" whether they will gain anything from the authors: "If he can neither teach us anything which we do not know, nor convince us of anything of which we are in doubt, nor strengthen our faith in what we already receive, nor set old truths in new lights, nor warm our feeling into noble earnestness, nor entertain us with wholesome jokes, nor excite us to honest laughter, then *he* is not the man and *his* is not the book for *us*. Whatever he and his book may be to others, they have no claim upon us, and we should be quite ready to show both the door."[15] Porter here envisions an author as a person knocking on the doors of houses with his book in hand, asking to be let in to entertain their inhabitants. In Porter's vision of reading, "We place ourselves in communication with a living man," and if we don't like what he has to say, we, as readers, can cut off communication by showing him the door. Once again, the focus is on reading taking place within domestic space, and on the author being present and in dialogue with the reader during reading.

On the reverse side of the same coin, magazine articles and books presenting sketches of "authors at home" encouraged readers to imagine visits to the *author's* home for an inside glimpse of the domestic space where works of literature were produced.[16] In 1895, the year before the serialization of *Pointed Firs* in the *Atlantic Monthly*, Jewett herself became the object of such an extended "author at home" portrait, written for syndicated publication in the Sunday newspaper supplements, and she (and even her dog and cat) made many briefer appearances in book and periodical accounts giving readers access to authors' domestic lives and spaces. The writer of the syndicated article, her journey made arduous by rainy weather and the lack of a South Berwick train station, is immediately put at ease by "the face of the woman who stood in the broad paneled hall with its great doors at each end," a face she finds "cheery enough to make up for any imaginable lack of sunshine" (the image of a female figure standing in "The Old Hall" next to the staircase with an open door behind her accompanies the piece, along with a conventional portrait of Jewett, a sketch showing the entire house, and another of a corner of the dining room).[17] The writer repeatedly draws attention to Jewett's claims to elevated social standing (because of both her authorship and her impeccable New England ancestry, embodied in the house and its furnishings), and she apologizes for the unseemliness of describing Jewett's private residence and the writer's private conversation with her. However, she also describes Jewett as graciously and willingly telling her about her house, her family, and the relationship of her writings to both, without being asked.

She goes on to describe Jewett's daily production in numbers of words, her writing of some works in a single sitting and others across days and weeks, and the periods between of rest and contemplation. Having prepared her newspaper audience with a full tour of the house and this description of Jewett's work habits, the writer finally leads readers into Jewett's "den," a scene marked by its scattered papers as the place where Jewett writes: "it is the most delightful I've ever seen. It is in the upper hall, with a wide window looking down upon the tree-shaded village street. A desk strewn with papers is on the one side and on the other a case of books and a table. Pictures, flowers, and books are everywhere." After a tour of the library and a leisurely conversation with Jewett about books, modern literature, and "the new woman" (a conversation that somehow seems enabled by the writer's access to Jewett's writing desk), the journalist leaves, ending the piece with a second set-piece of Jewett standing in the doorway of her house. As the writer tells us, she will always remember the whole visit, but particularly "the strong, reviving personality of the slender, dark-haired, dark-eyed woman who looked out on a wet world so cheerily as she stood in the doorway in her simple summer dress to bid me goodbye."

The high realist aesthetic was a world away from such scenes of authorial domesticity as that of Jewett in her doorway bidding adieu to her reader-visitor; the realist aesthetic instead insisted on authorial absence and distance rather than presence and personal engagement. As Borus argues, realist authors were sometimes suspicious and resentful of the increasing commodification of literature and authors in the expanding literary marketplace. The realists' decision to break with the literary tradition of engaging narrators and thus to withdraw themselves (or at least figures of themselves) as personal, easily identifiable presences from their texts was a response to these market pressures. The narrator in the new Jamesian model of fiction became an omniscient but unobtrusively literary presence who focused the reader's attention on the represented social "reality" of the text and on the psychological complexity of its fictional characters rather than on the author (at least according to the realists' own self-justifications). However, as Nancy Glazener argues, such authorial distancing and withdrawal was also a part of a strategy to "professionalize" realist authorship by simultaneously constructing the sentimental and sensational modes of authorship as *un*professional.[18] As Glazener notes, sentimental fiction by writers like Stowe relied on an author-reader relation that Richard Brodhead has labeled "disciplinary intimacy," a relation "modeled on the loving counsel of a parent that a child internalized because of her identification with the parent," with the author taking the role of the mother and the reader the role of the child. Because "disciplinary intimacy was the function of mothers," argues Glazener, "in becoming professionals who withheld their personalities rather than quasi-parental counselors, authors distanced themselves from this feminine coding" of sentimental authorship (111). Claiming the authority of detached professionals, realists accused authors who continued to use strategies of narrative familiarity of "unprofessional laxness" in their artistic practices.

Despite the disappearance of the author from the realist text, many readers apparently continued to seek authors in those texts, and readers violating realist standards of decorum in their reading practices also came under attack. Henry James's story "The Birthplace," part of the epigraph for this essay, subtly mocks the typical nineteenth-century-style reader looking for the author in the author's works. The main character, Morris Gedge, is a failed schoolmaster and librarian, fleeing a librarianship at the town of "Blackmore-on-Dwindle," where, much to his horror, most of his patrons are young women who read nothing but popular fiction by women writers (a circumstance that identifies the "wrong" style of reading with woman readers reading woman writers). He is hired with his wife as caretaker of the cottage where a famous author was born, and although everyone refers to the author only as "He" or "Him," the cottage is clearly Shakespeare's cottage. Gedge suffers a crisis of conscience when he comes to realize that all of the stories he and his wife tell tourists about Shakespeare's childhood in the house are false, merely "the Show" put on for "Them," the people who come to see it all because their tourist guidebooks tell them to. In an unguarded moment, he proclaims to a sympathetic visitor that "there is no such Person" as Shakespeare, "there *is* no author. . . . There are all the immortal people—*in* the work; but there's nobody else" (521). When Gedge's conscience leads him to hedge and qualify his statements when giving tours, the public won't have it. They want "Him" (Shakespeare), and if Gedge won't give Him to them, Gedge will lose his job. He finally resolves his dilemma by learning to lie, by carrying on the Show so well that the board of overseers doubles his salary. The Author is not at home, but Gedge learns to conjure up a bogus vision of Him anyway.

James scorned direct address to readers as breaking the illusion of naturalness in fiction by introducing just such an authorial presence into the consecrated space of the fictional text. In his influential essay "The Art of Fiction," he complains of Anthony Trollope's "want of discretion" in speaking to his readers directly in digressions, parentheses, and asides because "such betrayal of a sacred office seems to [James] a terrible crime" which "shocks" him.[19] Trollope is an author at home in his novels, and James wishes he would disappear, like the false specter of Shakespeare in "The Birthplace." In a review of a published collection of Gustave Flaubert's letters, James explicitly connects impersonal narration with resistance to demands for authorial presence in the marketplace. James praises Flaubert's insistence on the "impersonality" of the literary text: "His constant refrain in his letters is the impersonality, as he calls it, of the artist, whose work should consist exclusively of his subject."[20] In light of this drive for impersonality, James deplores the publication of Flaubert's private letters and the revelation of that personality that Flaubert deliberately chose not to reveal through his works: "He kept clear all his life of vulgarity and publicity and newspaperism only to be dragged after death into the middle of the marketplace, where the electric light beats the fiercest."[21]

In an unsigned *Atlantic Monthly* review of Jewett's story collection *Old Friends and New* published sixteen years before the publication of *Pointed Firs* in the *Atlantic*, editor Horace Scudder explicitly urges Jewett to imitate Henry James's narrative techniques, precisely because of the unseemliness of her personal presence in the stories through the voice of the engaging narrator:

> [She should make] her characters act for themselves. At present they cling to her skirts, and she leads them about with her. . . . In *Deephaven* and these later sketches, the author has not yet felt the confidence which would enable her to withdraw her direct support from her characters. She cautiously holds, for the most part, to the form of the story which permits her to be present during most of the action. We suggest, as a practice experiment in story-telling, that she avail herself of the method which is sometimes used in Mr. James's stories, where one of the characters, not identified with the

storyteller, is charged with this duty. It might gradually strengthen her in an ability to conceive of a story which had its own beginning, middle, and end, and was not taken as a desultory chapter of personal experience.[22]

We can see here precisely how, as Glazener argues, an older style of narrative familiarity becomes identified with an unprofessional laxness coded as maternal and feminine. By being "present" as a narrating voice in her stories, argues Scudder, Jewett is like a mother with her children hanging about her skirts. Simultaneously, she is herself a literary child, immature and cautiously holding on to the prop of first-person narration to get her through her stories, much as her characters hang on to her maternal skirts to walk. Scudder here accuses Jewett of the same sort of literary transgression for which James would soon chide Trollope—being a personal authorial presence in her text.

As Daniel Borus argues, James's influential critiques of earlier fiction aside, the device of the engaging narrator "did function to establish the novel as a direct and personal communication between narrator and individual reader" (100). In contrast, readers of high realist narrative, "unable to pinpoint precisely the source of the narrative . . . find their interpretive space constricted and their role at times akin to that of a dazed spectator" (101). James's quotation of one formulation of Flaubert's aesthetics in his review captures nicely the paradoxical power of this authorial absence: "It is one of my principles that one must never write down *one's self.* The artist must be present in his work like God in Creation, invisible and almighty, everywhere felt but nowhere seen" (332). Extending the metaphor backwards to Fern, Harland, and their contemporaries, one might say that the personal author present in the prerealist text through the engaging narrator or the figure of the author-heroine is like Christ, the personal, fully human presence of God, who enters the homes of ordinary people to serve them, rather than like James's author as God the Father, whose creation contains and imagines the reader by presenting a fully formed "objective" world open to neither an "author's" nor a reader's intervention.

In the 1890s, a time of contention and transition in narrative method, what would Jewett's original readers have done with the figure of the author-narrator of *Pointed Firs*? As heirs to the realists, modern critics have often felt compelled to take pains to distinguish the narrator from

Jewett and to remind us, as Jewett herself did, that *Pointed Firs* is fiction and Dunnet Landing a fictional place.[23] However, most of Jewett's readers in the 1890s, schooled to read for authors, would not have felt the same compulsion to draw such distinctions, and even professional critics slipped easily into conflating Jewett with the figure of the narrator in their reviews of *Pointed Firs* after its publication in book form. An anonymous reviewer in *The Critic*, for example, observes: "The *author* tells the story of a seaside summer on the coast of Maine. *She* lives with a fine old countrywoman . . . *she* talks to a sea-captain . . . *she* sails out to the island" (emphasis added).[24] While finding the subject of the tales to be slight, the reviewer attributes the appeal of the book to "the writer's fine and constant appreciation of whatever is individual and excellent and nature and humanity as it lies about her. We do not see that Dennet [*sic*] is absorbing, but that Miss Jewett is absorbed. Her interest is unfailing and she invests each incident for the reader with the same gentle glamour which it obviously has for herself." If pressed to state whether the book was memoir or fiction, this reviewer might have drawn a distinction between the narrator and Jewett; but the reviewer does not make this distinction clear, leaving open the possibility that "the writer's" appreciation is so clear to the reader because "the writer" is a character in the book who clearly demonstrates her appreciation through words and actions. In a similarly unstable formulation, an anonymous reviewer in *The Nation* remarks, "The casual observer could see little of interest here, the average writer could make little of what he sees; but the acute and sympathetic observer, the exceptional writer, comes on the scene, looks about, thinks, writes, and behold! a fascinating story."[25] But is that observer and writer coming on the scene Jewett herself in a figurative sense, or has the reviewer conflated Jewett with the narrator as a character "coming on" Dunnet Landing as a visitor? Or both simultaneously?

We as modern readers are accustomed to pick up a paperback edition of *Pointed Firs* that is clearly labeled "fiction" (even if the text's status as a "novel" always remains in doubt), but readers of *Pointed Firs* in its serialized version in the *Atlantic Monthly* faced no obvious or even subtle cues or clues that would have prompted them to draw a distinction between the narrating "I" and Sarah Orne Jewett. The first installment in the January 1896 *Atlantic* begins in the third person, describing an unnamed traveler and "lover of Dunnet Landing" returning to the Maine coast for a second visit. Several paragraphs into section 2 of the installment, the narrating voice abruptly shifts to the first person, and the narrator reveals herself to be the traveler and also discloses that she is a writer. For the rest of the sketches, the narrator remains unnamed and relatively unspecified. We know more about the facts of Almira Todd's life history than we do hers. The two facts that she discloses about herself, that she writes and that she spends most of the year living in some other place that is more populous than Dunnet Landing, would also not have prompted an *Atlantic* reader to draw distinctions. Most readers of the magazine would have recognized Jewett as a regular contributor of both tales of country life narrated by an omniscient narrator and of first-person accounts of country excursions; and because Jewett was a literary celebrity, most readers would have known Jewett both as a Maine native and as a sometime resident of Boston and a participant in its literary life. For *Atlantic* readers, these known facts of Jewett's life and literary career would not have distinguished her from the narrator.

The *Atlantic* did not clearly label or segregate "fiction" and "nonfiction" in its issues or in its index, and the first installment of *Pointed Firs* shares the January issue with other prose pieces whose fictional status is similarly indeterminate. "A Farm in Marne" by Mary Hartwell Catherwood features a similar unnamed first-person narrator who is both a traveler and a writer; she describes a visit to a French convent and its farm, detailing the domestic economy of French peasants. Agnes Repplier, also writing as an unnamed "I," describes French peasants celebrating the Catholic "Fete de Gayant." In such a context, a reader could have easily read any of these pieces either as nonfictional narratives by authors directly describing their experiences of travel or as fictional pieces told through the character of a first-person narrator; or readers could simply have chosen not to draw such distinctions at all, relating to all of these first-person narrators as expressions of authorial character and perception, regardless of the fictional status of the events narrated.[26] Although the original book publication of *Pointed Firs* was removed from this particular context, it contained no preface or other additional matter distinguishing Jewett from the narrator.

An instructive comparison can be made between the first installment of *Pointed Firs* in the January 1896 issue of the *Atlantic* and one of Henry James's artist tales, "Glasses," which appeared in the February 1896 issue.[27] Although the first-person narrator remains unnamed throughout the story, the rapid accumulation of detail about him and his life, including his profession as a painter, quickly marks him as a fictional character. Readers of the *Atlantic* would have known James and his reputation as they would have known Jewett and her reputation, and they knew he was not a professional portrait painter. As James critic Barbara Hochman argues, James's use of first-person narrators with clearly delineated personalities in his artist tales "inevitably drives a wedge between the act of narration and the figure of the writer." Indeed, Hochman argues, such first-person narration creates even more of a distance between narration and the figure of the author than James's use of a distant, impersonal narrator in his later novels whose narrative voice merges with characters who serve as narrative "reflectors."[28] In James's later novels, a reader can still catch glimpses of a narrating voice and the personality of that voice, even if such a personality is harder to locate than that of an engaging narrator; but when the first-person narrator is a fictional character, a voice that the reader might identify with the author's is nowhere to be found. The narrator of "Glasses" often self-consciously draws attention to himself as a writer, if not a professional one, and to his act of constructing his tale, beginning the story with a reflection on the act of narration: "Yes, I say to myself, pen in hand, I can keep hold of the thread, let it lead me back to the first impression."[29] The "I" holding the pen at the opening of "Glasses," however, is a fictional character, his act of narration doubly displaced from the figure of James, the man holding the pen behind the man holding the pen. The figure of the author in the text disappears altogether, and a reader seeking the author's personal presence in the text will be frustrated.

I would emphasize, however, that a first-person narrator only creates distance between the act of narration and the figure of the author when that first-person narrator is clearly distinguished from the author. The first-person narrator of *Pointed Firs* does not drive a wedge between the act of narration and the figure of the author, but instead allows for the possibility of bringing the two together, thus satisfying reader desire for authorial presence. From the realist perspective, we might read the narrator of *Pointed Firs* as functioning as the sort of Jamesian character-narrator that Horace Scudder urged Jewett to adopt, a figure detached from the author as teller (and thus detaching the author from her readers). However, from the perspective of a reader reading for the author, the narrator functions as a clear stand-in for Jewett, who thus remains in her text and accessible to her readers. Through this invocation of authorial presence, the text maintains a connection to the tradition established by Jewett's female predecessors, adapting a realist strategy to distance herself from the represented world of her text while simultaneously allowing and even encouraging conflation of her as author with her author character who narrates the action. Of course, Jewett's strategies are not entirely the same as those of her predecessors. On a formal level, her narration is less intrusive. Although the narrator occasionally comments on the action before her, she does so because she is a direct observer and sometime participant, not because she is an engaging narrator. Although she draws attention to herself and her perceptions, she does not directly draw attention to her reading audience through direct address to that audience. On a thematic level, Jewett's narrator as a character belongs to a different cultural moment than Isabel Oakley or Ruth Hall. The description of her profession is presented matter-of-factly, and no crisis or conflict between authorship and domesticity structures the book. However, *Pointed Firs* still crucially aligns the narrator as an author figure with domestic scenes of production and consumption of story. She often drifts away from the professional labor of writing to observe and participate in the life of Dunnet Landing, or, on a metaphorical level, the author "disappears" to become an audience for oral folk culture.

The narrator only engages in the business of writing in the first few chapters of the book, a period of time during which she feels torn between her role as writer and her role as audience. She sits alone in her room in Mrs. Todd's house, and she finds it "impossible not to listen, with cottonless ears . . . with an idle pen in my hand, during a particularly spirited and personal conversation" between Mrs. Todd and one of her customers.[30] After she lets herself abandon her writing to become Mrs. Todd's assistant in the spruce beer trade, she rents the empty schoolhouse in which to write, but once she is there, the "half-written page" (21) on her desk becomes a mark of her separation from the Dunnet Landing community. Although her encounter with Captain Littlepage in the schoolhouse at first seems like an answer to her longing for a "companion and for news from the outer world" that is "half-forgotten" in her authorial pursuits, the Captain is not the representative of oral folk culture that he at first seems to be. As his name suggests, he is a "little page," a man trapped in the world of intensively read works of "great" literature (Milton, Shakespeare, and the unnamed but obviously implied Coleridge). Littlepage derides the modern townsfolk for getting "no knowledge of the outside worlds except from a cheap, unprincipled newspaper," but despite his world travels, he appears to have gotten all of his knowledge of the world from Milton, acquired while he spent his time in solitary reading below deck in order to avoid getting too "familiar" with his crew (25). After escaping the Captain and his print-induced, Coleridgean phantasmagoria, she obligingly ingests a mysterious draught from Mrs. Todd's stock, and this draught seems to break her ties to authorship, the schoolhouse, and the overly literate world represented by the Captain.

Despite her claim that she rented the schoolhouse for the remainder of her stay in Dunnet Landing in order to have a quiet, private place to write, after her encounter with Captain Littlepage, the narrator never mentions writing again (and considering her report of her activities for the remainder of the summer, one is led to assume that she had no more time in her schedule for writing). Instead, the narrator turns to a more authentic oral culture of stories passed from mouth to mouth, often at the hearth, the center of the home, and to direct experience of the world.[31] In a typical progression surrounding the story of "Poor Joanna" and Shell Heap Island, the narrator first actively solicits the story from Mrs. Todd and Mrs. Fosdick, with prompting statements and questions ("What time of year was this?" [61]; "How large an island is it? How did she manage in winter?" [62]), until Mrs. Fosdick and Mrs. Todd begin prompting each other, and the narrator's questions and her narrated analysis drop away, the storytellers taking over. After she hears the story, the narrator makes a pilgrimage to see the island firsthand, with Mrs. Todd's and Mrs. Fosdick's words motivating her trip and shaping her perceptions.

The eating of the pies inscribed with text at the Bowden Reunion represents, I think, the apotheosis of the oral recapture of the abstract world of print publication and circulation. In what Elizabeth Ammons calls a "feast of language," a sacrament in which "a modern women writer find[s] renewal and nurture in a matrifocal community" through eating a pie that "fuses the realms of literary art (language) and domestic arts (cooking),"[32] the act of eating fuses not only domesticity and literature, but orality and the written word. "[D]ates and names were wrought in lines of pastry and frosting on the tops" of the pies, says the narrator, and there was "even more elaborate reading matter" on one pie at her table, which the guests "began to share and eat, precept upon precept" (96).

Mrs. Todd specially selects the word "Bowden" for the narrator to eat, while Mrs. Todd selects the word "Reunion" for herself. The cook, echoing the world of print, inscribes the pie with text, and the "author," a guest at the table, returns the world of print to its source, the mouth. The metaphorical equation of reading with eating is an old one and, as critics have recently pointed out, in late-nineteenth-century America the metaphor usually served to simplify and hierarchize the relation between reader and text, figuring the text as a thing that readers simply swallowed; the object swallowed rather than the act of swallowing produced either a positive or negative effect on the swallower. The metaphorical equation of reading with eating thus often reinforced the notion that readers (particularly less-educated and female readers) were mindless, passive consumers.[33] In the reunion scene, however, Jewett reclaims and revises the metaphor by making it clear that *eating* is not a mere matter of swallowing and incorporation. In Jewett's reworking, reading *is* eating, but eating that happens in the rich, interactive social context of the meal, the banquet, or the feast. Here, "author" and "reader" sit together, with the "book" passed from hand to hand, the pieces tasted, savored, and commented upon. And the narrator, in an act of community and reciprocity, takes the role of the reader, the one who eats as opposed to the one who prepares and serves the food.

The narrator has been a guest at many houses during her stay in Maine, and in the end, she fittingly eats a house, the gingerbread representation of the Bowden Homestead, which is not covered in text, but which she describes as "an essay in cookery." After consuming the word Bowden and eating the Bowden Homestead, the narrator's sojourn in Dunnet Landing, her time as a guest and as audience, must end. She must leave so that she can again enter the abstract world of print, and, implicit in the logic of the book, write the narrative that is *The Country of the Pointed Firs*.[34] Mrs. Todd's placing of a bay twig in her basket when she departs implicitly recognizes this necessity; she must leave and take up her laurel wreath (bay being another name for laurel), reassuming the mantle of authorship. The "author" has been a guest contained within the homes of ordinary people, but now she will return to the city and literary professionalism and recontain those homes inside the world of the text she creates. Or, to use the narrative's own imagery, she will bake her own big pie, inscribed with many more words, a representation of the world of Dunnet Landing, for others to consume in their homes.

The design of the book thus allows readers to imagine a very personal and immediate relationship between an author and her readers, including a reciprocity and exchanging of roles. Jewett herself often engaged in just such a personalized, author-centered mode of reading. In her letters, she writes of spending long evenings with authors whose works engaged her on a very personal level. She supplemented her heavy diet of literary reading with authors' memoirs, biographies, and collections of published letters. No doubt she enjoyed the "Memories of Hawthorne" by his daughter Rose Hawthorne Lathrop and the excerpts from Dante Gabriel Rossetti's letters that ran concurrently with *Pointed Firs* in the *Atlantic.* On her trips abroad with Annie Fields, she went on literary pilgrimages to visit living authors she admired, such as Tennyson, and to retrace the steps of dead ones. In a letter to Sarah Wyman Whitman, she describes with satisfaction her visit to Haworth for a pilgrimage to the Brontë home, even though she had been warned that things had changed since the death of the Brontë sisters: "Never mind people who tell you there is nothing to see in the place where people lived who interest you. You always find something of what made them the souls they were, and at any rate you see their sky and their earth."[35] In *Atlantic Monthly* sketches appearing alongside and between installments of *Pointed Firs*, Mary Argyle Taylor and Alice Brown shared their own literary pilgrimages with readers. Taylor describes with sensuous detail her stay in a house in Nohant, France, where George Sand once lived. She lingers over the oddly eroticized thrill she feels each night, when her "brain was strangely fired" as she "lay down to rest in the great curtained bed of George Sand."[36] In "Latter-Day Cranford," Brown describes her trip to Knutsford, England, which, she is careful to say, "is emphatically not the Cranford of Mrs. Gaskell's lovely chronicle, but it glitters with links of similitude" nevertheless because Gaskell had lived there.[37] Nineteenth-century readers of *Pointed Firs* would, I believe, have felt just such a sense of intimacy with Jewett through the figure of the author-narrator, just as many latter-day pilgrims to Martinsville, Maine, have recognized that it is emphatically not the Dunnet Landing of Jewett's chronicle, though they still seek links of similitude and traces of Jewett's presence.

Describing the shrinking size of her stories in an 1890 letter to Annie Fields, Jewett says, "They [the stories] used to be long as yardsticks, they are now as long as spools, and they will soon be the size of old-fashioned peppermints."[38] As Sarah Sherman says of this typically puckish Jewett self-analysis, it is crucial that Jewett envisions her art as something to be eaten or consumed, like a "domestic communion wafer: a sweet designed to disappear into the substance of the reader, *not* to remain outside experience like a yardstick."[39] A yardstick is also, of course, an instrument of measurement and judgment, and Jewett chose not to stay outside of her readers to measure and judge them, like the Jamesian author, God the Father. Jewett's fictional strategies in *Pointed Firs* are more akin to those of Harland and Fern than those of James. Serving readers' desires to connect imaginatively to the author, Jewett created an author figure who puts aside the task of writing to listen to ordinary people and to be an honored guest in their homes. Jewett's author heroine allows herself to be taken into the home, away from the call of "Art" and professionalism; through her author figure, Jewett built a personal relationship with her readers rather than stage a Jamesian withdrawal from them. Although in the act of fiction writing she necessarily assumed a controlling position outside or above the world of her readers, she was not an impersonal, omniscient Author-God, but a woman who strategically allied herself with the domestic values of her readers without surrendering strong authorship.

Notes

1. Henry James, "The Birthplace," in *The Short Stories of Henry James*, ed. Clifton Fadiman (New York: Modern Library, 1945), 521. This story was first published in James's collection *The Better Sort* in 1903, and then also appeared in the New York Edition.

2. *Letters of Sarah Orne Jewett*, ed. Annie Fields (Boston: Houghton Mifflin, 1911), 79.

3. Michael Holstein, "Writing as a Healing Art in Sarah Orne Jewett's *The Country of the Pointed Firs*," *Studies in American Fiction* 16 (1988): 39–49; Elizabeth Ammons, "Going in Circles: The Female Geography of Jewett's *Country of the Pointed Firs*," *Studies in the Literary Imagination* 16 (Fall 1983): 83–92; Margaret Roman, *Sarah Orne Jewett: Reconstructing Gender* (Tuscaloosa: University of Alabama Press, 1992); Sarah Way Sherman, *Sarah Orne Jewett: An American Persephone* (Hanover, N.H.: University Press of New England, 1989); and Richard H. Brodhead, *Cultures of Letters: Scenes of Reading and Writing in Nineteenth-Century America* (Chicago: University of Chicago Press, 1993).

4. I take the term "literary field" from Pierre Bourdieu, *The Field of Cultural Production: Essays on Art and Literature*, ed. Randall Johnson (New York: Columbia University Press, 1993).

5. For the useful and evocative phrase "reading for the author," I am indebted to Barbara Hochman, who applies the phrase in a different manner. See "Disappearing Authors and Resentful Readers in Late-Nineteenth-Century American Fiction: The Case of Henry James," *ELH* 63 (1996): 177–201.

6. Daniel Borus, *Writing Realism: Howells, James, and Norris in the Mass Market* (Chapel Hill: University of North Carolina Press, 1988). My account relies on Borus's central insight: that realism advocated effacement of personal authorial presence in literary texts at least in part in reaction to the commodification of the author in the expanding literary marketplace. However, Borus focuses exclusively on male realists. Although he claims that he is mapping the intellectual terrain of realism and that his narrative would look the same if he discussed women writers (10), as my argument will suggest, the aesthetic dicta of high realists were a gendered response to the practices of popular women writers. Jewett, as a woman writer who valued the tradition of women writers who came before her, does not break as radically from their literary practices. For the sake of simplicity, I will be using the term "realism" throughout to indicate the literary strategies sometimes called "high realism" that emerged in late-nineteenth-century America, while recognizing that the term "realism" is problematic.

7. Borus reads high realism much more sympathetically than I do, seeing the withdrawal of the author as an attempt to reestablish direct, personal communication with the reader who has been alienated from the celebrity author. Considering the tenor of male realists' critiques of the excesses of sentimentality practiced by their female predecessors and contemporaries, however, I tend to see their pronouncements more as a turf war with a popular, female-identified tradition that apparently served the needs of many readers very well. For a very different reading of Jewett's work as reacting to the aesthetic dicta of male high realists, see Michael Davitt Bell, "Gender and American Realism in *The Country of the Pointed Firs*," in *New Essays on "The Country of the Pointed Firs,"* ed. June Howard (New York: Cambridge University Press, 1994), 61–80. For Henry James's antagonism toward his female predecessors and contemporaries, see Alfred Habegger, *Henry James and the "Woman Business"* (Cambridge: Cambridge University Press, 1989).

8. Mary Kelley, *Private Woman, Public Stage: Literary Domesticity in Nineteenth-Century America* (New York: Oxford University Press, 1984), passim. See viii–ix for her explanation of her choice of the term to designate these writers.

9. Robyn Warhol, *Gendered Interventions: Narrative Discourse in the Victorian Novel* (New Brunswick: Rutgers University Press, 1989).

10. See, for instance, the closing chapter of the book publication of the novel: "I beseech *you*, pity those mothers that are constantly made childless by the American slave trade!" (emphasis added). Harriet Beecher Stowe, *Uncle Toms' Cabin, or Life among the Lowly* (New York: Penguin, 1981), 623–24.

11. Nina Baym, *Novels, Readers, and Reviewers: Responses to Fiction in Antebellum America* (Ithaca: Cornell University Press, 1984), 129.

12. Fanny Fern, *Ruth Hall and Other Writings* (New Brunswick: Rutgers University Press, 1986), 174. Subsequent page references are cited in the text.

13. Marion Harland (pseud. Mary Virginia Terhune), *The Hidden Path* (New York: J. C. Derby, 1853), 231. Subsequent page references are cited in the text.

14. Among other novels of this genre that employ similar tropes are Harland's *Phemie's Temptation* (1869), Susan Warner's *Queechy* (1852), Augusta Jane Evans's *Beulah* (1859) and *St. Elmo* (1867), and Helen Hunt Jackson's *Mercy Philbrick's Choice* (1876). Mary Kelley discusses many of these novels in chapter 5 ("Secret Writers") of *Private Woman, Public Stage*. I am greatly indebted to Kelley's work, which interprets these novels as unconscious expressions of psychic conflict in the author's own lives, but I prefer to read the novels as means of strategic authorial placement in the literary field. Evans's novels, particularly *St. Elmo*, are better known to modern readers than Harland's, and many (including Kelley) have commented on Edna Earle's *failure* to reconcile authorship and domesticity and have taken this failure as typical. However, despite the conflicts that also appear in the other novels named above, reconciliation of domesticity (with or without marriage) and authorship, not Edna's forswearing of one for the other, is the norm. Note also the stark contrast between these fictions of female authorship and Melville's *Pierre*, which reveals the author-hero, Pierre, to be incapable of accommodating himself to the market (and its many female readers). He bars himself in a room alone to write, away from the bizarre female menage that lives with him, and commits suicide when his publisher tells him that his book, then in page proofs, will not be published because it would be a fraud on the public.

15. Noah Porter, *Books and Reading; or, What Books Shall I Read and How Shall I Read Them?* (New York: Scribners, 1871), 50.

16. See Borus, *Writing Realism*, chapter 5, for a discussion of this genre. Again I read the primary materials quite differently. Borus sees the "system of celebrity" elaborated through the author-at-home genre as causing the "author's status [to dwarf] the reader's" (127), thus introducing distance and mystery. Instead, I see the genre as potentially closing the distance between author and reader and allowing for personal communication.

17. "Pleasant Day with Miss Jewett," *Philadelphia Press*, August 18, 1895, n.p. I have surmised that this article was syndicated based on the appearance of an apparently identical article on the same date in both the *Press* and the *Boston Sunday Herald*. See descriptions of these items in Gwen L. Nagel and James Nagel, *Sarah Orne Jewett: A Reference Guide* (Boston: G. K. Hall, 1978), 28–29. On the development of the fiction syndicates generally, see Charles Johanningsmeier, *Fiction and the American Literary Marketplace: The Role of the Newspaper Syndicates in America, 1860–1900* (New York: Cambridge University Press, 1997). Not coincidentally, Jewett sold at least four stories to the Bacheller newspaper syndicate in 1895, suggesting both Irving Bacheller's and Jewett's recognition of the promotional value of a biographical sketch in the same venue. See

Charles Johanningsmeier, "Sarah Orne Jewett and Mary E. Wilkins (Freeman): Two Shrewd Businesswomen in Search of New Markets," *New England Quarterly* 70 (March 1997): 58.

18. Nancy Glazener, *Reading for Realism: The History of a U.S. Literary Institution* (Durham: Duke University Press, 1997), 13. Subsequent page references are cited in the text.

19. Henry James, "The Art of Fiction," in *The Norton Anthology of American Literature*, ed. Nina Baym et al. (New York: W. W. Norton, 1989), 456–70.

20. Henry James, "Gustave Flaubert," *Macmillan's Magazine* 67 (February 1893): 332.

21. James is aware of the irony of his review, which, after proclaiming that the letters shouldn't have been published, proceeds to quote from those letters at length in his analysis of Flaubert's "artistic temperament." Thus, after a brief protest, James nevertheless takes on the task of probing Flaubert's tortured psyche with great relish.

22. [Horace Scudder], "Recent Novels" (review of *Old Friends and New*), *Atlantic Monthly* 45 (May 1880): 686.

23. See, for instance, Jewett's letter to a young fan, Mary E. Mulholland, who asked where on the Maine Coast Dunnet Landing was: "I cannot tell you just where Dunnets [*sic*] Landing is . . . . It is not any real 'landing' or real 'harbor'" (*Sarah Orne Jewett Letters*, ed. Richard Cary [Waterville, Maine: Colby College Press, 1956], 89). Note also the attempt of residents of Port Clyde, Maine, a town close to Martinsville, where Jewett vacationed before and perhaps during the writing of *Firs*, to claim the Port Clyde schoolhouse as the place where she wrote *Firs*, thus conflating the town with Dunnet Landing and the narrator with Jewett (Paula Blanchard, *Sarah Orne Jewett: Her World and Her Work* [Reading, Mass.: Addison-Wesley, 1994], 75).

24. Review of *The Country of the Pointed Firs*, *Critic* (February 13, 1897): 110. The review continues to conflate Jewett with her narrator by using this unspecified "she."

25. Review of *The Country of the Pointed Firs*, *Nation* (April 15, 1897): 288.

26. Although Catherwood and Repplier are relatively obscure figures now, they were also regular *Atlantic* contributors who would have been familiar to many readers. Several more installments of the Repplier and Catherwood travel sketches appeared in the following 1896 issues of the *Atlantic*, alongside or between appearances of subsequent installments of *Firs*, as do strikingly similar first-person travel and nature accounts by other writers, such as Bradford Torrey's descriptions of birdwatching in the Southern states (February and September), Maurice Thompson's account of bird specimen collecting in the Okefenokee (April), several sketches by Lacfadio Hearn of life in Japan (May and September), and yet more birdwatching memoirs (Olive Thorne Miller in Maine in May, June and July).

27. The four installments of *Firs* appeared in the January, March, July, and

September 1896 issues of the magazine. A serialized version of James's "The Old Things," narrated by an omniscient narrator, later published in book form as *The Spoils of Poynton,* also appeared in the 1896 *Atlantic.* For an interesting account of the influence of *Atlantic* editor Horace Scudder on the work of both Jewett and James for the *Atlantic,* see Ellery Sedgwick, "Horace Scudder and Sarah Orne Jewett: Market Forces in Publishing in the 1890s," *American Periodicals* 2 (1992): 79–88.

28. Hochman, "Disappearing Authors," 186.

29. Henry James, "Glasses," *Atlantic Monthly* 77 (February 1896): 145.

30. Sarah Orne Jewett, *The Country of the Pointed Firs and Other Stories* (Garden City: Doubleday Anchor, 1956), 18. All subsequent page references are to this, until recently the most widely available edition. However, my analysis focuses only on those chapters that appeared in the original book publication in 1906 (that is, I ignore "William's Wedding," "A Dunnet Shepherdess," and "The Queen's Twin").

31. Many scholars have examined the dynamics of storytelling in *Firs* (see, for just two examples, Marilyn Sanders Mobley, *Folk Roots and Mythic Wings in Sarah Orne Jewett and Toni Morrison: The Cultural Function of Narrative* [Baton Rouge: Louisiana University Press, 1991], and Sandra A. Zagarell, "Narrative of Community: The Identification of a Genre," *Signs* 13 [1988]: 498–527), so I will not discuss these dynamics in detail here. Recent ideological critiques of regionalism have alerted us to the possible conservative impulse behind Jewett's claiming of Maine rural culture as "authentic" and of the cosmopolitan narrator's appropriation of that authentic culture (see Brodhead, *Cultures of Letters;* Sandra A. Zagarell, "*Country's* Portrayal of Community and the Exclusion of Difference," in *New Essays,* ed. Howard, 39–60; Elizabeth Ammons, "Material Culture, Empire, and Jewett's *Country of the Pointed Firs,*" in *New Essays,* ed. Howard, 81–100; and Susan Gillman, "Regionalism and Nationalism in Jewett's *Country of the Pointed Firs,*" in *New Essays,* ed. Howard, 101–17). Without denying the validity of the concerns raised by the critique of regionalism, I want to suggest that the relationship between the narrator and the people of Dunnet Landing operates on more than one axis. "Urban" and "rural" are not the only operative terms structuring these relationships; the characters also exchange the roles of "authors" and "readers," "tellers" and "audiences." As Johanningsmeier argues in "Two Shrewd Businesswomen," the newspaper syndicates allowed Jewett to reach many poor and rural readers, readers that Brodhead insists were *not* readers of regional fiction, but were instead only the objects of a fiction that was consumed by middle- and upper-middle-class readers of magazines like *Harper's* and the *Atlantic Monthly.*

32. Ammons, "Material Culture, Empire, and Jewett's *Country of the Pointed Firs,*" 81. In this, Ammons's most recent essay on *Firs,* she emphasizes not the matrifocal celebration of the feast, but the way that the feast and attendant reunion ceremonies transform Dunnet into a center of empire. Ammons's read-

ing flattens the text down to one level of meaning; I cannot agree with Ammons's insistence that the reader has no choice but to enact that meaning, consciously or unconsciously.

33. For the deployment of the metaphor by late-nineteenth-century American librarians to institute hierarchies of value and to control reader access to materials, see Catherine Sheldrick Ross, "Metaphors of Reading," *Journal of Library History* 22 (1987): 147–63. On the gendering of the metaphor in Louisa May Alcott's *Little Women* and Thomas Bailey Aldrich's *The History of a Bad Boy*, see Steven Mailloux, "The Rhetorical Use and Abuse of Fiction: Eating Books in Late-Nineteenth-Century America," *Boundary 2* 17 (1990): 133–57.

34. Although Jewett added the chapters featuring the narrator's visit with Elijah Tilley for book publication, the serialization fittingly ends with the reunion and the implicit recognition that the narrator's visit must draw to a close with the closing of the summer. The final chapter, describing the narrator's departure, was also added for book publication.

35. *Letters of Sarah Orne Jewett*, ed. Fields, 158.

36. Mary Argyle Taylor, "In a Famous French Home," *Atlantic Monthly* 77 (June 1896): 754.

37. Alice Brown, "Latter-Day Cranford," *Atlantic Monthly* 77 (April 1896): 526.

38. *Letters of Sarah Orne Jewett*, ed. Fields, 81.

39. Sherman, *Sarah Orne Jewett*, 273.

"To Make Them Acquainted with One Another"

Jewett, Howells, and the Dual Aesthetic of *Deephaven*

Paul R. Petrie

When Sarah Orne Jewett entered into correspondence with the *Atlantic Monthly* regarding prospective publication of the sketches that later became her first book, *Deephaven* (1877), it was W. D. Howells with whom she communicated. Howells, then in transition from assistant to chief editor, was already guiding the *Atlantic*'s editorial policies in accordance with a nascent conception of literature's social-ethical mandate, which would gain full expression a decade later in his "Editor's Study" columns in *Harper's Monthly* (1886–92).[1] The American regionalism that came into vogue during the postwar decades—of which Jewett's work was an example—was well suited to Howellsian literary purposes, and it was on the grounds of these ideals that he accepted Jewett's early sketches of life along the southern Maine coast for publication and later encouraged her to revise them into book form.

Jewett's unique variant of the Howellsian social-ethical agenda for American literature is clearly implemented in both *Deephaven* (1877) and *The Country of the Pointed Firs* (1896), but while the latter is almost universally acclaimed as Jewett's most successful work, the earlier book is usually considered a promising but uneven apprentice work. *The Country of the Pointed Firs* immerses its readers in a powerfully realized local culture, detailing the network of everyday events, objects, and relationships that comprise the commonplace life of a Maine coastal village. But at the same time, the vivid impression of regional authenticity derives in large measure from the book's evocation of further dimensions of these realities: the sense that mundane social life resonates with an intuited spiritual immanence that both transcends and informs everyday existence. In *Country*, these tendencies exist within an aesthetic "fusion" (to borrow a term from Elizabeth Ammons) "that is so subtle and complex as to appear quite simple."[2] In the earlier book, however, this fusion is only fitfully successful; despite the narrator's dogged attempts to do justice to both aspects of her local subjects, she is apt to vacillate from one agenda to the other, her narrative mode lurching uncomfortably back and forth between the two.

Perhaps because of this disparity in achievement between otherwise analogous fictions, *Deephaven* reveals the process by which Jewett arrived at the seamless unification of ethically purposeful social description with mystically evocative symbolism in *The Country of the Pointed Firs*. Rereading *Deephaven* through the lens of a Howellsian conception of literary purpose reveals how Jewett reshaped the literary-ethical imperative she shared with her editor, adapting it to her own conceptions of both the nature of commonplace experience and the literary mode best suited to communicating it. *Deephaven* comprises Jewett's adoption and extension of Howells's model of ethically purposive social fiction, to include a supra-social, spiritual dimension of commonplace reality. Further, *Deephaven* reveals the terms of Jewett's struggle to transform linear Howellsian narrative mediation into a more reader-participatory, metaphysically evocative narrative experience.

The keystone of W. D. Howells's nascent literary vision, which would gain ever-expanding currency as a cultural ideal of literary practice in the final decades of the century, was an increasingly explicit conception of literary fiction as an ethically purposeful vehicle for fostering social understanding and cohesion in an age of societal fragmentation. Howells's active encouragement of regionalist writing occurred on the basis of its use value as cultural mediation between an urban, upper-middle-class readership and the other sectors of a postbellum U.S. society riven by regional, ethnic, and class divisions. Literature, he consistently asserted, should dedicate itself to introducing to each other citizens from the various divided sectors of society, in the hope that literary acquaintance would lead to constructive alteration of behavior, from reformed personal morality to comprehensive reconsideration of national economic and social priorities. The best of the new writing, Howells would proclaim in the *Editor's Study*, was filled with "conscience and purpose," dedicated to communicating commonplace experiences across cultural boundaries in order to make all corners of the democracy better know and understand each other: "The whole field of human experience was never so nearly covered by imaginative literature in any age as in this; and American life especially is getting represented with unexampled fullness. . . . [A] great number of very good writers are instinctively striving to make each part of the country and each phase of our civilization known to all the other parts; and their work is not narrow in any feeble or vicious sense."[3] On the contrary, the fulfillment of literary art's primary goals depended on precisely this sort of diffuse, collective, incremental representation of each constituent part of the society. "Men are more like than unlike one another," Howells wrote; "let us make them know one another better, that they may all be humbled and strengthened with a sense of their fraternity. Neither arts, nor letters, nor sciences, except as they somehow, clearly or obscurely, tend to make the race better and kinder, are to be regarded as serious interests; they are all lower than the rudest crafts that feed and house and clothe, for except they do this office they are idle" (96).

Jewett implements her version of the Howellsian social-ethical agenda from the first pages of *Deephaven*, launching a narrative that has all the earmarks of a regionalism aimed at mediating the cultural differences between the lives of the narrated and those of the audience. Jewett deftly introduces the enabling situation: the narrator, Helen Denis, and her friend Kate Lancaster will spend their summer vacation in the vacant mansion of Kate's deceased grand-aunt Brandon, in the sleepy coastal village called Deephaven. While Kate and Helen's family members summer at more usual holiday destinations (the Berkshires, Newport, Lake Superior, Britain), the two young Bostonians (accompanied by Kate's house-servants) will join the postwar vogue for roughing it in quaint, rural backwaters.

The first chapter of *Deephaven* allies its readers with Kate and Helen, as educated, upper-middle-class, urban outsiders eager to experience the local culture; the regionalist narrative, in a process explored by Richard Brodhead, enables an audience comprised chiefly of people who more closely resemble the narrators than the narrated to share vicariously in Kate and Helen's vacation.[4] Before Kate, Helen, and Jewett's readers have even arrived in Deephaven, we have already met our first authentic local character: Mrs. Kew, the lighthouse keeper's wife. Jewett has her narrators[5] travel by train from their native Boston to an outlying station—the last outpost of their civilization—whence they share a coach ride to Deephaven with Mrs. Kew. The travel arrangements themselves serve to emphasize the cultural distance between Deephaven and the world of its narrators and readers.

Subsequent chapters are devoted, in regionalist fashion, to the visitors' fascinated observations of provincial life, focusing on the details that most clearly mark Deephaven, its residents, and their way of life as "Other." Helen makes passing mention of city visitors whom the young women periodically receive, but even these visits serve primarily to provide occasions for Deephaven-based storytelling. Pages are devoted to detailed descriptions of the Brandon mansion and its furnishings, presented as harbingers of a lost eighteenth-century heritage. Frequent calls upon Mrs. Kew give Jewett's narrators opportunity for close observation and description of the lives and accouterments of those quintessential shore-dwellers, the lighthouse-keeper and his family. Another local denizen, Mrs. Patton, an old friend of the deceased Aunt Brandon, provides Kate and Helen entrance into the homes and domestic histories of other Deephaven citizens. Kate and Helen, as sympathetic outsiders who yet win their way into the confidence and intimacy of the natives, provide us readerly access to a wealth of local experience, mediating between two different cultural worlds.

Toward this end, the narrators assume a relatively objective yet clearly appreciative stance toward the subjects of their narration, rendering culturally representative characters, events, and objects in transparently mimetic prose readily amenable to regionalist social documentation. The account of Kate and Helen's visit with Mrs. Patton in chapter 3, for instance, faithfully transcribes the old woman's Downeast dialect, using it to reveal local culture through the memories associated with quotidian household objects.[6] "She had all genealogy and relationship at her tongue's end" (31) and "had either seen everything that had happened in Deephaven for a long time, or had received the particulars from reliable witnesses" (32), Helen Denis writes; via Mrs. Patton, Helen communicates family and community history through the stories that attach themselves to the implements of everyday life in the village. Thus the appearance of a battered earthenware mug that Kate and Mrs. Patton had once used for picking currants becomes the occasion for rehearsing the social history of the mug itself: its various owners, the uses it has served, the emotional associations it has acquired through decades of constant service. Likewise, the rediscovery of a quilt buried in a forgotten trunk leads to a rehearsal of the history of the watered-silk gown from which it was made, complete with the personal drama of local history memorially annexed to it. When Mrs. Patton serves the young women some cake, she includes with it a complete oral history of the recipe and the circumstances of its transmission from England to her hand. Jewett productively mines the local culture for all its resources of regionally representative events, objects, characters, and relationships.

Deephaven's union of local cultural content with a literary form ideally equipped for close description of that content testifies to Jewett's regionalist intentions. Despite her public disavowals of any actual prototypes for her Maine village, internal and biographical evidence reveal close adherence to many of the features Jewett had observed during her own summer vacations in York and Wells, on the southern Maine coast, during the late 1860s and early 1870s—the very years of *Deephaven*'s genesis. The narrative places a premium upon the authenticity of these coastal scenes and adopts a literary form well suited to their documentation. Formally, the book proceeds as a series of sketches, linked primarily by locale and narrative voice rather than by elaborate plotting. Howells's suggestion to Jewett that she try to write something more lengthy led the two eventually to agree, in their correspondence concerning *Deephaven*, that the openendedness and descriptive flexibility of the sketch form made it ideal for Jewett's gifts and purposes—a realization that may have been aided, on Howells's part, by his analogous experiments in *Suburban Sketches* (1871).[7] To make literature from "the every-day life" of such "a quiet old-fashioned country town" as Deephaven, Helen asserts (in a directly narratorial comment anticipating the *Editor's Study*'s pronouncements of the literary value of the commonplace), "one must care to study life and character, and must find pleasure in thought and observation of simple things, and have an instinctive, delicious interest in what to other eyes is unflavored dulness" (37).[8]

Jewett aligns her narration of the culturally normative aspects of commonplace Maine coast life with a Howellsian vision of social-ethical literary purpose. Her 1894 preface to a newly illustrated edition of *Deephaven* comments explicitly on the origin of the sketches in an ethical imperative for literary mediation of postbellum social divisions. The sketches, she writes, responded to new national conditions; urbanization, increased prosperity, and expanded rail service "brought together in new association and dependence upon each other" rural districts and "crowded towns," making possible "a new and national circulation of vitality."[9] But "the young writer of these Deephaven sketches was possessed by a dark fear that townspeople and country people would never understand one another, or learn to profit by their new relationship" (3). To bridge this social chasm became the informing goal of Jewett's writing.

The basis for this mediation, Jewett explains, consists in an underlying human commonality that may form a new foundation for community. In words distinctly reminiscent of one of Howells's most pointed statements of literature's ethical *raison d'être* in the *Editor's Study*, Jewett wrote in her preface that "Human nature is the same the world over" (6) despite the vagaries of local cultural difference. In national terms, she writes: "There is a noble saying of Plato that the best thing that can be done for the people of a state is to make them acquainted with one another" (3). This goal, she continues, can be achieved only when literature abandons the malicious impulse inherent in caricature and dedicates itself to the accurate representation of the lives and circumstances of the Other; "the caricatured Yankee" (3) of conventional fiction must be replaced with "a more true and sympathetic rendering" drawn from life rather than literature.[10] "The people in books," Jewett writes elsewhere, "are apt to make us understand 'real' people better, and to know why they do things, and so we learn to have sympathy and patience and enthusiasm for those we live with, and can try to help them in what they are doing, instead of being half suspicious and finding fault."[11]

Thus Jewett, in accordance with Howellsian literary imperatives, ties her literary practice, through its potential for real ethical effect on an actual audience, to a specific conception of the social uses to which literature should be harnessed. A Howellsian model of literature's ethical functions assigns primary value to fiction's mediation between an audience and subjects in some way alien to that audience. Fiction promotes the readerly sense of belonging to a common culture with the represented Other, by incorporating the Other into the audience's enlarged sense of its own group identity. Socially alien subjects thereby come to appear in the minds of readers as recognizable, if still distant, kin. Jewett and Howells both place their faith in the notion that the literary promotion of cross-cultural sympathies will lead not only to an audience's feeling or thinking differently, but also to their acting differently. Jewett's sympathetic adherence to realistic depictions of places and people, rather than to preexistent literary models, is thus an instrument for moving a society of readers to ethical action—to behaving differently toward the provincial outlanders with whom they were more and more brought into contact.[12]

Jewett subordinates choices of form and style—as Howells would do in the *Editor's Study* in theoretical terms—to this ethical formulation of literature's socially mediatory purposes, insisting that fiction's value as truthful social communication should be the primary determinant of aesthetic choices. Thus, for instance, Jewett's adoption of the sketch, as we have already seen, derives from its relative lack of prescribed form: its formal characteristics would arise on an *ad hoc* basis directly from the requirements of the social "materials" that the fiction sought to document. Likewise, Jewett's deployment of a transparently referential language subordinates literary style to clear communication. "Don't try to write *about* people and things," her father, Theodore Jewett, had counseled her; "tell them just as they are!"[13] If the informing goal of literature is to make the Other known to an actual readership, then "literary" concerns must efface themselves in the interests of unimpeded reference.

Deephaven's enactment of a socially mediatory ethical agenda also leads Jewett to her book's particular configuration of its narrators, Kate and Helen. In order to communicate provincial realities successfully to an audience of cultural outsiders, Kate and Helen must somehow simultaneously claim membership in both the narrated culture and the culture of their audience; the "girls" (as Jewett consistently refers to them) participate in a "double insider/outsider positioning" that, as Francesco Loriggio points out, "regionalist writing unavoidably generates."[14] But Jewett's narrative arrangements emphasize this inevitable relationship, first by choosing a first-person narrative voice, and then by carefully specifying Kate and Helen's claims to dual cultural citizenship. Thus the narrative begins in the city, emphasizing the girls' solidarity of outlook with their educated, urban audience, thereby staking a claim to narrative reliability. Having arrived in Deephaven, Jewett uses the girls' natural sympathies and, more prominently, Kate Lancaster's local family connections to grant the narrators plausible access to the "inside knowledge" of the life of the local culture. Anxious to capitalize on *Deephaven*'s mediatory capacities, Jewett goes out of her way to establish her narrators' double credentials.

What first meets the eye in *Deephaven*, then—in Jewett's choices of narrative stance, subject matter, language, form, and style—is a text dedicated to sympathetic documentation of regional cultural realities, allied with a Howellsian program of ethically purposeful social mediation. Gradually, though, it becomes clear that *Deephaven* aims at significantly more than this socially mediatory agenda. The narrative begins to focus on elements of the local culture and character whose signification is not only mundane and social but simultaneously spiritual and supra-social. As *Deephaven* turns its attention to such occult concerns as telepathy, madness, and death, the book reveals Jewett's struggle to enact, in Josephine Donovan's words, "a theory that erases the divide between spiritual and material, seeing the transcendent as incarnate in the physical."[15] *Deephaven* increasingly strives (to quote again from Donovan) to "evoke, suggest, hint at the existence of a higher realm, a transcendent realm, by means of earthly objects, characters, and relationships"[16] whose full significance can only be apprehended through these mystical connections. Jewett's book begins to expand the basis of regionalist representation, from the Howellsian field of social-ethical relationship to a less easily specifiable realm of spiritual signification. Only by taking account of both these dimensions of reality, Jewett maintains, can her book truly communicate the essence of life in Deephaven.

More than any other influence, Jewett's encounters with an Americanized version of Swedenborgianism during the writing and revision of *Deephaven* served simultaneously to strengthen her solidarity with Howellsian literary goals and to push her beyond its social boundaries. As Josephine Donovan has established, Jewett's involvements with the Swedenborgian spokesperson Theophilus Parsons, whom Jewett had met at Wells Beach in 1872 and with whom she corresponded over the next decade, played several important roles in the formation of her aesthetic. The Swedenborgian "doctrine of uses" reinforced Howellsian realist ethics by enabling Jewett to see literature as an ethically useful instrument; at the same time, it situated the origins of ethical obligation in a realm transcending temporal human relationships. The "doctrine of correspondences" strengthened Jewett's sense that "the spiritual interpenetrates the material"; but Jewett replaced Swedenborg's elaborate system of allegorical correlations with "a theory that erases the divide between spiritual and material, seeing the transcendent as incarnate in the physical."[17] Significantly, those passages of *Deephaven* that most conspicuously employ occult materials date from after Jewett's discovery of Swedenborg, during her revision of the original *Atlantic* sketches into book form. Parsons's variety of Swedenborgianism, modified further by Jewett herself, thus gave Jewett both a further incentive to adopt a Howellsian model of literary enterprise and a basis for expanding its range of representation.[18]

Significantly, Helen's Howellsian narratorial comment—that the regionalist "must care to study life and character, and must find pleasure in thought and observation of simple things, and have an instinctive, delicious interest in what to other eyes is unflavored dulness" (37)—arises from a visit to the village churchyard, symbol of a realm of existence that is intimately integrated with, yet simultaneously transcendent of, the everyday life of the community. Here Helen and Kate begin to piece together the interwoven stories of Deephaven's past, soon to be further embroidered by the memories of the village's still-living residents; here they receive early intimations, as Julia Bader writes of Jewett and her contemporaries more generally, "that an external reality hitherto objectively perceived and transparently visible can blur and dissolve, that the firm, knowable texture of a familiar world can be shaken and lost," revealing other possibilities of meaning beyond.[19] On one level, the graveyard is but another detail of authentic local culture; but it stands also as a subtle indicator that Jewett seeks the full significance of commonplace social life on a plane that transcends social signification. The graveyard is an apt metaphor both for the Howellsian regionalist's documentation of quotidian social realities, and for Jewett's dawning sense that such realities are thoroughly suffused with a mysterious, spiritual immanence.

Deephaven's first extended foray into the realm of the supernatural occurs in Kate and Helen's encounters with Captain Sands, a "peculiar and somewhat visionary" (64) retired seafarer with an endless supply of true tales of mental telepathy. In accordance with her Howellsian social-ethical agenda, Jewett narrates the Captain's appearance, personal history, possessions, and conversation as further examples of authentic local culture. But the content of Captain Sands's conversation, the recurring themes of which are telepathy and death, points to a further level of significance in the Captain's experiences. The girls' interaction with

Sands culminates in an episode that pointedly demonstrates Jewett's mystical interests.

The Captain and his two guests are fishing on the bay when Sands unexpectedly turns the boat toward shore and announces the onset of a storm, no sign of which is yet visible to any of the boat's occupants. Safely landed, he explains, "Folks may say what they have a mind to; I did n't see that shower coming up, and I know as well as I want to that my wife did, and impressed it on my mind. Our house sets high, and she watches the sky and is al'ays a worrying when I go out fishing" (93). Encouraged by Kate and Helen, the Captain continues his ruminations, citing several other instances of "one person's having something to do with another any distance off" (96), and culminating with a brief disquisition on the metaphysical implications of such experiences:

> "It's the thinking that does it," says I, "and we've got some faculty or other that we don't know much about. We've got some way of sending our thought like a bullet goes out of a gun and it hits. We don't know nothing except what we see. And some folks is scared, and some more thinks it is all nonsense and laughs. But there's something we have n't got the hang of. . . . I guess we shall turn these fac'lties to account some time or 'nother. Seems to me, though, that we might depend on 'em now more than we do." (96–97)

Through Helen, Jewett acknowledges that such ideas are usually considered eccentric "by even a Deephaven audience, to whom the marvelous was of every-day occurrence" (93). But as the Captain goes on to cite his evidence, anecdote after anecdote about people's having sure knowledge of the lives of relatives and close friends separated from them by immense physical distances, it becomes increasingly clear that Jewett means us to accept this evidence with as much respect and sympathy as Kate and Helen do. Jewett carefully distinguishes such occurrences from the "dream-books" and "spirit-rappings" (172) of crass, commercialized spiritualism, which Sands himself regards as superstitious foolishness, and Helen's narrative interpolations encourage us to suspend our skepticism. "It loses a great deal in being written," Helen writes (in a comment that predicts narrative difficulties that I shall discuss presently), but "it was impossible not to be sure that he knew more than people usually do about these mysteries in which he delighted" (174).

By the end of the chapter, it is clear that Jewett intends the Captain Sands episode as much more than another regionally representative description of a provincial Other. While it is certainly that, the content of the Captain's conversation pushes Jewett's readers to take seriously further dimensions of commonplace reality. The primary difference between Sands's tales and the spirit-rappings and dream-books that the text disparages is, as the Captain himself notes, that "You don't get no good by" (96) the latter, while the former signify a supernatural order wholly congruent with ordinary village life. The spiritual, Jewett maintains, permeates the normal, everyday social interactions that constitute the life of the village; any account of local realities that neglects this dimension of the communal life fails to do full justice to its subject. The Captain Sands chapters comprise Jewett's first extended effort to move her regionalist narrative onto a new plane, one concerned not only with the social aspects of the quotidian but with their metaphysical connections as well.

Helen and Kate, as the figures of the Howellsian narrative mediator, faithfully translate the meaning of Sands's stories into terms more amenable to a cosmopolitan audience. Jewett uses their speculations to steer her readers toward a sense of spiritual interconnection that transcends the web of social and ethical relationship more usual to Howellsian literary purposes. Kate transposes the Captain's theory of undeveloped mental capacities into Greek mythological terms, citing the myth of Demeter and Persephone to amplify the meaning of Sands's experience:

> I was just thinking that it may be that we all have given to us more or less of another nature, as the child had whom Demeter wished to make like the gods. I believe old Captain Sands is right, and we have these instincts which defy all our wisdom and for which we never can frame any laws. We may laugh at them, but we are always meeting them, and one cannot help knowing that it has been the same through all history. They are powers which are imperfectly developed in this life, but one cannot help the thought that the mystery of this world may be the commonplace of the next.[20]

Helen in her turn extends the thought beyond the human, to include a sense of the spiritual animation of all physical Nature. Deephaven folks' readiness to believe in "supernatural causes," she speculates, arises not from provincial ignorance but from proximity to natural facts that are fully saturated with supernatural energies. "The more one lives out of doors," she observes, "the more personality there seems to be in what we call inanimate things. The strength of the hills and the voice of the waves are no longer only grand poetical sentences, but an expression of something real, and more and more one finds God himself in the world, and believes that we may read the thoughts that He writes for us in the book of Nature" (104). Such asides make it very clear that Jewett intends in *Deephaven* not only a narration of provincial culture for Howellsian social-ethical ends, but also a widening of readerly sympathies beyond the realm of social reality to include the perception of an all-pervasive metaphysical order, which includes the social and the material but is not limited to it. The sympathy that Jewett's supra-Howellsian regionalism seeks to promote between wealthy city reader and poor country subject seeks its basis in an all-inclusive spiritual interconnection.

But the presence of this expanded agenda in *Deephaven* is hampered by Jewett's allegiance to a mediatory model of regionalist narration, which has the unintended effect of distancing her readers from narrated experiences that require more direct readerly participation to convey their full significance.[21] This observation returns us to Francesco Loriggio's insight into the inevitable insider/outsider tension in regionalist writing. Writing under a Howellsian model of literary purpose that intentionally emphasized literature's role as a mediator between divided subcultures, Jewett chooses to incorporate in *Deephaven* a first-person narrator whose overt presence *as a mediator* would presumably help forward the process of mediation to which Jewett's text is devoted. But by making literature's mediatory function so conspicuously a feature of the book's narrative configuration—in other words, by embodying it in a first-person narrator who relies on linear representation of provincial social and material reality—Jewett unintentionally obstructs the other half of *Deephaven*'s project: its concern with spiritual aspects of reality that defy linear, "objective" recounting.

Jewett signals her partial awareness of this problem of regionalist narration in an incident that occurs during one of Helen and Kate's frequent visits to Mrs. Kew's lighthouse. When a boatload of city visitors arrives to tour the premises, just as Kate and Helen themselves have done earlier, they mistakenly assume that Kate is a local denizen, a family member of the lighthouse keeper. Kate plays along with the visitors' mistake, consenting to guide them on their tour. She reveals her true identity only when one of the visitors, who clearly occupies a lower social stratum than does Kate, innocently offers to provide Kate with a reference for employment in a Boston department store. The incident simultaneously establishes both the degree to which Helen and Kate fit in with the local culture, and the degree to which, as figures of the regionalist narrator, they remain separate from and above it. Their role in Deephaven society grants them the appearance, at least to other outsiders, of belonging wholly to the provincial culture. But Kate's willingness, as Ann Romines puts it, to invoke "'superior' class or sophistication or erudition to stave off Deephaven, when it comes too close," points to the curious in-but-not-of status of the regionalist narrator. Successful mediation of regional realities depends on Kate and Helen's dual membership in two different subcultures, but the first-person narrative arrangement that arises from it reemphasizes the very divisions it is intended to bridge.[22]

Helen's attempts to mediate between Captain Sands's reality and that of her audience result in a story, as Romines points out, that "vacillates between admitting the possible influence of such uncontrollable powers in [the women's] own lives, and placing them at a safe and interesting distance" (211). Since we rely for our access to Deephaven directly on Kate and Helen, as first-person narrators whose cultural solidarity with their audience enables their mediation, their vacillation is recapitulated in our readerly relationship to *Deephaven*'s characters and events. Experiences like those of Captain Sands, when related from and for the perspective of educated outsiders, can hardly avoid retaining a hint of the ludicrous no matter how strenuously the narrator may explicitly endorse their validity. The thematic content of the Captain's storytelling signals Jewett's expanded literary intentions, but because she has not yet learned sufficiently to manipulate the regionalist narrator's ambiguous status, they remain "trapped" within the objective reporting of Sands's character, circumstances, and speech; the spiritual truths into which the Captain's stories open a window are stranded in a linear recounting instead of gaining an evocative, emotionally involving reality of their own. The narrators, consequently, are saddled with the job of explaining the metaphysical significance of these occult materials in a series of asides. As readers, we are left, along with Kate and Helen, as sympathetic outsiders observing someone else's spiritually suggestive experiences, rather than participating in them in our own right.

Ensuing chapters continue this pattern: the mediatory logic of linear narration interferes with the impact of Jewett's metaphysical agenda. The chapter entitled "Miss Chauncey" attempts to use another Deephaven native both to communicate the nature of the local culture and to suggest further, transcendental dimensions of that reality. On the one hand, Miss Sally Chauncey presents Kate and Helen with another opportunity to describe a regionally representative local character. The old woman and her house, relics from an age of seafaring and mercantile prosperity, comprise a treasure trove of provincial history, which the girls are eager to exploit. So eager are they to satisfy their curiosity, in fact, that they actually take advantage of Miss Chauncey's deafness to steal a self-guided tour of her mansion—this after having been thwarted in an earlier attempt to break into the house, thinking it uninhabited. Jewett emphasizes the voyeuristic, culturally appropriative aspects of the regionalist project by establishing the girls' initial involvement with Miss Chauncey on the basis of their insatiable appetite for authentic examples of the local culture.

Gradually, as the girls establish a personal relationship with their hostess, this narrative voyeurism gives way to a more sympathetic identification with the old woman's experience, which enables Jewett to deploy Miss Chauncey's precarious mental state as a thematic doorway—analogous to Captain Sands's almost obsessive interest in telepathy—into the realm of metaphysical transcendence that comprises Jewett's expansion of the Howellsian project. Miss Chauncey's madness, on one level, is of a piece with her value as a regionalist resource: it results from the emotional impact of the violent deaths and partial insanities of both her father and her brothers, victims of the precipitous decline of the Maine coastal economy. But the nature of her madness suggests the existence of a realm of transcendental significance. Miss Chauncey's present, quite literally, is her past. She sees around her the undimmed splendor of the familial estate of genteel and prosperous seafarers, despite the fact that the house is actually in a state of advanced dilapidation. In her visitors she sees contemporaries of her own bygone youth; she asks Kate and Helen for news of long-dead Boston acquaintances as though they still enjoyed a healthy middle age. The very idea of death is alien to her: "Ah, they say every one is 'dead', nowadays. I do not comprehend the silly idea!" (129). In her insanity, Miss Chauncey lives in an eternal, historically transcendent present that simply obliterates the everyday boundaries of time and space.

As it was in Kate and Helen's narration of Captain Sands's tales, Miss Chauncey's thematic significance as a symbol of transcendent spiritual realities is at odds with her status as a regionalist exhibit. Miss Chauncey functions both as a sign of eternal wisdom and as a picturesque local nut case. The narrators' moments of intimacy with Miss Chauncey seek to draw us into participation with her expanded sense of reality, but the mediatory logic of the narration will not let us forget either the nature of their relationship to Miss Chauncey nor the plain fact that the woman is mentally incompetent. Once again, by the chapter's end the narrators are reduced to making abstract pronouncements about the spiritual significance of their subject, in lieu of full readerly participation in that experience.

Jewett's struggle to fuse her two major aesthetic goals is even more evident in the chapter entitled "In Shadow." Kate and Helen's story of their acquaintance with a severely impoverished farm family makes a pitch for our sympathetic identification with these living examples of rural privation; the girls' excursion to the rock-bound, exhausted soils of a coastal farm offers an opportunity to describe yet another phase of local life and culture. The sudden deaths of the farmer and his wife, killed by years of fruitless struggle with the rocky soil, provide the perfect occasion for a union of socially mediatory description with a more evocative, metaphysically symbolic narrative mode. Death—absolutely mundane yet undeniably mysterious—becomes the nexus for Jewett's attempted fusion of aesthetic goals. On the one hand, the farmstead funeral is an opportunity for sympathetic observation of a central rite of local culture; on the other hand, the proximity of Death brings near a realm of occult signification that pervades and transcends commonplace social realities.

At their best, Helen's funeral observations effectively couple social and natural description, in a prose highly evocative of the enigmatic presence of Death. She observes, for instance:

> The minister and some others fell into line, and the procession went slowly down the slope; a strange shadow had fallen over everything. It was like a November day, for the air felt cold and bleak.

> There were some great sea-fowl high in the air, fighting their way toward the sea against the wind, and giving now and then a wild, far-off ringing cry. We could hear the dull sound of the sea, and at a little distance from the land the waves were leaping high, and breaking in white foam over the isolated ledges. (122–23)

Descriptive detail here is so thoroughly invested with the emotional and spiritual significance of the event that we cannot help experiencing natural facts as metaphysically charged markers; Jewett blends natural and human to evoke our emotional participation with the mourners in response to the presence of Death. But the mood is shattered when Helen abruptly reverts to a more linear narration, reminding us that she is observing the scene from the perspective of an outsider and reporting it for other outsiders: "We had never seen what the people called 'walking funerals' until we came to Deephaven." Representative details of Deephaven's "rigid funeral etiquette" (122) follow, narrated as a parcel of interesting items in a touristic travelogue, interfering with the attempt to evoke the mystical dimensions of the experience of Death.

No matter how much the narrator may wish to participate in the metaphysical dimensions of the reality transpiring before her, no matter how clearly Jewett's thematic intention is to read the supernatural through the social, the linear, mediatory narration of the Howellsian regionalist never quite allows it. Kate can assert the "sudden consciousness of the mystery and inevitableness of death" (123) among the funeral participants, she can speculate on the power of the occasion to make her feel "how close to this familiar, every-day world might be the other" (123); but the powerful logic of narration-as-social-mediation effectively precludes—except in fits and starts—our feeling as though we are engaged, to the extent Jewett so clearly intends us to be, in the fullest significance of commonplace local experience. Helen's careful descriptions of the funeral rites have the unintended effect of distancing the reader from the narrated experience, leaving us with Kate and Helen on a hillside neighboring the farmstead, uninvited guests, observing the rites from a respectful distance.

Deephaven reveals an author struggling to find the narrative means to enact a new set of aesthetic ends. The central inclusion of occult materials and themes expresses Jewett's extension of purposes in writing about

Maine coast people and places, beyond Howellsian mediation of a fundamentally social and ethical reality to evocation of a metaphysical realm both transcendent and inclusive of commonplace social reality. Jewett's mysticized sense of human commonality necessitates an enlarged aesthetic agenda for her work, which in turn calls for a new narrative mode of engaging readers in represented reality: one that will replace the distancing effect of linear, socially mediatory documentation undertaken on the Howellsian plan with a more evocative, symbolic, reader-participatory reading experience. Since every "'thing' is animated with a spiritual presence," language must move beyond the mimetic and mediatory in order to "directly express this unmediated spiritual reality."[23] Howellsian mediatory narration must give way to a narrative mode providing more direct access to orders of reality that by their very nature defy linguistic specification.

A pair of literary advices that Jewett received during the writing of *Deephaven* pointed the way toward realization of a new narrative mode that *Deephaven* itself would achieve only sporadically. In an 1871 diary entry, Jewett again quotes her father: "A story should be managed so that it should *suggest* interesting things to the *reader* instead of the author's doing all the thinking for him, and setting it before him in black and white."[24] The tendency of the advice, reinforced by a second passage from Flaubert, which Jewett pinned above her writing desk in South Berwick, is away from the content of literary representation, away from close observation and specification of material and social realities, and toward the quality of readers' imaginative involvement with the represented experiences of literature.[25] Where Howells would aim at readerly immersion in the experience of the text through mimetically faithful representation of commonplace social life, Jewett's emerging aesthetic relies more heavily on a process of readerly concretion of literary experience. Jewett's "imaginative realism" (as Josephine Donovan has christened it, borrowing from Jewett's letter to a young artist)[26] aims to employ the literary documentation of the quotidian not only to further Howellsian social-ethical mediation, but also to evoke full readerly emotional involvement in the spiritual underpinnings of commonplace experience.

Nearly two decades after *Deephaven*, in *The Country of the Pointed Firs*, Jewett would discover the aesthetic means to unify her social-ethical purposes with a spiritualized understanding of the significance of local realities. The result is a book that, while roughly homologous in form and intent to *Deephaven*, fuses powerful evocation of the spiritual with a definitively descriptive regionalism, transforming the earlier book's disruptive tensions into a new narrative unity. In *Deephaven* we see Jewett's promising but uneven attempt to unite two distinct yet overlapping sets of literary purposes within a single aesthetic practice. The fusion of literary goals that would result in *The Country of the Pointed Firs* is only partially accomplished here, but for that very reason, *Deephaven* lays bare the terms of Jewett's later triumph.

Notes

1. William Dean Howells, *Editor's Study*, ed. James W. Simpson (Troy, N.Y.: Whitston, 1983).

2. Elizabeth Ammons, *Conflicting Stories: American Women Writers at the Turn into the Twentieth Century* (New York: Oxford University Press, 1991), 45.

3. Howells, *Editor's Study*, 3, 98. Subsequent references are cited in the text.

4. Richard H. Brodhead, *Cultures of Letters: Scenes of Reading and Writing in Nineteenth-Century America* (Chicago: University of Chicago Press, 1993). See especially 119–26 on the parallel social uses of regionalism and the vacation for the rising leisure class, and 145–54, where these insights are applied more specifically to Jewett's career, concentrating primarily on *The Country of the Pointed Firs*. See also Allison T. Hild's article on touristic "narrative mediation" in *Pointed Firs*, "Narrative Mediation in Sarah Orne Jewett's *The Country of the Pointed Firs*," *Colby Quarterly* (1995): 114–22. Brodhead, in my opinion, exaggerates the extent to which regionalism constitutes an act of cultural imperialism, and he consequently suppresses the genre's innate potential for productive resistance to social and cultural hierarchization.

5. Technically, Helen Denis is the sole narrator of *Deephaven*, but in fact she comprises with Kate Lancaster a sort of hybrid narrator. The women experience everything in the book together, and although Helen alone writes about their experiences, she relies heavily on the more voluble Kate for the content of her narration. Here and throughout, therefore, for the sake of convenience I refer to Kate and Helen collectively as "the narrators."

6. Sarah Orne Jewett, *Deephaven*, in *Novels and Stories* (New York: Library of America, 1994). Subsequent references are cited in the text.

7. Jewett notes her adoption of the sketch form in an 1873 letter to Horace Scudder, in which she confesses a lack of "dramatic talent" and ability for plot construction: "It seems to me I can furnish the theatre, and show you the actors, and the scenery, and the audience, but there never is any play! I could write you entertaining letters perhaps, from some desirable house where I was in most charming company, but I couldn't make a story about it." She therefore finds the

sketch more conducive to her strengths in description and characterization: "I am certain I could not write one of the usual magazine stories. If the editors will take the sketchy kind and people like to read them, is not it as well to do that and do it successfully . . . ?" This early and decisive artistic choice arose in part, as Paula Blanchard notes, from Jewett's correspondence with Howells concerning the early *Deephaven* sketches published in the *Atlantic* between 1873 and 1876. See *Sarah Orne Jewett Letters*, ed. Richard Cary (Waterville, Maine: Colby College Press, 1967), 29, and Paula Blanchard, *Sarah Orne Jewett: Her World and Her Work* (Reading, Mass.: Addison-Wesley, 1994), 61–62.

8. Howells's review of *Deephaven*, published in the June 1877 issue of the *Atlantic Monthly*, testifies to the book's primary quality as sympathetic documentation of regional social realities: "No doubt some particular sea-port sat for Deephaven, but the picture is true to a whole class of old shore towns, in any one of which you might confidently look to find the Deephaven types." The narrators' "sojourn is only used as a background on which to paint the local life," Howells continues, and the narration itself "subtly delights in the very tint and form of reality," informed by a "conscientious fidelity" that produces "a sympathy as tender as it is intelligent" (25). William Dean Howells, Review of *Deephaven* by Sarah Orne Jewett, in *Critical Essays on Sarah Orne Jewett*, ed. Gwen L. Nagel (Boston: G. K. Hall, 1984), 25–26.

9. Sarah Orne Jewett, Preface to *Deephaven* (Boston: Houghton Mifflin, 1894), 2. Subsequent references are cited in the text.

10. *Sarah Orne Jewett Letters*, ed. Cary, 84. The latter quotation is from a letter of May 22, 1893, to Frederick M. Hopkins, which seems to have served as a prototype for the 1894 *Deephaven* preface. See *Sarah Orne Jewett Letters*, 83–85 and n. 6. The maxim from Plato may be found in this letter also, as well as in letters to Samuel Thurber (164) and Elizabeth McCracken (*Letters of Sarah Orne Jewett*, ed. Annie Fields [Boston: Houghton Mifflin, 1911], 228).

11. Blanchard, *Jewett: Her World*, 230.

12. My interpretation of Jewett's mediatory and hence democratic aesthetic resists recent assertions in Michael D. Bell, *The Problem of American Realism: Studies in the Cultural History of a Literary Idea* (Chicago: University of Chicago Press, 1993), 175–204, and Brodhead, *Cultures of Letters*, 142–76, that Jewett belongs to a "high-art" tradition embodied most significantly by Henry James. Both critics depend on fundamental misreadings of W. D. Howells's relation to this tradition: Brodhead by insisting on Howells's full alliance with James as a symbol and proponent of a putative high culture, and Bell, conversely, by declaring Howells's supposed opposition to "art" and especially to women's art. That both readings can emerge from the same writer's works testifies both to the complexity of Howells's thinking and to these critics' lack of attention to that complexity.

13. *Sarah Orne Jewett Letters*, 19. Jewett pinned a parallel piece of advice, from Gustave Flaubert, above her writing desk: "Ecrire la vie ordinaire comme

on écrit l'histoire" ("Write about daily life as you would write history") (Blanchard, *Jewett: Her World*, 84). While this quotation from the French realist raises too many issues about differences between Howellsian and other varieties of realism to be unambiguously useful here, Jewett seems to have understood by it a second piece of counsel toward referential documentation of commonplace realities in literature. See Blanchard's discussion.

14. Francesco Loriggio, "Regionalism and Theory," in *Regionalism Reconsidered*, ed. David Jordan (New York: Garland, 1994), 11. From this fact, more than any other, derives the long-running arguments over possible distinctions between "local color" and "regionalism," and over regionalism's and/or local color's possible relationships to realism. The discussion usually reverts to some version of the local color versus regionalism distinction found, for instance, in Donald Dike (although Dike eschews the term "regionalism" altogether): local color writers "were related to local material in two dissimilar ways," Dike writes. The first sort write as "tourists," exploiting "the eccentric and picturesque" aspects of "a local community, struck by its singularity, its differences from the norm of their own social group," which includes their audience. The second sort (regionalists) "identified themselves with the community which was their subject matter," and sympathetically rendered local difference as "cultural relativists," granting local culture a validity equal to that of the metropolis (82). For Dike, realism and local color "overlap" but have "no necessary connection" with each other (86). See Donald Dike, "Notes on Local Color and Its Relation to Realism," *College English* 14 (1952): 81–88.

More recently, Judith Fetterley and Marjorie Pryse, in their redefinition of regionalism as a women's literary tradition distinct from both "local color" and "regional realism" (which they seem to regard as interchangeable terms) recapitulate the distinction between the empathetic, insider regionalist narrator, and the exploitive, outsider local color narrator. See Judith Fetterley and Marjorie Pryse, Introduction to *American Women Regionalists, 1850–1910* (New York: W. W. Norton, 1992), xi–xx. See also Richard Brodhead's extended discussion in *Cultures of Letters* of nineteenth-century American regionalism generally (107–41), and more particularly of Jewett as regionalist (142–76).

The regionalist debate significantly predates these modern authorities. As Ann Douglas [Wood] points out, Howells used local color women writers as exemplars of the new realism in the very first of his "Editor's Study" columns for *Harper's Monthly*. See Ann Douglas [Wood], "The Literature of Impoverishment: The Women Local Colorists in America, 1865–1914," *Women's Studies* 1 (1972): 3–45. For Howells, such writing was valuable not only for its mimetic accuracy but for the fact that it was written by insiders from a local point of view, as numerous "Study" columns avowed. Further, to cite just one more historical example, Howells's disciple Hamlin Garland, in pushing Howellsian ideas of local literary perspective to more subjectivist extremes, calls the literature of the insider "local color," not regionalism. See Hamlin Garland, *Crumbling Idols:*

Twelve Essays on Art and Literature (Gainesville, Fla.: Scholars' Facsimiles, 1952), esp. essays 5 and 6, entitled "Local Color in Art" and "The Local Novel," respectively. For fuller discussion of these issues, see also Bernard A. Bowron, Jr., "Realism in America," *Comparative Literature* 3 (1951): 273–75; Marjorie Pryse, "Reading Regionalism: The 'Difference' It Makes," in *Regionalism Reconsidered*, ed. David Jordan (New York: Garland, 1994), 47–63; Marjorie Pryse, "'Distilling Essences': Regionalism and 'Women's Culture'," *American Literary Realism* 25.2 (Winter 1993): 1–15; and Judith Fetterley, "'Not in the Least American': Nineteenth-Century Literary Regionalism as UnAmerican Literature," in *Nineteenth-Century American Women Writers: A Critical Reader*, ed. Karen L. Kilcup (Malden, Mass., and Oxford: Blackwell, 1998), 15–32.

15. Josephine Donovan, "Jewett and Swedenborg," *American Literature* 65 (December 1993): 731–50.

16. Josephine Donovan, *New England Local Color Literature: A Women's Tradition* (New York: Ungar, 1983), 100.

17. Donovan, "Jewett and Swedenborg," 732.

18. Significantly, Howells shared Jewett's awareness of contemporary Swedenborgianism, but could not, as she did, grant it his full belief. As Donovan points out, Theophilus Parsons "became a neighbor of William Dean Howells (on Concord Avenue in Cambridge) in July 1873" ("Jewett and Swedenborg," 732). Another Boston acquaintance, Henry James, Sr., was a Swedenborgian as well, as was Howells's own father. The younger man shared his father's interest in Swedenborgian ideas throughout the latter's lifetime, corresponding periodically about the philosophy and about the junior Howells's inability to place his faith in it. Howells's rationalist skepticism rendered him permanently doubtful about the mystical aspects of Swedenborgianism, but its ethical aspects played an important role in the formation of his aesthetic. In effect, Howells became, in the phrase of his biographer Edwin H. Cady, an "ethical Swedenborgian." See Edwin H. Cady, *The Road to Realism: The Early Years 1837–1885 of William Dean Howells* (Syracuse: Syracuse University Press, 1956), esp. 145–51.

19. Julia Bader, "The Dissolving Vision: Realism in Jewett, Freeman, and Gilman," in *American Realism: New Essays*, ed. Eric J. Sundquist (Baltimore: Johns Hopkins University Press, 1982), 176. Subsequent references are cited in the text.

20. Sarah Way Sherman treats Jewett's literary and biographical involvements with the myth of Demeter and Persephone at length. Here, though, I am primarily interested in the use of the myth by Kate and Helen as a mediatory narrative tool. Sherman, *Sarah Orne Jewett: An American Persephone* (Hanover, N.H.: University Press of New England, 1989), 103.

21. Judith Bryant Wittenberg has suggested that *Deephaven* is "Jewett's exploratory metafiction," in which the "author overtly considers various aspects of her narrative craft, exploring such basic artistic issues as the posture of the writer *vis-a-vis* her material" (153). See Wittenberg, "*Deephaven:* Sarah Orne Jewett's

Exploratory Metafiction," *Studies in American Fiction* 19 (1991): 153–63. While the scope and conclusions of Wittenberg's study differ from mine, her insight into *Deephaven*'s experimentation with narratorial configuration supports my argument. Most recent critics of *Deephaven* take for granted its narrative limitations and turn their attention to Helen and Kate as characters within the tale Helen tells. See, for example, Ann Romines, "In Deephaven: Skirmishes Near the Swamp," *Colby Library Quarterly* 16 (1980), and especially Judith Fetterley, "Reading Deephaven as a Lesbian Text," in *Sexual Practice/Textual Theory: Lesbian Cultural Criticism*, ed. Susan J. Wolfe and Julia Penelope (Cambridge: Blackwell, 1993), 164–83. Fetterley reads *Deephaven* as the suppressed record of Helen's lesbian attachment to Kate. My reading, on the other hand, focuses more centrally on Kate and Helen as narrators rather than characters, although the success of their narration depends in part on their filling both roles simultaneously.

22. Romines, "In Deephaven," 209. Subsequent references are cited in the text. Romines makes a similar point about the quality of Kate and Helen's interaction with the rituals which she sees as the central constituents of *Deephaven*'s collective life. Try as they might to enter the local life unreservedly, Romines asserts, "the two young protagonists quietly crash into a transparent, unbreakable partition" (205), erected by themselves, which reduces their attempts at full participation to "ritual as spectator sport; ritual as a kind of sympathetic voyeurism" (209).

23. Donovan, "Jewett and Swedenborg," 744.

24. Quoted in Donovan, *New England Local Color Literature*, 100.

25. Flaubert wrote, "Ce n'est pas de faire rire, ni de faire pleurer, ni de vous mettre à fureur, mais d'agir à la façon de la nature, c'est à dire de faire rêver" ("It is not to provoke laughter, nor tears, nor rage, but to act as nature does, that is, to provoke dreaming") (Blanchard, *Jewett: Her World*, 84). In Jewett's own words, extracted from a letter to Sarah Whitman: "You bring something to the reading of a story that the story would go very lame without; but it is those unwritable things that the story holds in its heart, if it has any, that make the true soul of it, and these must be understood, and yet how many a story goes lame for lack of that understanding" (*Letters of Sarah Orne Jewett*, ed. Fields, 112). A lack of understanding of "those unwritable things" that constitute the core of the story, Jewett continues, causes us to "confuse our scaffoldings with our buildings" (112).

26. See Josephine Donovan, *Sarah Orne Jewett* (New York: Ungar, 1980), 134, and *Sarah Orne Jewett Letters*, 91.

Part II

Contemporaries

Jewett and the Writing World

Challenge and Compliance

Textual Strategies in *A Country Doctor* and Nineteenth-Century American Women's Medical Autobiographies

Judith Bryant Wittenberg

A major problem for readers and reviewers of Jewett's *A Country Doctor* over the past century has been finding the proper grounds for appraising the novel's strengths. Reviewers of the 1880s assailed the work, calling it "simply an expanded sketch" lacking "the material for a novel proper" and containing "little or no plot,"[1] a judgment Jewett herself seems eventually to have internalized. In a 1904 letter, she conceded that she generally lacked "dramatic talent" and that *A Country Doctor* "is of no value as a novel." Yet in that same letter, she also elucidated what may be the most useful basis for judging her 1884 novel, its "many excellent ideas," ideas for which she expressed gratitude to her physician father and his teachings.[2] Those "excellent ideas" have to do with issues surrounding the challenges faced by a young woman wishing to prepare for the demanding and male-dominated profession of medicine, as viewed within the context of nineteenth-century American social history.

The purpose of this essay is to consider the topic of professional preparation, looking at *A Country Doctor* intertextually with a group of contemporaneous autobiographies by actual female physicians of the mid-and later nineteenth century. Indeed, the novel tacitly invites the investigation of such contextual interrelationships with its comment on the "renown some women physicians had won,"[3] which suggests that Jewett was familiar with Nan Prince's real-life counterparts. An intertextual consideration of Jewett's novel in conjunction with comparable nonfiction works of the era reveals the textual strategies all of them employ to function in partial compliance with some of the prevailing notions about gender, education, and professionalism, along with the ways in which they distinctly challenge them. The enormous difficulties confronted by a woman attempting to embark on a career in a field essentially closed to her are apparent in this group of texts, not only in the explicit depiction of the obstacles faced by individual females, but also in more subtle fashion, in the form of rhetorical and ideological capitulation to conventional attitudes toward women. The texts thus function so as to mask some of the radicalism of their portraiture.

The women depicted in these works are to a large degree the sort of subversive "border cases" that expose the artificiality of binary logic as defined by Mary Poovey in her analysis of the ideological work of gender in mid-Victorian England. Such "border cases"—of which a strong-minded woman like the would-be lady doctor of the later nineteenth century is a primary example—served to challenge, says Poovey, the social arrangement of separate spheres for men and woman and the sexual division of labor. They thus had the potential to destabilize ideological certainty.[4] At the same time, the texts in which these several women physicians who pose threats to the existing order appear also variously disclose the ways in which discursive practice, as elucidated by Foucault in "The Order of Discourse" and other works, governs by exclusion and regulation; the production of discourse, says Foucault, is "at once controlled, selected, organized and redistributed according to a certain number of procedures." All texts are constrained by cultural assumptions and delimited by "internal rules." They "cannot speak of just anything."[5]

The autobiographies I wish to discuss in conjunction with Jewett's *A Country Doctor* are all by women of great significance in American medical history—Harriot K. Hunt, often described as the first woman physician to practice in the United States, Elizabeth Blackwell, the first woman to graduate from an American medical school, and Marie Zakrzewska, the first woman faculty member at the first American medical school expressly for women, the New England Female Medical College in Boston. Although their autobiographies were published at different times—Hunt's *Glances and Glimpses* in 1856, *A Letter from Marie Zakrzewska* in 1860, and Blackwell's *Pioneer Work* in 1895—all three women became visible in the field of medicine in the northeastern United States between 1847, the year Hunt and Blackwell were rejected by several American medical schools, and 1859, when Zakrzewska arrived in Boston to take up her faculty position.

All four of the texts I am discussing reflect a certain cultural dynamic; in similar ways they treat the topic of self-development and explore the specific issues surrounding the entry of women into a preponderantly male profession, managing to pay homage to the dominant culture even as they contest it on a number of fronts. Although distinguished from each other by their respective autobiographical and novelistic formats, collectively these works employ a revealing series of thematic elements and logical arguments in their portraiture of revolutionary figures. Despite the apparent generic differences, all are writerly, self-conscious projects that construct the life of an individual; moreover, as women-authored texts of an earlier era, all face the special challenges posed by standard, distinctly masculine assumptions about the nature of individual and social identity.

The context in which these works appeared is salient, for it was an era in the United States when women became increasingly interested in entering the medical profession. Medical historians such as Paul Starr, Carol Lopate, and others have identified several factors that probably facilitated women's entry into the profession: the fact that medical care had its original locus in the home, so that women often functioned as healers; the acceptance of a wide variety of approaches to medicine, some of them linked to practices associated with women, such as herbalism; and the increase in sexual fastidiousness during the Victorian period that made it seem not only proper but morally necessary that women patients be able to turn to doctors of their own gender.[6] Samuel Gregory, the somewhat eccentric individual who was instrumental in founding the first medical school for women, asserted that the practice of obstetrics by males was "indelicate," even "indecent," and cited the need for female physicians "to attend to the peculiar complaints of their own sex."[7] The more feminist voice of Caroline Dall made the same argument on slightly different grounds, citing not only the commonality of women doctors with their patients but also the fact that their abilities were enhanced by the addition of "sympathetic intuition" to professional skills.[8] By the late nineteenth century, seventeen medical colleges for women had been established in the United States, and the number of women physicians increased to a total of nearly 2,500 by 1880. This relatively halcyon period came to an end at the beginning of the twentieth century, in part because of a waning of the Victorian concern with sexual privacy but more because a growing emphasis on professional standards, evident in increased requirements for licensure and internships, closed off some of the routes into medicine taken by women. The absorption or closing of some of the women's medical colleges, along with strict admission quotas for women at the remaining medical schools, further decreased their numbers.

At all times, however, the obstacles faced by a woman who wished to enter the medical profession were considerable. Even beyond the explicit barriers presented by the hostility of most medical schools and male physicians, intense pressures were exerted by cultural precepts, many of which are directly assailed by the autobiographies and by Jewett's novel. These precepts include the notion that women were physically and mentally the weaker sex, that advanced education was destructive to both the physiques and psyches of women, and that women's efforts to achieve professional status were likely to make them masculine. Women in Victorian America were designated as the weaker sex by a combination of evolutionary law—visible in Herbert Spencer's argument that women's physical evolution had terminated at an earlier stage than men's—and craniometric studies that assumed a correlation between skull capacity and intellectuality and thus identified women and blacks as inferior.[9] Quite possibly the outgrowth of this so-called scientific evidence, the ideas about women and higher education represented in E. H. Clarke's controversial 1874 work, *Sex in Education*, had an impact; in it, Clarke retracted his earlier support of women to argue that advanced education had a negative impact on them.[10] Professionalism in women, too, was seen as deleterious; a physician named Henry Smith asserted in 1875 that women should remain at home, that involvement in any "public matters" was likely to make them "mannish."[11] More subtle than such outright attacks but equally problematic, the Cult of True Womanhood, identified by Barbara Welter as pervasive in popular works of the era, mandated piety, purity, domesticity, and submissiveness in women.[12]

Given this cultural context, it is surprising that any women were courageous enough to pursue medical studies. Yet the lives of the actual women physicians as depicted in their autobiographies, along with Jewett's fictional portrait, serve as a direct refutation of the more hostile ideas, even as they clearly subvert most of the prescriptions of the Cult of True Womanhood. At the same time, however, they accede to some of the dominant precepts as if to alleviate the threat they pose to the prevailing gender ideology.

Piety, for example, the first of the womanly qualities named by Welter, is a recurrent, if perhaps unconscious, strategy in this group of texts—evident even in the autobiography of Harriot Hunt, in many ways the angriest of them all, who readily pays tribute to her religion's "life-giving principles" and to her pastor.[13] Elizabeth Blackwell is clearly pious in recording her belief in the "living Spirit" of Jesus Christ, which "dispels all evil" and "produces peace unspeakable."[14] She describes her early stages of medical study as assisted by "Divine help," particularly in one visionary moment in which she felt surrounded by "Spiritual influence" and knew that her decision was "in accordance with the great providential ordering" (34–35). Jewett's Nan Prince, too, refers to her God-given gift for the study of medicine and to her belief that "God . . . made me a doctor" (242), and her guardian, Dr. Leslie, compares her work to Christ's, saying that both came to it "not to be ministered unto but to minister" (251). Of course such passages not only accord with conventional religious views of the time but also serve to mitigate the drastic nature of these women's earthly decisions by attributing them to Divine Providence.

Another strategy by which these texts partially defuse their challenge to the social order takes the form of a hesitancy in espousing the sort of pervasive women's rights being propounded at, for example, the 1850 Worcester Convention. Zakrzewska describes the convention as "ridiculous" and herself as initially "shocked" by the demands for the emancipation of women; only gradually did she allow herself to be persuaded by arguments in its favor.[15] Blackwell asserts that she is unable to sympathize fully with what she calls the "anti-man movement," because she has had "too much kindness, aid, and just recognition from men" (178). Although she does not speak of the conventions per se, Nan Prince acknowledges that reformers "are apt to develop unpleasant traits," a consequence of their having "to fight against opposition and ignorance" (208).

Rather than presenting themselves as social reformers, the women physicians tend to couch discussion of their decisions in individualistic terms, arguing that they are exceptional cases. Hunt notes that she always "felt I was to do something different in the future from other people" and that her search was for her own "true vocation" (22). Nan, too, points out that she is "very far from believing that every girl ought to be a surgeon" (208) but is instead following the "laws" of her own nature, fulfilling a destiny that is the almost inevitable outgrowth of her particular combination of inherited skills and vocational interests. Elizabeth Blackwell says that her concern is not with woman's rights or man's rights but "with the development of the human soul and body" (179). As a result, all four texts reveal a similar pattern in their depiction of the female at their center up to the moment in which she begins medical study—the identification of crucial influences and the pinpointing of important developmental stages. In focusing almost exclusively on the individual and her growth—the recognition of her proclivities and her subsequent movement toward useful knowledge and practical accomplishment—the texts describe the women's early years, with an emphasis on childhood experiences and family support.

The focus on childhood in these texts obviously hearkens back to the work of Romantic poets such as Wordsworth and in certain ways anticipates Freud's emphases, although their pre-Freudian status is apparent in the sort of highly suggestive issues that are sometimes raised without much apparent awareness of their implications. Hunt in particular is explicit about the importance of her childhood years, asserting that "It is the early life that makes the after life" and, despite worrying that she may have burdened her reader with an excess of detail, notes that such details "are the little rivulets, brooks, and streams that give power and volume to the broader after-current of my life" (48, 41). A similar metaphor appears in *A Country Doctor:* Nan's life is described as seeming to flow in one steady, unchanging current before the "great change" of her grandmother's death (59).

Jewett's novel is particularly rich in the description of childhood moments and formative experiences. Nan's physical energy and willingness to defy conventional notions of ladylikeness are evident in several early scenes, such as those in which she steals away at dawn in order to build a raft and chase young wild ducks on the river or pulls down the ends of pasture fences at neighboring homesteads, allowing cattle to escape. Similarly, her potential talent for, and interest in, medical practice is displayed in a series of youthful incidents, including those in which she accompanies Dr. Leslie on his morning rounds, "always watching for chances when she might be of use," or is discovered having folded the papers of medicinal powders with "quick and careful fingers" and reading a medical dictionary "as if it were a storybook" (66, 79–80). Nan's proclivities are encouraged by her guardian, who allows her to grow up "as naturally as a plant" (77).

While none of the texts attempts any precise definition of the nature-nurture proportions in the central figure's development, the autobiographies all provide relevant information, and Elizabeth Blackwell offers something close to an assessment of the proper balance with her comment that a positive situation is one in which "free play" is given to one's "natural disposition, under wise but not too rigid oversight" (1), a description that obviously fits the conditions in which Jewett's Nan Prince grows into young adulthood.

The one way in which Nan's position differs sharply from the other three is her orphaned state, probably a result of the novelistic convention that independent and motivated young women tended to be those free from the encumbrances of family. Other fictional women physicians of the time, such as those in novels by W. D. Howells (*Dr. Breen's Practice* [1881]) and Elizabeth Stuart Phelps (*Dr. Zay* [1882]), lacked at least one parent, having experienced loss at an early age. By contrast, the actual women physicians whose autobiographies are being discussed here all matured in so-called intact families. Moreover, assuming one can accept the autobiographical assessments at face value, all the women seem to have had parents who were both admirable individuals and, with one exception, remarkably enlightened about fostering their unusual daughters' development. The family recollections are uniformly positive: Harriot Hunt pays homage to her parents as individuals and notes the value of the household ambiance, with its emphasis on the discussion of ideas and on "argument, fresh and varied" (3–4). Marie Zakrzewska, too, describes the exemplary nature of family members such as her midwife mother and her physician grandfather and comments on the early supportiveness of her parents, who "gave me full scope to follow out my own inclinations" (25).

Jewett's Nan Prince, although orphaned at an early age, has some pleasant years under the loving and laissez-faire guidance of her maternal grandmother before being taken into the household of a kindhearted physician, Dr. Leslie, whose helpful endorsement of Nan's personal freedom is augmented by his intelligent interest in her academic and professional development. Dr. Leslie's housekeeper and other caring neighbors in the small-town milieu provide additional affection and assistance.

Nan's guardian, Dr. Leslie, is a benign and helpful paternal presence, one of a series of such figures who recur in these texts. In fact, paternal or quasi-paternal influence is a central element in all four works. Harriot Hunt praises her father's enthusiasm for his profession, and Blackwell describes hers as "a beneficent Providence" memorable for his "warm affection and sense of fun" (3), while Zakrzewska cites a whole series of helpful males who figured in her life. Jewett's Dr. Leslie was modeled on the author's own father, a talented physician in South Berwick, Maine, who early recognized his daughter's abilities. Like his fictional incarnation, Dr. Jewett took his daughter along on visits to patients and provided her with a wide array of reading material.[16] From the beginning to the end of Jewett's novel, Dr. Leslie is for Nan Prince a crucial exemplar as well as a compassionate father-surrogate.

Although the maternal figures in these works do not, perhaps, receive "equal time," they are portrayed as playing significant roles in their daughters' lives. Sarah Sherman and Josephine Donovan have noted the way in which Nan Prince's resolve to become a doctor occurs on the river shore associated with her mother's anguished journey home at the beginning of the novel; the reconnection with her mother's spirit in this epiphanic moment clearly enables Nan's "great decision."[17] The autobiographies all pay tribute to the physician's mother, particularly that by Marie Zakrzewska, whose midwife mother was an exemplar herself, along with providing consistent encouragement to her daughter.

With supportive family—or, in the case of Nan Prince, surrogate-family—providing a nearly ideal background for the development of their particular talents, all four women are able to give more or less free play to their own predilections. Indeed, literal play in the form of childhood games and physical activities is identified as important to the growth of these young women. Nan Prince is described as having read Defoe's *Robinson Crusoe* and Edgeworth's *The Parent's Assistant*, fictions with apparent relevance to the youthful recreation of the women physicians. Elizabeth Blackwell discusses playing Robinson Crusoe with her brothers and sisters, and Marie Zakrzewska comments on her time spent as an "appendage" to her midwife mother. Exuberant physicality seems also to have played a significant role in the development of these young women. Sharon O'Brien has written about the nineteenth-century advice manuals that advocated outdoors activity for girls as a means to foster resourcefulness and self-confidence as well as physical well-being,[18] and Harriot Hunt is also explicit about the value of allowing girls to play sports. Both Blackwell and Zakrzewska mention the joy of playing outdoors as children, and the young Nan Prince is a tomboy par excellence, playing pranks, climbing trees, and roaming the countryside fearlessly on foot or horseback.

Because tomboyism fosters qualities such as independence of spirit unlikely to be fully compatible with such social strictures as school attendance, it is hardly surprising that the young women sometimes find themselves at odds with their schooling. Zakrzewska notes that her teachers saw her as "unruly" and "obstinate" (24) because she would not always obey their commands, and Nan Prince, whose "wildness" is repeatedly noted by members of her community, manifests a discomfort with school sufficient that her sympathetic guardian at one point "rescues" her from it, taking her instead on his daily rounds. This freedom occurred within certain boundaries, however; even the manuals that advised outdoor activities for girls did not intend to challenge traditional notions of woman's essential role and asserted that such activities should cease when a girl entered puberty so that she could begin acquiring proper feminine traits such as submissiveness and an interest in the domestic arts. Yet such an evolution often proved far from "natural," and all of the texts discussed here manifest an obvious struggle with the pressure to conform to domestic ideology.

Although the females allow themselves to be socialized to some degree as "feminine"—Zakrzewska concedes the "necessity of attracting others by an agreeable exterior and courteous manners" (40) and of learning to be more attentive to dress and deportment, while Nan Prince acquires facility at tea drinking and ladylike conversation with her female elders—all experience unease and intense restlessness when they confront the expectation that they will become fully domesticated. Hunt says she realized early that she was unlikely ever to be "useful" in many of the "domestic arts," that indeed she was cut out "to do something different . . . from other [women]" (14, 22), and Zakrzewska rails at the injustice of stereotypical ideas that "forced" her to do housework when she wanted to read (39). For both Blackwell and Prince, the crisis brought on by a period spent at home facing the specter of a future dominated by domesticity engenders their resolve to become physicians.

Unsettled by her felt need for a "more engrossing pursuit" than housekeeping, Elizabeth Blackwell decides to follow a suggestion that she study medicine (27), while Nan, after her return from boarding school, finds herself "restless and dissatisfied," unable to "content herself" with household duties (122). In the difficult period that follows, Nan spends much of her time outdoors, physically active and intermittently reflective. Finally, in an epiphanic moment, she decides to study medicine, and feels herself turning away from her "fog"-like former existence and "toward a great light of satisfaction" (125).

Nan's interlude of self-confrontation and subsequent resolve is an enriched fictional version of what is depicted in the autobiographical texts, portended in all but one of the cases by a recognition of the specific predilection for medicine; the exception is Elizabeth Blackwell, who appears to have been more taken with the "great moral struggle" of obtaining admission to medical school than she was compelled by the prospect of medicine itself. The doctoring skills of the young Nan become apparent in the moment when she bravely splints the broken leg of a turkey, aided by the memory of having seen Dr. Leslie mend a man's broken arm. An instance of amateur medical practice was also crucial for Marie Zakrzewska, "a decisive event" (47), when she nursed a gravely ill aunt and cousin, while for Hunt it was the experience of observing the treatment of her sister's illness and realizing that a more humane and consultative approach was called for. This was, she says, the "great turning-point of my life" (81).

For each of the females, such crucial moments of resolve are followed by a struggle with the personal implications of her decision and a confrontation with the professional obstacles. Not one of the women marries—the texts are explicit about the difficulty of integrating professional and family life and about the threat marital alliance would represent to personal independence. Hunt is openly hostile to the institution of marriage, preferring that women be educated for "useful occupation" (52), and seeing herself as "married" to her profession. Zakrzewska concedes that she had been "inclined toward men" but quickly tired of them, thus "proving that my desire for independence was innate."[19]

Nan Prince believes that her choice of profession is incompatible with marriage, which would force her to "bury the talent God has given me" (210). Privately congratulating herself for having "repelled all possibility" of a successful outcome to George Gerry's suit and for being "proof against such assailment," Nan regards the prospect of romance as "a new enemy, a strange power, which seemed so dangerous that she was at first overwhelmed by a sense of her own defenselessness" (222). Elizabeth Blackwell's autobiography even more vividly discloses the threat represented by marriage and its attendant intimacy, as the author comments at one point on "the hideousness of modern fornication" and notes that when she confronted "the disturbing influence of the other sex" and realized "what a life association might mean, I shrank from the prospect, disappointed or repelled." She came to view medicine as a means to "place a strong barrier between me and all ordinary marriage" (79, 28).

Certainly the obstacles to the attainment of professional goals are presented in all the texts as enormous, likely to consume most of the attention that might otherwise be devoted to intimate relationships. Moreover, they reveal the strength and inertia of the "established system" analyzed in the 1860s by John Stuart Mill in his treatise *The Subjection of Women* as he argued against the continued "social subordination" of women and for their admission to "the occupations hitherto retained as the monopoly" of men.[20] The resistance of the "system" to change was striking, and all of the actual women physicians faced difficult obstacles and outright rejections by medical schools. Blackwell describes a whole series of problems, ranging from the well-meant advice to desist from her efforts to enter medical school to a series of outright rejections, followed eventually by hard-won admission to the school at Geneva and the challenging years of study. Harriot Hunt, too, faced repeated rejections, in her case from Harvard Medical School, which finally offered admission in 1850 only then to confront her with a petition against it signed by all of the students. Zakrzewska faced several barriers in Germany in a difficult process that culminated in the death of her sponsor and led her to set sail for the United States.

Jewett's novel has little to say about the process of applying to medical school but elucidates some of the other challenges for a woman determined to pursue a medical career. Some of these are set forth in a conversation between Nan's guardian Dr. Leslie and his old friend Dr. Ferris, which explores Nan's fitness for medicine and the hazards of letting her pursue such a course, a course that Ferris believes may "risk her happiness" (78). Others are found in Nan's spirited and memorable confrontation with Mrs. Fraley in which she asserts her confidence in her aptitude for medicine and her belief that comparable opportunities should be made available to all women who wish them, because God "[gave] us the same talents" (210).

In arguing for equal opportunity for women, Jewett's *Country Doctor*, like the three medical autobiographies, reveals a divergence from the cultural norm; even more of a challenge is posed by direct and sometimes fierce assaults on the stereotypical thinking that made entry into the medical profession difficult. Both Hunt and Zakrzewska, for example, assail what Hunt calls the "polarized" view of the sexes then prevalent, the essentialist view that men and women are inherently different. The two physicians reveal a more constructionist vision of gender in their assertions that males and females alike should receive equal treatment in order to remove what Hunt calls the "deadly miasma" of difference that "poisons alike the sons and daughters" (395). Nan Prince, too, sees a fundamental error in the argument that "what [is] right for men [is] wrong for women" (210), and broods about the inequities that make it difficult for her to be "trained as boys are, to the work of their lives" (123).

Indeed, the argument that both sexes need to have similar educational and professional options available to them plays a significant role in all the texts; the moment in which some of Blackwell's well-meaning mentors advise her to disguise herself as a man in order to enter medical school crystallizes the issue memorably. Blackwell refused the masquerade, saying it was to her "a moral crusade . . . a course of justice and common sense, and it must be pursued in the light of day, and with public sanction, in order to accomplish its end" (62). In recording the terrible hurdles she faced in attempting to gain access to a medical faculty, Zakrzewska confronts the fundamental question of how women should be educated and "what is their true sphere" (67).

The anger felt by the actual and fictional women physicians occasionally pierces the generally temperate surfaces of their narratives. At one point, Nan Prince feels she is becoming a "reformer, a radical," even "a political agitator" in her efforts to proceed "against the wind" (131), and she has a brief moment of "savagely rebuking society in general for her unhappiness" (123). Hunt's frustration is the most visible, in keeping both with her advocacy of women's rights and her especially frustrating experience with medical school rejections. She expresses outrage at girls being educated for "nothing but marriage," at their "sale" for a home and social position (48–49), at women's lack of equal pay and equal professional opportunity, and at their inability to participate in the political process. "Men rocked" the "cradle of liberty!" Hunt exclaims (44), going on to exhort her readers, "Let every girl see to it that she has the means of her own support" (52).

Such outbursts are rare in these texts, however, as indeed is much in the way of straightforward cultural critique. Though perhaps radical in many of the ideas they explore and in their portraits of articulate, independent, intelligent women pursuing professional goals and refusing to submit to traditional expectations, they are rather restrained in their tone, as if in tacit recognition that, to recall Foucault, they "cannot speak of just anything." Moreover, they employ a variety of strategies, such as the deferral to some conventional precepts of female behavior, the focus on arguments for professional development for special individuals, and their acknowledgment of powerful paternal presences, in order to play a mediative role, to negotiate the difficult space between compliance and confrontation. Thus all four texts succeed in doing a certain amount of ideological work on behalf of the prevailing culture even as they contest many of the gender prescriptions and memorably plead for the sort of professional opportunity for women that would not become widely available for another hundred years.

Notes

1. *Literary World* 15 (June 28, 1884): 211; *Continent* 6 (November 4, 1884): 127. Reprinted in *Critical Essays on Sarah Orne Jewett*, ed. Gwen L. Nagel (Boston: G. K. Hall, 1984), 31–32.

2. *Letters of Sarah Orne Jewett*, ed. Annie Fields (Boston: Houghton Mifflin, 1911), 195.

3. Sarah Orne Jewett, *A Country Doctor* (1884; rpt., New York: New American Library, 1986), 144. All subsequent references are cited in the text.

4. Mary Poovey, *Uneven Developments: The Ideological Work of Gender in Mid-Victorian England* (Chicago: University of Chicago Press, 1988), 12, 14, and passim.

5. Michel Foucault, "The Order of Discourse [1971]," in *Modern Literary Theory*, third edition, ed. Philip Rice and Patricia Waugh (London: Arnold, 1996), 239.

6. Paul Starr, *The Social Transformation of American Medicine* (New York: Basic Books, 1982); Beatrice L. Levin, *Women in Medicine* (Metuchen, N.J.: Scarecrow

Press, 1980); Carol Lopate, *Women in Medicine* (Baltimore: Johns Hopkins University Press, 1968); Regina Morantz, "The Lady and Her Physician," in *Clio's Consciousness Raised*, ed. Mary Hartman and Lois W. Banner (New York: Harper, 1974), 38–53.

7. Quoted in Frederick C. Waite, *History of the New England Female Medical College* (Boston: Boston University School of Medicine, 1950), 14, 17.

8. Caroline Dall, in *Sex and Education: A Reply to Dr. E. H. Clarke's "Sex in Education,"* ed. Julia Ward Howe (Boston: Roberts Brothers, 1874), 89–90.

9. John S. Haller and Robin M. Haller, *The Physician and Sexuality in Victorian America* (Urbana: University of Illinois Press, 1974), 48–62.

10. Howe, "Sex and Education," in *Sex and Education*, 13–31.

11. Quoted in Haller, *Physician and Sexuality*, 80.

12. Barbara Welter, "The Cult of True Womanhood: 1820–1860," *American Quarterly* 18.2 (Summer 1966): 151–74.

13. Harriot K. Hunt, M.D., *Glances and Glimpses: or, Fifty Years Social, Including Twenty Years Professional Life* (Boston: John J. Jewett, 1856), 23. All subsequent references are cited in the text.

14. Elizabeth Blackwell, *Pioneer Work in Opening the Medical Profession to Women* (1895; rpt., New York: Schocken, 1977), 32. All subsequent references are cited in the text.

15. *A Practical Illustration of "Woman's Right to Labor": or, A Letter from Marie E. Zakrzewska, M.D.*, ed. Caroline Dall (Boston: Walker, Wise, 1860), 154. All subsequent references are cited in the text.

16. F. O. Matthiessen, *Sarah Orne Jewett* (Boston: Houghton Mifflin, 1929), 15, 50.

17. Sarah Way Sherman, *Sarah Orne Jewett: An American Persephone* (Hanover, N.H.: University Press of New England, 1989), 122, 169–88; Josephine Donovan, "Nan Prince and the Golden Apples," in *After the Fall: The Demeter-Persephone Myth in Wharton, Cather, and Glasgow* (University Park: Pennsylvania State University Press, 1989), 31–41.

18. Sharon O'Brien, "Tomboyism and Adolescent Conflict: Three Nineteenth-Century Case Studies," in *Woman's Being, Woman's Place*, ed. Mary Kelley (Boston: G. K. Hall, 1979), 351–72.

19. Quoted in Agnes Vietor, *A Woman's Quest: The Life of Marie E. Zakrzewska, M.D.* (1924; rpt., New York: Arno, 1972), 173.

20. John Stuart Mill, *The Subjection of Women* (1869; rpt., Cambridge, Mass.: MIT Press, 1970), 50 and passim.

From Transcendentalism to Ecofeminism

Celia Thaxter and Sarah Orne Jewett's Island Views Revisited

Marcia B. Littenberg

More than a century separates Transcendentalism, the mid-nineteenth-century literary and philosophical movement that proposed a new, more vital relationship between Man and Nature, and ecological feminism (ecofeminism),[1] a philosophical, political and literary movement that proposes a new, more vital environmentalist ethic emphasizing the connection between perceptions of gender and nature. While obvious parallels exist between these two movements, especially the radical critique of politics, religion, and the conceptualization and "management" of nature that each offers, little attention has been paid to the role of New England women regionalist writers in providing an important historical link between them.

Because the New England women regionalists have been closely identified with the development of literary realism, their ideological and aesthetic connections to Transcendentalism have not received sufficient attention by literary historians. Moreover, because both Jewett and Thaxter self-consciously identified their literary perspective as regionalist, critics have focused on its representational fidelity, its nostalgic evocation of country life, and, most recently, its place in an elitist "culture of letters" that capitalized on picturesque stories of rustic places.[2] Except for early appreciations of Jewett's fiction as literary pastoralism,[3] relatively little attention has been paid to the significance of her perspective toward the natural landscape or the conceptual and ethical values it reveals. Thaxter's literary reputation has been even slighter, warranting new consideration of her reputation as a nature writer largely after Lawrence Buell's attention to *Among the Isles of Shoals* (1873) in his *The Environmental Imagination* (1995).[4] Both Jewett and Thaxter can be fruitfully reconsidered in relation to Transcendentalism and to more recent ecofeminist theories.

Feminist criticism, notably that by Marjorie Pryse, Elizabeth Ammons, and Sarah Way Sherman,[5] has afforded important historical recontextualizations of women's regional writing. Part of the difference between the regional texts by women and those by men, these critics observed, was their perspective on and sympathy for their subject. Karen Warren identifies this sympathy as a distinctively feminist perspective, noting in her essay "The Power and the Promise of Ecological Feminism" that an ecofeminist perspective "gives central place to the voices of women," in particular historical circumstances and regions. She also differentiates this empathetic, feminist stance from a traditional, patriarchal relation to the natural world: one that judges, contains, and objectifies.[6] Feminist philosopher Marilyn Frye draws a similar distinction between "arrogant" and "loving" perception to differentiate between the idea of conquest or mastery of nature and an ethic of care, concern, and reciprocity.[7] The power of Jewett's and Thaxter's writing lies in its expression of female sensibility, its sympathetic portrait of women's lives and women's perspectives, and its "loving" relationship to the natural world. By examining Jewett and Thaxter's historical and aesthetic ties to New England Transcendentalism and suggesting how and even why they transformed this earlier Romantic ideology, I hope not only to recover their aesthetic roots but to explain how Jewett and Thaxter sowed the seeds of an early ecofeminism in the rocky New England coastline.

The first tenet of Transcendentalism, as every student learns, is a reemphasis on feeling, for it is one's sympathy with nature, one's ability to "see into the very heart of things"[8] that allows one to discover nature's beauty, and with it, transcendent meaning. Tracing the history of Romanticism, Walter Jackson Bate noted, "feeling *transcends* what is usually regarded as 'reason' not only because it offers a more spontaneous vitality of realization, but also because it is aware of nuances of significance and of interrelationships to which the logical process is impervious."[9] The Romantics' emphasis on feeling underscored the "sympathetic intuition" of the imagination. Writing about Thoreau, Emerson pointed out the importance not only of Thoreau's patient, detailed observations of the natural world but also of the counterrealist tendency of Transcendentalism to identify with what one sees and imbue it with meaning. Emerson notes, "The tendency to magnify the moment, to read all the laws of Nature in the one object or one combination under your eye, is

. . . comic to those who do not share the philosopher's perception of identity. To him, there was no such thing as size. The pond was a small ocean; the Atlantic, a large Walden Pond. He referred every minute fact to cosmical laws."[10]

It does not take a Transcendental leap of imagination to perceive that this same literary aesthetic informs the regional writing of Sarah Orne Jewett and Celia Thaxter. Not only do they share with the New England Transcendentalists a deeply personal response to nature conveyed through detailed observations of the natural world, but the central tenet of each writer's literary vision is sympathetic identification with the places she describes. Indeed, as Sandra Zagarell has pointed out, Jewett's representation of the natural landscape and the community emphasizes their harmonious, organic identity.[11] Like Thoreau, Jewett and Thaxter find a world in a pond, an emblem of society in a teacup, the power of nature in a wildflower. It is, Willa Cather noted in her appreciative commentary on Jewett's work, "this gift of sympathy" that marks Jewett's greatest gift; "it is a gift from heart to heart."[12]

In addition to reaffirming the sympathetic ties between "man" and "nature," much of the effort of New England Transcendentalism was directed toward a radical critique of capitalism and the abstract order of mechanical forces represented by industrialization and urbanization. Both Emerson and Thoreau opposed these man-made, amoral forces to the moral order of nature. Indeed, Thoreau undertook his experiment in living because he wanted to learn to live simply and truly, in harmony with nature. His experiment was both philosophical and preservationist. How can we live without destroying nature? What can we do to preserve what we value and what progress threatens? Offering a passionate defense of the wilderness, the Transcendentalists opposed the exploitation of natural resources for commercial gain. As Carolyn Merchant notes in *Ecological Revolutions*, "The romantic movement cast a golden light on wild nature,"[13] often turning metaphor into literal representation in paintings, poetry and prose. Mountains, forests, meadows, and rivers inspired emotional outpourings from poets and artists. Unspoiled nature was viewed as an emblem of spiritual truth as well as a source of serenity and personal fulfillment. Endowing the natural world with moral power, mythologizing it as "Virgin Land," mother and savior,[14] the Romantics equated nature with the highest ideals, even with divine revelation.

To Emerson, America offered visible proof that Mother Earth was still alive: "There in that great sloven continent still sleeps and murmurs and hides the great mother, long driven away from the trim hedgerows and over-cultivated gardens of England."[15] Thoreau writes of Nature not only as teacher, friend, nurse, and lover, but repeatedly as Mother. "Sometimes," he wrote, "a mortal feels in himself Nature—not his Father but his Mother stirs within him, and he becomes immortal with her immortality."[16] Since Thoreau's emotional response to nature as maternal principle went hand in hand with his preservationist message, it should be evident that within Transcendentalism lay the seeds of ecofeminism. What was required, however, was a shift in gender and philosophical perspective that Thoreau, for all his genius, was not able to achieve.

Contemporary ecofeminist analysis helps us to understand more fully the historical conditions that attracted the women regionalists to Transcendentalism and also to explain how they extended and revised its perspective. Writing not only about nature but about men and women who lived close to nature, who accept not only its power and beauty but its rhythms and cycles, Sarah Orne Jewett and Celia Thaxter are able to make that necessary juncture between the admiration for unspoiled nature and the possibility for living meaningfully in harmony with nature that lies at the heart of ecofeminism. Jewett and Thaxter's evocative, sympathetic portraits of island days and backwater communities, their stories of people whose lives are shaped by their environment, prefigure the revaluation of women and nature that marks the more self-conscious political agenda of contemporary ecofeminists.

The aim of ecofeminism is the creation of a nonexploitive political and social structure. Ecofeminist analysis makes clear that the exploitation of nature is bound to an oppressive conceptual framework and a logic of domination used to "justify" subordination. Such analysis points out that the patriarchal structures that reinforce the domination of women and nature are historically, politically, economically, and ideologically connected.[17]

Ecofeminism has been described as a new term for the ideal of pastoralism because it seeks to reclaim those bonds to the earth that industrialization and urbanization have threatened. In addition, it attempts to reconnect ties between women and nature that have been obscured or devalued by patriarchal culture and to create a conceptual framework of reciprocity and inclusiveness. By combining environmental ethics with feminist theory, not only our ways of knowing but our way of living in nature and with others could change. Notions of moral superiority and domination could be replaced by an ethic that emphasizes conservation, mutual respect, and acceptance of variety and difference. Ecofeminists believe that an exploitive, value-hierarchical, patriarchal ethic that places greater value on progress and use has defined relations between men and women, nature and culture in ways that are both destructive to the environment and limiting of women's place and power. Ecofeminist practice would replace this ethic with more reciprocal and inclusive paradigms. Liberal, radical, and socialist feminist theorists approach these objectives from somewhat different political perspectives, which shape and color their analyses of both the means and ends of ecofeminism.[18] Ultimately, however, all forms of ecofeminism share a common environmentalist vision that Jewett and her contemporaries would have recognized and to which they were committed. For ecofeminism in essence is the reclaiming of our ancient connection to the natural world and to each other, a "reweaving" of old stories with new perspectives that acknowledge and value the interconnectedness of all living systems. These themes are central to Jewett's as well as Thaxter's portraits of their region.

As Merchant points out in *Ecological Revolutions*, the expansion of the market economy and the subsequent emphasis on turning natural resources into profit divided public attitudes toward nature in the nineteenth century, "split[ing] human consciousness into a disembodied analytic mind and a romantic emotional sensibility" (2). The former was concerned with land use and land management; its motive was profit. The latter regarded nature aesthetically and sought unspoiled nature for spiritual and moral comfort. In this latter sense, Nature, like women, occupied a necessary but subordinate separate sphere. Much as in our own time, the same middle-class individuals who profited from the use of nature's resources also sought the antidote of weekend excursions to New England's lakes and mountains. The same merchants and industrialists who were subjected to the stresses of competition sought unspoiled nature's psychic comfort, flocking to Maine's rocky coasts, among other places.

At the Appledore Hotel on the Isles of Shoals, Celia Thaxter entertained almost every major writer and artist of New England from the mid-1860s until her death in 1894.[19] Aside from the attraction of her daily poetry readings and her magnificent wildflower garden, Appledore was an artists' and writers' retreat, a place where some of the original members of the Brook Farm community, as well as the next generation of Transcendentalists, along with many of New England's elite, came to contemplate the glories of nature made more precious by the growing pressures of urban American life. Entertaining her guests at Appledore, Thaxter was able to maintain a balance between the wild, natural geography of the region and the domestic ideal of a well-run and beautiful "home." It may well have been Thaxter, Jewett's beloved "Sandpiper," who evoked Jewett's description of Mrs. Blackett in *The Country of the Pointed Firs:* "Her hospitality was something exquisite; she had the gift which many women lack of being able to make themselves and their houses belong entirely to a guest's pleasure. . . . Sometimes, as I watched her eager, sweet old face, I wondered why she had been set to shine on this lonely island of the northern coast. It must have been to keep the balance true, and make up to all her scattered and depending neighbors for other things which they may have lacked."[20]

Partly as a result of his own Transcendental inclinations and partly because of their isolation at the White Island lighthouse, Thomas Laighton educated his daughter Celia using the principles prescribed by Margaret Fuller in *Woman in the Nineteenth Century.* Celia was taught first by her father and later by Levi Thaxter, her tutor,[21] to observe the natural world around her, to learn from daily life, to record her observations, and to be self-reliant. While Celia's education lacked formal academic discipline, it encouraged her love of nature and her intimate connection to the Isles of Shoals. Like Jewett, who was also instructed by her father to recognize and appreciate nature, Thaxter was by temperament and training prepared to extend the Transcendentalist appreciation for nature through evocative portraits of her region in poetry and prose. She was also prepared to make the connection between the joys of living in solitude with nature and the potential for communal harmony that she observed in the life of the island people.

Like her friend Jewett, Celia Thaxter suggests an "organic" connection between the natural environment and the community. Not only the trees, plants, and rocky coastline but the way of life is represented as indigenous and natural. Using a seasonal structure in her portrait of the Isles of Shoals, Thaxter emphasizes even narratively how nature shapes life there. In a description of Appledore she writes:

> Appledore is altogether the most agreeable in its aspect of all the islands, being the largest, and having a greater variety of surface than the rest. Its southern portion is full of interest, from the traces of vanished humanity which one beholds at every step; for the ground in some places is undermined with ancient graves, and the ruined cellars of houses wherein men and women lived more than a century ago are scattered here and there to the number of seventy and more. The men and women are dust and ashes; but here are the stones they squared and laid; here are the thresholds over which so many feet have passed. The pale green and lilac and golden lichens have overgrown and effaced all traces of their footsteps on the doorstones; but here they passed in and out, old and young, little feet of children, heavy tramp of stalwart fishermen, lighter tread of women, painful and uncertain steps of age. Pleasant it is to think of the brown and swarthy fisherman, the father, standing on such a threshold, and with the keen glance all seafaring men possess sweeping the wide horizon for signs of fair or foul weather; or the mother, sitting in the sun on the step, nursing her baby, perhaps, or mending a net, or spinning,—for the women here were famous spinners, and on Star Island yet are women who have not forgotten the art. Pleasanter still to think of some slender girl at twilight lingering with reluctant feet, and wistful eyes that search the dusky sea for a returning sail whose glimmer is sweeter than moonlight or starlight to her sight, lingering still, though her mother calls within and the dew falls with the falling night. I love to people these solitudes again, and think that those who lived here centuries ago were decent, God-fearing folk . . . and all the pictures over which I dream are set in this framework of the sea, that sparkled and sang, or frowned and threatened, in the ages that are gone as it does to-day, and will continue to smile and threaten when we who listen to it and love it and fear it now are dust and ashes in our turn.[22]

This passage is marked not only by romantic nostalgia but by the connection between Thaxter's observation and her emotion. She emphasizes the relationship between the place and the people, between the past and the present, between her experience and the feelings of others. The description is sentimental in the best sense; it expresses what she feels and draws the reader into this emotional relationship. She gives voice to her sense of felt connection to the nonhuman environment and to the island people who once inhabited this region. While this description is certainly picturesque, the narrative encourages readers not just to look *at* this scene but to experience it as she does.

The idealization of nature in the nineteenth century occurred at the time that it was most threatened by industrial progress (Merchant, 250–51). Just as nature was imagined in two very different, separate realms, one in which it served the economy and the other the human soul, the ideal of utilitarian progress became associated with masculine values and Romanticism with feminine, private ideals. Although the first generation of Transcendentalists was dominated by a small group of elite males, the *values* of Transcendentalism were by mid-century identified culturally with "feminine" practice.[23]

How and why did nature become identified in the latter part of the nineteenth century with women's "sphere" and writing about nature become a woman-centered activity? As early as the 1820s, "Middle class women . . . found opportunities to influence [public] consciousness about nature by educating themselves in the natural sciences, by writing children's books and later by organizing women's clubs" concerned with protecting the environment or cultivating gardens. The study of natural history became popular during the 1820s and 1830s; plant collecting and identification gained acceptance in New England society and was encouraged in female academies as appropriate concerns for young women since they combined intellectual discipline with "feminine" sensibility. Painting flowers, describing them in travel diaries, collecting herbs, and planting gardens were seen as proper feminine pastimes, means of improving the graciousness and spirituality of domestic life. Middle-class women also became active participants in the conservation movement at the end of the century in organizations such as the Audubon Society. Celia Thaxter published an article in the first issue of the *Audubon Magazine* in 1887 entitled "Woman's Heartlessness" in which she describes the resistance she and other environmental activists met in their efforts to prevent fashionable women from wearing on their hats the feathers and stuffed bodies of birds.[24]

Because nineteenth-century New England culture so clearly emphasized these links between women and nature, it is not surprising that the women regionalists associate psychological fulfillment, moral insight, and the search for personal identity with particular landscapes, or that they write from what Julia Bader has called a "rooted" perspective.[25] The healing, protective, and affectionate relationship women demonstrate to each other in regionalist fiction often parallels and extends the affective role of Mother Nature herself. There is a deep appreciation for the beauty of nature and the joy to be found in one's connection to it. At times, as in Jewett's "A White Heron," a character must choose between nature and human society, but, more frequently, the ideal the regionalists envision is a proper balance, a harmony between the human community and the natural world. The celebratory Bowden family picnic in *The Country of the Pointed Firs* re-creates for Jewett's readers then as now this harmony and balance. As Sandra Zagarell notes, identifying the community as a family united through its mothers is another way of "naturalizing" the community and asserting its organic identity, particularly for nineteenth-century readers (45).

In looking backward toward more traditional communities, Jewett and Thaxter may well have been representing not an historical reality but a fictive one, as Richard Brodhead claims in *Cultures of Letters;* their aim, however, is to evoke for readers a palpable world as it might have been in order to intimate the lost potential of the past and perhaps to suggest a hope for restoring the balance upset by modern life. Rather than overtly critiquing urbanization, these portraits of rural life idealize an organic harmony perhaps attainable only in fiction. What has drawn generations of readers to Jewett's writing has been their sense of inclusion in this world, rather than of being merely summer tourists. Through their narratives, Jewett and Thaxter re-create for readers a sympathetic bond to the region and to the community. One listens to their stories, journeys with them to remote islands, shares their hospitality. One learns to see not as an outsider, but as a friend, a daughter, a sister, a welcome returning guest.

How does it help us to reevaluate Jewett and Thaxter's regionalism to see it as both growing out of Transcendentalism and transforming Transcendentalism through a female perspective? The fiction of Jewett and the natural histories of Thaxter (*Among the Isles of Shoals* [1873] and *An Island Garden* [1894]) offer different yet related answers to these questions. While Transcendentalist passages clearly emerge in the work of both Jewett and Thaxter, the writers also extend and revise the aesthetic principles of the early Transcendentalists by a subtle yet central shift in the way they employ the first-person narrative. This difference lies in representing oneself as connected to nature, not simply as a careful observer. It is also marked by the narrator's sensitivity to and acceptance of points of view different than her own. For example, when Jewett's narrator in *The Country of the Pointed Firs* climbs to the highest point of Green Island with Mrs. Todd, she experiences a transcendent moment "there above the circle of pointed firs" looking "down over all the island" and to the "ocean that circled this and a hundred other bits of island ground, the mainland shore and all the far horizons": "It gave a sudden sense of space, for nothing stopped the eye or hedged one in,—that sense of liberty in space and time which great prospects always give." William Blackett interrupts her transcendental reverie with the commonplace observation: "there ain't no such view in the world, I expect," to which the narrator agrees, adding this comment: "it was impossible not to feel as if an untraveled boy had spoken, and yet one loved to have him value his native heath" (45). While William's local pride in the view in no way matches the narrator's transcendent sense of "liberty *in* space and time," she honors it, acknowledging that his relationship to nature is not less valuable or true than her own. The narrative gives voice to both perspectives.

Transcendentalist narratives, in contrast, are more univocal, marked by the solitary presence of the observer. When Thoreau acknowledges his neighbors' points of view, he does so rhetorically, as, for example, in *Walden*, when he notes in "Spring": "In a pleasant spring morning all men's sins are forgiven. Such a day is truce to vice. . . . Through our own recovered innocence we discern the innocence of our neighbors."[26] In *Walden* forgiveness and understanding stem from spiritual principles inherent in nature, from an ideal of essential unity, not from a personal feeling of affection or identification.

There is also a shift in philosophy that affects this perspective. For Thoreau nature was both real ponds, ice, and woods and also an ideal principle. The connection between them was dialectical. The Transcendentalists lived in two worlds at once; in Emerson's words, "two states of thought diverge every moment in wild contrast."[27] Thoreau labored, particularly in his later journals, to resolve this philosophical dualism without satisfaction. Viewing nature in its purest form as necessarily excluding humanity, Thoreau offers his most evocative descriptions of the natural world always from the perspective of the isolated, contemplative Romantic observer.

In the following passage from *Cape Cod*, admittedly his bleakest work, Thoreau's description of the sea from the beach at Truro emphasizes his sense of isolation from nature in its rawest, most powerful, and even threatening form:

> Though there were numerous vessels at this great distance in the horizon on every side, yet the vast spaces between them, like the spaces between the stars . . . impressed us with a sense of the immensity of the ocean . . . and we could see what proportion man and his works bear to the globe. As we looked off, and saw the water growing darker and darker and deeper and deeper the farther we looked, till it was awful to consider, and it appeared to have no relation to the friendly land, either as shore or bottom,—of what use is a bottom if it is out of sight, if it is two or three miles from the surface, and you are to be drowned so long before you get to it, though it were made of the same stuff with your native soil?—over that ocean where, as the Veda says, "there is nothing to give support, nothing to rest upon, nothing to cling to," I felt that I was a land animal.[28]

As this description dramatizes, what Thoreau experiences looking at the ocean is alienation. The human and the natural world stand in opposition to each other; they constitute an ontological dichotomy that Emerson called *Me* and *Not Me.* Standing in front of nature's raw power, Thoreau feels awe, fear, and isolation.

Contrast this passage with another description of the sea from Thaxter's *Isles of Shoals:*

> Swept by every wind that blows, and beaten by the bitter brine for unknown ages, well may the Isles of Shoals be barren, bleak, and bare. At first sight nothing can be more rough and inhospitable than they appear. The incessant influences of wind and sun, rain, snow, frost and spray, have so bleached the tops of the rocks, that they look hoary as if with age, though in the summer-time a gracious greenness of vegetation breaks here and there the stern outlines, and softens somewhat their rugged aspect. Yet so forbidding are their shores, it seems scarcely worth while to land upon them,—mere heaps of tumbling granite in the wide and lonely sea,—while all the smiling "sapphire-spangled marriage-ring of the land" lies

> ready to woo the voyager back again, and welcome his returning prow with pleasant sights and sounds and scents that the wild wastes of water never know. But to the human creature who has eyes that will see and ears that will hear, nature appeals with such novel charm, that the luxurious beauty of the land is half forgotten before one is aware. Its sweet gardens, full of color and perfume, its rich woods and softly swelling hills, its placid waters and fields and flowery meadows, are no longer dear and desirable; for the wonderful sound of the sea dulls the memory of all past impressions, and seems to fulfill and satisfy all present needs (13–14).

Thaxter invites the onlooker to relinquish self-consciousness, to view the familiar sea and islands "islandly," as she does. In contrast to Thoreau's sense of alienation, Thaxter invites a sympathetic identification with both land and sea that transfigures the scene. Even the rhythm of this passage, imitating as it does the rhythm of the waves, obliterates the opposition between the viewer and the natural scene. By identifying with the natural landscape she knows so intimately, Thaxter is freed from the anxiety and alienation that Thoreau experiences in looking at the bottomless expanse of ocean from the beach at Truro. She urges readers of *Among the Isles of Shoals*, as does Jewett's narrator of *The Country of the Pointed Firs*, to learn to see with native eyes, to appreciate the connections between all things in this place.

Like Thaxter's, Jewett's narrative encourages us to feel an intimate connection with nature. The lyrical passage from "A White Heron," when Sylvia climbs the great pine tree and looks out from this great height to the sea, embodies this connection:

> Sylvia's face was like a pale star, if one had seen it from the ground, when the last thorny bough was past, and she stood trembling and tired but wholly triumphant, high in the tree-top. Yes, there was the sea with the dawning sun making a golden dazzle over it, and toward that glorious east flew two hawks with slow-moving pinions. How low they looked in the air from that height when before one had only seen them far up, and dark against the blue sky. Their gay feathers were as soft as moths; they seemed only a little way from the tree, and Sylvia felt as if she too could go flying away among the clouds. Westward, the woodlands and farms reached

> miles and miles into the distance; here and there were church steeples, and white villages; truly it was a vast and awesome world.[29]

This scene re-creates the transcendent moment in which self and nature merge. It achieves the exhilarated oneness with nature that Thoreau often strives for but rarely trusts. How different is the liberation of Jewett's young heroine Sylvia, as she imagines herself flying with the hawks, from Thoreau's estrangement at Cape Cod, where nature's raw power reminds him only of his own mortality, and he expresses the need for something "to cling to."

Part of this difference is the perspective that each writer employs. Thoreau stands alone on the shore, looks outward to sea, and finds nothing but undifferentiated vastness. Nature here is something savage and awful, not man's familiar Mother Earth, but the realm "of Necessity and Fate."[30] His concern for finding bottom reflects his need for an anchor, a grounding place. Bottoms "teach man to know his place in nature,"[31] he wrote. Jewett's perspective is fluid; Thoreau's is fixed. We first see Sylvia's face as we might if we could see it from the ground; then we see what Sylvia does, and, like her, soar on our imagination, like the hawks or the white heron itself, across the landscape. Because Jewett connects her character's imagination with what she sees, Sylvia can soar outward and not experience the terror of losing herself or, like Melville's Ishmael, fear falling into the vast unknown. Thus, while Jewett allows us a Transcendental leap into space, her character's imagination expands through her emotional connections with the natural world, which extend rather than obliterate her identity. She defines herself in connection with the natural world, part of the "web of life," whereas Thoreau remains a solitary self on the shore.

For Jewett and Thaxter, the philosophical split between Nature as an ideal and nature as real trees, rocks, birds, or sea is resolved through the sympathetic, emotional identity the writer affirms with the natural world. The dualism Thoreau experienced between his careful empirical observations of the natural world and his intuitive grasp of higher mysteries is resolved for the regionalists by a crucial shift in point of view. Instead of looking *at* nature, they invite one to identify with those who live within a particular place. The term that environmentalists use for this perspective is "bioregionalism." Bioregionalism examines how the ecology of a region reflects not only where but *how* one lives. It also has a political agenda, in that to truly become "native to a place," to obtain a "rooted" perspective, we must learn to understand not only a region's ecology but its sociology and its history. We must become part of the total life of a region and experience, albeit vicariously, our sense of belonging to a community. While Thoreau self-consciously undertakes the first task in *Walden*, becoming a close observer of nature's particulars, and includes in *Cape Cod* discussions of the local history, he remains most typically a solitary wanderer in the wilderness. It is Jewett and Thaxter who extend their island views to include the sympathetic connections to their region that transform both that region and nature itself.

By reaffirming the historical and theoretical missing links between Transcendentalism and women's regionalist writing, particularly that of Jewett and her contemporary Thaxter, I hope to shed new light on the distinctive qualities of their aesthetic vision. There is no question that "the American environmental imagination" (Buell, 2) has been profoundly shaped by Transcendentalism and by Thoreau in particular because he gave voice so eloquently to our desire to be connected to our world not only physically but spiritually and morally. But Jewett and Thaxter also transformed Transcendentalist language, perspective, and attitude. Their appreciation for nature went far beyond a simple nostalgia for bygone days and country ways. They revitalized nature writing, reclaiming the "elegiac resonance" (Buell, 233) of Thoreau's best writing and providing readers with vivid examples of what it might be like to live in greater harmony with nature. By focusing on women's experiences and narratives, Jewett and Thaxter also offer distinctively feminist perspectives. By listening to stories, offering their nonjudgmental observations, caring for others, and expressing sympathy and concern, they place readers in a different relationship with their region and nature than the Transcendentalists' more self-consciously philosophical agenda. It is this crucial shift in point of view, tone, and intent that links their literary vision with the goals of contemporary ecofeminism.

Notes

1. The term was first employed by Francoise d'Eaubonne in *Le Feminisme ou la Mort* (Paris: Pierre Horay, 1974), 213–52.

2. Richard H. Brodhead, *Cultures of Letters: Scenes of Reading and Writing in Nineteenth-Century America* (Chicago: University of Chicago Press, 1993), chapters 4 and 5.

3. See for example, Charles Miner Thompson, "The Art of Miss Jewett," *Atlantic Monthly* 94 (October 1904): 485–97; reprinted in *Appreciation of Sarah Orne Jewett*, ed. Richard Cary (Waterville, Maine: Colby College Press, 1973).

4. Lawrence Buell, *The Environmental Imagination: Thoreau, Nature Writing, and the Formation of American Culture* (Cambridge, Mass.: Harvard University Press, 1995). Buell calls *Among the Isles of Shoals* "the first extended work of environmental nonfiction produced by the late nineteenth-century regional realist movement" (233).

5. See esp. *American Women Regionalists, 1850–1910*, ed. Judith Fetterley and Marjorie Pryse (New York: Norton, 1992); Elizabeth Ammons, "Going in Circles: The Female Geography of Jewett's *Country of the Pointed Firs*," *Studies in Literary Imagination* 16 (Fall 1983): 83–92; and Sarah Way Sherman, *Sarah Orne Jewett: An American Persephone* (Hanover, N.H.: University Press of New England, 1989).

6. Karen Warren's essay originally appeared in *Environmental Ethics* 12.3 (Summer 1990): 125–46, and was reprinted in *Environmental Philosophy*, ed. Michael Zimmerman et al. (Englewood Cliffs: Prentice-Hall, 1993, 1998), 325–44.

7. Marilyn Frye, "In and Out of Harm's Way: Arrogance and Love," in her *The Politics of Reality* (Trumansburg, N.Y.: Crossing Press, 1983), 66–72.

8. This phrase appears in William Wordsworth's poem "Tintern Abbey" (line 49) and refers to the ideal balance between nature seen by the eye (sensation) and nature perceived from within by the imagination. The ideal is "a balance, an ennobling interchange / Of action from without and within . . . Both of the object seen, and eye that sees" (*The Prelude* [XIII.375–78]).

9. Walter Jackson Bate, *From Classic to Romantic* (New York: Harper and Row, 1946), 130.

10. Quoted in *Henry David Thoreau: Modern Critical Views*, ed. Harold Bloom (New York: Chelsea House, 1987), 7.

11. See, for example, Sandra A. Zagarell, "*Country*'s Portrayal of Community and the Exclusion of Difference," in *New Essays on "The Country of the Pointed Firs,"* ed. June Howard (New York: Cambridge University Press, 1994), 39–60.

12. Willa Cather, "Miss Jewett," in *Not Under Forty* (1922; rpt., New York: Knopf, 1964).

13. Carolyn Merchant, *Ecological Revolutions: Nature, Gender, and Science in New England* (Chapel Hill: University of North Carolina Press, 1989), 251.

14. For further discussion of the land-as-woman metaphor in American literature, see Annette Kolodny, *The Lay of the Land: Metaphor as Experience and History in American Life and Letters* (Chapel Hill: University of North Carolina Press, 1975).

15. Emerson, *Complete Works* (Boston: Houghton Mifflin, 1903–4), 5:288.

16. *Portable Thoreau*, ed. Carl Bode (New York: Penguin, 1977), 222.

17. See Warren, "The Power and the Promise of Ecological Feminism" and

"Feminism and Ecology: Making Connections," *Environmental Ethics* 9 (1987): 3–20.

18. See also *Feminist Literary Criticism: Explorations in Theory*, ed. Josephine Donovan, second edition (Lexington: University Press of Kentucky, 1989). Ecological feminist literature includes works from a variety of scholarly perspectives and sources. See esp. Ynestra King, "Feminism and the Revolt of Nature," *Feminism and Ecology* 4 (1981); Judith Plant, *Healing Our Wounds: The Power of Ecological Feminism* (Boston: New Society, 1989); and Ariel Kay Salleh, "Deeper than Deep Ecology: The Eco-Feminist Connection," *Environmental Ethics* 6 (1984): 339–45, and "Epistomology and the Metaphors of Production: An Eco-Feminist Reading of Critical Theory," *Studies in the Humanities* 15 (1988): 130–39.

19. Jane E. Vallier, *Poet on Demand: The Life, Letters, and Works of Celia Thaxter* (Camden, Maine: Down East, 1982), 18.

20. Sarah Orne Jewett, *The Country of the Pointed Firs and Other Stories*, ed. Mary Ellen Chase (1896; rpt., New York: Norton, 1981), 46–47. Subsequent references are cited in the text.

21. See Vallier, *Poet on Demand*, 56–58, for a discussion of the disastrous marriage between Celia and Levi Thaxter.

22. Thaxter, *Among the Isles of Shoals* (Boston: James Osgood, 1873; rpt., Portsmouth, N.H.: Randall, 1994), 29–31.

23. Merchant discusses the nineteenth-century gendering of nature at length in *Ecological Revolutions*.

24. For a brief discussion of this essay, see Karen L. Kilcup, Introduction to *Nineteenth-Century American Women Writers: An Anthology* (Cambridge, Mass., and Oxford: Blackwell, 1997), xlix. Thaxter's essay is reprinted in this collection (281–83).

25. Julia Bader, "The 'Rooted' Landscape and the Woman Writer," in *Writing from a Regional Perspective*, ed. Leonore Hoffman and Deborah Rosenfelt (New York: MLA, 1982), 23–29.

26. Thoreau, *Walden*, in *Henry David Thoreau* (New York: Library of America, 1985), 573.

27. Quoted in Loren Eisely, "Thoreau's Vision of the Natural World," in *Henry David Thoreau*, ed. Bloom, 36.

28. Henry David Thoreau, *Cape Cod*, in *Henry David Thoreau*, 934–35.

29. Jewett, "A White Heron," in *American Women Regionalists*, ed. Fetterley and Pryse, 203.

30. F. O. Matthiessen, *American Renaissance* (New York: Oxford University Press, 1941), 162–63.

31. See Walter Benn Michaels, "Walden's False Bottoms," in Bloom, *Henry David Thoreau*, 79–95.

The Professor and the *Pointed Firs*

Cather, Jewett, and Problems of Editing

Ann Romines

In recent years it has been exhilarating to see the Sarah Orne Jewett–Willa Cather relationship becoming a frequent subject of literary discourse. However, our accounts of that relationship have tended to concentrate on the last sixteen months of Jewett's life, when she and Cather became friends,[1] and the years immediately after Jewett's death, when Cather attended to her friend's advice and radically revised her writing life, terminating her career as a journalist in order to devote herself entirely to fiction. This increasingly familiar—and important—story often culminates with the 1913 publication of *O Pioneers!*, which Cather dedicated "to the memory of SARAH ORNE JEWETT, in whose beautiful and delicate work there is the perfection that endures."

However, the Cather-Jewett story did not end in 1913. In this essay, I will argue that the memory of Jewett and *The Country of the Pointed Firs* was an "enduring" but far more conflicted presence in the next decade of Cather's career, the mid-life mid-1920s, when she concurrently edited an influential edition of Jewett's fiction and wrote *The Professor's House.* Both were published in 1925. By 1925 Willa Cather had achieved much that her mentor, Sarah Orne Jewett, must have wished for her. She had published eight acclaimed works of fiction, won a Pulitzer Prize for *One of Ours,* and was supporting herself handsomely as a fiction writer. Her biographer James Woodress summarizes: "She had reached the top of her profession. She was a world-class author."[2] And she was fifty-three, the age of Jewett when her carriage accident ended her writing career. Despite her steady productivity, this was a period of malaise and disjunction for Cather; later, she famously wrote that "the world broke in two in 1922 or thereabouts," consigning her to "the backward," those over forty.[3]

Sharon O'Brien sees Cather's edition of Jewett as a project intended to resist that 1922 rupture. Cather, whose reputation was by then larger than Jewett's had ever been, aimed to become a competitor in the game of canon-building that such contemporaries as D. H. Lawrence were playing with a vengeance in the mid-1920s.[4] In her preface, Cather proposed her own nineteenth-century short list; she wrote, "If I were asked to name three American books which have the possibility of a long, long life, I would say at once, 'The Scarlet Letter', 'Huckleberry Finn', and 'The Country of the Pointed Firs'."[5] Only the last of these books would have come as a surprise to 1925 readers, of course. As O'Brien observes, by including Jewett "in the male-dominated literary canon from which [Cather] had once felt excluded, as her literary inheritor Cather was also including herself,"[6] thus confirming an ongoing tradition of female authorship.

The Jewett edition was the only full-scale editing task of Cather's mature career after she renounced journalism, and she took it very seriously. She chose all the stories, vetoing at least one that Jewett's sister Mary—Cather's good friend and frequent hostess—wanted to include, and she insisted on writing the preface herself. Much of the best-known language associated with Cather's discussion of art comes from that preface and its 1936 expanded version.[7] The artist's "gift of sympathy," language that is "a gift from heart to heart," the necessity of knowing both "the world and the parish"—Cather scholars will recognize these phrases as touchstones that have become titles of well-known works of Cather scholarship. All come from her celebratory description of Jewett's art.

However, celebration and canon-building are not the only tasks of Cather's preface. For this essay is also a confirmation of the *critic's* and the *editor's* magisterial power. The title itself emphasizes the importance of the editor's contribution: she has chosen and certified *The* Best *Stories of Sarah Orne Jewett* (emphasis added). Cather emphatically lets us know that *she* chose the eleven stories that accompany *The Country of the Pointed Firs* in her slim selection; she points out flaws in at least two of these stories. She intimates that these stories are really *enough* of Jewett to read and emphasizes that stringent criticism is essential to the recognition of art: "To note an artist's limitations [and Cather claims Jewett has several] is but to define his genius." Even in her highest praise, Cather seems somehow to deny the fact of Jewett's *work* as an artist: "The 'Pointed Fir' sketches are living things caught in the open . . . they are not stories at all but life itself."[8] (In 1936, she added that Jewett's stories "were but reflections, quite incidental," of her "love of the Maine country and seacoast," restating her subtle deprecation of Jewett as conscious artist.)[9] Finally, the preface invokes a male contemporary that Cather admired, Robert Frost, and celebrates the discernment of Jewett's future critical reader, who is—perhaps not incidentally—conventionally male: "I like to think with what pleasure, with what a sense of rich discovery, the young student of American literature in far distant years to come will take up this book and say, 'A masterpiece!' as proudly as if he himself had made it" (xix).

Cather commented during this period that Jewett was, after all, "a minor writer," and "very uneven. . . . A good balance of her work is not worth preserving. The rest, a small balance—enough to make two volumes—is important."[10] In one sense, of course, Cather herself was the *maker* of those two volumes. Like the future student she imagined, she might consider herself the discerning creator of this "masterpiece." Perhaps that is why she committed what most Jewett readers consider the most egregious error of her edition, fracturing the formal unity of the 1896 version of *The Country of the Pointed Firs* to insert three later stories, an editorial judgment that seems to violate the ethic of sympathy that she describes as central to Jewett's art.

These contradictions in Cather's editing project all signal that she was in the process of rethinking her inheritance from Jewett. A more subtle indication of how deeply that process was a part of Cather's working life is apparent when we compare *The Professor's House*, her 1925 novel, with the Jewett text Cather most admired, *The Country of the Pointed Firs.* Both these books emphasize issues of reconnection with an earlier American culture that is perceived by contemporary observers as seductively coherent. In Jewett's text, that culture is a preindustrial Maine maritime community, and in Cather's text it is an Anasazi cliff village on a New Mexico mesa. But both sites are described almost identically as refuges. On Green Island, one of the farthest outposts of pointed fir country, Jewett's urbane autobiographical narrator says "it was impossible not to wish to stay on forever,"[11] while Cather's Tom Outland also describes the mesa country as "the sort of place a man would like to stay in forever."[12]

To Jewett's narrator, a returning "lover of Dunnet Landing," the village culture seems univocal, like "a single person" (1–2). Tom Outland sees the Cliff City as similarly unified: it is "like sculpture," grouped around a "fine" (and phallic) central tower "that held . . . the . . . houses together and made them mean something" (180). Such constructed coherence compels Jewett's narrator and Cather's Tom Outland and his professor to return, again and again, to these remote little cities. According to Tom's first mentor, the Belgian-born priest Father Duchene, that coherence was what made the long-vanished cliff dwellers "a superior people." They had "a distinct feeling for design. . . . Buildings are not grouped like that by pure accident" (197). This resembles the language in which Cather's preface frames its highest praise of Jewett's fiction as "tightly built and significant in design . . . the design is the story and the story is the design" (x). In her single published comment on *The Professor's House,* Cather describes her own book as an experiment in design influenced by Dutch paintings that feature domestic interiors with a window open to a glimpse of sea. "In my book," she says, "I tried to make Professor St. Peter's [midwestern] house rather overcrowded and stuffy. . . . Then I wanted to open the square window and let in the fresh air that blew off the Blue Mesa," where the cliff city was built, centuries earlier.[13] The Professor's writing study in his old house, which he perversely refuses to surrender, is distinguished by one "fine thing" that the Professor *must* have, a view of blue water: "a long, blue, hazy smear—Lake Michigan, the inland sea" (20). In the Dunnet Landing schoolhouse, where Jewett's narrator—like the Professor—has staked out a writing place at a strategic distance from the domestic entanglements of traditionally feminine pursuits, there is a strikingly similar water prospect: "I spent many days there quite undisturbed, with the sea-breeze blowing through the small, high windows" (9). And, perhaps not incidentally, both these problematically cloistered writers are *autobiographical* characters.[14] In fact, the disaffected Professor is exactly Cather's age as he reflects that his own passionate writing life may be at an end—as Jewett's working life *did* end, at that same age, fifty-three.

Such a close web of correspondences strongly suggests that Dunnet Landing, as well as Dutch landscapes, must have been an insistent presence in Cather's mind as she wrote *The Professor's House.* Equally telling are the alterations she made in Jewett's model. Dunnet Landing is inhabited by elderly but emphatically *living* storytellers—most of them women—who insist on complicating the narrator's initial naive view of

Dunnet as a place that speaks with a single voice. Her published narrative, which we read as *The Country of the Pointed Firs*, becomes increasingly multivocal as she writes it. But the long-dead native people of the Blue Mesa speak only through the remnants of their material culture: architecture, pottery, stone tools, bone implements, yucca mats. The twentieth-century men who discover these ancient things do not consider themselves qualified to read such texts; Tom keeps a scrupulous descriptive journal, but he seals it up behind a rock, instead of publishing, as Jewett's narrator does. He takes his instructions from Father Duchene, who advises that Tom "must go to the Director of the Smithsonian Institution. . . . He will send us an archaeologist who will interpret all that is obscure to us . . . in a scholarly work" (199). The worldly priest invokes a male hierarchy of privileged interpretation that will produce sanctioned writing, a "scholarly work." Young Tom dutifully travels to Washington and makes the futile rounds of government agencies. But no one is interested; he finds no highly skilled readers who will attend to his mesa. Back in New Mexico, hearing of Tom's failure, his friend and collaborator Roddy Blake sells all the portable Cliff City objects to a profit-minded German collector.

In *The Country of the Pointed Firs*, such everyday objects—a bunch of herbs, a piece of jewelry, a broken teacup—were often the means by which the narrator began to read (and write) the multiple Dunnet Landing stories. By the book's end, a dead woman's parlor furnishings are an open book to her: "I looked at the unworn carpet, the glass vases on the mantelpiece with their prim bunches of bleached swamp grass and dusty marsh rosemary, and I could read the history of Mrs. Tilley's best room from its very beginning" (124). Tom Outland's experience is very different. Although he protests and breaks with Roddy over the artifacts' sale, it is only after those things are gone (including a few preserved human bodies) and the mesa is swept clean of other human traces that he spends his most exalted and focused time there. For a summer, the young man lives blissfully alone in the buildings he has named Cliff City, studying European languages—Spanish grammar and Latin poetry—to prepare for college admission. His surroundings become continuous with the texts he studies; later, he explains that "When I look into the Aeneid now, I can always see two pictures: the one on the page, and another behind that": the stone town on the mesa (228). Tom makes this empty place his own: "Something had happened in me that made it possible to co-ordinate and simplify, and that process, going on in my mind, brought with it great happiness. It was possession" (226).

Empty, the Cliff City becomes entirely the textual property of twentieth-century patriarchal storytellers: the boyish explorers, their tutor-priest, the anthropologists and archaeologists they hope to attract, and finally the history professor of Cather's title, who visits the mesa village with Tom as his guide. The city's putative unified "design" is *their* construction, their story. Eve Kosofsky Sedgwick aptly describes Tom's story of the Blue Mesa as a "gorgeous homosocial romance."[15] Women, like the problematic Indian corpse that the men patriarchally christen "Mother Eve," are primarily an impediment to this male enterprise. Father Duchene posits that this youthful murdered female had a strong will and insistent sexuality, suggesting a purely "personal tragedy" that he cannot tie into the men's seamless hypothetical story about the Cliff City. Perhaps her husband found her in "improper company" and disposed of his unruly property as he desired? "In primitive society the husband is allowed to punish an unfaithful wife with death," says the priest (201). In *The Professor's House,* histories are written only by men, and women are unproblematic only when they remain within a narrative frame of domestic faculty and contained sexuality or when they facilitate men's projects, as does a helpful young secretary Tom meets in Washington.[16] As Judith Fetterley has observed, "in *The Professor's House* . . . Cather accords cultural meaning to the male body [only] and permits no celebration of the female body and its desires."[17]

The Country of the Pointed Firs can be read as a preservationist project if we see the work of the female narrator, a publishing writer, as an effort to preserve a connection to an earlier, woman-centered culture through the contemporary resources of *print.*[18] Cather regendered this publishing enterprise, casting it as the male problem of a dispossessed writer-professor and an orphan boy. First, she made "Tom Outland's Story" the insistently masculine centerpiece of her book, and it became one of her best-known works because it was one of the few stories she allowed to be reprinted. Also, within that story, Tom Outland himself writes a book, a careful diary of his Cliff City discoveries and observations. At the novel's end, Tom is dead, a casualty of World War I, and the Professor is editing his manuscript for publication. This process confirms Tom's youthful assumption that the Cliff City artifacts and stories are his male intellectual legacy: "they belonged to *boys* like . . . me that have no other ancestors to inherit from" (219, emphasis added). St. Peter's editing project reinforces that assumption. Although he will take no money from Tom's estate, he boldly claims Tom's manuscript to edit and market, thus circulating the homosocial, colonial narrative of Tom's blue mesa. The Professor finds the young man's "plain account . . . almost beautiful, because of the stupidities it avoided and the things it did not say. . . . [T]hrough this austerity one felt the kindling imagination, the ardour and excitement of the boy" (238). This is praise as ardent as Cather's for the "best" of Jewett. Yet, as Cather did with her Jewett project, St. Peter sees his own editing contributions as crucial to the success of Tom's manuscript. He must "edit and annotate" and "write an introduction" if the published book is "to mean anything" (150), he believes. His editing will ensure the preservation of a patriarchal inheritance.[19]

Both *Country* and *The Professor's House* are preoccupied with such issues of inheritance. (As middle-aged women writers with no children, both of whose estates would include major bequests to female contemporaries, Jewett and Cather may also have been reflecting on traditions of inheritance in their personal lives.) As many of us have observed, Mrs. Todd's gift of the coral pin, a family heirloom and an emblem of female solitude, proposes a female model of inheritance, beyond primogeniture, that is based in women's chosen affinities and not in patriarchal law. Choosing a writer as her heir, Mrs. Todd also ensures that her legacy will be perpetuated in print. In *The Professor's House*, Tom Outland's will is a major problem. Conventionally, he left everything to his fiancée, the Professor's daughter Rosamund, who profits handsomely from Tom's lucrative scientific discovery. But even to the Professor, Tom's great champion, such a will is unsatisfactory, for it privileges only heterosexual commitments and does not acknowledge Tom's intense homosocial alliances with such men as Roddy Blake, his nurturing companion of the Blue Mesa, and his physics professor, Dr. Crane, who facilitated his scientific success.[20]

St. Peter's daughters, Rosamund and Kathleen, are at the center of the book's controversies about Tom's legacy. When they were children, Tom was their favorite companion, and they "used to live in his stories" of the Blue Mesa (112). Rosamund is now married to Louie Marsellus, an enterprising, expansive Jewish electrical engineer who has marketed Tom's invention, "the Outland engine," profitably. The Marselluses spend their new riches liberally and enthusiastically, and Kathleen, who is married to a journalist and living on his modest income, is often jealous. Their most troubling appropriation, in the family's eyes, is one of language: they take Tom's name, *Outland*, and bestow it upon their luxurious new country house, a decidedly unindigenous dwelling, an architect's fantasy of a "Norwegian manor" on the shores of Lake Michigan. As "Outland," Tom's name, story, and inheritance become part of an expanding postwar multiethnic and multicultural world economy, which the living Tom resisted when he protested the mesa artifacts' transportation to Germany. In such an economy, Louie Marsellus can imagine himself and Tom (whom he never met) not as competitors, but as men of the same, and thus mixed, blood: "'I never think of him as a rival', said Louie. . . . 'I think of him as a brother'" (145). Meanwhile, Kathleen indignantly resists the Marselluses' appropriations by claiming a piece of Tom for her own. She too had a secret romantic attachment to Tom, and she stakes her claim to his enticing tales: "Now that Rosamund has [the house] Outland, I consider Tom's mesa entirely my own" (112).

Such issues of inheritance reflect the problems that recent post-colonialist commentators on Cather's career have seen as central to Cather's malaise of the early 1920s. The concerns of Elizabeth Ammons are typical and pertinent:

> What went wrong for Cather after 1922 . . . was the obvious, undeniable emergence of a new world composed of multiple, competing, cultural perspectives struggling against white, Eurocentric, monocultural hegemony. This new world was not composed of interesting ethnic differences finally and comfortably dominated by Western European values (as in the happy worlds of *O Pioneers!*, *The Song of the Lark*, and *My Ántonia*, for example). Rather, it was a world in which the old securities of global, white, European cultural supremacy were starting to give way to something new and frightening: Jews with power, "dark" people making demands, immigrants writing literary criticism, lesbians out of the closet. What Cather longed for after 1922 was the return of hegemonic, white, patriarchal control.[21]

It is not difficult to see such longings expressed in *The Professor's House*, in the "problem" of Louie, a Jew among gentiles, who is powerful, seductive, and globally peripatetic, and in the controversies about how to make an ancient Indian culture into a profitable legacy for non-Indian men. Less obviously, these longings are also implied by Cather's Jewett preface, which privileges present and future male readers and places Jewett in a tradition of classicist and/or canonical male-authored texts: Homer, Theocritus, Hawthorne, Mark Twain. The 1936 expanded version, "Miss Jewett," more explicitly denigrates readers "of foreign descent" who cannot understand and appreciate the native "Yankee" qualities of Jewett's language and characters.[22] Both versions of the preface, as I have already suggested, undercut Cather's advocacy of her mentor's writing and of the tradition of female authorship that Cather and Jewett shared.

This troubling and conflicted agenda also surfaces in *The Professor's House*, most interestingly through the Professor's two daughters. At his darkest moments, as St. Peter formulates his own story of mid-life malaise and writer's block in his mind, he tends to cast himself as a Lear without a Cordelia. His wealthy, acquisitive daughter Rosamund most appalls him when she exercises a "faultless purchasing manner" while buying antique European furniture; "she was like Napoleon looting the Italian palaces" (135), a *male* master of cultural appropriation. (And in this image, she has also appropriated her father's name, for one of St. Peter's secrets is that he was christened "Napoleon.") At her vulnerable moments, Kathleen seems a more likely candidate for Cordelia. But Kathleen's jealousy of her sister is literally fearsome to her father, as he watches her "pale skin" become greenish; and when he sees her pluckily walking alone, he is also disturbed and hurries to "make her take his arm and be docile" (52). Women with agency trouble the Professor, as "Mother Eve" troubled the white men on the Blue Mesa. St. Peter's work is about men—Spanish explorers in North America; his readers are men; his students—of whom Tom Outland is the best—are men. The world of his writing has no place for living women.

Thus both his daughters are cut off from the possibilities of writing. Kathleen, a "quick" student, was good at watercolor portraits, but her attempts to paint her mother and sister failed. "I can't really do anybody but Papa" (52), she says, suggesting the limitations of a woman artist for whom patriarchs are the only possible subject. And Rosamund never puts brush or pen to paper. When she is traveling with her mother and husband in Europe, both Mrs. St. Peter and Louie write frequent, fluent letters home. But Rosamund is entirely silent. The trip ends abruptly when she becomes pregnant and the family returns "home to prepare for the advent of a young Marsellus" (249). The baby, bearing its father's surname, is the only text this daughter produces. The economy of *The Professor's House* offers no place for a writing woman. When Augusta suggests to the Professor that the Magnificat was "composed" by the Virgin Mary "just as soon as the angel had announced to her that she would be the mother of our Lord" (84), he is amused by the sheer implausibility of a composing (and pregnant) woman.

The central problem of *The Country of the Pointed Firs* is a composing woman, the narrator. Where will she work? What are her subjects? How is her work of composition related to the various domestic lives she begins to know in Dunnet Landing? Physically and psychically, she works out relations to her "half-written page" (15), although the difficulties of these relations are expressed by the form of the 1896 edition and its relation to the four later "Pointed Firs" stories.

Early in "Tom Outland's Story," the most Edenic moments occur when Tom, living with Roddy and their cook/housekeeper, "old Henry," seems to have solved such composition problems. The men set up "housekeeping" in a cabin on the mesa. There they spend their days excavating, "and every night after supper, while Roddy read the newspapers, I sat down at the kitchen table and wrote up an account of the day's work" (189), his surviving journal. But this Eden is soon terminated by a snakebite, which kills Henry, and then by Tom's quarrel with Roddy over the sale of the artifacts. Years later, St. Peter takes up Tom's writing problems again—the issues of domicile, mobility, homosocial community, and relations with domestic life with which he, like Jewett's narrator, is entangled—from a clearly patriarchal perspective. In the last section of Cather's novel, the Professor's writing problems intensify, as he unsuccessfully labors to claim the most problematic part of Tom Outland's legacy, his journal, by editing it.

In Willa Cather's work as Jewett's editor, which most readers would now consider at best a partial success, she redesigned and framed the 1896 text of *The Country of the Pointed Firs,* working as St. Peter attempted to do with Tom Outland's diary. For at least fifty years, Cather's edition of Jewett was widely circulated and influential; most readers who were introduced to Jewett before 1981 probably first encountered *The Country of the Pointed Firs* in Cather's 1925 version, which is still widely available in paperback.

Even the publications of 1925 do not represent the last chapter in the Jewett/Cather relationship. *The Professor's House* offers cues to continuities; at the end of that book, the near-suicidal Professor is rescued from asphyxiation by the intervention of Augusta, an elderly seamstress/nurse/housekeeper (and a character who would be at home in Dunnet Landing), to whose domestic stability St. Peter is newly drawn. On the book's last page, he thinks that "Augusta was like the taste of bitter herbs; she was the bloomless side of life that he had always run away from,—yet when he had to face it, he found that it wasn't altogether repugnant" (256). This description, with its herbal motifs, is reminiscent of Mrs. Todd, with whom Jewett's narrator shares a house and a profound (and possibly erotic) friendship in Dunnet Landing.[23] In fact, Judith Fetterley suggests that Augusta is "perhaps Cather's emblem for Edith Lewis," Cather's longtime companion and literary executor, who provided much of the domestic continuity in her life, as Annie Fields did for Jewett.[24] Thus, when Cather turns to (autobiographical) St. Peter's relations with Augusta at the end of *The Professor's House*, even in this insistently male-centered novel she may be obliquely broaching issues of a lesbian writer's working life that are also present in *The Country of the Pointed Firs*.

Augusta and the Professor have long shared a workspace, she sewing by day and he writing by night. When they attempt to separate their materials—their "life work," the Professor calls them—they find that domestic work and writing have cohered into a single text; "in the middle of the box, patterns and manuscripts interpenetrated" (13). This image of pages suggests that the issues between St. Peter and Augusta are very much those of *textual* relations. At the end of Cather's novel, Tom Outland's diary is still unedited, and St. Peter's relations with his work and his family are unresolved. But his relations with Augusta are solid: "There was still Augusta . . . a world full of Augustas, with whom one was outward bound" (257). Thus *The Professor's House* ends where *The Country of the Pointed Firs* began, in an author's rapprochement with domestic culture as enacted by Augusta and Mrs. Todd.[25] As I have argued elsewhere, that probing and troubled rapprochement is evident throughout the remaining decades of Cather's career, in such great texts as *Shadows on the Rock*, "Old Mrs. Harris," and *Sapphira and the Slave Girl*, all clearly touched by the influence of Jewett.

My final example of this influence is from the very next year. In 1908, Jewett had advised Cather not to write in a male voice, "always . . .

something of a masquerade" for a woman—advice that Cather had ignored with stunning success.[26] But in 1926, in the book that follows *The Professor's House,* Willa Cather introduced her first specifically female narrative voice—the voice in which Jewett wrote almost exclusively—in *My Mortal Enemy.*[27]

Another of Willa Cather's gifts from Jewett was a necklace, which she displays prominently in a famous 1910 portrait photograph,[28] and which we have speculatively connected with Mrs. Todd's gift of jewelry to another writer. It is telling, I think, that *My Mortal Enemy* ends with the legacy of a necklace, a gift from an older woman to a young woman writer. For this writer, the legacy is troubling. It distracts her from conventional storytelling—such as "the bright beginning of a love story"—and forces her to hear the voice of the necklace's former owner, a passionate, disaffected aging woman who loved both women and men (104–5). It is the presence of that intruding voice, of course, that gives *My Mortal Enemy* its subject and its troubling power. Finally, I would remind you that that power, as in much of Willa Cather's fiction, is intimately connected to her complex relationship with Sarah Orne Jewett.

Notes

1. Willa Cather spent much of 1907–8 in Boston, working on a biography of Mary Baker Eddy for *McClure's Magazine,* of which she was an editor. Jewett was in Boston at the home of her companion, Annie Fields.

2. James Woodress, *Willa Cather: A Literary Life* (Lincoln: University of Nebraska Press, 1987), 334.

3. Willa Cather, Prefatory Note to *Not Under Forty* (New York: Knopf, 1964).

4. Lawrence's *Studies in Classic American Literature* (1923; New York: Viking Press, 1964) is a classic example of this game.

5. Willa Cather, Preface to *The Best Stories of Sarah Orne Jewett* (Boston: Houghton Mifflin, 1925), xviii.

6. Sharon O'Brien, *Willa Cather: The Emerging Voice* (New York: Fawcett Columbine, 1988), 352.

7. The expanded version was published in 1936 in *Not Under Forty.*

8. Cather, Preface, xv, x.

9. Cather, "Miss Jewett," in *Not Under Forty,* 87.

10. Quoted in Woodress, *Cather,* 356. This quotation cited by Woodress is from the 1924 Rascoe interview. Willa Cather, interview by Burton Rascoe, in

Willa Cather in Person, ed. L. Brent Bohlke (Lincoln: University of Nebraska Press, 1986).

11. Sarah Orne Jewett, *The Country of the Pointed Firs and Other Stories*, ed. Mary Ellen Chase (New York: Norton, 1981), 52. Subsequent references are cited in the text.

12. Willa Cather, *The Professor's House* (New York: Vintage, 1990), 168. Subsequent references are cited in the text.

13. Willa Cather, "On *The Professor's House*," in *Willa Cather on Writing* (Lincoln: University of Nebraska Press, 1988), 31–32.

14. Both James Woodress, *Willa Cather* (368–69), and David Harrell (184–85) see important autobiographical elements in Cather's characterization of St. Peter. David Harrell, *From Mesa Verde to the Professor's House* (Albuquerque: University of New Mexico Press, 1992).

15. Eve Kosofsky Sedgwick, *Tendencies* (Durham: Duke University Press, 1993), 174.

16. The secretary, whom Tom describes patriarchally as "a nice little thing" (206), is named Virginia. She and her mother are kind and attentive to Tom while he is Washington, but ultimately they cannot help him get the official male support he seeks there. Since "Virginia" is the name of both Willa Cather's mother and her native state, the young woman's brief friendship with (motherless) Tom may suggest a story about the powers and limits of maternal origins and support, one with autobiographical implications.

17. Judith Fetterley, "Willa Cather and the Fiction of Female Development," in *Anxious Power: Reading, Writing, and Ambivalence in Narrative by Women*, ed. Carol J. Singley and Susan Elizabeth Sweeney (Albany: State University of New York Press, 1993), 231.

18. I developed such a reading of *The Country of the Pointed Firs* in Ann Romines, *The Home Plot: Women, Writing, and Domestic Ritual* (Amherst: University of Massachusetts Press, 1992), 48–90.

19. Early in the development of this essay, I was influenced by comments from my graduate student David Tritelli about postcolonial issues in *The Professor's House*, particularly problems of ownership as they might be reflected in the Professor's editing of Tom Outland's diary.

20. David Harrell points out Tom Outland's "social irresponsibility," as expressed in his will (*From Mesa Verde*, 187).

21. Elizabeth Ammons, "Cather and the New Canon: 'The Old Beauty' and the Issue of Empire," in *Cather Studies*, ed. Susan J. Rosowski (Lincoln: University of Nebraska Press, 1996), 3:256–66. Other critics who have recently discussed such issues of empire in Cather's fiction of the 1920s include Walter Benn Michaels, *Our America: Nativism, Modernism, and Pluralism* (Durham: Duke University Press, 1996), and Joseph T. Urgo, *Willa Cather and the Myth of American Migration* (Urbana: University of Illinois Press, 1996).

22. Cather, "Miss Jewett," 93–94.

23. For example, the Professor's evocation of the childless Augusta as "bloomless" recalls the description of Mrs. Todd's garden as "plain" with "Hardly a flower in it except your [herbal] bush of balm" (86).

24. Fetterley, "Willa Cather," 223.

25. Yet another problem of Cather's edition of *The Country of the Pointed Firs* is that, by inserting four later stories—especially "William's Wedding"—before "The Backward View," the final sketch of Jewett's 1896 edition, she upset the delicate calibrations of the narrator's departures from and returns to Mrs. Todd and her house, calibrations that suggest the constant and ongoing readjustments of that complex relationship.

26. *Letters of Sarah Orne Jewett*, ed. Annie Fields (Boston: Houghton Mifflin, 1911), 246.

27. Willa Cather, *My Mortal Enemy* (New York: Vintage, 1961).

28. This photograph from about 1910 shows a richly dressed and authoritative-looking young Willa Cather as managing editor of *McClure's*. Her long, tasseled necklace, Jewett's gift, is highlighted against her dark clothing. The photograph has been frequently reproduced; for example, it appears as the frontispiece in Sharon O'Brien's *Willa Cather: The Emerging Voice*.

Visions of New England

The Anxiety of Jewett's Influence on *Ethan Frome*

Priscilla Leder

Edith Wharton's memoir, *A Backward Glance*, refers frequently to other writers of fiction, but she seldom connects their work so specifically with her own as she does when describing her motivation for writing *Ethan Frome:* "For years I wanted to draw life as it really was in the derelict mountain villages of New England, a life . . . utterly unlike that seen through the rose-coloured spectacles of my predecessors, Mary Wilkins and Sarah Orne Jewett."[1] In her introduction to *Ethan Frome*, Wharton resolves to reveal the "granite outcroppings" of conflict and suffering that fictional depictions of New England "overlooked" in favor of "abundant enumeration of sweet-fern, asters and mountain-laurel."[2] Given the popularity of *The Country of the Pointed Firs*, Wharton's acquaintance with Jewett, and the structural similarities of the two works, it seems likely that *Pointed Firs* provided a paradigm of the vision Wharton wished to correct.

R. W. B. Lewis reports that in July 1905 Edith, her husband Teddy, and their friend Bay Lodge drove from The Mount "as far as South Berwick, Maine, the home of Sarah Orne Jewett."[3] Lewis's language implies that they visited South Berwick because of Jewett and/or her house, but there is no record of an encounter. In fact, though the two women must have met (Wharton's letters include a 1902 note to Annie Fields accepting "your kind invitation for Friday" and anticipating "seeing you and Miss Jewett")[4] and certainly knew each other's work, Wharton's remark about rose-colored glasses is virtually the only published comment by either upon the other's work.[5] That comment, with its skepticism toward Jewett's world, perhaps grows out of the differences between the two writers' attitudes about their backgrounds. Wharton, who expressed her ambivalence toward her own upbringing through her concern with distinctions and formal perfection, may have been uneasy with Jewett's habit of identifying herself with her own background and emphasizing unity rather than distinction.

The expression of that unity in *Pointed Firs* through the emphasis on connections—between people, between human beings and nature, between past and present—perhaps disturbed Wharton and kept her from seeing Jewett's many depictions of loss, conflict, and suffering—the granite underlying the lush vegetation. Wharton implies that Jewett has oversimplified; however, in *Ethan Frome* she herself reduces Jewett's living landscape to a stark tableau and replaces an elaborate web of connections with a series of gaps. In effect, she extracts the granite boulders from the landscape and isolates them under harsh electric light.

Like *Ethan Frome*, *Pointed Firs* employs a narrator who recounts a sojourn in a New England village and whose account combines direct observation with the villagers' stories. *Pointed Firs* blends the two in a smooth progression—observation leads into someone's story, which in turn informs another observation. For example, the tale of Joanna Todd emerges as the narrator first hears about Mrs. Fosdick, then observes Mrs. Fosdick directly, hears Mrs. Fosdick and Mrs. Todd recount Joanna's story, and finally visits Shell-Heap Island and re-creates Joanna's experience in her own imagination.

In *Ethan Frome*, on the other hand, the narrator's observations, his imaginative re-creations, and the villagers' accounts remain separate, punctuated by gaps both within and between them. In considering Harmon Gow's account of Frome's life, for example, the narrator notes that "there were perceptible gaps between his facts, and I had the sense that the deeper meaning of the story was in the gaps."[6] Since Gow tells his story at the beginning of the novel, we might expect the gaps to be filled by the end. However, the last account, Ruth Varnum's, though fuller and emotionally richer, also contains gaps, in the form of repeated ellipses. Though many of these mark the pauses and hesitations natural to a painful recounting, they nevertheless conceal, most notably Mattie Silver's first words upon regaining consciousness after the coasting accident. Does Mattie blame Ethan? God? Herself? Unarticulated, Mattie's despair cannot undergo the kind of redeeming contextualization Jewett gives to Joanna Todd's experiences.

The narrator's own imaginative re-creation of Ethan, Mattie, and

Zeena's story does offer insights into their thoughts and motivations, but he takes pains to detach what he calls his "vision" from his observations. Though he reports finding "the clue" to Ethan during the night he spends at his house, he recounts only the first two or three minutes of that night, leaving the reader to infer the connection between the house and the story it contains. In finding the "clue" to his "vision" in the connection between dwelling and people, Wharton's narrator recalls Jewett's story-generating "click" when an old woman and old house come together in her mind.[7] Yet, while Jewett in *Pointed Firs* describes the dwelling and its contents as extensions of its inhabitants, Wharton's narrator presents such connections as subjective and arbitrary.

By labeling the narrative his "vision," Ethan Frome's narrator invites the reader to remain detached from it and to see it as merely an extension of himself. As Cynthia Griffin Wolff puts it, his tale "is not 'true' except as an involuntary expression of his own hidden self."[8] In *Pointed Firs*, on the other hand, the smooth connections between observation and story, dweller and dwelling encompass the reader as well. For example, in recreating Joanna Todd's isolation, the narrator invites the reader to identify with it: "In the life of each of us . . . there is a place remote and islanded, and given to endless regret or secret happiness."[9]

In *Ethan Frome*, the narrator's distance from his audience may reflect his distance from his creator, Edith Wharton. Her male, scientifically minded engineer seems almost the antithesis of her female, artistically minded self. While she resided comfortably at The Mount and observed rural New England by taking leisurely drives, her narrator "had been sent up by my employers on a job connected with the big power-house at Corbury Junction"—a declaration that sent Henry James into gales of laughter. "The notion of dear Edith being sent anywhere by anyone, he commented, boggled belief."[10]

Certainly, the narrator's employment gives him a plausible reason for being in Starkfield, and his gender gives him a mobility and a potential rapport with Ethan Frome that an Edith Wharton might not have had. However, in discussing her choice of narrator, Wharton does not mention those advantages. Rather, she cites his sophistication relative to the "simple" people he "interprets": "If he is capable of seeing all around them, no violence is done to probability in allowing him to exercise this [interpretive] faculty."[11] Notably, he sees *around* rather than *into* them, unlike the omniscient narrators Wharton usually employs. The preposition emphasizes his emotional distance from the characters and renders them dense, opaque, and limited—like granite boulders.

Jewett's narrator, a well-traveled woman writer like her creator, at first seems similarly separated by her sophistication from the people she observes. However, as many readers have noted, she eventually enters the lives of the characters and begins to learn from and revere them. Her knowledge of life and literature, rather than distancing her from them, becomes a means of comprehending them, as in the much quoted passage when she sees Almira Todd as "Antigone alone on the Theban Plain," possessed by an "absolute, archaic grief" (49). Furthermore, as an artist, she can appreciate the skill with which they arrange their houses, their lives, and their stories; and she can associate their artistry with her own.

For the characters in *Ethan Frome*, artistry and the appreciation of beauty merely emphasize their distance from narrator, author, and audience. Mattie's genteel accomplishments have no practical value for her, and Wharton's list of them invites the reader to feel superior to their genteel conventionality: "She could trim a hat, make molasses candy, recite 'Curfew shall not ring to-night', and play 'The Lost Chord' and a pot-pourri from 'Carmen'" (59). As if to underscore that such conventionality is essential to Mattie rather than imposed upon her, Wharton employs it to express the love of natural beauty that draws Ethan to Mattie: "When she said to him once [as they looked at a landscape]: 'It looks just as if it was painted!' it seemed to Ethan that the art of definition could go no farther, and that words had at last been found to utter his secret soul" (34). Ethan's response to Mattie's comment reveals the limitation of his own sensibilities. His appreciation of nature tends toward the scientific, as he identifies the constellations and holds Mattie "entranced before a ledge of granite thrusting up through the fern while he unroll[s] the huge panorama of the ice age" (34), an image that, though powerful, has as little to do with their everyday experience and their emotional lives as "The Lost Chord."

In fact, Ethan's scientific perspective, like the narrator's, gives the landscape of *Ethan Frome* an atomistic, inorganic quality: "The night was perfectly still, and the air so dry and pure that it gave little sensation of cold. The effect produced on Frome was rather of a complete absence of atmosphere, as though nothing less tenuous than ether intervened between the white earth under his feet and the metallic dome overhead.

'It's like being in an exhausted receiver', he thought" (27). The explicitly scientific metaphor belongs to Frome (that is, the Frome of the narrator's vision), but the narrator's own descriptions of the winter landscape have a similar tone—evoking metallic images ("silver-edged darkness," pine cones like "bronze ornaments") and inexorable, mechanical processes (mist is "burnt away," the landscape "whiten[s] and shape[s] itself under the sculpture of the moon") (135).

In contrast, the elements of Jewett's landscapes seem to interact with each other rather than being acted upon by scientific laws: "There was a great stretch of rough pasture-land round the shoulder of the island to the eastward, and here were all the thick-scattered gray rocks that kept their places, and the gray backs of many sheep that forever wandered and fed on the thin sweet pasturage that fringed the ledges and made soft hollows and strips of green turf like growing velvet" (40). Her description evokes movement ("wandered"), relationship ("fringed" and "made"), and, most importantly, volition. Jewett's rocks have chosen to "keep their places," in community with the other elements of the landscape; Wharton's "ledge of granite" forms part of an inexorable scientific process that continues regardless of the boulder's placement in the forest.

While Jewett's landscapes extend a chain of interaction that links characters, narrator, author, and reader, Wharton's stark, schematic landscapes reflect the characters' isolation; "[Ethan] seemed a part of the mute melancholy landscape, an incarnation of its frozen woe" (14). Zeena and Mattie, like Ethan, seem "frozen" in their unarticulated emotions. Even the brief glow of passion between Mattie and Ethan remains largely unexpressed, buried under the restraint of everyday routine. Moreover, Mattie's initial warmth is literally frozen into the paralysis that makes her an invalid, her voice the same "querulous drone" that the sickly Zeena's once was. Zeena's shift from invalid to nurse reverses her earlier change from nurse to invalid after the death of Ethan's mother, like a mirror image. Similarly, as Wolff points out, the narrator resembles Ethan, and the lives of the three characters, trapped by circumstances in an apparent eternity of privation and suffering, resemble the frozen landscape they inhabit.

In *Ethan Frome*, such resemblances seem static, one unchanging image mirroring another. In *Pointed Firs*, similarities between incidents and characters form part of an ongoing, cyclical process. The marching participants in the Bowden family reunion resemble "a company of ancient Greeks going to celebrate a victory," but they also move into the future: "we carried the tokens and inheritance of all such households from which this had descended, and were only the latest of our line" (100). This sense of process allows for the assimilation of conflict and suffering and thus for the broader scope of Jewett's vision. The suffering of characters like Joanna Todd and Elijah Tilley yields stories, which in turn yield meaning for the narrator, Mrs. Todd, and the reader. Elijah Tilley's broken china teacup, though useless in itself, remains part of a set that, like his relationship with his late wife, was complete and satisfying. The narrator, though she finds Mr. Tilley's parlor and the seldom-used items that furnish it "a much sadder and more empty place than the kitchen," nevertheless appreciates it as an extension of the couple and their aspirations (124).

Like Sarah Tilley's teacup, Zeena Frome's red glass pickle dish, that delight of Freudian critics, ornaments a parlor. Unlike the teacup, the pickle dish, which is never used, is an apparently unique item whose singularity symbolizes Zeena's alienation from her surroundings; it initiates strife rather than fond memories. The pickle dish, which like the teacup is broken and then hidden at the back of a shelf, aptly signifies Wharton's re-vision of *Pointed Firs.* Like her use of a visiting narrator, it suggests that, whether she was conscious of it or not, her resolve to correct the "rose-coloured" vision of New England was especially focused on that work. In revising Jewett's broken teacup and Jewett's New England, Wharton replaces connection and community with isolation and atomization, as if too much closeness engenders discomfort.

For some readers, Wharton's desire to correct the vision of her predecessors explains the "frozen woe" of *Ethan Frome.* They argue that, through writing *Frome*, Wharton repudiates a stultifying passivity associated with her own secure but restricted upbringing. Marlene Springer maintains that Wharton "wrote out of her own fears of what her own emotional life . . . could become if she did not risk change."[12] In a similar vein, Wolff sees *Ethan Frome* as representing the effects of remaining in "the world of childhood, obedience, limitation, and emotional starvation." According to Wolff, Jewett depicts the pleasures of remaining in the static world of idealized childhood, and thus Wharton needed to repudiate her vision.[13] Like Springer and Wolff, I believe Wharton's upbringing to be the source of her attitude toward Jewett's fictional world. However, that attitude arises not only from her desire for emotional autonomy; more importantly, it reflects the complex process through which she defined herself as a literary artist both against and within the restrictions of her class.

In *A Backward Glance*, Wharton describes a childhood ritual that dramatizes her use of literature to create an identity for herself within her family: "The imagining of tales . . . had gone on in me since my first conscious moments; I cannot remember the time when I did not want to 'make up' stories. . . . [F]rom the first I had to have a book in my hand to 'make up' with, and from the first it had to be a certain sort of book. . . . [I]f the book was in reach, I had only to walk the floor, turning the pages as I walked, to be swept off full sail on the sea of dreams."[14] Wharton does not dwell here on the content of her "tales," inviting the reader to assume that, like most fantasies, they offered their creator escape and empowerment. Rather, she emphasizes her need for the physical book, whose possession legitimized her antisocial activity by confirming her participation in the consumption that characterized her class. Although in "making up" the four- or five-year-old Edith "abandon[ed her] 'nice' playmates" and "distressed" her parents by her "solitude," in "reading" a book from her father's library she affirmed her possession of the accouterments that made her Miss Jones of New York.[15] Noting Wharton's account of "parents and nurses, peeping at [her] through cracks in doors," Judith Fryer concludes that "making up," though ostensibly a form of withdrawal, was actually a way of seeking approval.[16] If so, "making up" provides an especially appropriate metaphor for the relationship between literary artistry and class in Wharton's life. On the one hand, writing could expose the limitations and restrictions of upper-class life; on the other, her insistence on distinctions and standards in writing expressed the exclusivity of her upbringing.

Wharton's parents, "who were far from intellectual, who read little and studied not at all, nevertheless spoke their mother tongue with scrupulous perfection, and insisted their children should do the same." In *A Backward Glance*, Wharton provides examples of words and phrases her parents deemed impure or vulgar, implying that the use of such expressions revealed the speaker's inferior class: "I still wince under my mother's ironic smile when I said that some visitor had stayed 'quite a while', and her dry: 'Where did you pick *that* up?'"[17] The question not only condemns the phrase but also insists upon its disreputable origins.

Though her account reveals that linguistic purity reinforced class exclusivity, Wharton also associates it with a kind of detached idealism: "My parents' ears were wounded by an unsuitable word as those of the musical are hurt by a false note."[18] Her depiction of her parents' concern with language as at once snobbish and idealistic typifies the ambivalence with which she recounts her upbringing. Toward the end of her equivocal discussion of the roles language and literature played in her upbringing, she finds her "clue" in the word "standard"—a concept she could incorporate into her own identity as an artist.[19]

In 1924, Wharton articulated her literary standards in *The Writing of Fiction*. Significantly, the "first assumption" of her theory is not the need to convey experience directly and immediately, which fiction writers often consider primary. Rather, it is "the need of selection"—the need to sort through "details more and more remotely relevant"—that is "the first step toward coherent expression." In defending her first assumption, Wharton declares that there would be no need for such an obvious "rule" if contemporary literary practices such as slice of life and stream of consciousness were not so much exaggerated that "their very unsorted abundance constitutes in itself the author's subject."[20] Just as her parents insisted upon discrimination in language as the mark of the upper-class writer, Wharton emphasizes discrimination among experiences as the mark of the genuine literary artist.

Though Jewett offered advice about writing, most notably to Willa Cather, she never attempted the kind of extensive analysis Wharton undertook in *The Writing of Fiction* and a number of magazine articles. There may, of course, be many reasons for this, but certainly she did not share Wharton's compelling need to make distinctions. Elizabeth Ammons appropriately locates both Wharton and Jewett among the late-nineteenth and early-twentieth-century women writers whose break with their predecessors "consisted in their avowed ambition . . . to be artists."[21] However, while Jewett's correspondence with editors and publishers reveals that she learned to act as a professional as she gained experience,[22] Wharton assumed the role more self-consciously. After delivering *The House of Mirth* to her publisher, she declared, "It was good to be turned from a drifting amateur into a professional."[23]

In his introduction to *A Backward Glance*, Louis Auchincloss finds Wharton's central motive in that very professionalism: "In short, her life was a revolution against the idea that a lady should be in everything a mere amateur. Mrs. Wharton was always determined to be surrounded with a beautiful world, even if she had to build it herself."[24] Auchincloss's language reveals, once again, the complex relationship between Wharton's upbringing and her literary artistry. Though her life was a "revolution" against the shallow, limited existence of the society woman, her need to be "surrounded by a beautiful world" grew out of her parents' expression of their upper-class identity. Asked as a child what she wanted to be as an adult, young Edith declared, "The best-dressed woman in New York" because "you know Mamma *is*."[25] The older Wharton adopted loftier goals, but she still aspired to distinguish herself by creating formal perfection.

Such formal perfection flourished best when isolated from the everyday. Noting that her father's, brothers', and husband's contemporaries were "men of leisure—a term now almost as obsolete as the state it describes," Wharton recalls "the delightful week-day luncheons of my early married years, where men were as numerous as women, and where one of the first rules of conversation was . . . [n]ever talk about money."[26] In the absence of mundane concerns, "delight" was possible. As readers of Wharton and her dear friend Henry James cannot help observing, leisure seems necessary not only for delight but also for the unfolding of the tensions and desires that are the raw material of fiction. Desire and betrayal flourish in the elaborately furnished rooms of the wealthy; ethical dilemmas play out between summer and winter houses. Work takes place largely in the background, as it did in Wharton's young womanhood: "almost all the young men I knew read law for a while after leaving college, though comparatively few practiced it in after years."[27]

For Jewett, in contrast, work generates storytelling: the young women of *Deephaven* observe the lighthouse keepers; Nan Prince finds her vocation as a country doctor; the narrator of *Pointed Firs* fishes, sells herbs, and hears tales of profit and loss at sea. In recounting the lives of doctors, sea captains, and a vast variety of homemakers, Jewett draws on her own experience as the granddaughter of a sea captain and the daughter of a doctor and on the lives of the families she visited while accompanying her father on his rounds. Although "her grandfather had left the family financially independent,"[28] Jewett and her family seem to have felt no special need to distinguish themselves from their neighbors. Their house, where Jewett lived most of her life, stands in the center of the village of South Berwick—imposing but not inaccessible.

To make the two-hundred-mile journey from Jewett's house to Wharton's New England home, The Mount, near Lenox, Massachusetts, is to see in wood and stone the relationship between each writer's background and her art. Jewett's house offers ten well-appointed rooms to accommodate all the activities of its inhabitants. At the center of those activities, in the upstairs hall, Jewett's desk looks out over the village. There, she created fiction out of, and in the midst of, the world she knew. While Jewett's house provides a comfortable accommodation for family and visitors, Wharton's house constitutes an artistic production. It embodies the principles of order and proportion that Wharton and the architect Ogden Codman articulated in their book *The Decoration of Houses*. In building and decorating the house, Wharton rejected the elaborate, fussy interiors of Victorian New York to create a formal perfection of her own, which opposed the world she knew while retaining its concern for standards and distinctions.

Jewett's house, in contrast, embodies the domestic ideal of the home as the center of experience. For Wharton, Jewett's emphasis upon the everyday lives of women, and her consequent identity as a "woman" writer may have been especially disturbing. Elizabeth Ammons theorizes that the group of late-nineteenth and early-twentieth-century women writers who aspired to be "artists" tended to identify with the masculine model of the artist and thus to alienate themselves from each other: "The often-remarked distance that Edith Wharton established between herself and other creative women is just one obvious, if exaggerated, example of this distinction . . . part of the author's historically explicable professional determination not to be categorized and dismissed as a woman writer."[29] Such determination is perfectly consistent with Wharton's concern with professionalism and with form.

Just as an identity as a woman writer contradicted the ideal of professionalism, the details of domestic activity were inconsistent with the ideal of formal perfection articulated by Wharton and Codman. Though published in an era when the design of kitchens had begun to command attention, *The Decoration of Houses* pays almost no attention to the kitchen.[30] Almost forty years later, Wharton's attitude toward domesticity seemed to soften along with her perspective upon her past. In *A Backward Glance*, she devotes two pages of lyrical description to the dinners of her childhood. However, instead of dwelling on details of food preparation and sharing, she emphasizes the finished product and the "great artists"—the African American cooks—who created it. Domestic production thus becomes simply another example of the search for formal perfection in "the complex art of civilized living."[31]

Ethan Frome does not depict "civilized living," but the writing of it was a formal exercise. Wharton reports that "its first pages were written—in French!" and explains that she began writing the story in Paris to provide her French tutor, who was "too amiable" to correct her spoken mistakes, with a sample of her French.[32] Wharton did not keep the "exercise," but later, at The Mount, she remembered the protagonist and wrote his story in Paris the next winter. Given its generation as an exercise and its setting in a relatively unfamiliar environment, *Frome* provided a kind of escape for Wharton. Significantly, Wharton remarked that it was "the book to the making of which I brought the greatest joy and the fullest ease."[33] Her sense of ease may have resulted from her liberation from the ambivalence she felt about her own New York world.

Nevertheless, insofar as Jewett's domestic vision of interconnectedness defined New England, that world held potential anxiety for Wharton. Thus, she used the narration of her story to insulate herself even further from her potentially disturbing subject. In fact, *Frome* seems almost an exercise in the kind of formal detachment Wharton advocated in *The Writing of Fiction*. In that work, she discusses a narrative technique she refers to as a "'hall of mirrors', a series of reflecting consciousnesses, all belonging to people who are outside of the story, but accidentally drawn into its current." This form, she believes, can create an admirably symmetrical solution to "the problem of coordinating consciousness"[34]—the need to tell a story that exceeds any one character's consciousness without leaping implausibly from one character's mind to another's or intruding on the narrative.

Wharton finds a perfect example of the hall of mirrors technique in Honoré de Balzac's short story "La Grande Bretèche," a story she cites as a source of the "method" of *Ethan Frome*.[35] "La Grande Bretèche," like *Ethan Frome*, employs a narrator who comes to a town from outside and pieces together one of its stories from his own observations and his conversations with people more directly involved in the events. Wharton implies that Balzac's narration provides objectivity without sacrificing richness of detail, but in the case of one character, objectivity gives way to the narrator's own desires and anxieties. Two of the narrator's informants, the real estate agent and the landlady, speak in their own voices, but the maidservant, Rosalie, has her part of the story retold by the narrator "in as few words as may be."[36] The narrator has made love to the maidservant in order to obtain her story, and his appreciative descriptions of her appearance replace her voice with her body. The narrator's summary of Rosalie's account of adultery punished by slow death reflects the anxiety underlying his seduction of her.

In *Ethan Frome*, Wharton employs the hall of mirrors technique insofar as the narrator combines his observations of Ethan with the accounts of Harmon Gow and Ruth Varnum. However, when the narrator pauses at the door of the Fromes' kitchen, Wharton abandons the hall of mirrors technique in favor of his "vision" of the story. Just as "Rosalie's" portion of "La Grande Bretèche" betrays the narrator's anxiety, the engineer's "vision" of Frome's story reveals his, and ultimately Wharton's, discomfort with the indiscriminate intimacy of a life centered around the kitchen. Moving into new geographic and cultural territory gave Wharton the freedom necessary for a formal experiment, but insofar as that territory had been claimed by Jewett and others as an extension of the kitchen, it seemed alien and threatening to Wharton. Her choice of narrator reflects her ambivalence. For Wharton's engineer narrator, as for Jewett's characters, work shapes life; thus, he represents a departure from the world of her New York novels. However, his profession represents the antithesis of domesticity and aligns him with Wharton's formalism.

In "The Engineer as Cultural Hero and Willa Cather's First Novel, *Alexander's Bridge*," Elizabeth Ammons explores the image of the engineer in the years just before Cather's 1912 novel appeared. She concludes that Cather created *Alexander's Bridge* "against a well-developed backdrop of literature and cultural mythology about the heroism, the patriotism, and the manliness of the American engineer: a figure repeatedly associated with conquest of the environment, expansion of Anglo hegemony, and veneration of the Wild masculine West."[37] Wharton, who herself published in *Scribner's*, one of the magazines that perpetuated this image, and who published *Ethan Frome* just one year before *Alexander's Bridge*, was writing against this same backdrop. Thus, her choice of the narrator's profession underscores his masculinity, figured in his distance from the world of domesticity.

His profession also associates him with Wharton's authorial vision. In a 1907 letter, she described a potential contradiction in that vision: "I conceive my subjects like a man—that is, rather more architectonically and dramatically than most women—and then execute them like a woman; or rather, I sacrifice, to my desire for construction and breadth, the small incidental effects that women have always excelled in, the episodical characterisation, I mean."[38] Wharton's language suggests that the large conception represents a desire to transcend a world of details—details upon which she must draw in order to realize her vision. Once again, form represents at once an ideal and a limitation. Writing *Ethan Frome* not long after this letter, Wharton embodied her "architectonic" conception and her "desire for construction and breadth" in her engineer narrator, who, she said, could "see around" the characters. The "small incidental effects," associated as they are with Jewett's world, appear isolated, frozen in painful tableau.

Wharton declared that in writing *Ethan Frome* she felt for the first time "the artisan's full control of his implements."[39] The phrase, with its emphasis on instrumental construction, recalls the language of her 1907 letter and the perspective of her engineer narrator. It asserts a kind of power—the masculine power of technology and controlled experiments. It also declares distance—the artisan shapes "his" material with implements, not with his hands. In confronting Jewett's world of closeness and connection, Wharton shaped herself against what she was not and brought her literary standards into relief like granite boulders.

Notes

1. Edith Wharton, *A Backward Glance* (New York: Charles Scribner's Sons, 1934), 293.

2. Edith Wharton, Introduction to *Ethan Frome* (New York: Barnes and Noble, 1995), v.

3. R. W. B. Lewis, *Edith Wharton: A Biography* (New York: Harper and Row, 1975), 150.

4. *The Letters of Edith Wharton*, ed. R. W. B. Lewis and Nancy Lewis (New York: Charles Scribner's Sons, 1988), 65.

5. In 1908, writing to Violet Paget about possible publishers for Paget's travel sketches, Jewett noted that "The Atlantic is just now printing some French sketches (rather more like useful tanks than hillside springs!!) by Mrs. Wharton." I have not discovered any comments other than this one, which is too specific to a single work to shed much light on Jewett's assessment of Wharton's work.

Sarah Orne Jewett Letters, ed. Richard Cary (Waterville, Maine: Colby College Press, 1967), 170.

6. Wharton, *Ethan Frome*, 7. Subsequent references are cited in the text.

7. Willa Cather, Preface to *The Country of the Pointed Firs and Other Stories* (Garden City: Doubleday Anchor, 1956), iv.

8. Cynthia Griffin Wolff, *A Feast of Words: The Triumph of Edith Wharton*, second edition (Reading, Mass.: Addison-Wesley, 1995), 177.

9. Sarah Orne Jewett, *The Country of the Pointed Firs and Other Stories* (New York: Doubleday, 1927), 82. Subsequent references are cited in the text. I have chosen the Cather edition because it is the one with which Wharton would most likely have been familiar.

10. Lewis, *Edith Wharton*, 310.

11. Wharton, Introduction to *Ethan Frome*, vii.

12. Marlene Springer, *Ethan Frome: A Nightmare of Need* (New York: Twayne, 1993), 10.

13. Wolff, *A Feast of Words*, 169, 178.

14. Wharton, *Backward Glance*, 34.

15. Ibid., 35.

16. Judith Fryer, *Felicitous Space: The Imaginative Structures of Edith Wharton and Willa Cather* (Chapel Hill: University of North Carolina Press, 1986), 154.

17. Ibid.

18. Ibid., 51.

19. Ibid., 52.

20. Edith Wharton, *The Writing of Fiction* (New York: Charles Scribner's Sons, 1925), 9, 12.

21. Elizabeth Ammons, *Conflicting Stories: American Women Writers at the Turn into the Twentieth Century* (New York: Oxford University Press, 1991), 4.

22. Richard Cary, Introduction to *Sarah Orne Jewett Letters* (Waterville, Maine: Colby College Press, 1967), 7.

23. Wharton, *Backward Glance*, 209.

24. Louis Auchincloss, Introduction to *A Backward Glance* (New York: Charles Scribner's Sons, 1934), viii.

25. Wharton, *Backward Glance*, 20.

26. Ibid., 56–57.

27. Ibid., 56.

28. *Sarah Orne Jewett Letters*, 7.

29. Ammons, *Conflicting Stories*, 11.

30. Fryer, *Felicitous Space*, 35. See Wharton and Ogden Codman, *The Decoration of Houses* (1897; rpt., New York: C. Scribner, 1926).

31. Wharton, *Backward Glance*, 60.

32. Ibid., 295.

33. Ibid., 293.

34. Wharton, *Writing of Fiction*, 92, 88.

35. Wharton, Introduction to *Ethan Frome*, ix.

36. Honoré de Balzac, "La Grande Bretèche," in his *The Lily of the Valley and Other Stories*, trans. James Waring (Philadelphia: Gebbie Publishing, 1898), 363.

37. Elizabeth Ammons, "The Engineer as Cultural Hero and Willa Cather's First Novel, *Alexander's Bridge*," *American Quarterly* 38 (1986): 754.

38. *Letters of Edith Wharton*, 124.

39. Wharton, *Backward Glance*, 209.

Part III

Conflicts

Identity and Ideology

"Whiteness" as Loss in Sarah Orne Jewett's "The Foreigner"

Mitzi Schrag

What can be gained by reading for "whiteness" in a time when, following works like Henry Louis Gates, Jr.'s *"Race," Writing, and Difference*, "race" is almost invariably set off with scare quotes?[1] Does the examination of "whiteness" re-secure "race"?[2] Or is it more dangerous to ignore the racial unmarkedness that underlies white material advantage and supremacist politics? In the past decade, as part of their respective projects to denaturalize "race," critics of "whiteness" such as bell hooks, David Roediger, George Lipsitz, Ruth Frankenberg, Eric Lott, Kobena Mercer, Vron Ware, and Coco Fusco have generally concurred that what we would abolish we must first make visible.[3] One area of antiracist work involves interrogating the production and historical specificity of "whiteness" in stories such as Sarah Orne Jewett's "The Foreigner" (1900). My examination of Jewett's narrative assumes, first, that "whiteness" is a fiction; I distinguish between "whiteness" as an imagined category and so-called white people or characters who experience themselves as white through an often unexamined identification with the category of "whiteness." Second, I assume that reading for historically variable constructions of "whiteness" is reading against "race" as a disciplinary concept dependent on a tacit sense of "whiteness" as normal, constant, and bio-logical.

But making "whiteness" visible may not by itself make "race" matter in a conscious way to those for whom "race" has long meant non-"whiteness."[4] What can we do with/about/against the "whiteness" we "uncover"? A partial answer lies in the work Toni Morrison advocates in *Playing in the Dark: Whiteness and the Literary Imagination*.[5] While volumes of literary criticism have sprung up using her "Africanist persona" to explore the imaginative force of slaves and slavery in the work of white American writers, white critics have paid too little attention to her suggestion that we study the "impact of racism on those who perpetuate it" (11).[6] We can begin to assess this impact when we read the work of white writers for evidence of an author's ambivalent, or reluctant, engagement with "whiteness" as a complicated, historically mutable nexus of identifications. We may then identify and publish the weaknesses of "whiteness," the ways in which it fails even those who take its privileges for granted.

Using a strategy that exposes an economy of "race"-linked advantage and disadvantage, historians like David Roediger and Alexander Saxton have described political and economic problems accruing to working-class "whites" whose racial identifications blind them to potentially beneficial coalitions based on other identifications.[7] In some fiction, too, a sense of loss underlies white characters' identifications with "whiteness," as other identifications and values are precluded or displaced to accommodate "whiteness" in the formation of white community. I hasten to add, however, that while "loss" connotes something once possessed, the sense of loss to which I refer is an affective experience in no way dependent on the ontology or ownership of a "lost" thing or quality. Like nostalgia, the sense of loss distorts the object of desire; the craving for wholeness, for example, is not a longing to return to an actual past but rather to a misrecollected imaginary moment of prior wholeness.[8] For reasons of time and space, I do not here explore the ethics of desire, though ethical issues clearly arise. Nonetheless, the *sense* of loss in some literature can be profound.

One goal of antiracist scholarship and pedagogy is to question the inevitability of the historically constructed categories we call "race" and to rethink relationships among social narratives, institutions, and human beings; therefore, discussions of "race" must avoid replicating those relationships. We must disable discourse that dead-ends in "white guilt." As AnnLouise Keating points out, "When self-identified 'white' students feel guilty, they become paralyzed, deny any sense of agency, and assume that their privileged position in contemporary U.S. culture automatically compels them to act as 'the oppressor'" (915). I propose that, if we are to expand the numbers of so-called white people to whom antiracism matters, a full accounting of that "possessive investment" must also consider the cultural and psychic *costs* of "whiteness," some of which become evident when we read literature using "whiteness"-as-loss as an analytical category that offers a marker for "whiteness" and a place where its power is both subverted and reestablished.

Some critics will argue that the search for "whiteness"-as-loss comes from or may lead to self-pity, consolation, or absolution on the part of white liberals eager to avoid responsibility for racism, whether actively or passively manifested. As a "white" woman who benefits from my "possessive investment in whiteness," I recognize the need to avoid slipping into an "isn't it awful to be white" mode that posits white guilt as a righteous burden, a "consciousness of kind"—uncomfortably resonant with the sentimental, paternalist concept of "the white man's burden" much in vogue in various turn-of-the-century religious, academic, legislative, and political power centers.[9] Though "whiteness"-as-loss may defamiliarize "whiteness," it is not a way for "white people" to "get in on the act" as victims of racism (Dyer, 44). Nor will exposing "whiteness"-as-loss directly empower those perceived as nonwhite. I agree with George Lipsitz's call for an examination of the "possessive investment in whiteness" that exposes the insidious methodology and scope of racially organized advantage.[10] I do not deny or minimize the enormous damage which that "investment" inflicts on non-"white" people. Even my phrase "the cultural costs of 'whiteness'" will, with justification, ring hollow for those weary of watching others enjoy the proceeds of "being white." But pointing to fissures in the construction of "whiteness" may expose "whiteness" as a false consciousness that both serves and damages its constituents.[11] At the very least, "whiteness"-as-loss suggests the historicity of "whiteness" and the energy expended to perpetuate white domination. In a reactionary climate where many grow deaf at the mention of racism, we might inspire new interest in antiracism by asking, "How and under what circumstances has 'whiteness' been a problem for so-called white people?"

Implying a sense of loss in the construction of "whiteness," several critics comment that "whiteness" is "precisely the absence of culture" (Roediger, *Toward the Abolition*, 13). Richard Dyer states that "when 'whiteness' *qua* 'whiteness' does come into focus, it is often revealed as emptiness, absence, denial or even a kind of death" (44); similarly, Ann-Louise Keating observes, "[T]he most commonly mentioned attribute of 'whiteness' seems to be its pervasive non-presence" (904). Whiteness, Morrison writes, "is mute, meaningless, unfathomable, pointless, frozen, veiled, curtained, dreaded, senseless, and implacable" (59). Despite the persistent figuring of "whiteness" as a terrible vacancy in U.S. literature, white emptiness or "whiteness"-as-loss is infrequently particularized.[12] If we historicize the sense of loss, spiritual death, cultural impoverishment, and the elision of other differences integral to some literary constructions of "whiteness," we may see, first, how "whiteness" is variously conceived, and, second, that it is sometimes experienced as a problem, not only by African American writers—like Ralph Ellison and James Baldwin, who told whites to look in the mirror for the source of what was once absurdly called the "Negro problem"—but also by turn-of-the-century white writers like Sarah Orne Jewett.

At the end of the nineteenth century, Jewett's white, middle- and upper-class readers were rapidly formulating and reformulating their ideas of race. During the "nationalist nineties," increases in immigration, accelerating imperialist sentiments, and fears caused by economic depression created a xenophobic climate.[13] Like the storm that haunts the telling of "The Foreigner" with the threat of "danger offshore among the outer islands," the rising tide of new immigrants was seen by many nativists as a menace to U.S. jobs and American homogeneity.[14] In this climate "the immigrant population . . . understood their 'Americanness' as an opposition to the resident black population"; aliens were socially, if not politically, naturalized as they demonstrated that they could leave behind anything that rendered them not "white."[15] "The American motto *e pluribus unum*—'Out of many, one'—forget[s] national origins," Alan Trachtenberg argues, "only to the extent that it assumes a state of '*whiteness*'—and a group of historically white states—from which the many were/are constituted as one." This process of "ethnic cultural cleansing" contributed to what Theodore Allen, who writes of the Irish immigrants during this period, calls *The Invention of the White Race.*[16] But, despite the fact that "race" was a widely debated concept in 1900, and despite Jewett's close personal and professional association with anti-immigrationist Thomas Bailey Aldrich, thus far Jewett's ideas of race have received far less attention than have her literary categorizations or her status as a "woman writer."[17]

Long celebrated for its universal, mythic, and transcendent properties, Sarah Orne Jewett's work is seldom seen as "racialized," in part because it so successfully constructs "whiteness" as "human nature," everywhere and nowhere at the same time.[18] However, some of Jewett's writings engage ideas of "race" that ought to complicate the critical reception of Jewett's Edenic community, particularly in "The Foreigner," where "whiteness" is knowable in ambivalent contrast to a nonspeaking, though central character who is *both* French and "American Africanist."[19] The combination is especially interesting in light of Jewett's lifelong pride in her French ancestry and her "American Hellenism," which "implicitly presented American culture as pure [and] worthy of preservation from the taint of alien [African and Semitic] ways" (Zagarell, "*Country*'s Portrayal," 54). Despite what many, including Willa Cather, have called its timeless qualities and despite the volumes of criticism that read Jewett as a regionalist who responds to national conflict by "turning [her] back on it," Jewett's fiction exhibits evidence of the nativist debates that took place during the turbulent era in which it was written.[20]

Jewett was indeed concerned with race, as several of her writings, including *The Story of the Normans* (1887), demonstrate. In this young people's history, which details the Normans' contribution to what Jewett saw as "the inferior race" of Anglo-Saxons, Jewett regrets what she calls the "mingling of the Norman's brighter, more enthusiastic, and visionary nature with the stolid, dogged, prudent, and resolute Anglo-Saxons."[21] Another text explicitly concerned with race, "The War Debt" (1890), describes the journey of an aristocratic young man of Boston who resurrects the dormant nobility of a vanquished Norman family from Virginia. North-South reunion and marriage save the Bellamy family, plagued with the duty to maintain the newly emancipated black men and women whom Jewett describes as "unequal to holding their liberty with steady hands."[22] But "The Foreigner" presents a far more complicated view of race than might be assumed from Jewett's connection with Aldrich or from her earlier writings, including *Pointed Firs*, where, as Zagarell shows, the Bowden family reunion "echo[es] the more genteel advocacy of racial exclusion articulated by members of Jewett's Boston circle."[23] Because the foreign woman embodies at once both Jewett's cherished Frenchness *and* the Africanist blackness she derides in "A War Debt," "The Foreigner" suggests that, in guarding against the taint of "alien ways"—seen as a threat to American "purity" from within and without U.S. borders in 1900—much of value is or could be lost.

To some extent, "The Foreigner" rethinks the implications of white racial solidarity inscribed in *Country of the Pointed Firs*.[24] In the 1896

Pointed Firs, the town of Dunnet Landing is textually constructed as an integral part—and perhaps the main "character"—of what Zagarell usefully identifies as a "narrative of community" that "portray[s] the minute and quite ordinary processes through which the community maintains itself as an entity."[25] And while "The Foreigner"'s frame narrative takes place in a time concurrent with *The Country of the Pointed Firs,* the events that Mrs. Todd describes occur some forty years earlier. Thus "The Foreigner" implies the need to reassess the foundations of *Pointed Firs'* community. "The Foreigner" was neither written nor published together with the *Pointed Firs* sketches that were first serialized in the *Atlantic Monthly.*[26] Nor was "The Foreigner" included when these sketches, together with two previously unpublished Dunnet Landing stories, came out later that year as *The Country of the Pointed Firs.*[27] Therefore some critics reject intertextual interpretations that read "The Foreigner" or any of the other three later Dunnet Landing stories together with the original book.[28] However, the two texts share characters, setting, and narrator, suggesting their common work as portraits of a single time and place; both contribute to the community of *Pointed Firs.*[29] An important Jewett character common to *Pointed Firs* and "The Foreigner" is Mrs. Almira Todd, who serves as the center of what Elizabeth Ammons calls Jewett's "female geography" and who practices herbal medicine. But in "The Foreigner" Mrs. Todd remaps this geography with the startling revelation that she gained her knowledge of plants through the "foreigner," who does not appear in *Pointed Firs.*

"The Foreigner" is a framed tale written by the same unnamed narrator, a visitor to Dunnet Landing, who writes *The Country of the Pointed Firs* during a summer's respite from the city. One stormy night in late August, as the narrator sits in the room she rents from Mrs. Todd, the latter comes in to confess her fear for the safety of her mother, the angelic Mrs. Blackett, who lives offshore on Green Island. To calm herself, Mrs. Todd tells the story of a "foreigner" whom she knew some forty years before. The narrative is structured as three loops or passes over the foreign woman's history. Conversation and comments about the storm frequently interrupt the story of past events. When Captain Tolland from Dunnet Landing is in Kingston, Jamaica, to load sugar, he finds the woman, whose "Portugee" husband and children have died of yellow fever. The foreigner, who lives almost her whole life in the West Indies, is described as "dark," of a "foreign cast," and "strange looking." The captain brings her back to Dunnet Landing, marries her, and leaves her behind when he returns to sea. Trying unsuccessfully to make friends in Dunnet Landing, Mrs. Tolland attends a church function where she sings and dances. The townspeople at first join in the music with pleasure, but the next day they feel outraged by what they have since decided was the foreign woman's indecent display. She retreats to her house; her only visitors are Mrs. Todd and Mrs. Todd's mother, Mrs. Blackett.

Their awkward friendship constitutes the story's second loop. Mrs. Todd admits that Mrs. Tolland was the source of much of the vital knowledge of plants and herbal medicine that augment Mrs. Todd's subsequent income and for which she is so valued in *The Country of the Pointed Firs.* When Captain Tolland dies at sea, Mrs. Tolland dies too, apparently of grief and loneliness. Later Mrs. Todd learns that, in addition to the knowledge she has inherited as Mrs. Tolland's protégé, she is the dead woman's only heir; she inherits Mrs. Tolland's home, her belongings, her flowers, and her money. Mrs. Todd's uncle, Captain Bowden, accidentally burns down Mrs. Tolland's house one night while searching by lantern light for the gold he believes remains hidden there. The third loop reveals that, on Mrs. Tolland's deathbed, she and Mrs. Todd see the ghost of the dying woman's mother. The storm of the frame narrative abates as this final part of the story reassures both Mrs. Todd and her auditor, "The Foreigner's" narrator, of an eternal connection with one's mother and with a feminine universal that persists beyond death.

The text explicitly states that Mrs. Tolland is French—she speaks French, she teaches Mrs. Todd to cook "like a child o' France," and she gives Mrs. Todd a memento of French imperialism, a French print of the "statue of the Empress Josephine in the Savanne at old Fort Royal in Martinique" (182). But her *arrival in* and her *exclusion from* the Dunnet Landing community are both directly tied to elements of her story that evoke the "Africanist persona" described by Morrison. While Mrs. Todd describes the extent of Mrs. Tolland's otherness, saying, "she come a foreigner and she went a foreigner, and never was anything but a stranger among our folks" (170), Mrs. Tolland's difference suggests "American Africanism"; the history of Mrs. Tolland's life in and rescue from Jamaica connects her with accounts of African slaves in the U.S. and in the Caribbean. The four ship captains from Dunnet Landing, themselves "three sheets to the wind," find her singing, playing her guitar, and dancing in a bar where white patrons are attended by "colored folks" (162). Later the four Dunnet men hear her "screech, an' they [see] a white dress come runnin' out through the bushes, an' tumbled over each other in their haste to offer help" (163). Mrs. Tolland apparently flees the sexual advances of the other white men from the bar only to encounter the four men from Dunnet Landing, whose own "haste" implies pursuit, if not sexual aggression. In the ensuing scene, evocative of narratives of slave capture and escape, the four sea captains from Dunnet Landing literally harbor the fugitive when they secret her "down to the wharves" (163). Before stepping onto the pier, "they [stop] in the street then and there an' dr[aw] lots who should take her aboard" (164). The first order of business, determining who will possess the woman, takes place in a lottery on the street before the ships depart Jamaica for the U.S. Like the African slave women that her history seems calculated to evoke, the "strange-looking" woman of the "foreign cast" is removed from her homeland, isolated from her family, stripped of her resources, subjected to sexual assault and humiliation, pursued, captured, "auctioned off," and shipped overseas.

The characterization of Mrs. Tolland also suggests Africanism. The rematerialization of Mrs. Tolland's dead mother connects both women with Jamaican obeah and with the spiritualism in which Jewett believed, which traced some of its ideas to West African roots.[30] Mrs. Todd observes, "[Mrs. Tolland would] act awful secret about some things too, an' used to work charms for herself sometimes, an' some o' the neighbors told to and fro' after she died that they knew enough not to provoke her" (170). Mrs. Tolland's ability to work charms, her too-free singing and dancing, and her strange looks raise suspicion among Dunnet Landing's white residents. When she sings "a gay tune" and "keeps time" drumming with her fingers on a Washington pie tin "like one o' them tambourines," the congregation decides that the woman "didn't have no sense but foreign sense" (179). Her difference from the people of Dunnet Landing results in her isolation and, when Captain Tolland dies, her isolation apparently causes her death.

While much is gained from the Jamaican woman, losses occur as a consequence of excluding her from the community. The losses fall into two categories: first, the town loses sight of its own values, and, second, it misses the opportunity to learn from the stranger. The failure to extend to Mrs. Tolland the hospitality that Jewett's fiction consistently endorses manifests itself as a kind of sin, a separation between values and behaviors that constitutes dis-integration. One might, for instance, connect the storm in which Mrs. Todd fears separation from her mother as a meteorological manifestation of Mrs. Tolland's exile, which abates only when Mrs. Todd recalls the nonwhite woman. This first area of loss or dis-integration is visible in part through Mrs. Todd's anxiety about the way that Dunnet Landing ostracized Mrs. Tolland. In a discursive paradigm similar to the script Susan Stanford Friedman calls a "narrative of confession," Mrs. Todd accuses herself of failing to establish sisterhood with the foreigner—a sisterhood that their similar circumstances, as the childless wives and then widows of seamen, ought to have compelled according to the terms of Jewett's matriarchal doctrine.

The foreign woman's reception in Dunnet Landing points to a gap between the spontaneity and openness to friendship valorized by Jewett and the cool New England rationality that literally closes a door on Mrs. Tolland. When Mrs. Tolland dances in the vestry, the townspeople join in an apparently natural response to the woman, who is "just as light and pleasant as a child" (167). "We all got to trottin' a foot, an' some o' the men clapped their hands quite loud, a-keepin' time, 'twas so catchin', an' seemed so natural to her" (167). But in the "sober" light of the following day, "there was an awful scandal goin' in the parish" (167). The woman leading the attack against the foreigner is Mari' Harris, described in *Pointed Firs* as looking like a "Chinee"; in effect the person most vigilant about maintaining the purity of the "Orthodox vestry" is the only character whose "whiteness" is suspect. Because Mari' Harris is known to readers of *Pointed Firs* as an unlikable character, Jewett's decision to use her as the warden who safeguards "whiteness" calls into question the action of safeguarding as well as the value and the "purity" of the "whiteness" she protects. But the extent to which Mari' Harris represents the rest of the town is suggested in three ways: first, Mrs. Tolland is at least indirectly chastised by "some o' the pastor's remarks" on the following Sunday; second, the rest of the congregation apparently joins in ostracizing Mrs. Tolland; and, third, Mrs. Todd's response to Mari' Harris is tempered by her knowledge that she will have to encounter Mari' again and again since both are members of the church. Eliza Tolland, sister to Mrs. Tolland's husband, helps to raise a "sight o' prejudice" against the foreigner as well (166). Even more damning is the townspeople's misreading of Mrs. Tolland's exit from the church: Mrs. Todd tells the narrator, "I wished she stayed [in church] . . . but she kind o' declared war, at least folks thought so, an war 'twas from that time. I see she was cryin' as she passed by me; perhaps bein' in meetin' was what had the power to make her feel homesick and strange" (167). In the terms of sentimental literature generally and in Jewett's own explicit code, Mrs. Tolland's tears call for connection with the other persons present—later Mrs. Tolland's tears do signal to and create a bond with Mrs. Todd (170)—particularly as Mrs. Todd recognizes that Mrs. Tolland's tears arise as a result of the foreigner's isolation from community.

To interpret Mrs. Tolland's desire for connection as a declaration of war perverts the most fundamental tenets of Jewett's neighborliness. The implied condemnation of the congregation is even more apparent in light of Jewett's belief in spiritualism and Swedenborg's teachings and her rejection of the Calvinist orthodoxy in which she was brought up. The kindness, intuition, hospitality, and sisterhood that characterize what Ammons and Josephine Donovan call Jewett's "woman's religion" are all repressed in order to preserve Dunnet Landing "from the taint of alien [African and Semitic] ways" (Zagarell, "*Country*'s Portrayal," 54). Mrs. Blackett—a virtual deity in *Pointed Firs* who epitomizes Jewett's canon of warmth, hospitality, and empathy—expresses what seems Jewett's own disapproval for the community's callousness when she shames her daughter Mrs. Todd by telling her, "Think if 'twas you in a foreign land!" (169). The exercise of rational control and the failure to extend hospitality, both linked to "whiteness," constitute the two most important elements of the dis-integration that "The Foreigner" laments.

The second area of loss, also associated with Dunnet Landing's assertion of white rationality, involves the failure to appreciate or emulate the values that Mrs. Tolland embodies. One of the values that Jewett endorsed and Mrs. Tolland typifies is childlikeness. Though Jewett's fiction is noted for its lack of young children, Jewett herself commented that she always thought of herself as "nine years old." She cherished the childlike qualities, "naiveté, innocence, and . . . vulnerability" with which Mrs. Tolland is consistently associated in "The Foreigner." By contrast, in "The Foreigner," Dunnet Landing seems comprised of "conservative, provincial . . . serious-minded adults, many of whom demonstrate little tender-hearted understanding [or] patient tolerance of . . . uninhibited display[s] of emotional feeling."[31] The Yankee culture that Jewett describes prizes sobriety, "ingenuity, pragmatism . . . and cautiousness" (Ammons, "Material Culture," 84). The dichotomy between these characterizations seems to echo the contrast delineated in Jewett's *Story of the Normans*, where Jewett prefers the "Norman's brighter, more enthusiastic, and visionary nature [to] the stolid, dogged, prudent, and resolute Anglo-Saxons" (364). While the Bowden family reunion scene in *The Country of the Pointed Firs* identifies that family as Norman, "The Foreigner" suggests that not all of Dunnet Landing exhibits those qualities that Jewett associates with the Normans; in fact, the resonance between the two sets of contrast—Mrs. Tolland's "child-like brightness" versus Dunnet Landing's "resolute" intolerance in "The Foreigner" and the Normans' versus the Saxons' qualities in *The Story of the Normans*—suggests an ambivalence about the way that "whiteness" (and/or "Americanness") became more closely linked with Anglo-Saxon than with Anglo-Norman "races" during this period. The implication in "The Foreigner" is that the exclusion of difference construed as "Africanist" simultaneously divests "whiteness" of the Norman influence Jewett held dear. In "The Foreigner," anti-African sentiments appear to have pushed white purists too far when Anglo-Saxonism and "whiteness" become synonymous.

The story suggests that Mrs. Todd, the narrator, and the reader might have learned a great deal more from Mrs. Tolland if Dunnet Landing had embraced rather than feared Mrs. Tolland's difference. Beyond the inscription of displaced values, the tale implies that knowledge of an "other world" is lost to the community as a consequence of excluding and forgetting the foreign woman. The end of international shipping to and from Maine had meant the loss of contact with places like Kingston and Tobago. In *Pointed Firs*, Jewett makes frequent mention of "curiosities" from "exotic" ports around the world, and, implicitly, she laments the increasing provincialism that characterized Maine after shipping died. But the real deprivation is diminished imaginative capital. Mrs. Todd tells the narrator that Mrs. Tolland "made me imagine new things, and I got interested watchin' her and findin' out what she had to say, but you couldn't get to no affectionateness with her. . . . I never give her a kiss till the day she laid in her coffin and it come to me there wa'n't no one else to do it" (172).

Lost imaginative capital is also signified by the destruction of Mrs. Todd's possessions. In Jewett's "material culture," "things" become texts. Objects await the myth(s) with which the storyteller will "fill them."[32] But objects remain haunted by the histories they can never tell when the objects are absent or destroyed or when those who love them die. The point is made in "The Foreigner" where the wind strikes Mrs. Tolland's guitar as she lays dying "and set[s] it swinging by the blue ribbon, . . . soundin' as if somebody begun to play it" (184). When she dies, the guitar is destroyed, silent. Mrs. Tolland's house suffers as well; its fate gestures at a conflict of values between storytelling objects and the Yankee thrift that, in this case, literally snuffs out that which it cannot take to the bank. Houses constitute the richest and most important of Jewett's material texts: Ammons refers to Jewett's fictional houses as "spiritual places, virtually shrines" ("Material Culture," 87). But on the night of Mrs. Tolland's funeral, Captain Bowden, the executor of her will, ransacks the house looking for a chest of gold. The "terrible sign o' dust" he raises condemns his search as an assault on Mrs. Tolland's tidy home. Mrs. Todd realizes a "real good lift" from the sale of some furniture, but Captain Bowden continues to tear apart the house: "He used to go up there all alone and search, and dig in the cellar, empty and bleak as 'twas in winter weather" until one night his lantern sets the house ablaze and Mrs. Tolland's home burns to the cellar (181). As a Bowden, as one of the most respected townsmen, as a man who understands wills and contracts, and as a retired navigator, Captain Bowden embodies the white community's ideal male citizen. His lack of regard for what Jewett suggests is the real value of Mrs. Tolland's legacy connotes a "bleak" gendered and racialized view of the world that leads him to destroy the home and garden Mrs. Tolland tended with love. The dead woman's flowers, however, continue to bloom in the door garden for years after she dies, reminding Mrs. Todd of Mrs. Tolland's beauty and her absence. Mrs. Todd is better able to appreciate and nurture the foreigner's legacy than is Captain Bowden; she *transplants* and thus saves some of the dead woman's perennials. But the death of the foreigner herself suggests that much is lost that cannot be "transplanted" or translated.

The loss of the foreigner, who "had so much information that other folks hadn't," demonstrates the limits of the feminine universal that so much of Jewett's fiction takes for granted (542). Mrs. Todd's fictional encounter with racial difference problematizes the ease with which the speaker and/or author can access—or make accessible—the woman's "way of knowing," which serves as a common denominator in the Jewett works that remain unconscious of their "whiteness." Mrs. Todd's machinations in the telling of the tale and her need to control the foreign woman's history complicate Jewett's customary use of gender codes; the act of recolonizing the matrifocal world exposes the racialization of that world while it positions Mrs. Todd as a conqueror. In the first two rehearsals of Mrs. Tolland's tale, Mrs. Todd skims over details that we discover are critical to the real import of the story. And when she reports on Mrs. Tolland's rescue in Kingston, she repeatedly downplays the captains' intoxication and their purpose in being at the bar, saying that "whatever they might lack o' prudence they more'n made up with charity" (164). Her handling of the story exhibits her need for control and her sympathy with the white men of Dunnet.

The power that Mrs. Todd wields allows her for forty years to "forget" the story of the foreign woman and to rematerialize Mrs. Tolland at will when she feels the need; Mrs. Todd's control is further emphasized by the fact that Mrs. Tolland says almost nothing in the text, a notable silence in Jewett's work, where the will and capacity to communicate empowers even dead women like Miss Tempy in "Miss Tempy's Watchers" (1888). While Mrs. Todd repeats apparently verbatim the remarks *about* the foreigner made by Dunnet Landing's white residents, the foreign woman's own speech is lost in the recitation, which privileges rationality and control over intimate contact. In this sense, Mrs. Todd's handling of the story suggests what Ammons calls an "ultramasculine Western way of knowing . . . preoccupied with . . . conquest" despite the weblike narrative structure that Ammons and others have venerated as a distinctly feminine way of telling.[33]

And if Mrs. Todd's narrative indicts Dunnet Landing for its failure to extend community to Mrs. Tolland, it is important to note that the religious congregation is not the only white community under construction in the story. Both *Pointed Firs* and "The Foreigner" construct community in two other ways: Community describes the cross-class relationship between the "local" Mrs. Todd and the unnamed narrator, as well as the relationship between the narrator and the urban, female leisure-class readers whom she teaches to "make friends with her characters."[34] Mrs. Todd's recollection of the ghost of the dark woman cements the relationship between the two white women in ways that resonate with the highly problematic white sisterhood in and around abolition writings like Stowe's, which Jewett valued so much.[35] In effect, the immigrant is sacrificed, not just to restore the harmony of Dunnet Landing or to effect a bond of community between Mrs. Todd and her listener(s), but also to perpetuate or resurrect a mythical American sorority of the past.

Yet to some extent "The Foreigner" deconstructs its own mythology; it raises "whiteness" and white exclusivity as an impediment to the eternal, maternal connectedness her readers cherished—epitomized by Green Island, where, Mrs. Todd tells us, nothing ever happened and nothing changed "since the world began" (158). In fact, as Mrs. Todd reminds the narrator that the foreigner was not welcome in Dunnet Landing, the branches outside the close circle formed by the two women scratch against the window like some poor "distressed creature trying to get in," just as they did on the night Mrs. Tolland died (168, 176). The language echoes that used to describe the foreigner whom Mrs. Todd repeatedly calls the "poor creature" or "poor distressed creature"; this echo implies that the foreigner represents a "branch" of this sisterhood that remains outside. "Who was Mrs. Captain Tolland?" the narrator asks, and Mrs. Todd answers, "I never knew her maiden name; If I ever heard it, I've gone an' forgot; 'twould mean nothing to me" (161). As Mrs. Todd says, Mrs. Tolland "come a foreigner, and she went a foreigner, and never was anything but a stranger among our folks" (170).

Mrs. Todd's rare inability to identify either the first name or the maiden name of a woman living in Jewett's matrifocal world illustrates Mrs. Tolland's marginality as much as or more than any other single piece of information.[36] In stark contrast to the histories of the other women with whom Mrs. Todd is acquainted, the foreigner's maternal line remains a mystery. While the "dark" women of the story—Mrs. Tolland and her mother—"naturally" possess reassuring knowledge of and access to an other world, the white women can access this knowledge only momentarily, only through the example of the other, and only after several tries. Though Mrs. Todd gains her most valuable knowledge from the "dark" woman, the tale suggests that Mrs. Tolland might have taught Mrs. Todd more but for her isolation and her premature death, both of which are linked with the white townspeople's perception of Mrs. Tolland's racialized difference from themselves. Despite the obvious racism implied in the dark woman's uninhibited dancing and her knowledge of the occult, and despite the story's concept of inclusion, which means speaking *for* the other, "The Foreigner" implies that white women distance themselves from the matriarchal ideal, "Green Island," when and if they fail to include and learn from their "dark sisters."

To say the story remains "haunted" by the dark specters of Mrs. Tolland and her mother is simply to state the obvious; the unnamed narrator asks for and hears a ghost story. But the story doesn't quite overturn the reader's expectation that ghost stories must be frightening, for while the foreigner's death assures Mrs. Todd and the narrator that "the doors stand wide open" between life and "the other world," the story's last two paragraphs sound another note. As the narrator comments on the "far complaining fog horn of a steamer up the Bay," Mrs. Todd remarks, "I do hate to hear the poor steamers callin' when they're bewildered in thick nights in winter, comin' on the coast" (187). The story's conclusion exemplifies Morrison's argument that "figurations of impenetrable whiteness . . . surface in American literature whenever an Africanist presence is engaged. These closed white images are frequently found at the end of the narrative" (33). Bewildered in the white fog as they approach the land, like strangers approaching a new territory or "white" citizens struggling to situate themselves in "whiteness," the ships lose their way.

While "The Foreigner's" expression of loss admits to a racist view of the other, it also implies a more complex understanding of "race" than is registered in Jewett's earlier writing. Moreover, "whiteness"-as-loss offers a way to consider what "whiteness" means to a particular writer in a specific historical context. This approach might prove useful in the analysis of current constructions of "whiteness" as well.[37] Examining the changing meanings of "whiteness" and looking at the places where "whiteness" connotes vulnerability, insufficiency, and loss may suggest new ways to discuss "race," new ways to forge alliances, and new ways to address bell hooks's question: "[W]hat's going on with whiteness?" (54).

Notes

1. Henry Louis Gates, Jr., *"Race," Writing, and Difference* (Chicago: University of Chicago Press, 1986).

2. AnnLouise Keating makes the argument that "theorists who attempt to deconstruct 'race' often inadvertently reconstruct it by reinforcing the belief in permanent, separate racial categories . . . their continual analysis of racialized

identities undercuts their belief that 'race' is a constantly changing sociohistorical concept, not a biological fact." Keating, "Interrogating 'Whiteness', (De)Constructing 'Race'," *College English* 57 (1995): 902.

3. In 1990, bell hooks commented on the need for a "discourse on race that interrogates whiteness. It would just be so interesting," she said, "for all those white folks who are giving blacks their take on blackness to let them know what's going on with whiteness" (*Yearning: Race, Gender, and Cultural Politics* [Boston: South End Press, 1990], 54). In *Yearning*, hooks quotes Coco Fusco as saying, "To ignore white ethnicity is to redouble its hegemony by naturalizing it" (171). David Roediger focuses on labor history in *The Wages of Whiteness: Race and the Making of the American Working Class* (London: Verso, 1991). A second Roediger book, *Toward the Abolition of Whiteness: Essays on Race, Politics, and Working Class History* (London: Verso, 1994), offers what Roediger calls "a survey of what we do not know" about the "interplay of racial and ethnic consciousness among whites in the US" (184). Ruth Frankenberg studies racial consciousness by interviewing women of various socioeconomic, politic, geographic, and sexual orientations who identify as "white" (*White Women, Race Matters: The Social Construction of Whiteness* [Minneapolis: University of Minnesota Press, 1993]). Kobena Mercer's "Skin Head Sex Thing: Racial Difference and the Homoerotic Imaginary," in his *How Do I Look: Queer Film and Video* (Seattle: Bay Press, 1991), examines the racialized gaze. For a recent review of work on whiteness from the perspective of an American Studies scholar, see Shelly Fisher Fishkin, "Interrogating 'Whiteness', Complicating 'Blackness': Remapping American Culture," *American Quarterly* 47 (1995): 428–38. For a bibliography of work related to whiteness (and to "race" generally), see Susan Stanford Friedman, "Beyond White and Other: Relationality and Narratives of Race in Feminist Discourse," *Signs* 21 (1995): 1–49.

4. This essay owes much to Carolyn Allen and Judy Howard, whose *Signs* seminar (University of Washington, Winter 1996) raised the question, "How do you get people to invest in antiracism?"

5. Morrison points to an "Africanist persona," represented as "a haunting," a "darkness," or a "black presence," which is "central to any understanding of our national literature and which should not be permitted to hover at the margins of the literary imagination" (33, 5). Morrison argues that the "fabrication of this Africanist persona is reflexive; an extraordinary meditation on the self; a powerful exploration of the fears and desires that reside in the writerly conscious" (17); she advocates critical attention to the question of how white-authored texts both reflect and enact definitions of "whiteness" as against or in complex relation to this fictional "Africanist presence" (*Playing in the Dark: Whiteness and the Literary Imagination* [New York: Random House, 1992]).

6. Though my focus here is on "whiteness," I do not suggest that racism is an issue exclusive to "black"/"white" histories. For an excellent analysis of other, not necessarily binary, racial narratives—Korean American/African American/

Latino, for example—see Susan Stanford Friedman, who points to the multiracial conflicts that erupted in Los Angeles in April 1992 after four white Los Angeles police officers were acquitted in the beating of Rodney King ("Beyond White and Other").

7. Roediger, *The Wages of Whiteness* and *Toward the Abolition of Whiteness;* Alexander Saxton, *The Rise and Fall of the White Republic: Class Politics and Mass Culture in Nineteenth-Century America* (London: Verso, 1990).

8. Roediger points out, "Historically, the use of an (often distorted) image of African American life to express criticisms of 'white culture', or longings for a different way of life, has hardly been an antidote to racism" (*Toward the Abolition of Whiteness,* 16). I suggest, however, that we need synchronic and diachronic studies that reveal the changing shape of the anxiety and the envy behind this usage in the construction of "whiteness."

9. Richard Dyer warns against the "isn't it awful to be white" mode in "White," *Screen* 29 (1988): 44–45. Subsequent references are cited in the text. "The white man's burden" was the subject of the chaplain's address to the 1900 Montgomery (Alabama) Race Conference, and the phrase "consciousness of kind" was coined by Franklin Henry Giddings, a turn-of-the-century sociologist whose *Theory of Socialization* (1897) included a graph detailing the declining degrees of sympathy or "fellow feeling" experienced by native-born whites when encountering first, white immigrants and then, people of color (George M. Fredrickson, *The Black Image in the White Mind: The Debate on Afro-American Character and Destiny, 1817–1914* [Hanover, N.H.: University Press of New England, 1987], 316). Though I cannot explore the idea in depth here, clearly the sense of a righteous burden, frequently attached to white guilt, endorses white supremacy.

10. George Lipsitz, "The Possessive Investment in Whiteness: Racialized Social Democracy and the 'White' Problem in American Studies," *American Quarterly* 47 (1995): 369–87. Cheryl I. Harris explores the value of white skin, arguing that "whiteness" is perpetuated as a legally protected "property" in U.S. law ("Whiteness as Property," *Harvard Law Review* 106 [1993]: 1707–91). See also Gayatri Chakrovorty Spivak, *In Other Worlds: Essays in Cultural Politics* (New York: Routledge, 1988); Ann du Cille, "The Occult of True Black Womanhood: Critical Demeanor and Black Feminist Studies," *Signs* 19 (1994): 591–629; and Harryette Mullen, "Optic White: Blackness and the Production of Whiteness," *Diacritics* 24 (1994): 71–89. As the title of Mullen's excellent essay suggests, Ralph Ellison's *Invisible Man* criticized "whiteness" as property long before the current wave of scholarship.

11. I do not advocate an appeal to white pride, which has operated as anything but a "purely" positive power in U.S. history. Nor do I suggest that so-called "white" antiracists indulge in a discourse of white "shame"; since guilt is other-directed, the victim toward whom one feels guilty is too easily figured as the "problem." I would argue, in fact, that what Susan Stanford Friedman calls

the "narrative of confession" cycles back to the "narrative of denial" at precisely that moment when victims of racism begin to look like the "problem." See Friedman, "Beyond White and Other." Current attacks on affirmative action, epitomizing this turn from "confession" to "denial" on a national scale, often couch Equal Employment Opportunity Commission programs in terms of whites' generosity toward blacks: equal opportunity is recast as white altruism.

12. The white whale of Melville's *Moby Dick* and the white wasteland in Poe's *The Narrative of Arthur Gordon Pym* come to mind as texts whose "whiteness" has been historicized. *Pym* is the subject of "Romancing the Shadow," chapter 2 in Morrison's *Playing in the Dark.*

13. See John Higham, *Strangers in the Land: Patterns of American Nativism, 1860–1925* (New Brunswick: Rutgers University Press, 1988).

14. Sarah Orne Jewett, "The Foreigner," in *The Country of the Pointed Firs and Other Stories* (New York: Norton, 1981), 157. Further references are cited in the text.

15. Morrison, *Playing in the Dark*, 47. This point is reiterated by many, including Cornel West (*Race Matters* [Boston: Beacon Press, 1993]) and John Higham (*Strangers in the Land*).

16. Alan Trachtenberg, "Conceivable Aliens," *Yale Review* 82.4 (October 1994): 42–65. Theodore Allen, *The Invention of the White Race* (London: Verso, 1994).

17. Recently, excellent works by Sandra A. Zagarell and Elizabeth Ammons, to which I am much indebted, read Jewett's world of women in *The Country of the Pointed Firs* as a metaphor for nationhood. See Ammons's "Material Culture, Empire, and Jewett's *Country of the Pointed Firs*" (81–91) and Zagarell's "*Country*'s Portrayal of Community and the Exclusion of Difference" (39–60), both in *New Essays on "The Country of the Pointed Firs,"* ed. June Howard (New York: Cambridge University Press, 1994). Other work that looks at "race" in Jewett's writing includes a brief 1957 article by Ferman Bishop, "Sarah Orne Jewett's Ideas of Race," *New England Quarterly* 30 (1957): 243–49; Howard's introduction to her collection; and Karen [Kilcup] Oakes's "'Colossal in Sheet-Lead': The Native American and Piscataqua-Region Writers," in *"A Noble and Dignified Stream": The Piscataqua Region in the Colonial Revival, 1860–1930*, ed. Sarah M. Giffen and Kevin M. Murphy (York, Maine: Old York Historical Society, 1992), 165–76. Joseph Church offers a useful discussion of Jewett's family connections with the slave trade in "Fathers, Daughters, Slaves: The Haunted Scene of Writing in Jewett's 'In Dark New England Days'," *American Transcendental Quarterly* 5 (1991): 205–24. As Church shows, the town of South Berwick, Maine, where Theodora Sarah Orne Jewett was born in 1849 and where she spent much of her life, depended for its economic life on shipping until the Jefferson Embargo. Theodore Furber Jewett, the grandfather for whom Jewett was named—and whose money largely supported Jewett throughout her life—owed his "sizable fortune to the 'flourishing West Indies trade of his time'"

(Church, 218). Curiously, however, Church's psychoanalytic reading of "The Foreigner" makes no mention of race. See his *Transcendent Daughters in Jewett's Country of the Pointed Firs* (Rutherford, N.J.: Fairleigh Dickinson University Press, 1994).

18. Keating, "Interrogating 'Whiteness'," 904. Richard Cary venerates what he calls "the universal grain [in Jewett] that underlies the veneer" of "thin particularization" (*Sarah Orne Jewett* [New York: Twayne, 1962], 27).

19. As Morrison uses it, her term "American Africanism" does not signal knowledge about Africa, "nor does it suggest the varieties and complexities of African people . . . rather [it is] a term for the denotative and connotative blackness that African peoples have come to signify, as well as the entire range of views, assumptions, readings, and misreadings that accompany Eurocentric learning about these people" (6–7). Keating points out, as have others, the near-impossibility of theorizing textual whiteness by any method except "a relational approach where 'whiteness' is examined in the context of 'blackness' or other non-'white' racialized categories" ("Interrogating 'Whiteness'," 905).

20. For example, Susan Gillman objects to the critical disconnection of Jewett's writing from national conflicts in "Regionalism and Nationalism in Jewett's *Country of the Pointed Firs*," in *New Essays*, ed. Howard, 101–17.

21. Sarah Orne Jewett, *The Story of the Normans; Told Chiefly in Relation to Their Conquest of England* (London: T. Fisher Unwin, 1887), 364.

22. Sarah Orne Jewett, "A War Debt," in *The Life of Nancy* (Boston: Houghton Mifflin, 1895), 73.

23. Zagarell, "*Country*'s Portrayal," 47. Zagarell notes that Thomas Bailey Aldrich wrote an 1892 poem, "Unguarded Gates," that asks the "white Goddess" of liberty whether she ought "to leave the gates unguarded" (Zagarell, 41).

24. The Bowden family reunion in *The Country of the Pointed Firs* smacks of what Ammons calls "clear protofacis[m]." Ammons points to "all those white people marching around in military formation ritualistically affirming their racial purity, global dominance, and white ethnic superiority and solidarity" (Ammons, "Material Culture," 97).

25. Sandra Zagarell, "Narrative of Community: The Identification of a Genre," *Signs* 13 (1988): 498–527. The events described three times over in "The Foreigner" take us back to a point prior to the beginning of *Pointed Firs*, which compels a reading of that story as a "narrative of community" according to theorists of literary structure, some of whom argue for an irrevocable link between historiography and narrativity. This link is particularly evident, says Paul Ricoeur, when a community, real or fictional, secures itself via the repetition of its "founding moments." Ricoeur, "Narrative Time," in *On Narrative*, ed. W. J. T. Mitchell (Chicago: University of Chicago Press, 1980), 165–86, 185.

26. The two stories added when *Pointed Firs* was published as a book were "Along Shore" and "The Backward View." The four stories written after this publication, which all treat the same characters and places, are "The Foreigner,"

"The Queen's Twin," "A Dunnet Shepherdess," and "William's Wedding." All are included in *The Country of the Pointed Firs and Other Stories* (Norton, 1981).

27. After its debut in the *Atlantic* in August 1900, "The Foreigner" was not reprinted until 1962; thus a further critical disconnection from *Pointed Firs* occurred. David Bonnell Green republished the story as part of a collection he edited entitled *The World of Dunnet Landing* (Lincoln: University of Nebraska Press, 1962). I am indebted for this information to Marjorie Pryse's "'Women at Sea': Feminist Realism in Sarah Orne Jewett's 'The Foreigner'," in *Critical Essays on Sarah Orne Jewett*, ed. Gwen L. Nagel (Boston: G. K. Hall, 1984), 98n. 1.

28. Exceptions to this critical "segregation" include Sandra A. Zagarell's "*Country*'s Portrayal," and Joseph Church's *Transcendent Daughters.*

29. I would also argue that, while a more conventional, linear, plotted novel would preclude reading "sequels" or "prequels" as part of the whole, the weblike narrative structure of the "sketches" that constitute *Country of the Pointed Firs,* which Elizabeth Ammons calls a "female geography" in her essay "Going in Circles: The Female Geography of Jewett's *Country of the Pointed Firs*" (*Studies in the Literary Imagination* 16 [1983]: 83–92), invites intertextual interpretation. The debate about whether or not to include "The Foreigner" when we analyze *Pointed Firs* foregrounds the issues of exclusion and boundary, suggesting the need for further study of Jewett's genre in its historical context.

30. Spiritualism was a popular movement in the nineteenth century, and Jewett was known to have participated in more than one séance. On several occasions she visited mediums after the death of those to whom she felt particularly close. The most fundamental principles of spiritualism held that one could communicate with the dead, consciousness persisted beyond life, and departed ancestors continued to care for and influence the living. Paula Blanchard, Richard Cary, and Elizabeth Ammons mention Jewett's spiritualism. Blanchard writes that Jewett was "convinced that her father was still present in her life, taking an active interest in everything she did" (*Sarah Orne Jewett: Her World and Her Work* [Reading, Mass.: Addison Wesley, 1994], 121). Elizabeth Ammons's essay "Jewett's Witches" (in *Critical Essays on Sarah Orne Jewett*, ed. Nagel, 165–83) notes that Jewett sent John Greenleaf Whittier a "fourteen-page letter about" a séance she attended. Ammons adds, "Certainly Jewett considered extrasensory communication possible between the living and the dead" (166).

For information on spiritualism and a brief mention of its connections with West African religions, see Ann Braude, *Radical Spirits: Spiritualism and Women's Rights in Nineteenth-Century America* (Boston: Beacon Press, 1989). See also Jon Butler, "The Dark Ages in American Occultism, 1760–1848," in *The Occult in America: New Historical Perspectives*, ed. Howard Kerr and Charles L. Crow (Urbana: University of Illinois Press, 1983), and George Brandon's essay in *Africanisms in American Culture*, ed. Joseph E. Holloway (Bloomington: Indiana University Press, 1991), 119–47, which explores the relationships in the Caribbean among Yoruba religions (such as *orisha*), Kardecan spiritism (which originated in France in the nineteenth century), Cuban *santeria*, and Jamaican *obeah*.

31. Edward J. Piacentino, "Local Color and Beyond: The Artistic Dimension of Sarah Orne Jewett's 'The Foreigner'," *Colby Library Quarterly* 21.2 (1985): 96–97.

32. I use the term "myth" as Roland Barthes describes it in *Mythologies* (trans. Annette Lavers [New York: Noonday Press, 1993]). Barthes writes that "*myth is depoliticized speech*," where political is understood to describe "the whole of human relations in their real social structure, in their power of making the world" (143).

33. The first phrase comes from Ammons's "Material Culture." Ammons describes Jewett's narrative structure as a feminine way of telling, as compared to the linearly plotted tale offered by Captain Littlepage in *The Country of the Pointed Firs* in "Going in Circles." Perhaps not coincidentally, Captain Littlepage's story describes a voyage in the fog (something like Pym's) that leads to a "waiting place between this world and the next," filled with "blowing grey figures" and frightened men "white as ashes," where whiteness connotes nothingness, a suspension between life and death (*Country of the Pointed Firs*, 27). One might conjecture that this narrative within *Pointed Firs* seems to anticipate "The Foreigner," in which, by contrast with Littlepage's experience of "frozen towns beyond the boundaries of human warmth" (Ammons, "Material Culture," 91), the narrator and Mrs. Todd learn through the example of the "dark" woman that "there's somethin' beyond this world; the doors stand wide open," and one need not feel "strange an' lonesome" after death ("The Foreigner," 187, 186).

34. The latter phrase comes from Marjorie Pryse's "Archives of Female Friendship and the 'Way' Jewett Wrote," *New England Quarterly* 66 (1993): 47–66, 48. The same point is made by Sarah Way Sherman in *Sarah Orne Jewett: An American Persephone* (Hanover: University Press of New England, 1988), 251. On the class to which Jewett's readers belonged, see Richard H. Brodhead, "Jewett, Regionalism, and Writing as Women's Work," chapter 5 in *Cultures of Letters: Scenes of Reading and Writing in Nineteenth-Century America* (Chicago: University of Chicago Press, 1993), 142–76.

35. The friendship between Mrs. Todd and Mrs. Tolland also exhibits the white woman's control. Extrapolating from Leslie Fiedler's models of interracial male friendships in *Love and Death in the American Novel* and *Return of the Vanishing American*, Elizabeth Schultz presents a critique of interracial friendships between women in American literature that seems apropos to Jewett's story. Schultz, "Out of the Woods and into the World: A Study of Interracial Friendships between Women in American Novels," in *Conjuring: Black Women, Fiction, and the Literary Tradition*, ed. Marjorie Pryse and Hortense J. Spillers (Indianapolis: Indiana University Press, 1985).

36. Several Jewett critics misidentify Mrs. Tolland, calling her "Eliza Tolland"

or "Eliza," which is the name of Captain Tolland's sister, for whom, Mrs. Todd says, "Even my mother had no regard" (166). This error alters the meaning of passages such as the one cited here. Critics who refer to Mrs. Tolland as Eliza include Josephine Donovan (*Sarah Orne Jewett* [New York: Ungar, 1980]), and Piacentino, "Local Color and Beyond," 92–98.

37. In several recent popular films "whiteness" connotes a myriad of anxieties, particularly anxieties associated with family and/or spirituality. These anxieties get worked out (or worked on) with assistance from a "nonwhite" character. Some recent mainstream "family" films, for example, seem to suggest that nonwhite characters hold a key that the "white" characters lack. *Clara's Heart*, *Grand Canyon*, *Karate Kid* (parts 1 and 2), *Free Willy* (parts 1 and 2), *Iron Will*, *Corinna, Corinna*, and *Pocahontas* all feature nonwhite guides who act as spiritual mentors to the well-meaning but confused white characters. Bonds of familial affection between white and nonwhite characters emerge, apparently as the result of the white character's contact with an ostensibly inherent nonwhite spirituality. In all of these films the "white family" is created and/or strengthened through contact with the nonwhite spiritual guide who enables some familial catharsis to occur.

"How Clearly the Gradations of Society Were Defined"

Negotiating Class in Sarah Orne Jewett

Alison Easton

Reading through Jewett's complete works can at first be a discomfiting experience, familiar as we still tend to be with only the handful of texts now commonly reprinted. What lies in the background of those well-known tales (tales primarily concerned with women's lives and identities) becomes foregrounded in others, and suddenly issues of class and race become as inescapable as those of gender. The essay that follows represents my early explorations of this territory and is part of what will be a full-length study of the intersections of class and gender in Jewett's writings.

So far the main critical reaction to matters of class in Jewett's texts (where indeed there has been any reaction) has been to identify Jewett as a conservative, nostalgic traditionalist and member of an exclusive Boston upper class. Early commentators, with varying degrees of approval, found in Jewett a New York–derived view of New England's cultural decline and a celebration of what they take to be an older set of values. This interpretation of Jewett's writings finds one of its first critics in Ann Douglas Wood, who sees women's regional writing as an exercise in nostalgia and a testimony to social despair. Some recent and more historicized readings have sought to place Jewett more precisely (and in their eyes, quite damningly) within a cultural aristocracy that was busy constructing a national culture with a nostalgic, indeed racist point of origin. This view identifies Jewett's participation not so much in cultural elegy, but more in the formation of an upper class with deep anxieties about the working class, especially immigrants. Jewett's work is seen as a fiction of "tradition," and again little distinction is made between her writings and the work of other regionalists.[1]

I have resisted such a conclusion for two main reasons. First, thinking biographically, it proves hard to place Jewett herself in terms of class. She does not seem to sit securely in any of the dominant class categories of the century, though she participates in a number of them. Her childhood was spent among the rural upper class in what historians now call an "island community," which in spite of some new manufactories still had a largely preindustrial agrarian and artisan economy, and where home was the place of work rather than the bourgeois refuge at the end of the working day. This kind of community seems to have retained a Revolutionary-era culture of deferential democracy and a mercantile conception of general welfare.[2] But Jewett was, of course, also a member of the Boston literary elite in a developed capitalist-based class system (and her "Boston marriage" to Annie Fields must have added a further, different dimension to this, and likewise Fields's involvement in Boston charities for the poor).[3] However, as an adult she continued to spend part of the year in Maine in what had become a stable and economically developed postbellum agrarian society. Hal S. Barron argues that this late-century Maine cannot, for all its continuities with the society she was raised in, be understood either in premodern rural terms or in terms of the contemporary urban, industrial scene. The world that Jewett had glimpsed in childhood was gone for good. Barron describes these rural communities as no longer servicing the world beyond their borders (western agriculture and distant industrialization had taken over from that economy), but with a stable population (endogamy, reduced in-migration, family continuity) they had resolved earlier distinctions and conflicts and organized their communities by the personal ties of kinship, propinquity, and friendship, thus evolving a consensus of values and beliefs.[4] It is this later version of rural society that may constitute the base of some of Jewett's fictional worlds, though one may note that Barron's consensus may not have been arrived at, or maintained, without effort.

Furthermore, while Jewett participated in the female friendship networks typical of the mid-nineteenth-century bourgeois world, she does not separate women from men in that middle-class ideology of spheres with its conservative, class-boosting cult of domesticity and the family. Her Boston marriage was a factor in this perspective, as was the general demographic shift to single working women toward the end of the century. Gender consciousness does not displace class consciousness as it had done, so David Leverenz argues, in texts earlier in the century. The nineteenth-century "female world of love and ritual" has distracted us from seeing the extent to which women's lives were part of wider social conditions, to be explained socioeconomically.[5]

My second reason for resisting simply consigning Jewett to nostalgic conservatism is that some of her stories seem quite consciously to make questions of class and racial division their central topic. I see her work as a series of experiments and negotiations at a time when many were denying that class was an important issue.[6] Here is someone responding creatively and in evolving ways to some of the class situations of her society. True, there are times when she writes unreflectingly, simply rehearsing ideologically formed views, or when her tales arrive at definitely conservative conclusions (and it would be worth asking why on those occasions this happens), but at other times she appears to explore, review, and question. We should also be careful to distinguish between the different approaches and positions taken by her various works over a long career. Class issues are not marginal, nor something she sidestepped. My intention in this study is to reflect on the range of positions and their complexities and confusions, rather than to resolve these complexities and confusions.

The attendant difficulties of this investigation I can only gesture to in as short a piece as this. First, I am aware that Jewett's personal class perceptions are not going to be simply replicated in her texts—who you are socially and what you write are not identical. Furthermore, the texts themselves are affected by their most common address to urban middle-class readers, many of whom, it seems likely, did entertain nostalgic, idealized notions of the rural.[7] This does not mean that the texts see the world in the same way as their readers did—I want to avoid that troubling elision made by some commentators on these texts.

Second, the whole issue of understanding what was happening in America throughout the nineteenth century in terms of class is historiographically a heavily debated problem that awaits yet further studies in a number of areas, and the applicability of the very category of "class" in relation to American society is still being explored.[8] I believe that it is not possible to understand large areas of social conduct within a capitalist society without some concept of class, but this essay will not use the term simply in its classic, essentialist Marxist form of a critique of capitalist wage-labor relations, but rather more broadly to indicate the experiences and subjectivities of a range of intermediate classes that shift and change over the period of Jewett's lifetime—as Stuart M. Blumin puts it, "the ways unequal distributions of wealth, income, opportunity, workplace tasks and authority, political power, legal status, and social prestige have organized the lives and consciousness of specific groups of Americans" (2–3). As Blumin shows, economic differences are translated into "significant differences in life-style, outlook, and aspiration" (3).

Third, I would wish to add to this already complex matter two further, possibly related considerations. We need to recognize that class categories tend to become greatly nuanced in individual experience. This may be clearer in a more consciously classed society like Britain, where individuals tend to modify and refine their understanding of their relation to a particular given class identity. We may attempt to place Jewett in a class (and, as I said, this is not a straightforward business), but we are still left to ponder her individual perception of this. The other insight that I find helpful in approaching the experience of class is one that Blumin adapts from Anthony Giddens: the distinction between class consciousness and class awareness. Class awareness lacks a definite sense of belonging to a class, and thus allows for a more individualistic perspective on social stratification. This is particularly useful, of course, if one is dealing with a social group like the American middle class and upper class, which were highly individualistic in their philosophy and likely to deny the significance of class. Class awareness also does not necessarily posit classes as conflict groups.[9]

And so, with all this in mind, I move to a consideration of selected texts. *Deephaven* (1877) is Jewett's first attempt to express the complexity of her experience of class in a changing America. Strikingly, its narrative structure is shaped, sometimes uneasily, by the class interactions going on. For all its simplifications, such as the construction of Deephaven mostly in terms of a past about to disappear entirely, the novel begins to find ways of addressing certain class situations. Jewett's own multiple position is figured in the doubling of the protagonist into two young women who are distinct but deeply attached to one another. Kate's family has inherited the Deephaven house, and Helen is her Boston friend who narrates the story. Even within this pair, there are class inflections to be noted: as Marjorie Pryse has pointed out, the two are not quite social equals in education and family property.[10] Neither of them is quite a tourist—the summer visitor, a figure scrutinized in several later tales, is represented here more by the protagonists' visiting town friends, who are briefly listed in the final chapter.

But the class position set up in the two women is further modified by their *ménage à deux*. I don't want to argue that the subliminal lesbian romance helps obliterate class boundaries with their neighbors (it seems to me a sentimental notion that gender commonalities are more powerful than class differences, and Jewett's later "Martha's Lady" faces up to this). But in this novel certain social structures are made flexible with the departure of parents, brother, and middle-class neighbors. Class boundaries are crossed: even before they reach the grand family residence we are shown them meeting Mrs. Kew, the lighthouse keeper's wife, and swapping seats with her in the coach they share.

Nevertheless, class boundaries are not transcended (as I believe they are uniquely in *The Country of the Pointed Firs*, a text that I have argued elsewhere is utopian in its aims and achievement).[11] Only once in *Deephaven*, in an early chapter, do class boundaries blur, and they are never allowed to do so again in the novel. This is a curious and clearly dangerous moment that forces an explicit reassertion on the narrator's part of the class differences of 1870s America. A shopgirl, seeing round the lighthouse where the protagonists are helping Mrs. Kew, mistakes Kate for one of her own class and offers to find her better work and lodging in Boston. That historically shopgirls belonged with white-collar workers, and were therefore aspirants to the middle class, means that her class was moving up toward Kate's, so that the Boston upper class had been taking steps to differentiate itself culturally from such people.[12] Helen as narrator copes with the situation by turning it into a discussion of good manners—a recurrent preoccupation of this novel. In this idea of manners, class is translated into a kind of social behavior whose origins are envisaged as lying in an older aristocracy but are deemed transferable to other classes—a paradox in which pre-republican values are democratically disseminated, and class divisions both validated and softened.

The novel's following two chapters then go on to address class issues directly: "It is curious to notice . . . how clearly the gradations of society were defined."[13] But this observation does not mean that the novel can shape these gradations into a consistent position. "Deephaven Society" defines Deephaven, twelve miles from any railroad, in terms of its difference from and distaste for industrial and immigrant America. The chapter does not dodge the problem of deference, which is not "consistent with the principles of a republican government" (69), but renders it innocuous in the persons of a nearly extinct aristocracy of a town that has "nothing to do with the present" (85). The effect is to locate certain unacceptable attitudes in antebellum upper-class Maine—thus disassociating them from the present—while simultaneously suggesting other continuities with postbellum Boston elite. It all presents a rather blurred picture.

The novel is glad then to move on to territory less uneasy in class terms—marginal places like the shore and the outlying farmhouses, where the rural and maritime workers monologue to ready listeners (there is no real dialogue presented). However, this impression of contact is modified by several things. The young women admit to asking for water as a way of gaining entry into the poorest farmhouses and have to learn that it is no "impertinence" to be expected by these lower-class people to talk about oneself (the novel appears to use their naiveté to criticize its big-city readers' unequal relationship to this material). Later, they come to a fuller understanding of this experience: they have no place at the funeral of a farmer dead from grief and poverty. The narrator's residual detachment (which no doubt masks difficulty) is further shown in the way that chapter after chapter ends with her stepping back from such scenes to reassert an upper-class Bostonian perspective.

Deephaven conjugates class using the differences among members of the antebellum Maine upper class, present-day Boston upper class, and present-day Maine farmers, sailors, and the servant class. Jewett was to reexamine all these elements, most notably through the trope of the Boston visitor and through an exploration of the historical roots of certain kinds of class difference, in increasingly complex ways in the course of her career. "The Life of Nancy," published the year before *The Country of the Pointed Firs*, in 1895, is the most complex orchestration of the Boston visitor theme. Through the experiences of its protagonists, the country woman, Nancy, and the city dweller, Tom, it presents the reader with a significant range of locales both geographically and historically. Boston is shown not only as the cradle of the American Revolution, but as a modern commercial city with traffic jams, business signs, spreading suburbs, and a moneyed, cultured upper class with close involvement in corporate finance. Four and a half miles away, but in a sense several decades distant, is Nancy's uncle's farm—a man who was "well acquainted"[14] with Tom's grandfather but of a totally different class and way of life to Tom's. The village in Maine lies far beyond even that, and since Tom does not return to it for nearly twenty years, the possible effect on it of a rapidly changing America is also considered. In Tom's modern Boston eyes it is "one of those nice old-fashioned country neighborhoods" (23) to which Tom had gone to look into his father's "land interests" (11), a place in which he had felt a born citizen; latterly it seems a good-sized town that had "grown up" (24), but with all the lumbering and building lots, described in terms of business investment, still standing as an untenanted country with its "untouched wall of firs and pines" (38).

Jewett refers twice in "The Life of Nancy" to "Rip Van Winkle," a tale in which the American revolution occurs while Rip sleeps. Arguably the hidden revolution in this text is that of urban industrial capitalism and the formation of new social classes, though it is one that had not changed the whole of America, and which left all kinds of differences to be negotiated. The way in which the tale is structured by both Tom visiting Maine and Nancy visiting Boston indicates that this is no simple opposition between "city" and "country." The question behind the text that I am adopting from Blumin is this: what is the relationship between what is happening in the cities and in the rest of the country? It is a question that twentieth-century historians are still addressing. Blumin has the idea of there being a "threshold": the point where rural communities became big enough, economically developed enough, close enough to the cities, and with a population turnover to be affected by them. Beyond that, Blumin speculates that there were presumably communities that were "organized into local networks and hierarchies that differed fundamentally from those of the city, and that imparted social identities far different from those generated within urban social networks."[15]

So is Nancy's East Rodney beyond that threshold? Economically there are links with the outside world, but, as we have seen, they are not strong enough to change the look of the place completely (unlike much of Boston). However, Nancy's teaching of dancing (a form of "manners") suggests effects and possible linkages that are not purely economic but nonetheless reflect class issues. Nancy seeks to prevent her young villagers feeling "hoggish an' left out" (32). Blumin cites evidence that farmers' daughters had aspirations of gentility, and they did understand the terms and means of social ascendancy (309–10). But Nancy's request to see dancing in Boston is the moment when Tom feels most acutely the "social barriers" (15) that exist in his Boston but had not existed, he felt, in East Rodney. The only way in which they can be removed in the city is at the innocuous pre-adult level of the dancing class. Nancy can teach dancing to the next generation, but she herself, afflicted by arthritis (too far from the benefits of modern medicine and modern class mobility) will never dance and never marry (the romance expected by most readers never materializes). The dancing may be a "measure to live by" (35) but something she can enjoy only "by proxy" (34). The tale's ending feels decidedly unresolved.

The works I have discussed so far made Jewett's handling of social class easier by not involving the industrial working class. *Deephaven* does not linger in the neighboring town of Denby, where we are told there are mills. However, there is a small cluster of tales that do deal with class relations within the classic terms of "labor" and "capital," a typical duality understood at that time. Jewett uses these terms herself. In these tales we meet factory workers and managers, company directors (in both self-made and inherited positions), investors in new enterprises, and what we would now call small businessmen (shopkeepers and craftsmen in a modern economy, people who now have to rent and borrow money at interest and are therefore caught up in the structures of capitalism).

Tales such as "The Growtown Bugle," "The Two Browns," "A Business Man," "The Failure of David Berry," and "The Gray Mills of Farley" deal with conscious deliberation, albeit on a small scale fictionally, with big changes in socioeconomic structures in the course of the nineteenth century, especially the widening differences between non-manual and manual work with the bifurcation of office and workshop.[16] It is notable that this particular take on class alters Jewett's handling of gender relations. Indeed, several middle-class female characters are depicted as greedy consumers of others' money making, as if their class/gender-based exclusion from the factory site blinkers them to the realities of working life. Several tales underline the divisions (not just gender ones) that industrial life creates. Sites are split, or even identity is split, showing an internal division in the subject and arguably in her middle-class readers: the New England spinster investing in a Kansas new town rather than in her local factory; an affluent businessman walking between his grand house and a shop in a working-class district of Boston, and, most notable of all, Mr. J. Benedict Brown of an old law firm, who is also Mr. John B. Brown, the director of a new engineering factory.

Divisions are clearly what Jewett is interested in, but it is not easy to place her politically. Obviously hers is not a Marxist analysis, nor is it a Progressivist one. Amy Schrader Lang argues that by the 1870s models of opposed interests had generally superseded the harmony of interests model with its ideology of free labor, though some then sought an "identity of interests" between labor and capital. Fictional critiques of capitalism in the last quarter of the century, Barbara Bardes and Suzanne Gossett explain, agree on the traditional fundamental values of equality, liberty, and democracy, but diverge in the debate between those supporting the capitalist system, those who suggest minor reforms, and those who propose more radical communitarian or socialist solutions.[17] Jewett's works do not fit securely into these categories. Her interest in labor and in farming, her questioning of the laws of supply and demand, and her positive attitude to Irish immigrants clearly set her apart from the classical Liberalism of an authoritarian, upper-class postbellum America.[18] Jewett had read some Ruskin, but that British model of romantic anticapitalism involves a nostalgia for a remote, medieval past to which it seeks to return.[19] Jewett places her utopia, *The Country of the Pointed Firs*, in the 1890s and constructs its world in ways that pick up and respond to current issues in America. It is not some timeless traditional world. A true conservative would locate her ideal society in the historical past; a social radical would place it in the future; so what are the politics of a writer whose utopia belongs in the present moment?

Her approach and attitudes resemble more closely antebellum reformist thinking that has been shown to be in certain ways a forerunner of reform movements at the turn of the century, that often had its origins in the rural, and that avoided political parties. Michael J. Heale discusses how these earlier reformers did not seek radical change but rather the restoration of what they saw as social harmony. They believed in the compatibility of classes and in a mobile, expanding social order. Sensitive to the plight of newcomers (Jewett's tales about immigrants are relevant here), they wanted to forge bonds. They were alarmed by signs of growing class conflict.[20]

In the cluster of Jewett's tales noted above there is a demystification of some of the processes of capitalism, most notably how profit from investment ruins others' lives. Her plots are structured to this end. Prudence Fellows (the name is an oxymoron) is such a bad neighbor because her amazingly successful investment in Kansas separates her capital from local labor; the directors of Gray Mills sell out their stock while it is rising after an imprudently high dividend; Brown agrees to sell his business while the going is good and retreats back to his high-caste status of lawyer. Most of the tales, however, are moralistic rather than polemical: their clear but simple and traditional (indeed Biblical) message is about caring for your neighbors in times of need.

But there are contradictions within this message that dissipate such meanings. The much-praised virtues of an earlier economic order (hard work, thrift, making it on one's own) seem paradoxically to bring the very success that makes you a modern big businessman (see "A Business Man"). Brown makes farm machinery that will "save hiring labor," we are told, but we are left to speculate whether the tale wished to imply that this will preserve the autonomy of the traditional small farmer (who usually had not hired much labor) or whether it will lead to rural unemployment. These issues are at least deliberately raised even though they are not pursued.

However, "The Two Browns" has a moment when issues to do with industrial capitalism are expressed more politically. Brown's experience of running the firm with a care for his employees (to whom he intends to offer a share in the business) has given him, we are told, a "chance to work out some experiments in the puzzling social questions of the day. He was ready now to be something of a statesman. He was willing to believe that he had got hold of the right thread of the snarled skein that linked labor to capital."[21] This passage suggests that Jewett is not naive in these tales, even though she handles Brown's subsequent selling-up with an irony so faint you can miss it, and the political possibilities vanish as if they had never been mentioned.

"The Gray Mills of Farley" (1898) is a far more radical text, depicting in an almost novelistic way a mill community from the perspective of the workers. Blumin's analysis of historical studies done on small industrial towns like Farley suggests that these places saw a division of society into two classes, without the presence of a middle class and its consequent fluidities (300–302). The tale's message is clearly that workers have the right to share the profits of their own labor. Its attack becomes savage when it depicts an old female worker curtseying to a director whom we have just seen rejecting any pay rise for the workers: his "They think they own the mills now" is placed against this curtsey, "as she had been taught to salute the gentry sixty years before."[22] This paralleling of old money, status, and power with new money, status, and power has multiple meanings: deference to one's masters brings no substantial change of status in any historical period; new money is the descendant of old economic inequalities and serves to perpetuate them (one young girl, whose only inheritance is work, is the fourth generation in the factory); the new order does not recognize some of the responsibilities that an older gentry class or even the early factory employers of young women might be deemed to have shown.[23] Being female only increases one's oppression—women are very important in this text as they were generally in the history of factory work in America. Furthermore, although historically speaking, there was more class awareness in small industrial satellite towns, Jewett does not imagine labor being organized (one worker says, "you cannot rebel against a shut-down; you can only submit" [273]), and in spite of tiny hints of leaders among the working class, only the Agent (the factory manager) is given agency in the text, and even this is limited to lending money and a field to plant. (There is a hint of more radical questioning in the choice of potatoes as this crop, recalling as it does the grossly mismanaged Irish Famine of the 1840s, which had driven so many Irish immigrants to work in American factories like this one.)[24] In sum, this polarization into labor and capital is too disturbing to admit a conclusion; Jewett never reprinted the tale.

Having avoided class war in those fictions, Jewett then moved to a consideration of civil war in her last novel, *The Tory Lover,* set in 1777. This novel makes best sense if placed in the context of Jewett's earlier explorations of class. Here current issues of class division are displaced sideways onto Loyalist/Patriot tensions in 1777 (and the novel does not underestimate the savagery of these tensions). I think too that racial divisions and the more recent conflict of the Civil War are also involved in some small way, given the novel's foregrounding of Maine's black servants early in the text and their definite slave trade origins. Like "Martha's Lady," another late tale published in 1897, this novel deals with earlier historical periods, not as a simple escape from present difficulties, but in order to imagine how earlier and different class relations were negotiated. Both these texts present clearly a class-stratified society, but one that is envisaged as far more interactive and nuanced than the capital/labor division previously discussed. This distinction may reflect a pattern of development identified by Blumin in various areas at different stages since the Revolution: some settlements initially developed a stratified society with a recognized superior class (something that usually we associate with a later advanced capitalist society), only then to mature and stabilize as small towns in a quite different society with more personalized relations (308–9).

What engages Jewett's imagination in *The Tory Lover* is the notion of neutrality (defined in terms of sympathy for both sides and the avoidance of armed conflict). This is both a political matter and, for Jewett, an issue raised by her own writings, with their open and only partially resolved handling of class tensions. The novel debates whether it is possible to maintain a neutral position in the middle of a "war" (and I would argue that this might be a class, race, or national war). To complicate matters, there are two kinds of division in operation in eighteenth-century Maine: first, the Loyalist/Patriot divide, and second, the lower classes and their "betters," the landed gentry. Tensions between rich and poor divide society differently than the Loyalist/Patriot struggle. While ideas of the great lady and of the country gentleman are endorsed by the novel, there is also a rhetoric of republican equality that confusingly cuts across this. The American reader might expect the wealthy and poor boats in an English harbor, but not the destitute woman with barefooted child whose husband is stuck wageless in Valley Forge. The novel's genteel hero, Wallingford, remembers with pleasure being treated as an equal by his shipmates when he belatedly enlisted on the *Ranger*, though its Revolutionary captain, Paul Jones, is less appreciative of the independent-mindedness of his Maine crew. Benjamin Franklin puts in an appearance, but so does French aristocracy. These disruptive ambivalences make it all rather confusing. Jewett loses control of her material through her attempt to hold open all positions, even though the plot itself takes her firmly to the conclusion that a neutral position is not possible.

Finally, "Martha's Lady" is particularly interesting in addressing not simply class, but the intersections of class and gender head-on. This was a peculiarly interesting class situation to write about, as well as the most familiar to her readers. In the bourgeois home upper-class and working-class women were brought into very close contact, but in a structure that reinforced unbridgeable distinctions even while it expected servants to create a home (which was not theirs) by standards which were not theirs. Relations between mistress and maid were notoriously fraught (servants, like Martha, were young, untrained, and unmarried). There were frequent complaints about servants and much advice to employers about their handling, such advice even envisaging the lady as a missionary encouraging genteel practices among the working class (a process of conversion that Jewett attempts to imagine in less oppressive terms but nonetheless still within class structures).[25]

Like *The Tory Lover*, the tale reaches back historically: the narrator carefully situates most of the events between the War of Independence and the Civil War, probably in the 1850s, but with further suggestions of the family's colonial origins. It also moves forward forty years over a major period of change for the country. The three characters offer a range, across time, of class and geography: the old-fashioned provincial gentlewoman in her mansion, the Boston visitor from "households of high social station,"[26] and Martha the maid from a "stony hill-farm" (146) with a bare wooden house.

The history of domestic service in America gives a better understanding of this tale's materials. Before the nineteenth century young women might go into service prior to marriage to learn to run a home—an idea that implied a certain classlessness and mutuality in relations between mistress and servant and that lingered longer as a life-cycle stage in the thinking of country people. Martha's predecessor left to marry. But, as Carol Lasser explains, the work's prestige fell in the nineteenth century, and native-born women found a maid's loss of independence degrading. The work was largely taken over by Irish women. In making Martha a native-born woman who, moreover, remains in the same household (as Lasser shows, migration to another post was the commoner pattern for the servant who never married), Jewett can explore how class interconnections might evolve from that older, pre-bourgeois base.[27]

But class is not transcended in this tale: separate though in relation, maid and mistress adhere to their class roles to the very last page. Unlike Nancy, Martha does not get to go to Boston (her mistress blocks the invitation from Miss Helena to her wedding). But this is also a love story (while the earlier "Life of Nancy" refused that plot and elevated "friendship" above marriage), though class so rules the relationship that it can be deeply uncomfortable to contemplate. The love is sublimated, but all the more passionately imagined for this sublimation. Because of this love, it is Martha, the daughter of impoverished farmers, who comes to represent the old ways of her mistress's mansion, its dignity, beauty, and stateliness. But she can never actually become a lady, that ideal which in the late eighteenth-century had superseded the earlier colonial working farming wife as a model of femininity[28] and ushered in some of the complex class relations of the nineteenth century.

The centrality of class relations with their attendant complexities and confusions is clear, then, even in the small selection of texts discussed in this essay. Explanations of Jewett's work in terms of gender alone are insufficient. The issues are all the more interesting for her refusal (or inability) to simplify or opt for easier resolution in at least some of her tales. Class/gender representations in her work need to be plotted in relation to a triple intersection: first, a shifting historical base where different stages in the development of a classed American society coexisted; second, Jewett's individual perspective on this, where simple class categories are not fully defining and where the textual situations are not necessarily identical to her own lived positions; and, third, her readership with a different experience and expectations in relation both to the worlds Jewett lived in and the worlds she created to negotiate class/gender difficulties. The evolution of Jewett's engagement with these issues and the variations in their representations demand now to be explored in detail.

Notes

1. See Perry D. Westbrook, *Acres of Flint: Sarah Orne Jewett and Her Contemporaries*, revised edition (Metuchen, N.J.: Scarecrow Press, 1981); Ann Douglas Wood, "The Literature of Impoverishment: The Women Local Colorists in America, 1865–1914," *Women's Studies International* 1 (1972): 3–45; Richard H. Brodhead, *Cultures of Letters: Scenes of Reading and Writing in Nineteenth-Century America* (Chicago: University of Chicago Press, 1993), esp. 142–76; *New Essays on "The Country of the Pointed Firs,"* ed. June Howard (New York: Cambridge University Press, 1994); and Brodhead, "Regionalism and the Upper Class," in *Rethinking Class: Literary Studies and Social Formations*, ed. Wai Chee Dimmock and Michael T. Gilmore (New York: Columbia University Press, 1994), 150–74.

2. See Robert H. Wiebe, *The Search for Order, 1877–1920* (New York: Hill and Wang, 1967), 1–10; Stow Persons, *The Decline of American Gentility* (New York: Columbia University Press, 1973); and Paula Blanchard, *Sarah Orne Jewett: Her World and Her Work* (Reading, Mass.: Addison-Wesley, 1994).

3. See Ronald Story, *The Forging of an Aristocracy: Harvard and the Boston Upper Class, 1800–1870* (Middletown, Conn.: Wesleyan University Press, 1980).

See also Brodhead, *Cultures of Letters*, though I wish to distinguish Jewett's participation in that class from identity with it.

4. Hal S. Barron, *Those Who Stayed Behind: Rural Society in Nineteenth-Century New England* (Cambridge: Cambridge University Press, 1984). David Leverenz, *Manhood and the American Renaissance* (Ithaca: Cornell University Press, 1989), 81, adopts the phrase "deferential democracy" from its use in a different context in Nick Salvatore, *Eugene V. Debs: Citizen and Socialist* (Urbana: University of Illinois Press, 1982).

5. See Carroll Smith-Rosenberg, *Disorderly Conduct: Visions of Gender in Victorian America* (New York: Knopf, 1985), especially 245–96, on writing against domesticity in the 1870–1900 period; and Mary P. Ryan, *The Empire of the Mother: American Writing about Domesticity, 1830–1860* (New York: Haworth Press, 1982). Brodhead, *Cultures of Letters*, 154–55, argues for too simple a continuation of that earlier female bonding.

6. See Stuart M. Blumin, *The Emergence of the Middle Class: Social Experience in the American City, 1760–1900* (Cambridge: Cambridge University Press, 1989), 285–90. Further references are cited in the text.

7. See Wiebe, *The Search for Order*, 39; Smith-Rosenberg, *Disorderly Conduct*, 167.

8. See Blumin, *The Emergence of the Middle Class*, 1–16; Sean Wilentz, *Chants Democratic: New York City and the Rise of the American Working Class, 1788–1850* (New York: Oxford University Press, 1984), 13–17.

9. Blumin, *The Emergence of the Middle Class*, 9–11.

10. Marjorie Pryse, in discussion, Jewett Centennial Conference, Portland, Maine, June 21–23, 1996. Elizabeth Silverthorne, *Sarah Orne Jewett: A Writer's Life* (Woodstock, N.Y.: Overlook Press, 1993), suggests this relationship between Kate and Helen is based on Jewett's friendship with the daughter of a Massachusetts senator.

11. See Alison Easton, "*The Country of the Pointed Firs:* History and Utopia," in Sarah Orne Jewett, *The Country of the Pointed Firs*, ed. Alison Easton (Harmondsworth: Penguin, 1995), vii–xxii.

12. See Blumin, *The Emergence of the Middle Class*, 293–95; Story, *The Forging of an Aristocracy;* and Brodhead, "Regionalism and the Upper Class."

13. Sarah Orne Jewett, *Deephaven* (Boston: Houghton Mifflin, 1886), 68. Subsequent quotations are cited in the text.

14. Sarah Orne Jewett, "The Life of Nancy," in *The Life of Nancy* (Boston: Houghton Mifflin, 1896), 7. Subsequent quotations are cited in the text.

15. Blumin, *The Emergence of the Middle Class*, 305. See also his entire final chapter, "Epilogue: City, Town, Village, Farm—The Geography of Class in Nineteenth-Century America," 298–310.

16. Blumin, *The Emergence of the Middle Class*, 258–97, sees this bifurcation as the key element in class formation at this period.

17. Amy Schrader Lang, "The Syntax of Class in Elizabeth Stuart Phelps's

The Silent Partner," in *Rethinking Class*, ed. Dimmock and Gilmore, 270–72; and Barbara Bardes and Suzanne Gossett, *Declarations of Independence: Women and Political Power in Nineteenth-Century American Fiction* (New Brunswick: Rutgers University Press, 1990), 108–17.

18. See John G. Sproat, *"The Best Men": Liberal Reformers in the Gilded Age* (New York: Oxford University Press, 1968).

19. See Michael Löwy, "Marxism and Revolutionary Romanticism," *Telos* 49 (1981): 83–95.

20. See Michael J. Heale, "Harbingers of Progressivism: Responses to the Urban Crisis in New York, c. 1845–1860," *Journal of American Studies* 10 (1976): 17–36.

21. Sarah Orne Jewett, "The Two Browns," in *A White Heron and Other Stories* (Boston: Houghton Mifflin, 1886), 250.

22. Sarah Orne Jewett, "The Gray Mills of Farley," reprinted in *The Uncollected Short Stories of Sarah Orne Jewett*, ed. Richard Cary (Waterville, Maine: Colby College Press, 1971), 270. Subsequent quotations for this work are from this edition and cited in the text.

23. See Alice Kessler-Harris, *Out to Work: A History of Wage-Earning Women in the United States* (New York: Oxford University Press, 1982), 64, 67–68.

24. Kessler-Harris, *Out to Work*, 63–64.

25. See Christine Stansell, *City of Women: Sex and Class in New York, 1789–1860* (New York: Knopf, 1986), 155–68, 219–20.

26. Sarah Orne Jewett, "Martha's Lady," in *The Queen's Twin and Other Stories* (Boston: Houghton, Mifflin, 1899), 149. Subsequent quotations are cited in the text.

27. See Carol Lasser, "'The World's Dread Laugh': Singlehood and Service in Nineteenth-Century Boston," in *The New England Working Class and the New Labor History*, eds. Herbert G. Gutman and Donald H. Bell (Urbana: University of Illinois Press, 1987), 72–88.

28. Ann D. Gordon and Mari Jo Buhle, "Sex and Class in Colonial and Nineteenth-Century America," in *Liberating Women's History: Theoretical and Critical Essays*, ed. Bernice A. Carroll (Urbana: University of Illinois Press, 1976), 284.

Party Out of Bounds

Gender and Class in Jewett's "The Best China Saucer"

Sarah Way Sherman

Who's to blame when parties get really *out of hand*?

—*The B-52s, "Party Out of Bounds"*

In the 1893 preface to her first book, *Deephaven* (1877), Sarah Orne Jewett recalls "a noble saying of Plato that the best thing that can be done for the people of a state is to make them acquainted with each other."[1] Her best-known attempt to illustrate this ideal is *The Country of the Pointed Firs* (1896), a book whose most moving scenes represent women of different classes forging utopian friendships over cups of tea and dishes of apple pie. However, the question remains whether acquaintance alone can heal a nation's differences. While empathy may overcome invidious distinctions between individuals, unconnected to broader analysis and action, it cannot undo the inequities of status and power that create them. Significantly, it may not be in *Pointed Firs*, but in more disturbing stories like "The Foreigner" (1900), where companionship between women of different backgrounds flickers or even fails, that Jewett's cultural critique is most searching and her narrative instabilities most revealing. This essay explores one such story of failed friendship and maps the cultural fault lines that failure exposes.

Included in an early collection of Jewett's children's stories, "The Best China Saucer" (1878) has as its centerpiece a tea party hosted by a middle-class girl and attended by a working-class girl and her baby brother.[2] However, unlike comparable situations in *Pointed Firs*, this one ends in disaster, not communion. A parable of endangered purity, dealing directly with middle-class civilization and its discontents, this narrative demonstrates graphically how female gentility was constructed not only through binaries of gender, but also through oppositions of class and, judging by its shadowy suggestions of savagery and primitivism, through oppositions of ethnicity and race as well.[3] The young hostess's temptation and fall reveal how fulfilling the demands of bourgeois womanhood meant purging oneself of the pollution of "natural" savagery, a savagery represented here not by the "removed" American Indian nor by the suppressed African American, but by the unruly working-class female, whose dangerous call to the unsocialized child's allegiance is initially stronger than the delights of respectability.[4] While the story's overt sermonizing marks it as transitional, still partially rooted in the sentimental ethos of Susan Warner and Harriet Beecher Stowe, its subtle ironies suggest the dynamics of Jewett's later work and reveal her covert resistance to the ideologies of womanhood represented by those mother texts. As the narrator warns in the beginning, "This is a story with a moral." And the moral, presented without further ado, is "Mind your mother,—unless, of course, you are perfectly sure she is a foolish and unwise woman, and that you are always the more sensible of the two" (71).

As the story opens, Mrs. Willis is leaving for the day and she forbids little Nelly to play with Jane Simmons, who is "a very naughty girl, and always teaches you bad words and bad manners, and tries to make you disobey me." Then she leaves Nelly all alone but for the servants and her dolls. Nelly cannot get the housekeeper to tell her stories and soon grows tired of dressing up in her mother's clothes. Bored and restless, she pesters her dolls: "Anything was better than sitting there, so she went to the doll's house and took dear Amelia, who had a very fair complexion and light hair, and looked so faded that Nelly always said she was ill. Poor thing! She had to take such quantities of medicine, and go without her dinner and stay in bed half her time . . . and when she went out, she was made into such a bundle with shawls that I was afraid the fresh air did her no good" (74).

Before examining this fictional relationship between girl and doll more closely, a look at the broader historical context of doll play reveals how Jewett's story captures the tensions in female development during the Gilded Age. According to Miriam Formanek-Brunell's *Made to Play House: Dolls and the Commercialization of American Girlhood, 1830–1930*, the period after the Civil War saw changes in doll play reflecting shifts in the larger society.[5] Earlier generations of girls had used these toys, often homemade, as aids to learning productive household skills such as sewing. After the Civil War, however, more elaborate, expensive, and often imported dolls served new purposes consonant with the demands of the emerging consumer culture and leisure classes. Fashionable dolls' dresses and furniture displayed family status, as the dolls themselves became participants in children's imitations of genteel social rituals such as visiting and tea parties. As middle-class women lost their productive role in the economy and emphasis on their "private" roles as wives and mothers heightened, so girls were encouraged to bond with their dolls in intense relationships anticipating both romantic and maternal love. Formanek-Brunell notes how middle-class daughters, perhaps like their mothers, led increasingly isolated and restricted lives. Although many girls, according to memoirs, diaries, and letters, preferred romping in the outdoors, parents often pressed them toward sedate imitations of adult gentility, with a wealth of material props as accessories to their socialization. Among these props were doll stories, stereographs, poems, and songs to serve as "seeds" to imaginative play.

Girls' responses to these expectations, Formanek-Brunell finds, were varied. While some enjoyed "appropriate" fantasy play, inviting friends and their dolls to mock housewarming and tea parties, others resisted the parental scripts in amusing and sometimes shocking ways. Some girls, for example, "preferred exhilarating 'indoor coastings'—sliding down the stairs while sitting on a tea tray—to dull tea parties." Others subverted adult expectations more directly. For example, the future feminist and author Zona Gale and a friend "wreaked havoc on their tea parties by smashing their unsuspecting dolls to bits." Thus while doll funerals were perhaps the most popular of these play occasions, Formanek-Brunell finds that it was often "not the passive grieving that provided doll players with pleasure." While the Gilded Age's domestication of heaven simply "made the afterlife sound fun" for some girls, for others "the staging of doll funerals was an expression of aggressive feelings and hostile fantasies." In these cases, emphasis switched from "ritualized funerals to cathartic executions." A *Pittsburgh Post* article described a five-year-old who broke her doll on purpose, then "declared with satisfaction, 'it was dead'. . . . Using available kitchen utensils she dug a grave in the backyard and then invited other little girls to do the same." Another former doll player recalls "vivid memories of harrowing games . . . during which our dolls became desperately ill and died." Yet another recalls that "funerals were especially popular, with [my doll] Becky ever the willing victim. . . . No day was too short for a funeral, just so [my friends] all got home for supper."[6]

Although at first glance "The Best China Saucer" seems to have been produced for the juvenile market, which offered such stories as adult-approved scripts, Jewett subtly subverts such expectations by dramatizing the social realities of doll play and its psychological tensions. Her portrayal of this childhood world, hidden from the eyes of judgmental adults, fits Formanek-Brunell's description perfectly. Nelly's isolation in the obviously wealthy Willis household, her sense of physical restriction, her empty leisure, her dependence on the doll for companionship and entertainment, all reflect the conditions of middle-class girlhood during the Gilded Age. The twist Jewett provides is the presence of Jane Simmons, the working-class wild card. While Formanek-Brunell describes middle-class girls joining up with their peers in exhilarating and cathartic bouts of rebellion, asserting their agency over repressive bourgeois ideologies, Jewett's story offers an even more complex and disturbing portrait of a divided society and psyche. Here class anxieties produce a response to social norms different from either simple acquiescence or outright defiance, and that outcome suggests much about Jewett's own conflicted loyalties.

These divided loyalties are manifested in Jewett's own life and work. Born to a privileged New England family, not unlike the Willis family, Jewett addressed her story to middle-class girls like Nelly, with whom she seemed to identify. After all, Jewett was a woman who, as her companion Annie Fields put it, "never put her dolls away." In fact, one of Jewett's dolls still holds a place of honor on her bed in the restored Jewett house in South Berwick, and lest one think it was placed there by a sentimental curator, historical materials make clear that this bedroom is the one room left intact after the author's death. However, an examination of the room reveals another side of Jewett. Her fishing gear is at the ready in one corner and her riding crops are crossed above the fireplace mantle. The woman who never put her dolls away is the same one who in middle age borrowed her nephew's sled one winter afternoon and coasted wildly down a neighborhood hill. In her novel *A Country Doctor* (1884) Jewett created a young heroine who actively struggles against the restrictions of bourgeois gentility and discovers her professional vocation after venting her frustration and rebellion in a furious run through the woods. And, of course, there is Sylvia of "A White Heron" (1886) who rejects the seduction of a charming hunter/ornithologist for the companionship of nature.[7]

However, as I have pointed out elsewhere, although Jewett gave both of these heroines working-class origins, they were preindustrial, agrarian origins, an identification she again stressed in *Pointed Firs.* This turn to the pastoral allowed Jewett to resolve some of the painful conflicts precipitated by the period's gender ideology. In the literary image of preindustrial women "close to nature" she found a way to resolve the conventional opposition between women's "earthiness" and their spiritual worthiness, their agency and their caretaking. Moreover, these figures gave her not only a literary subject, but also a model for her own adult identity as a woman writer, since here were women who were economically productive, yet retained their claims to moral dignity. However, this celebration of so-called "soft" primitivism is missing in "The Best China Saucer." In this earlier story there is no nostalgia for the preindustrial paradise and no redemption through communion with natural processes. The action takes place on bourgeois turf, rather than in pastoral landscape, and the ideological opposition between the "dirty" working-class girl and the "pure" genteel heroine dominates the story's action and its troubled resolution.[8]

To return to the story, we initially see Nelly dealing with the restriction and boredom of leisured gentility just as many grown-up ladies did, by lavishing attention on imaginary illnesses and manufacturing needs that demand her strict attention and care. She decides to take her best doll, the sickly Amelia, out for a stroll, making sure to dress her "warmer than usual, just to take up the time." However, even this game begins to pall, as is all too clear to Nelly's still unrepressed perceptions: "They walked up and down the garden some time, but it was stupid." In quest of real excitement, Nelly and her doll "went down by the carriage-gate to hunt for a bird's nest which Tom had said was near there in the hedge." It is important to note how the narrator empathizes with Nelly's boredom—"it was stupid"—and how she also understands the continued, felt presence of the doll: "They went down by the carriage-gate." Girls' identification with dolls is complex, but one aspect of it strongly resembles the identification of a mother with her child. Nelly's abandonment of her doll-playing, and the overly intense mothering it imitates, for the bird's nest reveals her lively curiosity about the natural world and her willingness to explore the boundaries of the domestic garden. The bird's nest by "the carriage-gate" is pointed out by her brother, Tom, and offers living creatures and actual reproduction rather than the "stupid" imitation of genteel motherhood. Like a magical response to this rebellious mood, Jane Simmons suddenly appears, and "Nelly is delighted." Remembering her mother's frequent admonitions not to play with the forbidden Jane, Nelly thinks, "I'll call her in for just a few minutes, and then I can go into the house and leave her; she doesn't dare to come near the house" (74). Alas, Jane is harder to control than Nelly suspects; even the house is not a protective amulet against her subversive powers.

Jewett presents Jane Simmons here as a kind of female Huckleberry Finn, who had entered U.S. literature in Twain's 1876 novel, *The Adventures of Tom Sawyer*, just two years before Jewett's own collection of children's stories. Huck "was cordially hated and dreaded by all the mothers of the town, because he was idle, and lawless, and vulgar, and bad—and because all their children admired him so, and delighted in his forbidden society, and wished they dared to be like him."[9] Middle-class Tom Sawyer "was like all the rest of the respectable boys, in that he envied Huckleberry his gaudy outcast condition, and was under strict orders not to play with him. So he played with him every time he got a chance." Huck's danger is clearly advertised by his clothing, for he "was always dressed in the cast-off clothes of full-grown men, and they were in perennial bloom and fluttering with rags." In fact, Twain's description of Huck's costume, with its trademark straw hat, has become a national icon of unfettered boyhood: "His hat was a vast ruin with a wide crescent lopped out of its brim . . . one suspender supported his trousers; the seat of the trousers bagged low and contained nothing; the fringed legs dragged in the dirt when not rolled up." In this first scene, Huck's ensemble is completed by a memorable accessory, a dead cat, which his illustrator depicts him dragging casually by its hind legs.

While Huck, in this novel at least, appears delightfully free of civilized restrictions and familial responsibilities, a similar "outcast condition" has saddled Jane prematurely with motherhood: the care of her baby brother. Significantly, it is the baby brother, rather than Jane, who echoes Twain's description of Huck:

> Jane looked unusually dirty that morning and very naughty. She was carrying her mother's parasol, and the brother, who was never

> called anything but "The Baby," was unbecomingly dressed in an old shawl, folded as small as possible; because he was so very short it trailed several inches upon the ground, and there were some little sticks and several burdock burrs tangled into the fringe. Jane had put a cast-off Shaker bonnet of her own upon his head; there was a great crack in the top of it, through which a tuft of hair showed itself, and fluttered in the wind. He had the dirtiest face you ever saw, and it always seemed to be the same dirt. Nelly hated The Baby. (74–75)

Although Jewett's representation initially plays off Twain's, with the inclusion of The Baby her tale takes a turn away from his idyll of boyish camaraderie across class boundaries: "'I don't see what made you bring The Baby . . .' said [Nelly], aloud. 'Oh, dear!' said Jane, 'I have to lug him everywhere. Long as he could n't talk I was n't bothered with him, for if worst came to worst, I used to tie him to the lilac-bush and clear out, and only be sure to unhitch before mother came; now he goes and tells everything. . . . Going to play dolls, are n't you?'" (76).

Here gender and class intersect to shape the drama that follows. As Nelly is being carefully initiated by a solicitous Mrs. Willis into the intricacies of domesticity, Jane is being forced by an absent mother to assume the real burdens of childcare. This live baby is grubby and demanding. And, while Nelly responds to her dolls with bursts of excessive, debilitating attention, alternated with bored neglect, her response to the real thing, The Baby, is hatred. Some years ago Annis Pratt, following Simone de Beauvoir's classic argument in *The Second Sex*, pointed out that "closeness to nature" might have different meanings and consequences for females than males, and the most significant consequence, in a world without reliable or easily accessible birth control, was pregnancy.[10] Without going into this vexed and intricate social historical problem in detail, let me just reiterate Nancy Cott's argument that, as middle-class women's social role narrowed to childrearing and they lost the prestige that their productive role in an earlier agrarian economy had conferred, they recovered their lost status by moralizing motherhood, a redefinition that required purging its sexual associations. Thus a crucial strategy through which middle-class women protected their genteel status from their own dangerous bodies was the convention of their passionlessness, and the displacement of their resultant anxieties around "natural functions" onto working-class women and women of color.[11]

It is a strategy that Gerda Lerner, Mari Jo Buhle, and Ann Gordon analyzed in their classic early studies of gender and class. For example, Buhle and Gordon noted that while more privileged women could confine their activities to the "domestic," poorer women were often forced to participate "in activities considered masculine. They shared with men a life in the world of business, a material existence which seemed inherently lacking in virtue and purity." "Easily identifiable through appearance, dress, rough manner, and attitude toward life," such women deviated from the widely held image of genteel womanhood, and therefore fell "outside the pale of respectability." Given this opposition between good ladies and bad females, "working women had only one advantage: they alone retained a right to sexual fulfillment." However, "without birth control and general sexual freedom, this right constituted a negative differentiation. Lower-class white and black women became recognized as prime objects of sexual exploitation, thus preserving the precious virtue of the Fair Lady."[12]

The implications of this analysis for related constructions of gender and race have been explored in a number of excellent recent studies. For example, Karen Sánchez-Eppler's *Touching Liberty: Abolition, Feminism, and the Politics of the Body* offers the Victorian "topsy-turvy doll" as an image of the interdependence of cultural constructions of black and white female bodies, and the displacement of sexual fears from one figure to the other. From one position, the doll appears white-skinned and genteel, but lift her skirts, turn her upside-down, and the caricature of a "wide-eyed pickaninny" appears in her place.[13] In *The Myth of Aunt Jemima: Representations of Race and Region*, Diane Roberts draws on Mikhail Bakhtin's contrast between the "classical" and the "grotesque" body to explore similar interdependent oppositions in Southern culture. Looking primarily at literary work, Roberts finds that "the ante-bellum South represented the middle-class white woman as asexual, spiritual, morally elevated, and angelic. If she deviated from certain codes, trespassing into the realm of behaviors relegated to black women (sexuality, 'dirt', passion), she lost her value in the white economy."[14]

Thus, in the system Roberts describes, white female bodies were "high" on a pedestal, while black bodies, female and male, had their place "below." They were "represented by the unspeakable, 'unclean' elements official culture would repress." And yet here as well the figures were interdependent: "Blacks in a slave society were powerless and marginal yet the whites who owned them built their culture around *not* being black. . . . Conservative whites insisted that blackness was low and therefore antithetical to the 'civilization', morality, and elevation represented by whiteness, yet the fascination betrayed with every nuance associated with 'the African', the many ways to slip 'down', speaks to the instability of the hierarchy."[15] Roberts quotes from Peter Stallybrass and Allon White's study of Renaissance class hierarchies, which describes parallel instabilities in the interlocking identities of the "upper" and "lower" members of early modern society: "A recurrent pattern emerges: the 'top' attempts to reject and eliminate the 'bottom' for reasons of prestige and status, only to discover, not only that it is in some way frequently dependent upon that low-Other . . . but also that the top *includes* that low symbolically, as a primary eroticized constituent of its own fantasy life."[16]

A similar pattern of opposition and displacement is clearly present in Jewett's story, where it serves to signify the class difference the story ultimately enforces. There is the imaginary baby, Amelia, who is purged of all biological messiness and serves as a simple vehicle for her "mother's" needs. Then there is the biological baby, who is smeared with dirt and remains obstinately unsocialized, "other." Drawing on Bakhtin's contrast between the "classical" and "the grotesque body," we find the classical represented by Amelia's miniature torso—with its hairless, hard body and absent orifices—and the grotesque by the nameless toddler—with its troublesome appetites and probably all-too-present and -productive bodily openings. The genteel Nelly overvalues, overnurtures the imaginary baby, while the "bad" Jane undervalues, undernurtures the biological one. The imaginary baby, smothered in woolens, is trundled about with tender care. The biological baby, trailing a forlorn shawl tangled with sticks, is hitched to the lilac bush like a dog.

However, if the story manifests a pattern of opposition and displacement, it also reveals a consequent instability. For if Nelly is forbidden to associate with the "dirty" girl and her equally dirty baby, she is still initially fascinated and "delighted" by her. Although the narrator has made it clear how "faded" Amelia's genteel attractions are, she coyly evades naming Nelly's motivation: "'What made her play with Jane?' Oh I'm sure I don't know. If Jane had not known any better, it would have been different; one would have pitied her, but she did know better than to be so naughty and so careless. There was certainly nothing to hinder her being good and kind and honest and clean except that she would not take the trouble" (75). This is a story about socialization and its disciplinary processes. Nelly is still a child. Not fully transformed to domestic angel, she still responds to the subversive, "natural" forces Jane represents. To use Stallybrass and White's formulation, Jane represents a "primary eroticized constituent of [Nelly's] own fantasy life": "In her heart, that day, Nelly was glad to see Jane, but she did not say much at first" (75).

From this encounter, the drama unfolds. Seeing Nelly's initial reserve and apparent hesitation, Jane applies her shrewd knowledge of character and accuses her hostess of being impolite. Nelly, who has been secretly searching for a rationalization to justify entertaining the forbidden Jane, seizes on this breach of etiquette. Her mother would never be so rude to one of *her* visitors. Her will to resist finally dissolves completely when Jane, promising to share a mysterious treat in her pocket, proposes a tea party. The two girls then set about their play in earnest, addressing each other by the names of their adult, married counterparts. Things are going so smoothly that Jane, anticipating some extra goodies, convinces Nelly to sneak inside the house for her mother's best china saucer and her dolls' cream pitcher. But when "Mrs. Simmons" subsequently sees that "Mrs. Willis" has not brought out any delicacies for their repast, she announces that she won't share the contents of her pocket after all:

> "I'm not a bit hungry," answered Mrs. Willis. "I had a splendid breakfast. I don't want any of your candy, or whatever it is. Mamma will bring me some from town."
>
> Mrs. Simmons was very angry. Her breakfast had not been "splendid," though she had had enough of it, and she had counted on Nelly's bringing out a quantity of good things. (77–78)

As the tempestuous Jane begins to get cross, Nelly begins to worry: "I wish I had thought to hide when I saw her coming. I must bring out something to eat, or nobody knows what she will do." And she scurries back to steal some plum pudding and macaroons from the pantry. Again, Jane's manipulation is shrewd. Like Huck, she is a streetwise kid, a con artist on a diminutive scale.

Then, as "Mrs. Willis" and "Mrs. Simmons" enjoy their tea party, another drama begins to form. Jane tells Nelly that she plans to open a little shop in her shed, where she will hawk "all sorts of delightful and useless things made of paper" in exchange for pins and cents from her neighbors. Nelly begins to imagine herself as the beneficent patroness of a female Horatio Alger: "Jane liked to get cents, and Nelly almost always had some in her pocket." As she imagines herself thus doling out liberal charity, "her heart warmed toward [Jane]: 'Poor thing!' she thought, 'she doesn't know any people but bad ones, and no wonder she swears and throws stones and does all sorts of things'" (79). However, this complacent reverie about the improvement of the deserving poor is suddenly broken, for "just now Mrs. Simmons happened to come closer to her, and Nelly saw for the first time a most shocking and heathenish decoration." Around her neck, Jane wears "a necklace of flies, on a long piece of white thread, to which the needle was still hanging. Oh! those dozens of poor flies. Some were dead, but others faintly buzzed" (79). This revelation—incidentally one of my favorites in all literature—proves that Jane's depravity is beyond doubt or redemption: "'Oh, Jane!' [Nelly] cried, 'what have you been doing to those poor flies, you horrid girl?' 'Want me to string you some?' said Mrs. Simmons with a grin. 'I did every bit of this this morning, before I came over. I'll bring you one that will go round your neck twice, if you will give me two cents'" (79).

Jane here manages to travesty both the domestic lady's formal "accomplishments" (the needle left hanging is an especially nice touch) and the self-made man's get-up-and-go (her sales pitch is a parody of Franklinesque enterprise). Like the working women described by Buhle and Gordon, Jane has retained masculine prerogatives and characteristics. While her premature childcare and bodily nonchalance may suggest sexual looseness, her free speech and aggressive hustling suggest ease in the commercial world. But unlike Tom Sawyer—whose response to Huck's dead cat is a prompt, "Lemme see him, Huck. My, he's pretty stiff. Where'd you get him?"—this customer's not buying. Suddenly overwhelmed with "feminine" squeamishness, Nelly's reply is a revolted protest that Jane must eat her pudding immediately and leave: "'I was going pretty soon, any way', said Jane. 'I guess there are flies enough left; you need n't make such a fuss. They let them stick on papers and die in your house. You r'e an awful little 'fraid cat. Who wants to play with you, any way?'" (79).

Openly subversive, Jane denounces female gentility's effort to transcend the element in which she must live and unmasks the hypocritical middle-class household's hidden savagery: trapping luckless flies with sticky paper is still insect torture, however discreet. Embedded in the world of dirt and biology, Jane is wise to its ways. Death does not revolt her any more than babies awe her. With her burdensome baby and her decoration of murdered trophies, she evokes the iconography, not of the "soft," but of the "savage" primitive: the cruel "squaw" who rejects the missionary's attempt at her enlightenment. She is unclean and unrepentant, impassive and impudent. Adorned like an infantine Kali—the Hindu goddess of birth and destruction who wore a necklace of human skulls—she ridicules Nelly's pretensions to purity.

Thus, like the English working-class men and women whom George Stocking describes in *Victorian Anthropology*, Jane carries a cultural signification similar to the "heathen" that the British Empire was then dominating overseas, or that the United States was "removing" farther and farther West. While the specific meanings assigned by bourgeois culture to American Indians, working-class poor, and African Americans varied, all shared to some extent in the negative connotations of the "primitive," and the dynamic of alterity and displacement is similar across cases, as the parallel between Stallybrass and White's analysis of Renaissance class symbolism and Diane Roberts's discussion of Southern racial symbolism makes clear. Moreover, as Stocking notes, the list of groups equated to "savages" or "primitives" was "quite extensive," including both working-class women and criminals, as well as "peasants, rustics, laborers, beggars, paupers, madmen, and Irishmen."[17]

The ostensible reasons for such categorizations were certain mental traits that placed these people "at a lower point on the unitary scale of intellectual and moral development: governed more by impulse, deficient in foresight, they were in varying degrees unable to subordinate instinctual needs to rational control." And yet, surveying the social geography of Britain, Stocking qualifies this supposed commonality in their mental deficiency by pointing to a more pertinent commonality in their social position: "Along different lines—of domestic life (woman, child), of socioeconomic status (laborer, peasant, pauper), of deviancy (criminal, madman), and of 'race' (Celtic Irishman, black savage)—they all stood in a subordinate hierarchical relationship to those who dominated economic life, who shared the political power, or who most actively articulated the cultural ideology of mid-Victorian Britain."[18]

And Jewett's dramatic conflict between heathen impulse and civilized rationality is not over yet. While Jane hurriedly wolfs down her pudding,

The Baby grabs the best china saucer and the little cream pitcher. A chase and a tussle ensue and then, "(how can I tell it?). . . . The Baby fell down and rolled over and over in the gravel, and the best china saucer and the cream-pitcher were both broken." "'What *will* Mamma say?' said Nelly. 'O Jane! It is one of the very best saucers that she likes so much, and I heard her tell Mrs. Duncan, the other day, that she could n't get any more'. If Jane had been at all sorry, Nelly would have considered her only her companion in misfortune, but instead of that she seemed to think it was a great joke, and said something very provoking" (80).

That evening a guilt-stricken Nelly hides the broken saucer from her mother. Then, like a diminutive and comical Eve concealing her transgression from the Lord of a domestic Eden, Nelly suffers her first taste of alienation from authority. In her bed that night she "wonders why she had played with Jane, and . . . remembers the fly-necklace with a shiver." Finally she sleeps, only to have such a "sad" and "odd dream . . . the moon was shining in brightly through the large hall windows, and Nelly dreamed she saw the funeral procession of the best china saucer" (82–83). Under Nelly's astonished eyes all the household crockery marches in solemn procession. There is "the cup, the poor lonely widow . . . dressed as usual with brilliant pictures of Chinese houses and tall men and women." Then come the rest of the near relations, with the portly punch bowl, "looking large and grand." After this "elegant company" comes her own "poor, sad little doll tea set": "It was remarkable that the cream-pitcher was the first of the family who had been broken, but Nelly had been very careful. There was a little plate badly cracked, and how dreadful if it should fall down the stairs and die on the way! It worried her terribly, the thought of this, as foolish things do worry us in dreams" (84).

In Nelly's dream the repressed content of her class anxieties becomes visible. First, the imagery of the funeral procession stresses both the decorum and the importance of its members. Judging by its lonely widow, the best china saucer was itself a rare piece of Canton porcelain, a link with the China Trade. Irreplaceable, it signifies the family's *history* of wealth, a history which the newly rich could never claim nor purchase. The patina on such goods, Grant McCracken writes, served "as a means of controlling status misrepresentation." It was "the terrible gatekeeper, the unforgiving test of who could, and could not, claim gentle standing."[19] According to Lloyd Warner and Paul Lunt's sociological study of privileged New England families in "Yankee City," "the inheritance of ritual objects from the past and their use by living lineal descendants provide the members of the upper-class group with a symbolic apparatus which ties the sentiments of the living with those of the dead. The house, its furnishing, and the gardens thus become symbolic expressions of the relations not only between household members but also between the living and the dead."[20] Significantly, the imperial dimensions of the Willis family's authority may also be signified by the china, which is here inscribed with the very image of the "heathen other," those Chinese men and women who seem here literally in service to white civilization.[21]

This fragile, prestigious china has become Nelly's fragile, prestigious family, for which *she* is responsible. That very fragility, and the constant vigilance it demands, here gives material form to the instability of the class hierarchy: the ever-present danger that those "on top" will slip "down," "fragment," and lose all integrity. The carnivalesque tea party caused the first breakage; will others follow? From Amelia's overprotective "mamma," Nelly has become an accomplice to negligent homicide, the mother's nightmare: "And next she thought, what if some of the other china should trip and fall, or if one of the heavy soup-tureens should go crashing down among the rest. She did not dare to watch any longer" (84).

Jane's influence threatens to bring the whole family crashing down. And that fall would be more than material. Painted porcelain and silver plate do more than display economic status. Becoming adept at manipulating these utensils is one of bourgeois childhood's central tasks for, as any middle-class Victorian mama would tell you, table manners are what separate people from pigs, civilized from savage. This family's domestic culture depends upon its formal rituals—those ceremonies that Jane Simmons has disrupted and whose sacred objects she has trashed—for they maintain the boundary between purity and pollution, clean and dirty, respectable and disreputable.[22] Suffice it to say that naughty Jane, brimming with class resentment and chaotic impulses, aimed straight for the heart of the genteel home. And at that heart is Nelly herself, for she is the family's true "fragile vessel." In her intact body and virginal reputation the Willis family's future prestige resides.

Alive to the danger, Nelly rushes up from bed to confess all in the morning. The admission purifies Nelly, but alas, poor Jane. The polluting agent cannot be purified. As Mrs. Willis explains, "I am sorry for the naughty little girl. I wish I could have done something for her; I tried, but she has always made you naughty, and I am afraid you cannot do her any good." Unlike those two other famous bad girls of sentimental fiction, Nancy Vawse of Warner's *The Wide, Wide World* (1850) and Topsy of Stowe's *Uncle Tom's Cabin* (1855), Jane is not a redeemable victim but a hardened perpetrator. Whereas the tears and earnest Christian love of Ellen Montgomery and Little Eva softened those other savage hearts and led them to embrace civilization's chastening rod, Jane's wickedness looms here as the stronger, more seductive influence. Indeed this is not the first time she has prevailed over Nelly's wavering and divided will. As with the nation's "Indian problem," the solution here is removal, virtually exorcism: the Simmons family "moves away the very next week." A nice little girl takes the place of bad Jane. But while Nelly is no longer bored nor lonely, "she has always wondered what it was Jane had in her pocket for the party." However, good girls must go without such interesting knowledge, which comes at too dear a price.

Unlike *Pointed Firs*, "The Best China Saucer" represents a character associated with nature as a destructive and subversive force.[23] In this early work we find Jewett grappling with the class divisions of bourgeois, industrialized society and, in what I believe is a direct consequence, with the polarized feminine images of the Victorian imagination: a miniature Virgin and Whore. What is interesting here, however, is the sly vein of humor running through the tale. The narrator's tone makes Nelly's boredom, and its sources, perfectly clear. We are in full complicity with her fall from grace. Although we see our heroine restored to the world of light, her walk on the wild side is presented as wholly normal behavior; little girls are not born little ladies, but must be taught the consequences of *not* being them. Though Nelly nurses her dolls, she is not a doll herself. However, "The Best China Saucer" ends with a sense of disappointment that Nelly's curiosity is not to be satisfied. She will get the compensation of a new friend—the compensation most Victorian genteel women found for their restriction—but she does not get to see what is in Jane's pocket. Nor do we know if Nelly will find the bird's nest she was originally seeking, or if she will ever explore the boundaries of the domestic garden or venture beyond its gates.

Indeed, though few would want Nelly to follow Jane's path, there is some truth to the bad girl's taunt that Nelly is a "'fraid cat." We see this "nervous" Nelly when she discovers, sometime after the disastrous party, that Jane has swiped Amelia's petticoat. In fact, this theft was a direct attack, for when Nelly went inside for the tea set she had entrusted Amelia's care to Jane: "'Amelia is my sick doll, you know, and you must be very careful of her'. 'Yes'm', said Jane, meekly, and as soon as Nelly was out of sight, she looked at poor Amelia's clothes and robbed her of her flannel petticoat, which was prettily embroidered and new only the week before" (76–77). Notice that Jane addresses her "friend" in the "meek" tones of a social inferior. But also notice that she knows just where to strike in retaliation for her subordination: the doll's underwear. While its obscurity ensures her crime will not be immediately detected, the dainty hidden slip, symbol of superfluous luxury and feminine gentility, must have been an irresistible target. And Nelly's response once this deliberate, and covertly sexual, violation is uncovered is an intensified campaign of anxiety-ridden nurturing: "the doll was at once taken very ill, and did not sit up much for half the summer. One of the rooms in the baby-house was kept dark, and the dolls took turns sitting with her at night" (77). Nelly, it seems, has mothered Amelia into neurasthenia.

Thus, as the dirty Baby and its heathen mother carry the genteel girl's displaced sexuality and aggression away with them, Amelia, as the representation of respectable womanhood, suffers a compensatory illness, a hysterical mourning. This disturbing outcome and its implications are illuminated by historian Carroll Smith-Rosenberg's analysis of hysteria "as a disease peculiar to the Victorian bourgeois family and as a disease related, as well, to the role changes and conflicts bourgeois matrons experienced between the 1840s and the 1890s."[24] Smith-Rosenberg finds "a complex interplay . . . between the character traits assigned women in Victorian society and the characteristic symptoms of the nineteenth-century hysteric: dependency, fragility, emotionality, narcissism." Moreover, she attributes the rise of these symptoms to "the elaborate child-rearing literature that began to appear during the first third of the nineteenth century." The authors of this literature "forbade overt anger and violence as unfeminine and vulgar and they did not reward curiosity, intrusiveness, exploratory behavior, in women. Indeed when such characteristics conflicted with the higher feminine values of cleanliness, deportment, unobtrusiveness, or obedience, they were criticized or punished." Punishment was usually not corporal, but emotional: "the inculcation of guilt and . . . threats of withdrawal of love or actual separation from parents," treatment that made girls "timid, anxious, dependent, and sensitive to rejection."[25] In other words, hysterical 'fraid cats.

Placed within the context Smith-Rosenberg describes, Formanek-Brunell's discussion of doll play in the Gilded Age demonstrates how middle-class girls resisted these pressures, a resistance particularly evident in those play funerals with their cathartic expressions of hostility and violence, followed by ceremonial recuperations of order, all ritually enacted away from the judgmental eyes of parents. Although Zona Gale's smashed dolls might have required an explanation, it seems that the rule was anything goes, as long as the girls "all got home for supper."[26] In "The Best China Saucer," however, the initiating act is not Nelly's travesty of the adult tea party, which she seems eager to imitate faithfully, but her subversion of middle-class visiting. Nelly invites the "wrong" girl, of the "wrong" class. She then tries to cover her disobedience by assuming the role of her own mother in educating Jane about bourgeois manners. Then it is Jane who resists socialization, not by her own working-class mother, but by her middle-class "friend." Indeed Nelly initially plans to control Jane by threatening to abandon her if she misbehaves. But given Jane's absent mother and her own childcare responsibilities, one suspects that this threat holds no terrors for her. Jane is always, already abandoned.

Finally, in Formanek-Brunell's cases, the girls are not alienated from their own antisocial impulses; but here, although Nelly is well aware of the boredom and "stupidity" of gentility and able to acknowledge the fierce resistance actual childcare arouses in her, she seems unable to act on these feelings. Instead, Nelly depends upon the working-class Jane to initiate the "naughtiness" she at once desires and dreads. In this sense she is at least partially alienated from her own rebelliousness, since her agency is displaced onto Jane. Like Young Goodman Brown tempted into the dark Salem woods "just this once," she toys with releasing her own rejected impulses while piously avowing her intention to contain them and self-righteously displacing them onto her working-class temptress. With the breaking of the saucer, however, Nelly's complicity is revealed, for this breach of decorum cannot be ritually restored before mother comes home.

Part of the story then also concerns surveillance and discipline, since by giving Nelly freedom to explore her choices her mother also gives her responsibility for the consequences. The aim of this new disciplinary "liberalism," as Foucault and later Richard Brodhead noted, was to prompt the individual's internalization of constant moral surveillance.[27] Finally you cannot hide from mother's eyes. Thus Nelly's dream of the mock funeral, rather than restoring the disrupted order as we see in Formanek-Brunell's examples, instead fearfully exposes the larger implications of Nelly's forbidden play. The result is her self-disciplinary act of confession.[28] Significantly, her mother grants her absolution by shifting the entire blame onto Jane: "She has always made you naughty, and I am afraid you cannot do her any good." A displacement at first only partial and unstable is now complete and confirmed, and whatever access Nelly had to her rebellious impulses is authoritatively denied. No wonder Amelia takes to her bed.

If we return, briefly, to the figure of Huckleberry Finn, the gender differences are again significant. In his revised *Imagined Communities* Benedict Anderson, picking up the thread traced by Leslie Fielder, notes how nineteenth-century white male characters often take the heathen other into their embrace: most famously Natty Bumppo and Chingachgook, Ishmael and Queequeg.[29] In *Huckleberry Finn*, of course, imagined fraternity across class lines produces not only Tom Sawyer's attraction to Huckleberry Finn, but also Huck's almost unswerving allegiance to Tom; across racial lines it produces not only Huck's willingness to sacrifice his soul for Jim's freedom, but also Jim's loyalty and paternal bond to Huck. Unlike these tales of constructing white masculinity, however, Nelly and Jane will never become "companions in misfortune." There is no representation of sorority across class lines here (let alone racial ones). Nelly is left a remorseful Eve while Jane, like Lilith, departs the domestic Eden with a curse.

And yet, it first appears as if there will be a similar bonding. Nelly, like Tom Sawyer, is drawn to the excitement of escape from gentility. Jane, like Huck, is ambivalently drawn to the sentimental comforts of middle-class family life. But if Huck's famous "innocent eye" registers middle-class pretensions and hypocrisy, he never unmasks those contradictions openly. While he expresses his rejection of civilization's requirements by slipping out the bedroom window (or off to the territories), he never musters Jane Simmons's bitter interrogation and outright denunciation. Nor does Huck leave the domestic settings he escapes trashed and broken. That job is left to his father, Pap, who in a drunken romp leaves a sentimental judge's guest bedroom so devastated that its features are unrecognizable. Finally, Tom Sawyer's status and masculinity are not threatened but curiously heightened by his adventures with Huck and his masquerade as a "gaudy outcast." What is "wild oats" for boys is "ruin" for middle-class girls.

Thus Jewett's surface story, far from offering a comforting democratic parable, apparently validates middle-class fears of working-class behavior and rationalizes the boundaries between the two groups. While the original *Pointed Firs* closes with the anonymous narrator receiving a treasured heirloom from her rural landlady as a sign of their friendship and an extension of family membership, here a similarly treasured heirloom is broken in the attempt to bridge the gulf between Nelly and Jane. It becomes a sign, not of differences transcended, but of differences transgressed. Whether or not good fences make good neighbors, this story suggests that they protect the purity of middle-class women within from the danger of working-class women without. Moreover, Jewett carefully protects the purity of her middle-class readers as well. While Nelly never discovers what was in Jane's pocket, we never get to hear her "very provoking" last words.

At the same time, however, Jewett's subtext suggests the subtle cost of such fences in personal and cultural pathology. There is, for example, that opening clause, permitting even a young reader to decide that her mother is perhaps not so wise after all. And although Jewett's narrator seems to turn away from the dangerous and dirty Jane, abandoning her to an unknown fate beyond the story's ending, as a reader I suspect this bad girl will survive, albeit outside the bounds of her author's future literary production. That is, if Jewett addressed her story to Nelly, she also imagined Jane, and gave her that rude, abrupt, and angry voice, with its wonderful "runaway tongue." Moreover, it is the doll who becomes hysterically ill, not its owner. While Nelly may have learned to deny her rebellious feelings, Amelia's prostration may also be read as the result of a covert and intensified campaign of passive-aggressive hostility: the symptomatic return of impulses Nelly has repressed. Here we may be seeing what Jewett's earliest readers praised as her "delicate" humor or what Willa Cather called her "arch" wit.[30] Although the narrator claims ignorance as to why Nelly played with Jane and withholds those "bad words" from our tender ears, her teasing silences invite readerly speculation and her overtly moralizing tone, as "faded" and cliched as Amelia's charms, slyly parodies its own reticence: "How can I tell it?"

There is a strange and subtle duplicity in this text, almost a countertext underlying its surface tale of brutal class antagonisms. The wit does not so much soften these antagonisms as unsettle and trouble them. Unlike Twain's fantasies of comradeship, this story gives its audience class conflict straight up, with a moral solidly in service of middle-class interests. And yet that arch voice invites us to question that moral, to revisit the scene of the crime and re-vision its meanings. By subtly suggesting that this encounter is not an outrage perpetrated against the haves by the have-nots, but a failed opportunity for "companionship in misfortune," Jewett's story may actually reenact the difficulty of overcoming class differences and the penalty paid on both sides for failure. Unlike the scenes of achieved friendship between women of different classes in *Pointed Firs*, with their sacramental sharing of apple pies and gingerbread houses, this story ends with its rituals disrupted, never to be completed. Its narrative silences suggest not ineffable sympathy but disturbing repression, "unspeakable things unspoken." As Toni Morrison saw in her brilliant exposition of white writers' "fabrication of the Africanist presence," Jewett's figuring of the banished Jane is "reflexive; an extraordinary meditation on the self; a powerful exploration of the fears and desires that reside within the writerly consciousness."[31] I recall Helen Papashvily's description of sentimentalism's subversive undertone, like a cup of sweet tea with just a slight taste of poison.[32] Here the aftertaste seems neither rage nor bitterness, but the faint, pervasive flavor of loss.

Notes

I particularly wish to thank Brigitte Bailey, Melody Graulich, Karen Kilcup, Marjorie Pryse, and Rachel Trubowitz for their insightful comments on earlier drafts of this essay.

1. Sarah Orne Jewett, Preface to *Deephaven and Other Stories* (1877; rpt., New Haven: College and University Press, 1966), 32. Also, *The Country of the Pointed Firs* (Boston and New York: Houghton Mifflin, 1896) and "The Foreigner," *Atlantic Monthly* (August 1900).

2. Sarah Orne Jewett, "The Best China Saucer," in *Play-Days: A Book of Stories for Children* (Boston: Houghton, Osgood, 1878). All subsequent references are cited in the text. To the best of my knowledge this work has not received previous critical attention. It is being reprinted in a forthcoming anthology to be edited by Paul Lauter and Anne Lauter.

Recent publications addressing issues of class, ethnicity, and race in Jewett's work include Richard H. Brodhead, "Jewett, Regionalism, and Writing as Women's Work," in his *Cultures of Letters: Scenes of Reading and Writing in Nineteenth-*

Century America (Chicago and London: University of Chicago Press, 1993); *New Essays on "The Country of the Pointed Firs,"* ed. June Howard (New York: Cambridge University Press, 1994); Amy Kaplan, "Nation, Region, and Empire," in *The Columbia History of the American Novel*, ed. Emory Elliott (New York: Columbia University Press, 1991); Karen [Kilcup] Oakes, "'Colossal in Sheet-Lead': The Native American and Piscataqua-Region Writers," in *"A Noble and Dignified Stream": The Piscataqua Region in the Colonial Revival, 1860–1930*, ed. Sarah L. Giffen and Kevin D. Murphy (York, Maine: Old York Historical Society, 1992). See also Marilyn Sanders Mobley's excellent study, *Folk Roots and Mythic Wings in Sarah Orne Jewett and Toni Morrison: The Cultural Function of Narrative* (Baton Rouge and London: Louisiana State University Press, 1991). My discussion is also informed by two valuable conference papers: Marjorie Pryse, "Sex, Class, and 'Category Crisis'," keynote address delivered at "Sarah Orne Jewett and Her Contemporaries: The Centennial Conference," Westbrook College, Portland, Maine (June 21–23, 1996), and Sandra Zagarell, "*Deephaven* and Regional Literature," paper delivered at "Borrowing Enchantment: Sarah Orne Jewett's Invention of Rural Maine," Berwick Academy, South Berwick, Maine (June 26, 1994). Pryse's revised essay appears in this volume as chapter 1.

3. The scholarship on this historical problem is too extensive to cite here. However, the following studies have informed my thinking for this essay: Elizabeth Ammons, *Conflicting Stories: American Women Writers at the Turn into the Twentieth Century* (New York: Oxford University Press, 1992); Hazel V. Carby, *Reconstructing Womanhood: The Emergence of the Afro-American Woman Novelist* (New York: Oxford University Press, 1987); Ann D. Gordon and Mari Jo Buhle, "Sex and Class in Colonial and Nineteenth-Century America," in *Liberating Women's History*, ed. Bernice A. Carroll (Urbana: University of Illinois Press, 1976); bell hooks, *Black Looks: Race and Representation* (Boston: South End Press, 1992); Winthrop D. Jordon, *White over Black: American Attitudes toward the Negro, 1550–1812* (Baltimore: Penguin, 1968); Gerda Lerner, "The Lady and the Mill Girl: Changes in the Status of Women in the Age of Jackson, 1790–1840," in *A Heritage of Her Own*, ed. Nancy F. Cott and Elizabeth J. Pleck (New York: Simon and Schuster, 1979); Marjorie Pryse and Hortense Spillers, eds., *Conjuring: Black Women, Fiction, and Literary Tradition* (Bloomington: Indiana University Press, 1985); Diane Roberts, *The Myth of Aunt Jemima: Representations of Race and Region* (London and New York: Verso, 1994); and Hortense Spillers, "Mama's Baby, Papa's Maybe: An American Grammar Book," *Diacritics* 17 (1987): 65–81.

4. My theoretical analysis of the cultural meanings of purity and pollution comes from Mary Douglas, *Purity and Danger: An Analysis of the Concepts of Pollution and Taboo* (London: Routledge, 1966). A thorough discussion of nineteenth-century concepts of savagery and civilization can be found in Roy Harvey Pearce, *Savagism and Civilization: A Study of the Indian and the American Mind* (Baltimore: Johns Hopkins University Press, 1953, 1965). For a discussion of

Victorian connections between the behavior of "primitive" tribes and that of the English-speaking working-classes, see George W. Stocking, Jr., "Victorian Cultural Ideology and the Image of Savagery (1780–1870)," in his *Victorian Anthropology* (New York: Free Press, 1987), 186–237.

Amy Kaplan's essay "Manifest Domesticity," *American Literature* 70:3 (1998): 581-606, appeared after this essay was completed. However, its argument parallels some of the points made here. For example, "domesticity," according to Kaplan, is a process "which entails conquering and taming the wild, the natural, and the alien. Domestic in this sense is related to the imperial project of civilizing, and the conditions of domesticity often become the markers that distinguish civilization from savagery" (582).

5. Miriam Formanek-Brunell, *Made to Play House: Dolls and the Commercialization of American Girlhood, 1830–1930* (New Haven: Yale University Press, 1993). See also Lynne Vallone, *Disciplines of Virtue: Girls' Culture in the Eighteenth and Nineteenth Centuries* (New Haven: Yale University Press, 1995), and *Small Worlds: Children and Adolescents in America, 1850–1950*, ed. Elliott West and Paula Petrik (Lawrence: University Press of Kansas, 1992).

6. Formanek-Brunell, 32. The interior quotations are from Ethel Spencer, *The Spencers of Amberson Avenue: A Turn of the Century Memoir*, ed. Michael P. Weber and Peter N. Stearns (Pittsburgh: University of Pittsburgh Press, 1983), 65. For an example of a text designed to supplement doll play, see Anonymous, *The Doll's Tea Party* (Boston: Lothrop, 1895).

7. For a discussion of these incidents and an overview of Jewett's life and career, see Paula Blanchard, *Sarah Orne Jewett: Her World and Her Work* (Reading, Mass.: Addison-Wesley, 1994). Blanchard also points out that, despite its rural image, South Berwick was an industrial center in Jewett's lifetime. A cotton mill was built on the Salmon Falls in 1832, and a woolen mill was founded, by a Jewett neighbor, on the Great Works River in 1855: "Both created jobs for young people from the farms and attracted growing numbers of newcomers, chiefly from Ireland and Quebec" (10). Given the mills and tenements within walking distance of Jewett's home, this story and its working-class characters may have had sources in the author's own childhood.

8. My 1989 study *Sarah Orne Jewett: An American Persephone* (Hanover and London: University Press of New England) treated the intersection of gender and class ideologies throughout its analysis (in fact, this article grows out of a chapter deleted from that earlier study). If I were to revise that book now, ten years later, I would want to explore the issues of race and ethnicity more carefully. For example, I then took note of the way constructions of white genteel femininity excluded black working women, but mentioned this crucial problem only in passing and without stressing its racial component (13). I would also want to emphasize the limitations of Jewett's pastoral resolution to the cultural conflicts underlying her work. Her celebration of the preindustrial world, while powerful and evocative, also evades the difficulty of applying its lessons to the

task of healing a society structured through the inequalities of imperialism and industrial capitalism. In stories like "The Best China Saucer" or "The Gray Mills of Farley" (1898) Jewett occasionally attempted to address directly the problems raised by a industrialized and urbanized society, particularly the problem of class. Thus, although this work may be seen as artistically less successful than *Pointed Firs*, that weakness may be due to Jewett's tackling of issues that she was not able to resolve in satisfying ways (perhaps because of her own conflicted loyalties). For an analysis of the pastoral genre's evasion of conflicts created by imperialism and industrial capitalism, see Raymond Williams, *The Country and the City* (New York: Oxford University Press, 1973).

9. Mark Twain, *The Adventures of Tom Sawyer* (1876; rpt. New York: Children's Classics, 1989), 39.

10. See Annis Pratt, "Women and Nature in Modern Fiction," *Contemporary Literature* 13 (1972): 476–90. Also, Simone de Beauvoir, *The Second Sex*, trans. H. M. Parshley (New York: Knopf, 1952).

11. See Nancy Cott, "Passionlessness: An Interpretation of Victorian Sexual Ideology, 1790–1850," in *A Heritage of Her Own*, ed. Cott and Pleck.

12. Gordon and Buhle, "Sex and Class," 290–91.

13. Karen Sánchez-Eppler, *Touching Liberty: Abolition, Feminism, and the Politics of the Body* (Berkeley: University of California Press, 1993), 133–34.

14. Roberts, *The Myth of Aunt Jemima*, 5. See also Mikhail Bakhtin, *Rabelais and His World*, trans. Helene Iswolsky (Bloomington: Indiana University Press, 1984), passim.

15. Roberts, *The Myth of Aunt Jemima*, 5–6.

16. Peter Stallybrass and Allon White, *The Politics and Poetics of Transgression* (London: Methuen, 1986), 5, quoted in Roberts, *The Myth of Aunt Jemima*, 6. Toni Morrison's important work on the Africanist presence in the "white" imagination and American literature is directly pertinent here. See Morrison, "Unspeakable Things Unspoken: The Afro-American Presence in American Literature" (1990), reprinted in *Within the Circle: An Anthology of African American Literary Criticism from the Harlem Renaissance to the Present*, ed. Angelyn Mitchell (Durham and London: Duke University Press, 1994), and *Playing in the Dark: Whiteness and the Literary Imagination* (New York: Vintage, 1992). When Morrison looks at white American writers' attempts to "imagine an Africanist other," she discovers that "the subject of the dream is the dreamer" (*Playing in the Dark*, 16–17).

17. Stocking, "Victorian Cultural Ideology," 229. According to Anne McClintock, in *Imperial Leather: Race, Gender, and Sexuality in the Colonial Context* (New York: Routledge, 1995), "by the latter half of the nineteenth century . . . an intricate dialectic emerged—between the domestication of the colonies and the racializing of the metropolis. In the metropolis, the idea of racial deviance was evoked to police the 'degenerate' classes—the militant working class, the Irish, Jews, feminists, gays and lesbians, prostitutes, criminals, alcoholics and the in-

sane—who were collectively figured as racial deviants, atavistic throwbacks to a primitive moment in human prehistory, surviving ominously in the heart of the modern, imperial metropolis" (43).

18. Stocking, "Victorian Cultural Ideology," 229–30. For further discussions of the iconography of the female "savage," see Donna J. Kessler, *The Making of Sacagawea: A Euro-American Legend* (Tuscaloosa and London: University of Alabama Press, 1996), 9–30. Also Pearce, *Savagism and Civilization;* Louise K. Barnett, *The Ignoble Savage: American Literary Racism, 1790–1890* (Westport, Conn., and London: Greenwood, 1975); Robert F. Berkhover, *The White Man's Indian: Images of the American Indian from Columbus to the Present* (New York: Knopf, 1978); and Rayna Green, "The Pocahontas Perplex: The Image of Indian Women in American Culture," *Massachusetts Review* 16.4 (1976): 698–714.

19. Grant McCracken, "'Ever Dearer in Our Thoughts': Patina and the Representation of Status before and after the Eighteenth Century," *Culture and Consumption: New Approaches to the Symbolic Character of Consumer Goods and Activities* (Bloomington: Indiana University Press, 1988), 41.

20. W. Lloyd Warner and Paul S. Lunt, *The Social Life of a Modern Community* (New Haven: Yale University Press, 1941), 107; quoted in McCracken, "'Ever Dearer'," 41. See also Mihaly Csikszentmihalyi and Eugene Rochberg-Halton, *The Meaning of Things: Domestic Symbols and the Self* (New York: Cambridge University Press, 1981). Analyzing the high value often ascribed to heirloom china, Csikszentmihalyi and Rochberg-Halton conclude that, given its fragility, "a china cup preserved over a generation is a victory of human purpose over chaos." Older people they interviewed especially valued such objects, perhaps because, "having witnessed the dissolution of many relationships, the decay of many forms of structured order, they appreciated the meaning of an unbroken dish" (83).

21. For a provocative discussion of imperialism and material culture in Jewett's work, see Elizabeth Ammons, "Material Culture, Empire, and Jewett's *The Country of the Pointed Firs*," in *New Essays*, ed. Howard, 81–99.

22. See Douglas, *Purity and Danger*, passim. According to Douglas, "uncleanness or dirt is that which must not be included if a pattern is to be maintained" (53). It is "matter out of place" and therefore "we must approach it through order." That is, the unclean or polluting is the anomalous or contradictory which must be excluded for a classifying system to remain consistent, "for any system of classification must give rise to anomalies, and any given culture must confront events which seem to defy its assumptions. It cannot ignore the anomalies which its scheme produces, except at risk of forfeiting confidence" (52). As I hope this essay shows, Jane Simmons transgresses bourgeois American culture's orderly system and unmasks its contradictions at several points.

See also Kaplan's "Manifest Domesticity," which argues that "domesticity not only monitors the borders between the civilized and the savage but also regulates traces of the savage within itself" (582). Further discussions of the

Victorian tendency to see white children as "savages" who must be domesticated and civilized may be found in Karen Sánchez-Eppler, "Raising Empires like Children: Race, Nation, and Religious Education," *American Literary History* 8 (1996): 399–425, and Ann Stoler, *Race and the Education of Desire: Foucault's* History of Sexuality *and the Colonial Order of Things* (Durham, N.C.: Duke University Press, 1995), 137–64.

23. Significantly, one other example is Mrs. Bonny, from *Deephaven*, published in 1877, the same period as *Play-Days.* Mrs. Bonny lives on Deephaven's wilder border in a house marked by its chaotic housekeeping. Here, as in "Best China Saucer," "savagery" and "dirt" are associated. Comparing her hostess to a "good-natured Indian," the young narrator of *Deephaven* is nevertheless too disgusted by the grimy cup Mrs. Bonny offers to drink from it. For a valuable discussion of this passage and the treatment of American Indians generally by Jewett and related writers, see [Kilcup] Oakes, "'Colossal in Sheet-Lead'."

24. Carroll Smith-Rosenberg, "The Hysterical Woman: Sex Roles and Role Conflict in Nineteenth-Century America," in her *Disorderly Conduct: Visions of Gender in Victorian America* (New York: Oxford University Press, 1985), 198. Revisiting this problem, Amy Kaplan argues that "the fear of disease and the invalidism that characterizes the American woman also serves as a metaphor for anxiety about contagion from the very subjects she must domesticate and civilize, her wilderness children and foreign servants, who ultimately infect both the home and the body of the mother" ("Manifest Domesticity," 591).

25. Smith-Rosenberg, "Hysterical Woman," 207, 212, 212–13, 214.

26. I cannot help thinking here of Maurice Sendak's classic *Where the Wild Things Are* (New York: Harper and Row, 1963), which similarly closes with a child safely returned from his rebellious journey to the land of monsters, only to find his supper waiting, "and it was still hot."

27. See Michel Foucault, *Discipline and Punish: The Birth of the Prison*, trans. Alan Sheridan (New York: Vintage, 1979), and Richard H. Brodhead, "Sparing the Rod: Discipline and Fiction in Antebellum America," in his *Cultures of Letters.*

28. Mrs. Willis's model of disciplinary liberalism seems similar to Marmee's strategies in Louisa May Alcott's *Little Women* (1868), a book Jewett certainly knew. See Richard Brodhead's "Sparing the Rod" for a Foucaldian analysis of that novel and its disciplinary practices.

29. See Benedict Anderson, *Imagined Communities: Reflections on the Origin and Spread of Nationalism* (London: Verso, 1983), 202–3.

30. Willa Cather, Preface to *The Best Stories of Sarah Orne Jewett* (Boston: Houghton Mifflin, 1925). For a study of narration and narrators in nineteenth-century women's literature, see Susan K. Harris, *Nineteenth-Century American Women's Novels: Interpretative Strategies* (New York: Cambridge University Press, 1990).

31. Morrison, "Playing in the Dark," 16–17.

32. Helen Papashvily, *All the Happy Endings: A Study of the Domestic Novel in America, the Women Who Wrote It, the Women Who Read It, in the Nineteenth Century* (New York: Harper and Brothers, 1956). I am reminded here as well of Toni Morrison's comment that "the trauma of racism is, for the racist and the victim, a severe fragmentation of self, and has always seemed to me a cause (not a symptom) of psychosis" ("Unspeakable Things Unspoken," 381).

Part IV

Connections

Jewett's Time and Place

"A Brave Happiness"

Rites and Celebrations in Jewett's Ordered Past

Graham Frater

In Jewett's stories for children, themes that underlie her principal work are often handled with notable transparency. *Betty Leicester's English Xmas* is a case in point.[1] Betty is with her father in England: Leicester's academic pursuits have taken him to work on Native American artifacts in the British Museum. He discovers evidence of ancient rites of passage and, in the central episode of the book, Betty is the prime mover in what becomes, in effect, a similar rite drawing past and present together. A Christmas guest in a great English house, Betty possesses social gifts that make the visit a success for two other young people: Edith, another visiting American, and, most significantly, Warford, the young heir to the estate. Still a schoolboy at Eton, Warford is consumed by an overwhelming diffidence that extends to the burden of his inheritance—the family title, the great house, its estates and traditions. Betty bonds the young people into an alliance; they devise a masque that they perform to the grownups at a grand Christmas supper. Their venture is a great success. Specifically, Betty's revival of an ancient celebration has the effect of reconciling the young heir to his inheritance: "For the first time in his life he felt a brave happiness in belonging to Danesly, and in the thought that it really belonged to him; he looked down the long room at Lady Mary, and he loved her as he never had before, and understood things all in a flash" (75). Through ceremony, Betty has linked past with present to secure the future: Warford's acceptance of his destiny has been achieved through a ritual revived by a young American. An affirmation of the past has brought together the young people from both sides of the Atlantic in a manner that recalls "the closest of kindred ties," which, when closing her Norman history, Jewett had urged that each should acknowledge.[2]

Other ritual affirmations of the past are readily found in Jewett's work: each is commonly allied to an abiding interest in notions of nobility, in inherited qualities, or in the achievement or restoration of order; and an interest in American roots and identity, found prominently in the Norman histories, is seldom far away.[3] However, Betty's reinforcement of the male line of an aristocratic English family sits oddly with Jewett's republican views and feminist sympathies. As will emerge, *Betty Leicester's English Xmas* is one of several tales where themes relating to the past are handled with variable degrees of explicitness and consistency.

Two Family Gatherings

In 1855, members of the Jewett family in the United States were invited to gather at Rowley in Essex County, Massachusetts, with the object of providing an opportunity for "mutual conference, and joyful greetings, for renewing and strengthening the bands of common brotherhood, and, in particular, to adopt measures for obtaining such historic facts as will perfect the genealogy of the Jewett Family and perpetuate those facts by publication in a well printed and neatly bound volume."[4] The reunion was scheduled for the 14th of June; a substantial and ceremonial occasion was planned, complete with an "Order of Exercises." These included a procession to "places of interest" in Rowley, a short address "under the stately elms" at the Old Jewett Homestead, and the singing ("to the music of 'Bonny Doon'") of "an original poem, entitled 'The Old Homestead'," composed by William Jewett Pabodie of Providence (*Jewetts*, x). The plan also entailed a procession to the meeting house, a service with a voluntary, hymns, an anthem, an oration by Professor C. C. Jewett of Washington, D.C., and a benediction by the Rev. Spofford D. Jewett of Colchester, Connecticut. Following the service, a further procession was scheduled and "those having tickets" were to dine, with additional "exercises," in the Town Hall. At the dinner, the President of the day was introduced by the Chief Marshal, and celebrations ensued: an invocation; a short genealogical address; "the singing of an original song, 'Our Family Pledge'," to the tune of "Auld Lang Syne"; and a sequence of "TOASTS, INTERCHANGE OF SENTIMENTS, and FAMILY CONGRATULATIONS, interspersed with music by the band" (*Jewetts*, x).

These ceremonies are recorded in *The Jewetts of America*, the "well printed and neatly bound volume"—two volumes in fact—that eventually emerged as a consequence of the occasion. They are rich with historical significance, showing us a New England family celebrating its origins, its connectedness as a clan, the successes of its members, the extent of its spread, and its rootedness in new soil. "Our Family Pledge" (*Jewetts*, xii–xiii), specially composed by Jedediah Jewett of Portland, Maine, is printed in full. It celebrates the family's gathering here "Upon old Rowley's shore," the spread of their branches "From Pine clad East and fertile West," the quest for freedom that first prompted their departure from England, and the emblems of the family crest; it concludes with the company's pledge to keep the name unsullied. Plainly, the Jewett clan was setting out its claim to be a founding family and to have lived up to its inheritance. In his introduction, Frederic Clarke Jewett notes, "The history of our family, quiet and unpretending as it has always been, is associated with the most stirring and impressive events of modern times. Our ancestors were actors in the most important scenes of the moving panorama of human progress" (*Jewetts*, xix). It is just this sense that New England families and towns had been engaged with the shaping of great events that animated "The Old Town of Berwick" and *The Tory Lover* in particular and may be felt throughout Sarah Orne Jewett's work.[5]

The writer herself was only six years old at the time of the Rowley exercises and neither she nor her parents are recorded in the invitation list. The two volumes took most of her lifetime to reach print. Nonetheless, it seems unlikely that she was unaware either of what had occurred or of these slowly accumulating family materials. Internal evidence suggests that her own entry in the genealogy, one of the more extensive, was composed around 1891.[6] It is improbable that she did not know of its existence. Moreover, the book tells of the Norman origins of the family, ponders the etymology of the name and takes the family line back to Bradford in Yorkshire, giving us facts that have become the biographical commonplaces of Jewett studies.

There are significant similarities and differences between the Rowley exercises and the Bowden reunion in Jewett's touchstone work *The Country of the Pointed Firs.* While the one event actually occurred and the other is fictional, as Bakhtin notes, "the boundaries between fiction and nonfiction, between literature and nonliterature . . . are not laid up in heaven."[7] In each case we have a text that mediates experience. Indeed, the chief differences between the Rowley exercises and the Bowden reunion lie in just this mediation, though structural similarities between the two occasions may, perhaps, be more instantly apparent; some, indeed, may be set out as a table:

Rowley Gathering	**Bowden Reunion**
Formal processions	A formal procession
Visit to Old Jewett Homestead	Old Bowden house is site of reunion
Ceremony under ancient elms at homestead	Feast in grove of trees on Bowden estate
Poetry composed for the occasion	A "faded garland of verses"
Formal speeches, including a short geneaology	Speeches and "some fine anecdotes of the family history"
The presence of a marshal or marshals	Santin Bowden
Family banquet	Family feast
Interchange of greetings, etc.	Greetings throughout, though perhaps less formally than at Rowley

Both events are celebrations of genealogy; both are ceremonial affirmations of the past, of survival and of family links. Each suggests a growing sense of national identity. F. C. Jewett's claim that the "panorama of human progress" may be found within his family history implicitly invokes an optimistic model of historical development of the kind found in Jewett's Norman histories. The rhetoric of Rowley's poetry and hymns echoes these uncomplicated sentiments; the heedlessly affirmative tone of the verse, of the introductory narrative materials, and of the individual entries in the genealogy is almost wholly unqualified. In the Rowley exercises and their book of genealogy, the Jewetts were creating and controlling the only coherent record of their dynasty, the one which they wished to remember for themselves and to be remembered for by others.

The Bowden reunion is much the more complex event and lacks the unclouded optimism of the equally mediated Rowley exercises. With "the likeness of 'most every sort of a foreigner . . . in our parish," the gathering becomes a microcosm.[8] The narrator, however, displays something of the preoccupation with genetic inheritance that may be found in Jewett's Norman histories. She picks out a "curiously French type of face . . . in this rustic company" (93); she adds, somewhat didactically, that a large "proportion of the early settlers on this northern coast of New England were of Huguenot blood" and urges dogmatically that "*it is the Norman Englishman, not the Saxon, who goes adventuring to a new world.*"[9] This comment underlines the Bowdens' status as representing the core of what is best in American history; elsewhere, Jewett had already urged that Americans were "the Normans of modern times."[10] The gap between Jewett and her implied author is perhaps at its narrowest here. The genetic determinism of the Norman histories formed an essential part of her understanding of the past; it was readily carried across into her fiction through authorial commentary (as here), where, just as readily, it could draw tension and inconsistency into her texts.

Genetic issues strike a melancholy note among the Bowdens: unfulfilled qualities contrast sharply with the high-achieving company at Rowley. Santin Bowden, the master of ceremonies, with his "fine resemblance to Mrs. Blackett" (91), is particularly significant: his "gift" for military drill ("'Taint nothin' he's ever acquired; 'twas born in him" [93]) is confined to strictly civic and social ceremonials—he was rejected for the Civil War as unfit. It is as if the strength of the Bowden strain is running out, and, indeed, we learn that there used to be "a great many more Bowdens" (88). Despite their "inheritance of good taste and skill and a certain pleasing gift of formality" (96), there is a sense of blighted potential about other family members too: "More than one face among the Bowdens showed that only opportunity and stimulus were lacking,—a narrow set of circumstances had caged a fine able character and held it captive" (97). When the narrator is prompted to wonder "at the waste of human ability in this world" (97), she conveys an implicit message that opportunities for development and personal fulfillment lie elsewhere—out West and in the newly burgeoning cities.

While Rowley's exercises celebrate the expansion of the Jewett clan across the States, the focus of the Bowden reunion is upon those who remained close to the roots they first put down. Where the Jewetts joined the expanding middle classes to become professors, doctors, and parsons, or, like Sarah's grandfather, left the sea to prosper as traders and ship owners, the Bowdens carried on the simple ways of the founding fathers, close to land and sea. The reunion can be read as an elegy for those ways of life. At Rowley, the Jewetts celebrated their past and expressed confidence in their future. With their diminishing numbers, courtly manners, and poignant burying ground, the elderly company of the Bowdens celebrates its survival, its bonds of love and kinship, but without reference to an expansive future. That it is also a threatened survival is signaled by the ceremonial pies and cakes with their edible reading matter: the "whole word Bowden" on an excellent early-apple pie was consumed, with perhaps special significance, by an urban outsider—the narrator herself (98). What makes the partings at the end of the reunion so prolonged and touching is the unspoken awareness that they may never be repeated.

The Bowdens and Dunnet Landing are isolated, not only in time and space, but from the tide of progress sweeping across America. While the Bowdens slip into the past, the reunion chapters place them within a longer historical context; their continuity has less in common with the fast-arriving machine age than with the order and archetypes of antiquity. The thrust of the classical references scattered throughout the book is at its plainest here. The narrator comments of the processing Bowdens that "we might have been a company of ancient Greeks going to celebrate a victory, or to worship the god of harvests in the grove above" (91). Indeed, she reaches further back to link the Bowdens of the New World with a wider human canvas—"we were no more a New England family celebrating its own existence and simple progress; we carried tokens and inheritance of all such households from which this had descended, and were only the latest of our line" (92). The accumulation of such references affirms that the New World, however raw, is in a clear line of descent from the old.

However, this long continuity, which is of the land and sea, a world powered by muscle, wind, and water, is itself drawing toward an end. In this regard, Sarah Way Sherman's study is especially helpful: she sees pastoral worlds as "defined by their position on the periphery of the urban, patriarchal world and by their mediation between that world and the wilderness."[11] Much of the book's elegiac power resides in the narrator's and reader's growing sense that the pointed firs country is being increasingly marginalized. While the expansive Jewett clan represents a new direction responsive to change, the Bowdens stand for a pastoral first phase of American history. They are part of a continuum that was faltering at much the same time on both sides of the Atlantic.

The Bowden reunion marks the end of pastoral within a rapidly developing Western civilization. In celebrating their fading clan, Jewett signaled a break with processional continuity, an end to old patterns and certainties. It is a melancholy note that contrasts sharply with the confident assertiveness of the Jewett family gathering at Rowley.

Civil War Aftermath

By contrast, "Decoration Day," though poignant and effective, shares something of the gentle didacticism of the Betty Leicester books; it is an adult tale where Jewett's assignment of values may be seen at its least complicated.[12]

The story is a triptych showing the village of Barlow and its veterans before, during, and after the first Civil War commemoration ever held there. The veterans are few and elderly: only nine are left. At the start, the three old men who are the instigators are shown in a tableau that is typical of Jewett's male figures: idling near the village store, they are impotent and neglected figures, not respected elders. All are veterans; their wartime experiences—barely understood even by themselves—continue to affect their lives, to isolate them from their peers and the younger generation alike. By the end, however, a change has occurred—"folks won't never say again that we can't show no public sperit here in old Barlow" (64).

Commemoration has been long delayed; while regular memorial ceremonies have been held in neighboring towns, none has occurred in Barlow ("'Tis a terrible scattered population . . . to favor with a procession" [50]). Partly owing to the delay, when it comes, the ceremony has something of the immediacy and directness of Betty's celebration at Danesly. The Barlow Decoration Day is an act of recognition and expiation, the community's settlement with its past. The rituals provide the element of transformation necessary for communal recognition to occur. The "brief evolutions" of the veterans' drill "were like a mystic rite" (52). The old soldiers' ancient accoutrements—not least because they are tattered—defamiliarize them, helping the townsfolk to perceive a new significance in these "old stick-in-the-mud" (45) figures and in the events they had undergone. No longer were they the "familiar men and neighbors alone,—they were part of that army which had saved its country" (54). In turn, the old men's transformations trigger others: watching from a window, an old woman whose sons and grandsons had gone to war "straightened her bent figure with all the vigor of youth. . . . [H]er old eyes flashed and then filled with tears," and she called out her thanks in a "quavering voice" (56). Too much had been unacknowledged for too long. Marthy Down, now a prosperous widow, had married another while her lover was at war; her soldier had returned to die in the poor house. Following the ceremony, as the old veterans reflect, she "must ha' kind o' harked back to the days when she was Marthy Peck" (62). She has been stirred to send flowers to his grave and to commission a headstone. "Sometimes folks has to get along in years before they see things fair" (63–64).

Indeed, new or revised perceptions occur throughout the story, including those of the veterans themselves. Planning and performing the ceremony help them recognize the scale and significance of the war—"It all looks a sight bigger to me now than it did then" (46). As with Marthy Down, time has helped them to see things fair; only now are they able to find any virtue in the soldiers of the South or to acknowledge that honor might also have impelled them. Asa Brown recalls a recent conversation about the patriotic inscription on a Southern soldier's grave—"I did feel kind o' red an' ugly for a minute, an' then somethin' come over me"; he can now agree that "the poor chap" (48) had patriotic motives too. Almost more than the conceded equality of motivation, it is the fellow feeling of "poor chap," the accepted suffering of the old enemy—especially after civil war—that signals the achievement of Barlow's Decoration Day. And, just as with Asa and the enemy, so in the village itself: perspectives are adjusted, the past is better understood, reconciliations are effected; the community is more coherent, at least for a while. The estranged veterans are better appreciated and more integrated into the life of the village.

Moreover, consistent with Jewett's composition of a short history of Berwick, her active engagement to secure the future of the Hamilton House, and the didactic line pursued by the adults in *Betty Leicester*, the ceremony prompts Barlow to attend to the preservation of its own history.[13] There is to be a series of "talks in the meetin'-house next winter"; the veterans will be invited to "tell where we was in the South . . . an' tell all we could about the boys that was killed" (61). Elder Dallas will gather the soldiers' surviving letters to "make out quite a history of us . . . for the benefit o' the young folks" (61).

"A War Debt" is more complex. It too turns upon an act of reconciliation, the restoration of war trophy, a ceremonial silver cup.[14] Tom Burton had brought it back from the Civil War only to be killed soon after. Knowing that the cup had belonged to a Southern friend and Harvard classmate of her husband's, Tom's mother urges her grandson, now a young man, to restore it to the defeated Bellamys. Young Tom sets off eagerly, hoping to combine his mission with some shooting. His journey takes him across a rich landscape still ruined by war. Colonel Bellamy gravely welcomes Tom to the remains of his grand house. For all their poverty and distress, the colonel and his crippled wife entertain Burton with ceremony; the cup is restored and, as the evening progresses, the family friendship is renewed. On his departure, in a spontaneous and symbolic gesture that reminds Bellamy of his old classmate, Burton Jr. gives the colonel his gun. The tale ends with the hinted possibility of closer links: the young man is smitten with the Bellamy granddaughter, whom, as he recognizes from a painting, he had encountered during his journey.

Though "A War Debt" is plainly a story of restoration and expiation, just below its harmonious surface several elements are more open to question, at least from a late-twentieth-century perspective. The issue of slavery emerges especially uncomfortably for contemporary readers. As the narrator contemplates the postbellum South, she takes a censorious and disappointed line regarding the public conduct of the freed slaves: they are seen as "lawless and unequal to holding their liberty with steady hands" (71). As represented by the Bellamys, the virtues of the ceremonious white elite, whose orderliness had encompassed slavery, are unquestioned. And Jewett's genetic preoccupation is seldom far from the surface. What attracts Tom in the Bellamy granddaughter is "this young Virginia lady's own look of high-breeding . . . her *advantage of race*" (73, emphasis added). The point is not made casually, it is emphasized: "she was the newer and finer Norman among the Saxons" (73).

"The Mistress of the Sydenham Plantation" gives us a Southern version of *Deephaven*'s Miss Chauncey; here too issues of nobility and order rest upon unresolved complexities below the surface.[15] On the Saturday before Easter Sunday, "the time of year to look after corn and cotton" (25), Mistress Sydenham takes it into "her poor daft head" (23) to revive the ritual inspection of her long-confiscated estates. Her "calm desire for obedience" (22) prevails over Old Peter, her enfranchised majordomo, and they set off. She reaches the estate to find the great house crumbled among the weeds. With no sign of outward disturbance, she appears calm at church next day—"as the calm sea shines back to the morning sun when another wreck has gone down" (35).

The story works on two levels: on one it is a study in pathos, on the other it carries hints of a strength of character and will that form part of what Richard Cary has described as "Sarah Jewett's belief in the nobility of the past."[16] If we read only slightly against the grain of the text, it soon becomes apparent that there is a third level: the admirable Sydenham will had been honed within a context—slavery—that renders that nobility equivocal. Though Cary notes accurately that "many of Miss Jewett's New England motifs are recognizable here" (129), he says little of this core ambiguity. Neither Old Peter's continued loyalty nor any hints of the Sydenhams' kindliness to their slaves in the past can disguise the massive abuse that the system itself had comprised. These tensions are clearly reflected in Jewett's narration. A key moment shows us the old Sydenham fields being actively farmed by their new owners, the freed slaves. The touches of color in the head kerchiefs and the sound of work-songs present a pleasing scene suggestive of a rural idyll—another kind of pastoral continuity.

In context, however, it is a continuity that is so problematic as to prompt a passage of authorial commentary: "It had a look of permanence, *this* cotton planting. It was a thing to paint, to relate itself to the permanence of art, an *everlasting duty of mankind;* terrible if a thing of force and compulsion and for another's gain, but the *birthright* of the *children of Adam*, and *not unrewarded*, nor unnatural when *one* drew by it *one's own life* from the earth" (28–29, emphasis added). Mieke Bal reminds us that "the argumentative parts of a text often give explicit information about the ideology" operating within it; here, style is at least equally telling.[17] The ponderous prose is less typical of Jewett's customary narrative mode than of the tropes and mannerisms of the Norman histories, where Jewett had ventured far from her usual territory. The features I have marked—the buttonholing demonstrative of the first sentence ("this"), the metonymic flourish ("children of Adam"), the distancing ("one"), the *litotes* ("not unrewarded"), and the emotive vocabulary ("everlasting duty," "birthright")—combine with stylistic inversion ("by it one's own life from the earth") and a cumulative sentence structure to emphasize, not resolve, the narrator's embarrassment. There is no escape: in this context, links with the past are reminders of abuse.

The unsteadiness betrayed by this rhetoric is underlined in what follows: by means of a blend of Old Peter's interior thoughts and more direct commentary, the narrator appears to mitigate the abuse of slavery. Where now there is disorder, the cabins "scattered all about the fields" (29), Peter recalls that there used to be order ("the long lines of the quarters"); and order is a quality that is almost always positive for Jewett. As he looks at the site of the quarters, Peter remembers that "It was gay there of a summer evening; the old times had not been without their pleasures. . . . 'I done like dem ole times de best'" (29). But these rose-colored memories, and the implication that Peter was well treated by the Sydenhams, merely serve to invoke the monstrosity of the system at large: "He had never been on the block; he was born and bred at old Sydenham; he had been trusted in house and field" (29). The exceptions of his case, with their anaphoric emphasis ("he had/he was/he had"), only highlight the norm. Moreover, though nominally free, in his fearfulness and deference toward his mistress, Peter, like the daughter in "The Landscape Chamber," is still in thrall to a patriarchal past. As if this were not enough, there is the case of Sibyl, still living on the plantation and, like her former mistress, now of uncertain mind. She had been on the block, sold off in hard times to the Sydenhams by Middleton, her white master and foster brother ("we push away from same breast" [32]). Neither Middleton's remorse when he seeks her out years later ("he kiss me an' kiss me"), nor her implied forgiveness, nor the hope of equality across the "ribber o' Jordan" (32) can conceal the fact that slavery had denied their intimately linked humanity. With little of Faulkner's deliberation and none of his irony, such examples bring Jewett to the fringes of his Yoknapatawpha County, where, for example, the McCaslin family tree displays the moral contradictions of slavery in full bloom.

A Yearning for Order

Jewett is perhaps clearest about the values she assigns to the past in her nonfiction, particularly in her short history of Berwick, the autobiographical essay on her Berwick childhood, and *The Story of the Normans.*[18]

As we might expect, she is also both clear and didactic in the two Betty Leicester books. As we move away from the nonfiction and children's books, the same values are found, sometimes securely, as in "Decoration Day"; elsewhere, complexities and tensions multiply more readily. At the extreme in this other direction come those moments when Jewett touches on the highly charged issue of slavery. On these occasions, it is as if she feels compelled to articulate a moral repugnance that contends with a yearning for order. In sum, her stance can become so unstable that a half recognition of its instability appears in comments and asides—often needless in themselves—and in an unusually florid narrative rhetoric that has more in common with the Norman histories than with the bulk of Jewett's adult fiction.

Between these two poles, more varying degrees of stability emerge. Positive values are clearly assigned to the worlds of *Deephaven* and *The Country of the Pointed Firs*, to most of the survivors of an earlier American elite, or of natural or pastoral worlds on the American continent. These are worlds whose survival is threatened. However, Jewett's interest in the past also lies in the evidence it provides of a growing American national identity. A new nation is essentially a developing one, yet part of what Jewett suggests has brought development about is the thrusting qualities of a Norman inheritance that her work has also associated with a waning older order. A genetic thesis is plainly involved, and the coherence of Jewett's stance commonly comes under strain whenever the expression of that thesis is most explicit. In "A War Debt," for example, there is hope for the future, a potential reconnection between North and South through the bonding of Burton Jr., a scion of the old Boston elite and the Bellamy granddaughter with her high Norman blood ("*refined still further by long growth in favoring soil*" [73; emphasis added]). But exactly the same Norman strain is weakening in the Bowdens: for all their French looks and ceremonial affirmations, the Bowdens and their way of life are in decline. The Norman strain, then, is seen variously as an invigorating influence and a declining force, as representing important developmental qualities and as displacing the valued coherence of the pastoral world. In short, Jewett's dream of order was self-subverting. The tensions noted in this essay remain largely unacknowledged in the texts concerned. Their presence, however, suggests that in her stories Jewett's treatment of the past possesses something of the unresolved and problematic property of progress itself—the dialectic character of historical development so valued by Lukács—to a degree that is greater, perhaps, than in her avowedly historical novel, *The Tory Lover.*[19]

Notes

1. Sarah Orne Jewett, *Betty Leicester's English Xmas: A New Chapter of an Old Story* (New York: Dodd, Mead, 1894). Further references are cited in the text.

2. Sarah Orne Jewett, *The Story of the Normans; Told Chiefly in Relation to Their Conquest of England* (London: T. Fisher Unwin, 1891), 366.

3. The sequel to *The Story of the Normans* was published as "England after the Norman Conquest," *Chautauquan* 12, n.s. 3 (1890–91): 438–42, 574–78, 707–11.

4. Frederic Clarke Jewett, *History and Genealogy of the Jewetts of America* (Rowley, Mass.: Jewett Family of America, Inc., 1908), ix. Further references are cited in the text as *Jewetts.*

5. Sarah Orne Jewett, "The Old Town of Berwick," *New England Magazine* 16 (1894): 585–609.

6. The evidence suggesting the date of composition is the sentence describing Jewett's mother as having died "within the last few months" (*Jewetts,* 648). Her mother died in 1891.

7. M. M. Bakhtin, *The Dialogic Imagination: Four Essays by Michael Bakhtin,* ed. Michael Holquist, trans. Caryl Emerson and Michael Holquist (Austin: University of Texas Press, 1981), 33.

8. Sarah Orne Jewett, "*The Country of the Pointed Firs" and other Fiction,* ed. Terry Heller (Oxford: Oxford University Press, 1996), 94. Further references are cited in the text.

9. *CPF,* 93, emphasis added. Jewett develops this idea more fully in *The Story of the Normans:* "England the colonizer, England the country of intellectual and social progress, England the fosterer of ideas and chivalrous humanity, is Norman England, and the Saxon influence has oftener held back in dogged satisfaction and stubbornness than urged her forward to higher levels" (356–57).

10. "It is ourselves, the people of the young republic of the United States, who might be called the Normans of modern times" (*Normans,* 360).

11. Sarah Way Sherman, *Sarah Orne Jewett: An American Persephone* (Hanover, N.H.: University Press of New England, 1989), 111–12.

12. Sarah Orne Jewett, *A Native of Winby and Other Tales* (London: T. A. Constable, 1910). Further references are cited in the text.

13. In *Betty Leicester,* both Mr. Picknell (205) and Aunt Barbara (217) urge the importance of acquainting the young with local history. Jewett, *Betty Leicester: A Story for Girls* (Boston: Houghton Mifflin, 1890).

14. Sarah Orne Jewett, *The Life of Nancy* (London: T. A. Constable, 1910). Further references are cited in the text.

15. Sarah Orne Jewett, *Strangers and Wayfarers* (London: James R. Osgood, McIlvaine, 1891), 22. Further references are cited in the text.

16. Richard Cary, *Sarah Orne Jewett* (New Haven, Conn.: College and University Press, 1962), 70. Further references are cited in the text.

17. Mieke Bal, *Narratology: Introduction to the Theory of Narrative*, trans. Christine van Boheemen (Toronto: University of Toronto Press, 1985), 129.

18. "Looking Back on Girlhood" has been reprinted in *Sarah Orne Jewett: Novels and Stories*, ed. Michael Davitt Bell (New York: Penguin, 1994).

19. Georg Lukács, *The Historical Novel*, trans. Hannah Mitchell and Stanley Mitchell (London: Merlin Press, 1962), 182.

We Do Not All Go Two by Two; or, Abandoning the Ark

Patti Capel Swartz

> I wish for your sake that I had been another sort of woman; but I shall never marry. I know you think I am wrong, but there is something which always tells me I am right, and I must follow another way. I should only wreck my life, and other people's. Most girls have an instinct toward marrying, but mine is all against it.
>
> —*Sarah Orne Jewett,* A Country Doctor

As a lesbian reader, I am delighted with acceptance of cross-dressing, of difference, of the woman-centered world I encounter in Sarah Orne Jewett's texts. I am delighted with a world that has the time and patience to allow people to follow their own ways. I come to each text that I read as what Bonnie Zimmerman would call a "perverse reader." In her 1993 essay "Perverse Reading: The Lesbian Appropriation of Literature," Zimmerman sees lesbian identity as "a way of knowing and acting—a mode of communication between the self and the world," one that is in process and that can overlap "heterosexual female or gay male perspectives."[1] Because of our socialization, we who are lesbians see and read with a "multiple perspectivity—a form of 'cultural bilingualism'—that can reinforce the connections, rather than the oppositions, between lesbian and heterosexual feminist perspectives" (136). Choice plays a large role in the ways in which lesbians read. This choice is not limited to "the gender of sexual partners," but rather it "may involve a totally transformed political stance in the world. But however it is understood by the individual, wherever she places herself on the 'lesbian continuum', lesbian identity is established when the individual sees the world anew as a lesbian, more than by a sexual act or by something she seeks and discovers, whether in the world or in herself. . . . The more self-reflective and self-conscious one is—the more defined one's lesbian perspective will be" (136).[2]

As a lesbian reader, I bring certain perceptions from the constructions of my own life to the texts I read. I believe that "lesbians come to literature with different emotions and experiences" and "that the lesbian resisting reader, reading perversely, is not merely demanding a plot or character study that the writer has not chosen to create. She is picking up on hints and possibilities that the author, consciously or not, has strewn in the text . . . bringing to the text an understanding of the world as *she* has learned to read and thus to know it" (Zimmerman, 144).

When I first contemplated and began writing about Sarah Orne Jewett's women, particularly women who chose to live alone by engaging in relationships with women that were sometimes but not always physical, or who choose never to marry, or not to remarry, I was living alone in Georgia, contemplating the solitary life I had myself chosen. My life had not always been solitary. I had married and had children. I had divorced. I had fallen in love with a woman and planned a life with her. When my relationship with that woman ended, I was sure that my life had crumpled. However, in continuing beyond that moment I realized that I had probably always known that I was a person who could engage in limited relationships, but that I needed freedom and the solitude to be alone: that neither marriage nor confining lesbian relationships worked for me. As this person, I came to read Jewett's texts in a particular way: as a woman who does not always find it necessary to go two by two but one who can create friendships and make both satisfying physical and spiritual connections with people in a woman-centered world.

Sarah Orne Jewett in *The Country of the Pointed Firs* provides a map for such living. She not only wrote of same-sex love in *Deephaven,* but in *The Country of the Pointed Firs* she also wrote of times of necessary solitude and communion with women away from an intimate sexual relationship, the kind of solitude that Jewett herself found necessary for her work. Jewett's own "Boston marriage" with Annie Fields seems to have been a most happy one, with close physical and spiritual caring. After Fields's husband's death, she and Jewett "began a pattern of intimate and shared life that lasted until Jewett's death in 1906."[3] However, that "pattern of intimate and shared life" included times when the women were separated, when Jewett lived and worked separately from Fields, realizing that she needed to do this for the sake of herself and her writing. In his chronology of Jewett's life, Michael Davitt Bell points out that for twenty years beginning in 1882, "with few exceptions, Jewett will spend spring in South Berwick, summer with Fields in Manchester, autumn in South Berwick, and winter with Fields at 148 Charles Street, where the two women will entertain many friends and literary figures; she will also continue to make shorter visits to other friends."[4]

Although the writer's relationship with Annie Fields was very strong, both Fields and Jewett seemed to understand the need to maintain closeness without creating constant ties that would keep either from her work. Fields was a fine reader and critic, and, as Jewett's letters to her friend show, she was often anxious that Fields read and comment on the writing in which she was engaged during their separations. The letters indicate, however, that that writing was often completed when Jewett was in South Berwick. Both women recognized the need for solitude and the need of some women not to follow a conventional path of pairings that joins one to the other throughout each day. As Fields points out in the introduction to the 1911 volume of Jewett's letters that she edited, Jewett was engaged in work that she believed essential: creating understanding between people as well as making sense of her own world. Fields quotes from Jewett's own second introduction to *Deephaven* in what may be the clearest statement of the intent of Jewett's work: to show that the differences that exist between people provide wellsprings of strength, and that the varying ways and desires of people from both country and town should not be condemned but rather understood and celebrated. Fields highlights Jewett's philosophy: "Human nature is the same the world over, provincial and rustic influences must ever produce much the same effects upon character, and town life will ever have in its gift the spirit of the present, while it may take again from the quiet of the hills and fields and the conservatism of country hearts a gift from the spirit of the past."[5]

Jewett's concern with the understanding of difference was not limited to her fear that city and country people would not understand each other, but also included her desire to amend prejudices about difference. Such differences encompassed life choices that do not include marriage, the necessity that women complete meaningful work, and the perceptual and sexual variations that emerge in many characters, including Dan'el

Gunn of "An Autumn Holiday," Mrs. Martin who was "The Queen's Twin," and, in *The Country of the Pointed Firs*, Joanna, Mrs. Todd, and the narrator herself.

The difference that marks each of these characters as they continue on the journeys of their lives, and the "state of society which admitted such personal freedom" as that Joanna chose,[6] is shown as well in the worlds that Jewett created. Mrs. Fosdick tells of cross-dressing in her youth. She had been part of a seafaring family and, in the course of one of her journeys, she had escaped from her feminine role. Her clothes had been left behind, and she spent much of the voyage dressed in her brother's clothes, reveling in a freedom gained with the replacement of her skirts by pants. Mrs. Fosdick's cross-dressing may have been from necessity, but such action was not censored but celebrated in Jewett's text.

In another story, "An Autumn Holiday," a man believes that he is his sister and dresses in women's clothes. Not only does Dan'el Gunn wear his sister's clothes about the house and believe he is she, on occasion he also escapes his caretakers, reappearing in church turned out in dress and bonnet. "After the first fun of it was over, most of the folks felt bad" for their amusement at Dan'el (*Novels and Stories*, ed. Bell, 582). Polly Marsh, a talented nurse who is not "one to marry for what she could get if she did n't like the man" (583–54), tells the story, and she respects the Cap'n despite the humor she imparts. Hearing at church of the women's missionary society meeting that Cap'n Gunn attends, Polly "always thought well of those ladies, they treated him so handsome, and tried to make him enjoy himself" (583). Finally, Polly tells of a visit from the deacon who had come to see the Cap'n's nephew about some fencing. As the nephew wasn't home, the deacon stayed to visit with the Cap'n, Polly, and her Aunt Statiry, whom Polly was visiting and helping. At the end of the visit, the Cap'n says "to Statiry, in a dreadful knowing way, 'Which of us do you consider the deacon come to see?' You see, the deacon was a widower" (583).

Like this story, Jewett's stories of aging men and women who have never married or who are left alone after marriage show her quiet understanding of the need for companionship and the bonds of varying kinds that can be formed between people. What Fields says of Jewett's letters, which unveil "the power that lies in friendship to sustain the giver as well as the receiver," could as well be said of all of Jewett's writing (*Letters*, 11).

As Fields notes, "Her *métier* was, to lay open, for other eyes to see, those qualities in human nature which ennoble their possessors, high or low, rich or poor; those floods of sympathy to be unsealed in the most unpromising and dusty natures by the touch of a divining spirit. Finding herself in some dim way the owner of this sacred touchstone, what wonder that she loved her work and believed in it?" (10).

Jewett's love of her work and her recognition of its importance is clear in *A Country Doctor.* This text, and the fact of its publication between *Deephaven* and *The Country of the Pointed Firs,* aids in the interpretation of both her earlier and later texts. When Dr. Leslie reveals his plan to allow Nan to study medicine if she likes, the reasoning he provides his friend Mrs. Graham is that "Nan is not the sort of girl who will be likely to marry. . . . I believe that it is a mistake for such a woman to marry. Nan's feeling toward her boy-playmates is exactly the same as toward the girls she knows. . . . [I]f . . . the law of her nature is that she must live alone and work alone, I shall help her to keep it instead of break it" (*Novels and Stories,* ed. Bell, 234). In a later conversation with George Gerry, Nan is even clearer about her need to live without domestic commitments or bonds: "I have never since I can remember thought of myself and my life in any way but unmarried,—going on alone to the work I am fit to do. . . . [S]omething tells me all the time that I could not marry the whole of myself as most women can; there is a great share of my life which could not have its way, and could only hide itself and be sorry" (355).

While *A Country Doctor* is the story of a woman who is different by virtue of her vocation, Jewett's first novel foregrounds women who diverge from social norms in their intimate relationships. *Deephaven* is a text in which women come together for a summer, a text in which bonding and love for women is foregrounded and in which marriage is not a present thought for either of the primary woman characters. In her examination of *Deephaven* as a lesbian text, Judith Fetterley proposes that the work "may have facilitated Jewett's life choice [with Fields] by allowing her first to imagine it in fiction" (165). Jewett wrote *Deephaven* after becoming engaged in deep and caring relationships and friendships with women, connections that are illustrated by an 1872 visit to Newport, when Jewett became "a particularly close friend" of Kate Birckhead (*Novels and Stories,* 918). A rich and compelling story of two young women who love and care deeply for each other, *Deephaven* reminds me of my own adolescence and life—of my bonds with and love for women.

I read between the lines to envision a confirmation of sexual preference in the scene in which the two young women dance and stay up all night talking, in an experience of mutual understanding and close companionship. Jewett creates a situation that does not need explicit sexual activity for love to occur, for there is an implicit eroticism and, between the lines, physical and psychical as well as sexual closeness in the account of Kate's and Helen's summer together.

Judith Fetterley has written about her preference for *Deephaven* over *The Country of the Pointed Firs* because the former includes implied lesbianism while she finds that *The Country of the Pointed Firs* "erased the lesbian content of [Jewett's] earlier work" (182). Unlike Fetterley, I do not believe this "erasure" occurs, but that Jewett is exploring other possibilities for difference and for lesbians, that the lesbian promise of Deephaven is reinscribed in different ways in *The Country of the Pointed Firs.* Indeed, *Deephaven* presages the possibility for silences as communion between spiritual partners that is continued in *The Country of the Pointed Firs*, as Helen observes of her relationship with Kate, "We are such good friends that we often were silent for a long time, when mere acquaintances would have felt compelled to talk and try to entertain each other" (*Deephaven*, 300).

At the close of *Deephaven* both Kate and Helen "were very dismal" (304) on their return to town and their separation, but both knew that memories of Deephaven would return after their departure, even though their lives together do not continue. The realization that some women can, should, and must live life with some separation from constant close domestic ties occurs explicitly and affirmatively in *The Country of the Pointed Firs.* Here is a world, woman-centered, in which all do not go two by two; a world in which women's lives are meaningful, and in which journeys alone are possible. In this world, sexuality does not rule: one is accepted as one is. In this world, I find possibilities for meaningful work, for exploration, and for the creation of a community in which sexual definition, sexual difference, and sexuality or gender are not essential—or even of much importance to the members. Women—and men—form bonds to create a woman-centered community in which they accept each other because they simply are.

The anchor for this story is not the narrator, although she focuses the telling, but rather Mrs. Todd. In fact, the importance of the story lies not in who the narrator is or what she believes, but in those narratives she encounters—narratives enlarged by connection to Mrs. Todd. The narrator has journeyed to a place where solitude and thus creation might be possible. She is a writer looking for the time and space to write. She does not need, nor does she want, the physical proximity of a life partner at this time. Instead she creates companionship with women in a woman-centered universe through involvement in lives and through listening to the stories of those who have journeyed or who are engaged in journeys, thus both finding and creating her text.

The journey of the women whose stories she tells, women related through blood or marriage, begins inland—with Mrs. Blackett's family and her birth on a farm. With her marriage and subsequent removal to Green Island, Mrs. Blackett's physical but not her emotional or psychical connection with her sister was broken. Green Island, however, is a world large enough for Mrs. Blackett. As she grew older, visitors and visits to the mainland and her care of her son William are enough to sustain her. The roots that nourished her are present on the island and are reinforced through these visits by the respect of others and by her continuing place in the extended family, although she is physically removed from much contact. She has a world big enough—William to do for, and a room for "that heart which had made the most of everything that needed love . . . a place of peace, the little brown bedroom, and the quiet outlook upon field and sea and sky" (*The Country of the Pointed Firs*, 54).

Mrs. Blackett realized, however, that this world would not be large enough for her daughter, and she encouraged Mrs. Todd to journey out into a larger world: "I always think that Providence was kind to plot an' have her husband leave her a good house where she really belonged. She'd been very restless if she'd had to continue here on Green Island. You wanted more scope, didn't you, Almiry, an' to live in a large place where more things grew?" (52). The world, however, is not without judgments on this score: "Sometimes folks wonders that we don't live together; perhaps we shall sometime" (52). But the judgments of others stopped neither from living in the ways best for them. These are women who are sure of themselves, unafraid to cross boundaries, who will not bow to public opinion.

Nor is Almira Todd, sibyl-like and magical, a woman contained. Past, future, and present merge in her wisdom; neither the natural nor the spiritual world are beyond her ken. She is saved from archetypical status, however, by her inability to know what to say or to do in situations when she is faced with people she cannot like. And we understand her pain and her assessment of herself when she relates that she is glad her husband never lived long enough to know the truth about their relationship. She had loved another, and felt she always would, but had married Todd anyway. The stories of her life have made Almira Todd wise, but they have also created a loneliness and solitude that could not be breached, for she realized that marriage simply for the sake of marriage was not enough to make a life. Similar to what the narrator says of Joanna's story, "It is not often given in a noisy world to come into the places of great grief and silence" (49). Mrs. Todd's grief did not prevent her from creating connections with others and showing love through the dispensing of herbs and the unquestioning acceptance of others.

Her husband's cousin, Joanna, however, could not accept such bridges. Joanna voyaged from the town to solitude on Shell-heap Island. She lived her life out on the island, alone but for her chickens, the birds she tamed, and an occasional visitor. Nevertheless, in the Dunnet Landing community, there is social acceptance of this choice and, even though Joanna chose solitude, the town did not forget her. Packets were landed, packets containing things that Joanna needed. Many attended Joanna's funeral, at which the song of a tamed sparrow was thought a fitter elegy than the voice of the pastor (78). When she visits the island, the narrator sees the mainland as Joanna must have seen it many afternoons from the spring where she came to get water. "There was the world, and here was she with eternity well begun. In the life of each of us, I said to myself, there is a place remote and islanded, and given to endless regret or secret happiness; we are each the uncompanioned hermit and recluse of an hour or a day; we understand our fellows of the cell to whatever age of history they may belong" (82).

Joanna's choice of solitude is one that resonates strongly for me. Mrs. Todd is a similarly powerful figure. It is no accident that she lives in the last house on the journey inland. In many ways, she seems a bridge between the world of land and sea, the present and the past, a bridge into a world of women. She is the connection or the port in which the tales of journeys begin and a place of memory in which they wait. She is the "conjure woman," the woman in communication with secrets of a world both beyond and within the life of a present world, animate in plants with healing powers, described through her relationship with herbs and healing. Just as plants have knowledge and physical presence beyond literal being and need a congenial place to grow, so do people need the proper space and spirituality. This space and spirituality will not be the same for all, nor will individuals' perceptions; but, unlike the world that labels and jeers, Mrs. Todd creates a space for difference, for acceptance of varying journeys. During Mrs. Todd's telling of the story of Joanna, for instance, the narrator reflects "upon a state of society which admitted such personal freedom and a voluntary hermitage" as Joanna's (69). The narrator also relates Mrs. Todd's anxiety that Captain Littlepage's sanity should not be judged when she approaches the narrator, who had spent the afternoon with the Captain. "Oh, then he's all right. I was afraid 'twas one of his flighty spells. . . . Some thinks he overdid, and affected his head, but for a man o' his years he's amazin' now when he's at his best" (29).

The difference that marks each of these characters as they continue on the journeys of their lives and in a "state of society which admitted such personal freedom" (69) as that Joanna chose shows that a kinder world is possible through the connections of friendships, connections and caring that often go beyond physical proximity (69). Indeed, Jewett's world exceeds the physical dimension, carrying over into the world of the spirit, where bonds between people remain possible over time and space, even beyond death. The focus that Jewett chooses for each of her characters is a focus of the spirit on the connections between people that are sustaining, a focus that I have found in lesbian and women-centered relationships.

It is this crossing of boundaries of the physical into the spiritual that provides so much depth to Jewett's work. Jewett has been identified as a "local color writer" and a "realist." Her close looks at the actual, however, go beyond the objective physical world, spiraling into realms in which possibilities for empathy, connections, and understanding are greater than merely physical links; love is not manifested always as physical presence or physical connection but rather as rising out of spiritual connections that do not always require physical presence. Such connections occurred in Jewett's life with Annie Fields and with her friends, showing that communion of spirit that she found necessary in her work and in her life that was at times without physical closeness. Jewett writes of these connections in her letters. From Europe Jewett wrote to her friend Sarah Whitman:

> I have been wishing to write to you ever since the day I went to Rheims from La Ferté, because I feel a little as if I had almost seen you there. Whether a little wind that blew against you when you were there, is still flickering among the pillars of the cathedral or not, who can say! but I think we went in together and I found something of you at every turn. It was a surprise of companionship, with all that surprise of beauty and strange solemnity which made me feel as if I had never seen a cathedral—even a French cathedral—before. Dear friend, I went at one step much nearer to you than ever before, and who shall say why?[7]

On the death of Celia Thaxter, Jewett wrote in a similar vein to Annie Fields: "It seems as if I could hear her talking, and as if we lived those June days over again. Most of my friends have gone out of illness and long weeks of pain, but with her the door seems to have open and shut, and what is a very strange thing, I can see her face,—you know I never could call up faces easily, and never before, that I remember, have I been able to see how a person looked who had died, but again and again I seem to see her. That takes me a strange step out of myself" (*Letters*, 110, 111).

A year after Sarah Whitman's death, Jewett observed in another letter to Fields: "I remember well that long bright day and the wonderful cloud I watched at evening floating slowly through the upper sky on some high current northward, catching the sun still when we were in shadows. I could not help the strange feeling that it had something to do with her. It was like a great golden ball or balloon, as if it wrapped a golden treasure; her golden string (that Blake writes about) might have made it. Those days seem strangely near. After a whole year one begins to take them in" (*Letters*, 203). Indeed, this passage parallels the way in which Fields viewed Jewett's life and letters: the "flickering lights and shadows of human life reflected on their pages. . . . She rested on the spirit within her, which was not of herself, and dared with a fearlessness that did not think on daring" (252). Jewett did not fear to make choices about life partners, but these choices contained necessary elements of solitude. She did not fear sharing her thoughts. She did not fear being alone. In Jewett's life and her writing, spirit and the need for solitude coexist with physical proximity and desire.

In *The Country of the Pointed Firs* Mrs. Todd points out the proper elements necessary to thrive. She illustrates these in her discussions of trees and of people, particularly Sant Bowden, in ways that could also be applied to Jewett herself, for, to recall Fields, Jewett's letters unveil "the power that lies in friendship to sustain the giver as well as the receiver" (11). It is this power to see and to accept difference, the power to sustain and be sustained, that Jewett passes on to her readers. On the way to the Bowden reunion, Mrs. Todd reins in the horse and nods her head as though to an acquaintance, and, looking at an ash tree, ruminates that it had looked poorly but was now doing well, as she had hoped that it would: "There's sometimes a good hearty tree growin' right out of the bare rock, out o' some crack that just holds the roots . . . right on the pitch o' one o' them bare stony hills where you can't seem to see a wheelbarrowful o' good earth in a place, but that tree'll keep a green top in the driest summer. You lay your ear down to the ground an' you'll hear a little stream runnin'. Every such tree has got its own livin' spring; there's folks made to match 'em" (92). What can seem to be lonely and solitary, like Jewett's map for a woman alone, is nourished by the need for solitude, nourished by the stream below the surface that cannot be seen yet makes a living connection.

We each must find connections that nourish without overwhelming us, those connections that Jewett writes of in her texts. Connections between people do not always depend on going "two by two." Solitude, as well as physical togetherness, is necessary for the work of our lives and for ourselves. Lack of physical proximity does not mean disconnection. Sarah Orne Jewett's work creates a map for the person who searches and works sometimes in solitary ways but still engages in spiritual connections like those between the narrator and Mrs. Todd. Her writing, her journey, like ours, is an "attempt to explain the past and present to each other" (Jewett, Preface to *Deephaven*, 6).

Notes

1. Bonnie Zimmerman, "Perverse Reading: The Lesbian Appropriation of Literature," in *Sexual Practice/Textual Theory: Lesbian Cultural Criticism*, ed. Susan J. Wolfe and Julia Penelope (Cambridge: Blackwell, 1993), 136. Subsequent references are cited in the text.

2. As Zimmerman notes, the phrase "lesbian continuum" was coined by

Adrienne Rich in "Compulsory Heterosexuality and Lesbian Existence," *Signs* 5.4 (Summer 1980): 631–60. Rich uses it to indicate the congruence between female friendship and lesbian love. I am using it to suggest the variety of self-concepts among lesbians.

3. Judith Fetterley, "Reading *Deephaven* as a Lesbian Text," In *Sexual Practice/Textual Theory: Lesbian Cultural Criticism*, ed. Susan J. Wolfe and Julia Penelope (Cambridge: Blackwell, 1993), 165. All subsequent references are cited in the text.

4. Michael Davitt Bell, "Chronology," in Jewett, *Novels and Stories*, ed. Bell (New York: Library of America, 1994), 920. All subsequent references to Jewett's novels are from this volume and are cited in the text.

5. *Letters of Sarah Orne Jewett*, ed. Annie Fields (Boston: Houghton Mifflin, 1911), 8. Also see Jewett, Preface to *Deephaven* (Boston: Houghton Mifflin, 1993), 6. All subsequent references to these sources are cited in the text.

6. Sarah Orne Jewett, *The Country of the Pointed Firs and Other Stories* (1896; rpt., New York: Norton, 1981), 69. All subsequent references are cited in the text.

7. *Letters of Sarah Orne Jewett*, ed. Fields, 155. For a detailed discussion of this relationship, see Sarah Ann Wider, "Books and Their Covers: Sarah Orne Jewett and Sarah Whitman Through My Daughter's Eyes," *Colby Quarterly* 34 (1998): 172–94.

Sarah Orne Jewett's Maine

A Journey Back

Carol Schachinger

In July 1898 Sarah Orne Jewett and her companion Annie Fields visited Haworth in Yorkshire, England, home of the Brontë sisters. They had been told there was nothing to see. The church had been pulled down and the rectory modernized; the village was irrevocably altered because of the railroad. But they went anyway and were not disappointed. The hill and the moor, wrote Jewett, "looked pretty much as it did when that household . . . burned their lights of genius like candles flaring in a cave . . . shut up, captives and prisoners, in the gloomy old stone house."[1] She was so struck by the mood of the place that she could "see the little pale faces of those sisters at the vicarage windows" (158). In a letter to her friend Sarah Whitman she concluded, "Never mind people who tell you there is nothing to see in the place where people lived who interest you. You always find something of what made them the souls they were, and at any rate you see their sky and their earth" (*Letters*, ed. Fields, 158).

Almost a hundred years later I journeyed to South Berwick, Maine, to experience Sarah Orne Jewett's earth and sky. I had recently read *The Country of the Pointed Firs* and was extremely moved by it. Part of the reason, I knew, was because, like the writer-narrator of the novel, I was homesick for Maine. And part of the reason was my affinity for an author who could evoke such powerful memories and nostalgia for a lost time and place. I wanted to know her better by gaining a sense of her world. I held to her written promise from her experience at Haworth: "Nothing you ever read about them can make you know them until you go there" (*Letters*, 158).

Every journey to Maine is a journey backward in time. Except for a brief heyday at the end of the eighteenth and beginning of the nineteenth century, Maine has always been a backwater. The decline that began in Jewett's day with the loss in shipping has continued right up to the present with the demise of fishing, agriculture, and manufacturing. Mainers still sense a closing down—a loss of old and better days. Today's major sources of revenue are from the paper industry and tourism. Much of the land is owned by corporations or out-of-staters. Maine people continue to be almost as poor as the families that Dr. Jewett, Sarah's father, visited on his rounds in the backwoods.

But this backwardness has certain advantages. Because change comes slowly here, the past is still very evident. The Jewett house, now managed by the Society for the Preservation of New England Antiquities, looks much as it did in the author's day. I can stand in her bedroom, surrounded by all her personal belongings—her riding crops, her photographs, her pincushion and jewelry—much as she left them. I can stand on the upper landing, where Jewett wrote, and look down on a town square not much different from her day: the Odd Fellows building on the left and the long brick block, with its street-level stores, on the right. I can sit at her desk, a large Sheraton secretary, and imagine her writing: "Today is town-meeting day and I am sitting by Mrs. Fields's desk at the front window . . . and it is very funny, beside giving rise to thoughts, to see the farmers and their country sleighs and their wives who come 'trading'! . . . I should like to shake hands hard with two or three of them, and they would say, 'Now which one o' the Doctor's *girls* be you!'" (*Letters*, 215).

Because change comes slowly here, I can stand on the banks of the Salmon Falls River near Hamilton House, as Jewett was so fond of doing, and look out at the same scene she saw. The old mansion, with its four tall chimneys, still stands alone on a promontory at a bend in the river. The countryside is absolutely silent. The river is like a mirror, watery black except where it reflects the peach color of the late afternoon sky. No houses are visible; the only signs of life are some cormorants floating in the water. It is still "a quiet place, that the destroying left hand of progress had failed to touch," as Jewett writes in her sketch "River Driftwood."[2] I can imagine Jewett standing in the window, absorbed in her own act of imagining: "One day I was in one of the upper rooms of the Hamilton house in a dormer window, and I was amused at reading the nonsense some young girl had written on the wall. The view was beautiful, and I thought she must have sat there with her work, or have watched the road or the river for some one whom she wished to see coming" (*Country By-Ways,* 17).

But there is a negative side to being the place that time forgot. It's what Captain Littlepage warns of in *The Country of the Pointed Firs:* "a community narrows down and grows dreadful ignorant when it is shut up to its own affairs, and gets no knowledge of the outside world."[3] It's what makes the young leave to seek their fortunes elsewhere, returning perhaps in their retirement years, both in Jewett's day and now. Although Jewett loved her home, she wrote in an 1882 letter to John Greenleaf Whittier that she found the boredom of the long winters, when she couldn't get out in the countryside, very trying as well as bad for her health.[4] In her diary, written in her twenties, she stated that she missed the excitement and company of friends that she found in city life; and if it weren't her home, she would be quite "miserable in Berwick" (Nail, 186).

Her solution was to live winters in Boston and summers in Manchester-by-the-Sea, with her companion Annie Fields, and spring and fall in Berwick with her sister Mary—an arrangement that began in her thirties and continued until her death. She found the stimulation her mind and art required among Annie Fields's large literary circle and in frequent travel. When she returned from the larger world, Maine seemed a haven rather than a prison. Jewett always returned to it as a lover, "so glad to be off the steamer; and next day, when I came here to the dear old house and home, it all seemed to put its arms around me." Much like the narrator in "William's Wedding," she gets "homesick for the conditions of life at the landing," weary of "the hurry of life in a large town."[5]

It's easy to understand her attraction. She was surrounded by beauty, within doors and out. The Jewett house is an elegant example of colonial Georgian architecture. It is filled with furniture and artwork from all over the world, attesting to the wealth of her merchant grandfather: Chippendale chairs and tables, Wedgwood china, Chinese vases, French wallpaper. I didn't appreciate the degree of luxury to which she was accustomed until I stood in the magnificent entrance hall, which she has described in *Deephaven:* "the lower hall is very fine, with an archway dividing it, and panellings of all sorts, and a great door at each end, through which the lilacs in front and the old pensioner plum-trees in the garden are seen exchanging bows and gestures" (*Novels and Stories,* ed. Bell, 14).

Outdoors there was an extensive and beautiful garden and beyond that the fields, hills, and coastline of an area well known for its scenic beauty. Ever since her childhood, when her father took her along with him on his rounds to visit his patients and taught her all he knew about the birds and animals and plants, she had a love for nature and for the beauty of her surroundings. She wrote in a letter to Annie Fields: "When one goes out of doors and wanders about alone . . . how wonderfully one becomes part of nature, like an atom of quick-silver against a great mass. I hardly keep my separate consciousness, but go on and on until the mood has spent itself" (*Letters*, 51).

I imagine her as a free spirit then, away from the constraints of Victorian ladylike behavior. She tells us in "An October Ride" that "I took off my cap to let the wind blow through my hair," and when her horse breaks into a run, "I feel as if I had suddenly grown a pair of wings" (*Country By-Ways*, 95).

She often went riding alone, exploring infrequently traveled paths and "by-ways," stumbling across signs of former human habitation—a lone grave marker, an abandoned house. On one particular fall day, as she writes in "An October Ride," she sheltered from the rain in an old, empty parsonage where she built a fire in the fireplace. There, in the late hours of a dark afternoon, she warmed herself to the glow of the coals and dreamed of the past. She imagined the former inhabitants, much as she did at Hamilton house, using the present setting to evoke the past: "The rooms which had looked empty at first were filled again with the old clergymen, who met together with important looks and complacent dignity" (*Country By-Ways*, 111).

Standing in her bedroom in South Berwick, walking along the tidal river near her home, seeing what she saw, feeling the textures of her life, I similarly try to evoke the writer who so moved me.

Her photograph, taken when she was a young woman, is before me as I write. People called her beautiful and she is. The lifted, rounded chin expresses a confidence of her place in the world. As one of the doctor's daughters, she was an aristocrat in Berwick circles—a "lady," as Willa Cather describes her. She wears her brown hair in a flattering upsweep, and her face is full, with a slight upturn to her nose. But most noticeable are her brown eyes—large, serene, almost melancholy with their heavy lids. An altogether sympathetic and approachable face—it's easy to see why so many people opened up to her and told her their stories.

The young Sarah was perhaps a lot like Sylvia in "A White Heron": wild and free, a child of nature. It is known that she did not do well in school and was not forced to go too often. She suffered from rheumatism, and her father's prescription was frequently to bring her on his rounds so that she could benefit from fresh air and sunshine. She writes, "I forgot I was under anybody's rule when I was out of doors" ("From a Mournful Villager," in *Country By-Ways*, 134).

Her first name was really Theodora, after her father and grandfather. I think, even though she didn't use the name, that it caused her to identify with these unusual men. Certainly she loved her father dearly and mourned his sudden death of a heart attack when she was twenty-nine: "I don't know how I can live without him."[6] She may well, like Nan Prince in *A Country Doctor*, have wanted to be a doctor herself. She had a sense that she was bound for something special; like Nan "She showed no sign of being the sort of girl who tried to be mannish. . . . She did not look strong-minded. . . . Yet everybody knew that she had a strange tenacity of purpose" (*Novels and Stories*, 249).

I can imagine that Jewett felt very different from her sisters and her neighbors—set apart by her gifts, her spirit, her ambition, her sexuality. She wrote in her diary on June 17, 1872: "I believe I am not like other people in anything and it never will amount to anything, all this trouble and perplexity and sorrow I have gone through with. . . . I have all that old feeling back again which used to come so often when I first knew Kate [Birckhead], when I used to wish with all my heart I could die and end it all. I would not live a day longer if it were not for my friends being troubled."[7] I can only guess at how difficult her adolescence must have been, as the walls closed in on her and the pressures increased to mold her into the marriageable Victorian lady. Her diary speaks of emotional outbursts, of rushing out of the house to go riding through the fields and forests, then coming back vowing to try to do better. Her struggle to define who she was, in a society that breathed conformity and encouraged secretiveness, must have been enormous.

She writes of being "watched." The Jewett house itself is part of the public arena, situated as it is in the center of town. The Jewetts were prominent townsfolk; a good deal of attention was focused on them. In the sketch "From a Mournful Villager" she writes, "I think there should be high walls around our gardens" (the Jewett house has a little white picket fence), so that "one can enjoy an afternoon nap in a hammock, or can take one's work out into the shady garden with great satisfaction, unwatched" (*Country By-Ways*, 126–27). She continues, "People do not know what they lose when they make way with the reserve, the separateness, the sanctity of the front yard of their grandmothers. It is like writing down the family secrets for any one to read" (127). She refers to the high fence as a "fortification around your home" (127).

People spoke of Jewett as a very private person. Her beloved companion Annie Fields writes of her, "with all her wit and humor and kind ways there was no suggestion leading to sudden nearness nor too great intimacy" (*Letters*, 9). We're allowed only occasional glimpses inside the fortress, as in "A Winter Drive":

> In the woods there was the usual number of stray-away trees to be seen, and they appealed to my sympathy as much as ever. It is not pleasant to see an elm warped and twisted with its efforts to get to the light, and to hold its head above the white pines that are growing in a herd around it and seem to grudge it its rights and its living. If you cannot be just like us, they seem to say, more's the pity for you! . . . If your nature is not the same as ours you ought to make it so. These trees make one think of people who have had to grow in loneliness; who have been hindered and crowded and mistaken and suspected by their neighbors, and have suffered terribly for the sin of being themselves and following their own natures (*Country By-Ways*, 177–78).

In a fascinating essay, "The Confessions of a House-Breaker," written when she was just beginning her relationship with Fields, Jewett writes of breaking *out* of the house in a pre-dawn walk through the village. Even so small an act of defying convention causes her to look over her shoulder: "I had a desire to go out farther into the world, and I went some distance up the street, past my neighbors' house; feeling a sense of guilt and secrecy that could hardly be matched. . . . But if any one had suddenly hailed me from a window I should have been inclined to run home as fast as my feet could carry me. In such fashion are we bound to the conventionalities of existence!"[8] Central to the experience is a clairvoyant connection to a distant friend—a feeling that another person is awake and close to her in spirit: "an understanding between us sprang up quickly, like a flame on the altar to Friendship, in my heart" (239). I imagine her in love with Annie Fields, unable to sleep, still struggling inwardly with what such an attachment means in a society that doesn't even have a word for love between women besides the euphemism "Boston marriage." Breaking through the bounds of convention causes her extreme anxiety: she "steals" out of the house, feels "astray" as she goes farther down the street, but soon is overcome by a sense of exhilaration at her daring. She jumps the fence on her return home (a decorous woman in her thirties) instead of opening the gate, then feels "dismayed afterward at such singular conduct" (243). I can imagine her stealing back upstairs in the dark house to her room, falling asleep in the dawn to awaken hours later still "delighted and puzzled" about the implications of her symbolic breakout (243).

Her room itself is a surprise: it's a nook, a hideaway at the back of the house, not one of the bright, imposing front bedrooms that look out on the street. It's dark, with woodwork painted the color of spruce trees in winter; and it has a steep, narrow, secretive stairway leading up to the garret and down to the breakfast room. It's a room to hide away in, to feel cozy in—a cave, but with a rear exit in case of trouble. Her initials are everywhere: carved into the wooden frames of the slates on her desk, "SOJ" etched into a windowpane. The design in the dark wallpaper can also be taken for an intertwined S and J. It strikes me as a place for a person who is both reticent yet eager to make her mark upon the world.

Jewett was born in this house, perhaps in this same bedroom—and it's the one she died in. Its access to the kitchen and the servants' quarters would have made it the logical choice for birthing and dying. When she was six her father built his family a smaller house next door, and they all lived there until her grandparents and finally her Uncle William died. Then, in 1887 her mother, her sister Mary, and Sarah moved back into the "great house," where she lived until her death in 1909. But it was always as much her home as the smaller house (which is now the town library). She writes in "From a Mournful Villager" that "The front yard I knew best belonged to my grandfather's house" (*Country By-Ways*, 134).

What does it mean to be born and die in the same house? It must give one a sense of rootedness and an understanding of place that we peripatetic moderns can only guess at. In his biography, Richard Cary ascribes Jewett's use of environment in her writings to this knowledge of place: "She does not merely describe, she works into the texture of her descriptions reserves of knowledge and experience drawn from long and sensitive intimacy with her milieu. She construes environment as a pictorial backdrop, but also as a powerful determining influence."[9] That this is so is obvious from Jewett's own words in "Lady Ferry": "there is a strong influence of place [upon character]; and the inanimate things which surround us indoors and out make us follow out in our lives their own silent characteristics. We unconsciously catch the tone of every house in which we live, and of every view of the outward, material world which grows familiar to us, and we are influenced by surroundings nearer and closer still than the climate of the country which we inhabit."[10]

In retrospect, Theodora Sarah Orne Jewett was lucky. She was beautiful, rich, and talented. She was the apple of her father's eye and probably somewhat spoiled. She enjoyed the advantages that Virginia Woolf found necessary for a woman writer: a private income and a room of her own. She had the good fortune to get in with the right crowd—editors, publishers, writers—who could inspire her and further her career. She happened to walk into a writing market that was hungry for "local color"; and she was published almost immediately, establishing a reputation at a very young age. She found a love relationship that would sustain her all her life yet leave her free to write. She had few responsibilities—even the running of the family home fell onto other shoulders: her sister Mary's. She traveled widely and lived in beautiful places. In fact, the only ill fortune she ever suffered was her terrible fall from a carriage, which injured her spine and left her in almost constant pain for her last seven years.

Why, then, this sadness like a hard kernel at the center of her stories and sketches, and especially in *The Country of the Pointed Firs*? So many of her writings are about loss, about time's passing, about death. One obvious answer might be that illness and death were more present companions to nineteenth-century life than they are now. Before her own death at fifty-nine, she experienced the loss of her father, mother, grandparents, uncles and aunts, a sister, and many of her close friends and mentors. One of her earlier memories is of her grandmother's death and how frightened she was at being left alone while all the grownups went next door to the great house ("From a Mournful Villager," in *Country By-Ways*, 137–38). Her stories abound with funerals. When she was forty-eight, she wrote in a letter to Annie Fields: "But how the days fly by, as if one were riding the horse of Fate and could only look this way and that, as one rides and flies across the world. Oh, if we did not *look back* and try to change the lost days! If we can only keep our faces toward the light and remember that whatever happens or has happened, we must hold fast to *hope*!" (*Letters*, 131).

Another possibility may lie in her sense of otherness, of being different from other people. Even though she was outwardly conforming, in her heart she was an unconventional woman living in the most conventional of times. It isolated her, much as Joanna in *The Country of the Pointed Firs* is isolated on her island. Her description of Joanna expresses a sense of pity and terror at such a sentence, even though self-imposed, for women who stray outside the culture's rigid expectations, combined with an almost envious respect for the courage it takes to be fully oneself. She writes, "In the life of each of us, I said to myself, there is a place remote and islanded, and given to endless regret or secret happiness" (132).

There is always a heart to every house—the place one is most drawn to. In the Jewett house, for me, it is the upstairs landing where she did her writing. I carry away one last picture of her sitting by that window, looking down into the square, separated from the common life by a twelve-over-twelve window. Sometimes she would descend to the public arena for a hearty handshake. But most often, I think, she would retreat into the richness of her inner world, where the people she imagined were more vivid than those she met on the street; and where the wild and shy child had the freedom to be fully herself.

Notes

1. Sarah Orne Jewett, *Letters of Sarah Orne Jewett*, ed. Annie Fields (Boston: Houghton Mifflin, 1911), 158. Subsequent page references are cited in the text.

2. Sarah Orne Jewett, *Country By-Ways* (Boston: Houghton Mifflin, 1881), 17. Subsequent references are cited in the text.

3. Sarah Orne Jewett, *The Country of the Pointed Firs* (Boston: Houghton Mifflin, 1896), 27. Subsequent references are cited in the text.

4. Rebecca Wall Nail, "'Where Every Prospect Pleases': Sarah Orne Jewett, South Berwick, and the Importance of Place," in *Critical Essays on Sarah Orne Jewett*, ed. Gwen L. Nagel (Boston: G. K. Hall, 1984), 187. Subsequent references are cited in the text.

5. Sarah Orne Jewett, "William's Wedding," in *Novels and Stories*, ed. Michael Davitt Bell (Library of America, 1994), 559, 556. Subsequent references are cited in the text.

6. Quoted in F. O. Matthiessen, *Sarah Orne Jewett* (Boston: Houghton Mifflin, 1929), 57–58.

7. Quoted in Paula Blanchard, *Sarah Orne Jewett: Her World and Her Work* (Reading, Mass.: Addison-Wesley, 1994), 71.

8. Sarah Orne Jewett, *The Mate of the Daylight and Friends Ashore* (Boston: Houghton Mifflin, 1884), 241. Subsequent references are cited in the text.

9. Richard Cary, *Sarah Orne Jewett* (New York: Twayne, 1962), 18.

10. Blanchard, *Jewett: Her World*, 17.

Contributors

Donna M. Campbell is assistant professor of English at Gonzaga University in Spokane, Washington. She is the author of *Resisting Regionalism: Gender and Naturalism in American Fiction, 1885–1915* (1997).

Alison Easton has taught at Lancaster University in England since 1973 and is senior lecturer in English. She has also been co-director of the university's Centre for Women's Studies. She is author of *The Making of the Hawthorne Subject* (1996), coeditor of *Women, Power, and Resistance: An Introduction to Women's Studies* (1996) and editor of the Penguin edition of Sarah Orne Jewett's *The Country of the Pointed Firs and Other Stories* (1995).

Thomas S. Edwards is associate academic dean at Castleton State College in Vermont. He was associate director of the Sarah Orne Jewett Centennial Conference in 1996 and of the American Women Nature Writers Conference in 1998. An award-winning teacher, he is currently editing a collection of critical essays, to be entitled *Such News of the Land: American Women Nature Writers.*

Graham Frater is an independent education consultant in the United Kingdom. On retiring from Her Majesty's Inspectorate (of schools) in England, he completed a doctorate on Jewett at the University of Warwick.

Melissa Homestead is assistant professor of English at Alabama State University, Montgomery, where she specializes in nineteenth-century American literature and the history of the book in America.

Karen L. Kilcup is associate professor of American literature at the University of North Carolina, Greensboro. Editor of *Studies in American Humor*, she has also published *Nineteenth-Century American Women Writ-*

ers: An Anthology (1997), *Nineteenth-Century American Women Writers: A Critical Reader* (1998), *Robert Frost and Feminine Literary Tradition* (1998), and *Soft Canons: American Women Writers and the Masculine Tradition* (1999). Her forthcoming work includes *Early Native American Women Writers: An Anthology*.

Priscilla Leder is associate professor of English and director of the Writing Center at Southwest Texas State University, San Marcos. She has published essays on Kate Chopin, Alice Walker, and Sarah Orne Jewett.

Marcia Littenberg is assistant professor of English at the State University of New York, Farmingdale. Her research interests focus on landscape and tradition in the work of Harriet Beecher Stowe, Sarah Orne Jewett, and Willa Cather.

Paul R. Petrie is assistant professor of English at Southern Connecticut State University, New Haven. He has published essays on Nathaniel Hawthorne and Willa Cather.

Marjorie Pryse is professor of English and women's studies at the State University of New York, Albany. She is the author of numerous articles on Jewett and of the introduction to the Norton edition of *The Country of the Pointed Firs* (1981). She coedited with Judith Fetterley *American Women Regionalists, 1850–1910: A Norton Anthology* (1992).

Ann Romines is director of graduate studies and professor of English at George Washington University. She is the author of *The Home Plot: Women, Writing, and Domestic Ritual* (1992) and *Constructing the Little House: Gender, Culture, and Laura Ingalls Wilder* (1997). She is volume editor of the Willa Cather Scholarly Edition of *Sapphira and the Slave Girl*, and editor of *Willa Cather's Southern Connections: New Essays on Cather and the South* (forthcoming).

Carol Schachinger is the author of numerous short stories, essays, and nonfiction articles. She has taught writing and literature at the University of Maine, Bridgewater State College in Massachusetts, and, most recently, Wheaton College.

Mitzi Schrag is professor of English at Clark College in Vancouver, Washington. Her current research focuses on American ghost stories.

Sarah Way Sherman is associate professor of English at the University of New Hampshire, Durham. Her publications include *Sarah Orne Jewett: An American Persephone* (1989). She is editor of a centennial edition of *The Country of the Pointed Firs and Other Stories* (1997).

Patti Capel Swartz is assistant professor of English at Morehead State University in Kentucky. She has published essays on Dorothy Allison, Barbara Kingsolver, the Harlem Renaissance, and the impact of Paulo Freire's philosophy of teaching, as well as reference entries in *Gay and Lesbian Literature II.*

Judith Bryant Wittenberg is professor and chair of English at Simmons College, Boston. Her articles on Sarah Orne Jewett have appeared in *Colby Quarterly* and *Studies in American Fiction.* She is the author of *Faulkner: The Transfiguration of Biography* (1979) and coeditor of *Unflinching Gaze: Morrison and Faulkner Re-Envisioned* (1997).

Index